D0710579

THE RISE AND FALL OF SOUL AND SELF

THE RISE AND FALL
OF SOUL AND SELF

An Intellectual History of Personal Identity

RAYMOND MARTIN AND JOHN BARRESI

CONTRA COSTA COUNTY LIBRARY

Columbia University Press · New York

Columbia University Press
Publishers Since 1893
New York   Chichester, West Sussex
Copyright © 2006 Columbia University Press

Library of Congress Cataloging-in-Publication Data
Martin, Raymond, 1941–
The rise and fall of soul and self : an intellectual history of personal
identity /Raymond Martin and John Barresi.
p.   cm.
Includes bibliographical references and index.
ISBN 0–231–13744–3 (hardcover: alk. Paper)—ISBN 0–231–51067–5
(electronic: alk. paper)
1. Self (Philosophy) 2. Self-knowledge, Theory of. 3. Identity
(Philosophical concept) I. Barresi, John, 1941– II. Title.
BD438.5 M375 2006

126.09–dc22   2005032273

Columbia University Press books are printed on permanent
and durable acid-free paper.
Printed in the United States of America
c 10 9 8 7 6 5 4 3 2

To
Dorothy Wang
and
Jolien Barresi

CONTENTS

THE RISE AND FALL OF SOUL AND SELF

INTRODUCTION

In Alfred Hitchcock's Rear Window, *a convalescing photojournalist, played by* Jimmy Stewart, is confined to his third-floor apartment. To amuse himself, he spies on his neighbors. As he spies, he begins to suspect, and then becomes convinced, that one of his neighbors, a middle-aged man, has killed his invalid wife. The Jimmy Stewart character tries to convince his girlfriend, played by Grace Kelly, to accept his theory. She shrugs it off, facilely explaining away his evidence. Then, one evening, suddenly realizing that his theory might be right, she comes over to the window next to where he has been sitting, peers out across the courtyard toward the murder suspect's apartment, and asks the Jimmy Stewart character to start from the beginning and tell her everything that happened and what it means.[1]

For those parts of the past that interest us, *everything that happened and what it means* is what many of us who are curious about the past really want to know. The word *everything* has to be taken with a grain of salt. In the example above, what the Grace Kelley character really wants to know is not literally "everything that happened" but *everything* that happened that it would be relevant and helpful to know in determining whether the Jimmy Stewart character's murder theory is correct.[2] Her request for what everything that happened *means* is for an explanation of how the different pieces of the puzzle—the evidence—fit together to yield a coherent picture of unfolding events. Similarly, in the present book, we are not going to try to tell literally *everything* that happened in the evolution of theories of the self and of personal identity. Rather, our goal is to tell *everything that happened that is relevant and helpful* to understanding why theory followed the course that it did—from its earliest beginnings to the present day. The meaning we are after is what this story can tell us about the enterprise of human self-understanding, including current attempts to understand the self and personal identity. By *theories of the self* we mean explicit theories that tell us what sort of thing the self is, if indeed it even is a thing. By *theories of personal identity*, we mean primarily theories of personal identity *over time*, that is, theories that explain why a person, or self, at one time is or is not the same person or self as someone at some other time.

In the West, views about the nature of the self and of personal identity first surfaced in ancient Greece. But at that time, so far as we know, there was no sustained, continuing discussion of these issues. That is, there is no record of theorists explaining what they did and did not like about earlier proposals and then suggesting new alternatives to better deal with outstanding issues. Rather, different theorists made proposals on a variety of related issues, for the most part without explicitly discussing what their predecessors had to say or why they themselves did or did not take a different view. For instance, in Plato's dialogue *Phaedo*, Socrates discusses self and personal identity in connection with his inquiry into the possibility of survival of bodily death, but when Aristotle made a radically different proposal for how the soul should be understood, he did so without directly discussing Socrates' (or Plato's) view.

A continuous tradition of discussion of self and personal-identity issues began in the second century C.E., during the Patristic Period. This discussion was motivated primarily by the need to make sense of the Christian dogma of the post-mortem resurrection of normal humans. At first, the church fathers, who had been trained in Greek philosophy, drew primarily upon Stoicism. Later, they drew upon Platonism. In the Latin West, Aristotelianism did not enter the discussion in a serious way until the thirteenth century. The other great tradition in classical Greece, materialistic atomism, of which Stoicism was one variety, reentered the discussion in the seventeenth century as the main theoretical underpinning for the rise of modern science. Since then, materialistic atomism, in one form or another, has remained the backdrop for the most influential discussions of the problems of self and personal identity.

As modern science came to the fore, the primarily religious concerns of the Patristic Period began to wane. Nevertheless, resurrection remained a preoccupation of most self and personal-identity theorists throughout the eighteenth century. Ironically, beginning in the 1960s modern equivalents of resurrection burst back onto center stage in the debate over personal identity. However, in our own times resurrection scenarios entered the discussion in the guise of science-fiction examples. The earlier discussion occurred in the context of developing a religious theology adequate to understanding personal persistence into an afterlife and the latter in that of developing a secular philosophy adequate to understanding the possibility of persistence in this life. In the former discussion, the issue was how to explain what we know to be true, in the latter, whether it is even possible to explain what we ordinarily assume to be true. Yet, as we shall see, in this case as in so many others in the debate over personal identity, the same issues keep recurring in a different guise.

So where to begin? In ancient Greece, of course. One of the earliest indications of interest in the problem of personal identity occurs in a scene from a play written in the fifth century B.C.E. by the comic playwright Epicharmus. In this scene, a lender asks a debtor to pay up. The debtor replies by asking the lender whether he agrees that anything that undergoes change, such as a pile of pebbles to which one pebble has been added or removed, thereby becomes a different thing. The lender says that he agrees with that. "Well, then," says the debtor, "aren't people constantly undergoing changes?" "Yes," replies the lender. "So," says the debtor, "it follows that I'm not the same person as the one who was indebted to you and, so, I owe you nothing." The lender then hits the debtor, who protests loudly at being abused. The lender replies that the debtor's complaint is misdirected since he—the lender—is not the same person as the one who hit him a moment before.[3]

An interesting—borderline amazing—thing about this scene is that it suggests that even in fifth-century-B.C.E. Greece, the puzzle of what it is about a thing that accounts for its persisting over time and through changes could be appreciated even by *theater audiences*. Another interesting thing about the scene is its more specific content: both debtor and lender have a point. Everyone *is* always changing. So, in a very strict sense of *same person*, every time someone changes, even a little, he or she ceases to exist: the debtor is not the same person as the one who borrowed the money, the lender not the same person as the one who hit the debtor. This very strict sense of *same person* is not an everyday notion but the product of a philosophical theory. It is also not a very useful sense of *same person*—unless you owe someone money!

In everyday life, we want to be able to say such things as, "I saw you at the play last night," and have what we say be true. If everyone is constantly changing and every change in a person results in his or her ceasing to exist, no such remarks could ever be true. Assuming that such remarks sometimes are true, there must be a sense of *same person* according to which someone can remain the same person *in spite of changing*. Saying what this sense is, or what these senses are, is *the philosophical problem of personal identity*.

In ancient Greece, the attempt to solve this problem took place in a larger philosophical context in which change and permanence, not just of people but of everything was an issue. At that time, many thinkers—apparently even many theatergoers—believed that all composite material objects, including human bodies, are constantly changing. They were aware that people often talk about objects that change, including human bodies and the people whose bodies they are, as if these things remain the same over the period in which they change. Finally, they were aware that some ideal objects, such as geometrical squares and triangles, seem not to change at all and also aware that sometimes we can have secure knowledge, such as the Pythagorean theorem, about such ideal objects. On what basis, if at all, they asked, can one talk meaningfully, and perhaps even acquire knowledge, about human bodies and persons that remain the same over time and through changes? This was their question.

Greek thinkers came up with three sorts of answers to this question. One was that there is a changeless realm, like the ideal realm of geometrical objects, which is beyond the ever-changing material world and that one's essential self—one's *psyche* (or, soul)—resides in this changeless realm and thereby ensures one's personal immortality. This answer, due to Plato and subsequently endorsed by Christianity, would inspire countless generations of Western thinkers. Another answer, due to Aristotle, was that there is a changeless dimension *within* every material object, which allows material objects, including human beings, to remain the same in spite of changing but which may not ensure one's *personal* immortality. Finally, the materialistic atomists, a third tradition of Greek thinkers, argued that both change and stability in material objects are the product of changeless, material atoms coming together and pulling apart. These thinkers reasoned that often more or less long-lasting configurations of atoms are named and, hence, become available to be known. People, or at least their material bodies, the atomists reasoned, are temporary configurations of this sort.[4] The question of which of these three theories best accounts for personal identity, or even for bodily identity, fueled subsequent personal-identity theory.

Today almost all theorists accept modern physical science as the backdrop against which self and personal persistence must be explained. Hence, they assume some version or other of materialist atomism. One difference this makes, as we shall see, is that whereas for Plato, and then subsequently for Platonic Christianity, the soul is something intrinsically unified and therefore available to explain lesser degrees of unity in other things, in our own times the soul's descendent, the self, has become theorized as something that lacks unity and that itself requires an explanation. In other words, whereas what used to do the explanatory work was the perfect unity of an incomposite immaterial soul, what now does it is the imperfect unity of a composite material body. In addition, theories of the self and of personal identity once invariably were parts of larger all-inclusive worldviews, but today they are so far removed from being connected to the big picture that self-theorists in different disciplines often lack even a common framework in terms of which they can understand and discuss one another's work. In sum, whereas previously theory was integrated and the self one, in our own times, theory has become variegated and the self fragmented. Accompanying this two-fold transition from unity to fragmentation has been a closely related one in which the soul began as unquestionably real and the self ended as arguably a fiction. What all of this means is something to which we shall return.

In telling the story of how thinkers in the West explicitly conceived of selves, or persons, and then tried on that basis to account for personal identity, we have tried to strike a balance between what would be required in order to tell two rather different types of stories. One of these would explain the views of thinkers in their specific historical contexts—on their own terms, so to speak. In this account, the story would be told with little regard to subsequent developments. The other would highlight those aspects of thought that were of more lasting interest or that seem relevant to contemporary concerns. There is tension between these two types of stories. Provided that one strikes a good balance between the two, this tension, we believe, is not destructive but creative. We try to strike a good balance.

We have also had to strike a different sort of balance, having to do with how much discussion to include of interpretational controversy over the views of the theorists we discuss. What we have tried to do, for the most part, is to write in a way that is sensitive to such controversy without actually discussing it explicitly. The alternative was to write a book that is substantially longer than this one. Instead of discussing interpretational controversy, our goal has been to provide a clear, concise account of the most consequential core of each theorist's views: what the theorist said and was taken to have said by his peers and by subsequent thinkers.

Even within these limitations, the story we want to tell is an ambitious one. We could not have told it without relying on the work of an army of scholars whose efforts have greatly aided us in understanding original sources, especially by directing us to the most important passages, providing translations, and suggesting interpretations. Throughout this book we will, in notes, acknowledge our indebtedness to these scholars. However, in the case of some of them just doing that seems insufficient since their works were so helpful. We want then also to acknowledge them here:

- Michael Ayers. *Locke*. 2 vols. (Routledge, 1991).
- Caroline Walker Bynum. *Resurrection of the Body in Western Christianity, 200–1336* (Columbia University Press, 1995).

- Marcia Corlish. *Medieval Foundations of the Western Intellectual Tradition, 400–1400* (Yale University Press, 1998)
- James C. M. Crabbe, ed. *From Soul to Self* (Routledge, 1999).
- Edward Craig, ed. *Routledge Encyclopedia of Philosophy*. 10 vols. (Routledge, 1998)
- Richard C. Dales. *The Problem of the Rational Soul in the Thirteenth Century* (E. J. Brill, 1995).
- Paul Edwards, ed. *Encyclopedia of Philosophy*. 8 vols. (Macmillan and Free Press, 1967).
- Daniel Garber and Michael Ayers, eds. *The Cambridge History of Seventeenth Century Philosophy*. 2 vols. (Cambridge University Press, 1998).
- C. Fox, R. Porter, and R. Wokler, eds. *Inventing Human Science: Eighteenth-Century Domains* (University of California Press, 1995).
- Neil Gillman. *The Death of Death: Resurrection and Immortality in Jewish Thought* (Jewish Lights Publishing, 1997).
- Paul Oskar Kristeller. *Renaissance Thought: The Classic, Scholastic, and Humanist Strains* (Harper & Row, 1961); and *Eight Philosophers of the Italian Renaissance* (Harper Collins, 1964).
- B. Mijuskovic. *The Achilles of Rationalist Arguments: The Simplicity, Unity, and Identity of Thought and Soul from the Cambridge Platonists to Kant: A Study in the History of an Argument* (Martinus Nijhoff, 1974).
- Colin Morris. *The Discovery of the Individual, 1050–1200* (Harper & Row, 1972).
- Jean A. Perkins. *The Concept of the Self in the French Enlightenment* (Librairie Droz, 1969).
- Roy Porter, ed. *Rewriting the Self: Histories from the Renaissance to the Present* (Routledge, 1997); and *Flesh in the Age of Reason: The Modern Foundations of Body and Soul* (W. W. Norton, 2004).
- E. S. Reed. *From Soul to Mind: The Emergence of Psychology from Erasmus Darwin to William James* (Yale University Press, 1997).
- Timothy J. Reiss. *Mirages of the Selfe: Patterns of Personhood in Ancient and Early Modern Europe* (Stanford University Press, 2003).
- C. B. Schmitt, Quentin Skinner, Eckhard Kessler, and Jill Kraye, eds. *The Cambridge History of Renaissance Philosophy* (Cambridge University Press, 1988).
- Roger Smith. *The Norton History of the Human Sciences* (W. W. Norton, 1997).
- Robert Solomon. *Continental Philosophy Since 1750: The Rise and Fall of the Self* (Oxford University Press, 1998).
- Richard Sorabji, ed. *Aristotle and After* (Institute of Classical Studies, 1997).

- J. Sutton. *Philosophy and Memory Traces: Descartes to Connectionism* (Cambridge University Press, 1998).
- Charles Taylor. *Sources of the Self: The Making of the Modern Identity* (Cambridge University Press, 1989).
- P. P. Wiener, ed. *Dictionary of the History of Ideas: Studies of Selected Pivotal Ideas*. 4 vols. (Charles Scribner's Sons, 1973–74).
- John P. Wright and Paul Potter, eds. *Psyche and Soma* (Oxford University Press, 2000).
- J. W. Yolton. *Thinking Matter: Materialism in Eighteenth-Century Britain* (University of Minnesota Press, 1983).
- Robert M. Young. *Mind, Brain, and Adaptation in the Nineteenth Century: Cerebral Localization and Its Biological Context from Gall to Ferrier* (Oxford University Press, 1990).

In addition to relying on the work of others, we have drawn on material, almost always substantially revised, from our own previously published work. Some of this material we published jointly, including:

- "Hazlitt on the Future of the Self." *Journal of the History of Ideas* 56 (1995): 463–81.
- "Fission Examples in the Eighteenth- and Early-Nineteenth-Century Personal Identity Debate" (with Alessandro Giovannelli). *History of Philosophy Quarterly* 15 (1998): 323–48.
- *Naturalization of the Soul: Self and Personal Identity in the Eighteenth Century* (Routledge, 2000).
- "Personal Identity and What Matters in Survival: An Historical Overview." In *Personal Identity*, ed. R. Martin and J. Barresi (Blackwell, 2003).
- "Self-concern from Priestley to Hazlitt." *British Journal for the History of Philosophy* 11 (2003): 499–507.

We have also drawn from Raymond Martin, *Self-Concern: An Experiential Approach to What Matters in Survival* (Cambridge University Press, 1998), and from his "Locke's Psychology of Personal Identity," *Journal of the History of Philosophy* 38 (2000): 41–61.

For their support of research that contributed to the writing of this book, we thank the Research Development Fund of Dalhousie University, the Social Science and Humanities Research Council of Canada, the General Research Board of the University of Maryland, and the Humanities Development Fund of Union College.

Finally, Ray Martin wishes to thank Dorothy Wang, who throughout the time he worked on this book was not only a continuous source of cultural stimulation and intellectual insight but his best friend. And John Barresi wishes to thank his wife, Jolien, for her boundless patience and sympathy while we were working on this project and for the many years of love and support she has provided him.

I

FROM MYTH TO SCIENCE

Pre-philosophical Greek attitudes toward the soul and the prospects for surviving bodily death found expression in Homer and subsequently in the mystery cults of Dionysus (Bacchus) and Orpheus. The earliest attempts to grapple with such issues philosophically occurred hundreds of years later, in the sixth century B.C.E., primarily in the philosophies of Pythagoras and Heraclitus.

In Homer, people had psyches, which survived their bodily deaths. But the survival of a psyche was not the survival of a person. Before bodily death, peoples' psyches, or life principles, were associated with their breath (*pneuma*) and movement. Other faculties, most of them associated with bodily organs or bodily activities other than breath and movement, were responsible for specific mental and emotional tasks. *Nous*, for instance, was associated with seeing and was responsible for reasoning; *thymos* was associated with the organism's immediate mental and physical response to an external threat and was responsible for courage; *phrenes* was associated with the midriff and responsible for strength; *kardia* was associated with the heart and responsible for passion, including fear.[1]

In the case of ordinary people, each of these mental faculties ceased at bodily death, at which time their psyches, in the form of breath, left their bodies to go to Hades, where they existed as shades or shadows. To ninth-century-B.C.E. Greeks, it seems to have been little consolation to know that one's psyche would survive one's bodily death as a shade. The life of a shade was not a life worth living. Heroes, on the other hand, survived bodily death in a more robust way, by becoming like gods. But the survival of heroes, it seems, was more for the community of living Greeks than for the heroes themselves. No one was encouraged to become a hero simply in order to survive. Honor, rather, was the objective. Whatever value mere survival may have had for the heroes themselves, Homer portrayed their godlike survival as a reward to the community for having produced heroes. Postmortem heroes provided the community with moral exemplars.

In later Greek literary works, such as in the poems of Pindar and the plays of Sophocles, there is a gradual movement away from Homer's merely imaginative conception of psyches in Hades, where the souls of everyone are treated more or less the same, to more moral conceptions, in which departed souls are more closely affected by how well they had lived. In Homer, living people are rarely if at all concerned with the fates of their psyches. The people portrayed in later literary works, whose accounts of postmortem existence tend to be more nuanced, show more concern.

In the early fifth century B.C.E., progressive Greek thinkers began to replace all such myths with science. So far as the self is concerned, their interest centered on the word *psyche*, which meant different things to different thinkers. Sometimes it meant *person* or *life*, sometimes personality, sometimes that part of one that could experience. In each case, psyche tended to be understood as a bodily function that has emotion and appetite.[2] But under the influence of Orphism and perhaps also Greek shamanism, later thinkers began to think of the psyche in more spiritual terms.

Pythagoras (fl. 530 B.C.E.) and Empedocles (fl. 450 B.C.E.), two of the earliest philosophers to have been concerned with the self, may have been shamans. Both of them combined what today we would call *science* with an Orphic-style mysticism. Pythagoras inspired legends but wrote nothing, so it is hard to speak with confidence about his views. Originally from Samos, he was an astronomer and mathematician who was said to have originated the doctrine of the tripartite soul, which resurfaced in the philosophy of Plato. Pythagoras also espoused rebirth, or transmigration, and was said to have been able to remember what happened in many of his previous incarnations. Empedocles, on the other hand, was preoccupied with medicine rather than mathematics. Admired widely as a miracle worker, he was said to have cured illness by the power of music. He was also said to have restored the dead to life.

According to the Orphism with which Pythagoras and Empedocles may both have been associated, when a human dies his or her soul (or psyche) persists. Those persisting souls that were pure remained permanently with the gods. Those that were impure remained in the company of the gods while they awaited incarnation again as humans, animals, or worse (Empedocles apparently believed that he had once been incarnated as a bush). The process of incarnation "soils" souls, augmenting their impurity. Their subsequent fates depend on the behavior of their new hosts, especially upon whether the hosts, if human, observe certain dietary restrictions and religious rituals. Pythagoras, for instance, prohibited his disciples from sacrificing animals and from consuming flesh or beans and encouraged them to participate in rituals that celebrated the superiority of the intellect over the senses. Orphism taught that ultimately all souls reunite with the universal deity. In sum, what Pythagoras and Empedocles seem to have shared, and what they encouraged in thinkers who would come later, was belief in a soul, or self, that existed prior to the body, that could be induced to leave the body even while the body remained alive, and that would outlast the body.[3]

These ideas were extremely consequential. Directly or indirectly, they seem to have powerfully influenced Plato and, through Plato, various church fathers, including Augustine and, through Augustine, Christian theology and, through Christianity, the entire mindset of Western civilization, secular as well as religious. It is ironic, perhaps, that ideas that eventually acquired such an impressive rational pedigree may have originated in the dark heart of shamanism, with its commitment to magic and the occult.

Subsequent to Pythagoras and Empedocles, Heraclitus (535?–475? B.C.E.), of whom more is known, had a scientific interest in the nature of the soul and a sagelike interest in its well-being. Impressed by what he took to be the extent to which people live divided from one another and themselves, he thought he saw the way toward unification (or *re*-unification).[4] Impressed with Pythagoras' method of "scientific inquiry," which he wrote was "beyond that of all other men," he was less impressed with Pythagoras himself, who he said was "dilettantish and misguided." Heraclitus would be more systematic: everything, including earth, air, and water, is made of fire.

In Heraclitus's view, humans have souls, which arise from water. Living properly causes one's soul to dry out. The dryer one's soul becomes, the more alive and noble one becomes. Desire, and its ally passion, keep the soul in ignorance, hence, moist. One whose soul is moist, like a drunk or a sleepwalker, is unaware of where he is. Such a person lives in a world of his own, with an "understanding peculiar to oneself." Wisdom comes from self-understanding. It is the same for everyone, and it involves awakening, as if from a dream. Those who "are awake have one world in common." In this world, the soul reveals its boundless nature: "You could not in your going find the ends of the soul, though you traveled the whole way: so deep is its Law (*Logos*)."[5] At bodily death, the soul separates from the body, at least temporarily. The souls of the foolish, which are moist, return to water. The souls of the wise, which are dry, join the cosmic fire.

Heraclitus was impressed with impermanence. He gets credit for the famous saying that you cannot step into the same river twice. What he meant by this saying is disputed. Probably he meant that because all material objects are always changing none of them is the same for more than an instant, hence none lasts for more than an instant. This is how Plato interpreted him. Cratylus, who became a follower of Heraclitus, is said by Plato and Aristotle to have carried Heraclitus's intriguing idea one step further, maintaining that since everything is constantly changing, not only does nothing persist but it is not even possible to speak truly. To dramatize this point, Cratylus pronounced, rather colorfully, that you cannot step into the "same" river even once.[6]

Whatever Heraclitus's actual view, he was the first thinker whose writings have survived who was concerned with explaining the conditions that would have to obtain for persons, or anything else, to persist. The introduction of this issue was the origin in Western thought of the philosophical problem of the identity over time of objects that change—that is, of how something that changes can nevertheless remain the same. Heraclitus's view was that nothing that changes can remain the same. Whether or not this view is true, it is not practical.

Once the issue of explaining persistence through change was introduced, it immediately struck a cord in Greek intellectual and artistic culture. By the beginning of the fifth century B.C.E., many Greek thinkers, probably including Epicharmus, believed that since everything is in constant flux, humans too are in constant flux. Whether a thing in flux could nevertheless continue to remain the same is, of course, a separate question.

In Plato's *Symposium*, which is thought to be one of his earlier dialogues, Diotima explains to Socrates, rather matter-of-factly:

> [Overtime,] each living creature is said to be alive and to be the same individual—as for example someone is said to be the same person from when he is a child until he comes to be an old man. And yet, if he's called the same, that's despite the fact that he's never made up from the same things, but is always being renewed, and losing what he had before, whether it's hair, or flesh, or bones, or blood, in fact the whole body. And don't suppose that this is just true in the case of the body; in the case of the soul, too, its traits, habits, opinions, desires, pleasures, pains, fears—none of these things is ever the same in any individual, but some are coming into existence, others passing away.

A few lines later, Diotima remarks that unlike in the case of divine things, everything mortal is preserved not by "being absolutely the same" but by replacement of something similar: "what is departing and decaying with age leaves behind in us something else new, of the same sort that it was."[7]

Diotima's view presented here—that the identity over time of every "mortal" thing is to be understood in terms of a relationship among its ever changing parts—is called a *relational view of the identity of objects over time*. It is the view to which virtually all current personal-identity theorists subscribe. Before it could gain ascendancy, the Platonic view had to be vanquished.

In the *Symposium,* Plato contrasts identity through change with unchanging, divine immortality. He goes on to suggest that to the extent that humans grasp the eternal forms—in particular, beauty—they also, if only in the moment, participate in immortality. But, as we shall see, in the *Phaedo*, which may have been written at about the same time as the *Symposium*, Plato focused not on our mortal nature but on the immortality of the soul—the only part of our nature that he thought persists after bodily death. Consistent with the *Symposium*, he also pointed out that there is a difference between the souls of ordinary people, which persist eternally but constantly change their nature due to their attention to earthly things, and the souls of philosophers, or lovers of wisdom (*philosophia*), like Socrates, who by seeking to know the eternal become one with it. Only such souls—Plato's heroes—achieve "real," that is, unchanging, immortality. Ordinary people, on the other hand, reincarnate, forgetting themselves in the process (*metempsychosis*).

Platonism

In the surviving literature in the West that predates the fifth century B.C.E., theories of the self were rarely articulated for their own sakes (Heraclitus's views are an exception) and even more rarely subjected to rational tests. Rather, they tended to be implied by views that were expressed about other things, such as social relationships or what happens to humans after bodily death. With the arrival of Socrates (470?–399), this situation changed dramatically. Socrates is depicted by Plato as someone who taught by deed as well as by word. In the mid-twentieth century, Mahatma Gandhi is said to have responded to a request for the essence of his teaching by replying, "My life is my teaching." Socrates, as depicted by Plato, could have truthfully answered the same question with the same reply. He claimed that life's most important project is care of one's own soul. And he tried not only to discover the truth but to live it. However, he cared for his soul largely by trying rationally to figure out the nature of things, including moral and aesthetic things. In this rational quest, he was a philosopher in the modern sense of the word, arguably the first of his kind in the West.

Socrates appeared on the scene in Greece just as the new scientific intellectualism that had been ushered in by Pythagoras, Heraclitus, and others had begun seriously to challenge traditional mythology. It was a time in Greek culture that in some ways is analogous to two later times in Europe when science challenged traditional Christian beliefs: in the thirteenth century, when translations of Aristotle, together with advances in Islamic science, were introduced to European thinkers; and in the seventeenth century, when mechanistic physical science began to displace Aristotelianism.

In fifth-century Greece, Socrates helped to pave the way for the eventual triumph of secular reason. If this were all that he did, it would have been enough to earn him a place of renown in Western intellectual history. But he did one other thing that was even more consequential. He inspired Plato (429?–348? B.C.E.). And unlike Socrates, who wrote nothing, Plato wrote a great deal. Plato, of course, wrote in the form of dialogues—philosophical plays—in which a character named *Socrates* was the spokesperson for Plato's own views. For a long time, people simply assumed that this character faithfully captured the historical Socrates. As depicted by Plato, Socrates was a vehicle for reason's triumph over tradition. As a consequence, what people took to be the historical Socrates became a cultural icon—the first *secular* saint. To most students of philosophy, he still has that status.

In the *Phaedo*, Plato recounts the jail-cell conversation that took place on the day that Socrates was put to death by the Athenian authorities. In this conversation, Socrates argued for the immortality of each person's soul, which he took to be "immaterial" and akin to the divine. His view was then subjected by Simmias and Cebes, his students, to intense rational criticism, to which Socrates replied with counterarguments. The view of Simmias and Cebes was that the soul's relation to the body is like that of harmony to a stringed instrument. Hence, they claimed, when the body decomposes the soul ceases. To a modern secular audience, it may seem that Simmias and Cebes have the stronger case, but in the dialogue they eventually succumb to Socrates' arguments. Nevertheless, their arguments are the first in the West that we know about to explicitly question the immortality of the soul.

In most modern, and perhaps even in many ancient contexts, Simmias and Cebes' sort of "deathbed behavior" would be ungracious in the extreme: they tried to convince Socrates, hours before he was to die, that bodily death is the end! Plato had a different view of the propriety of their behavior. In the dialogue, as Plato portrays it, Simmias and Cebes' display of independent thinking showed Socrates, as he was about to die, that they had gotten one of the main things that he had tried to teach them. That main thing was the importance of not believing anything dogmatically or unreflectively but instead subjecting every potential belief to intense rational criticism and being always prepared to follow an argument wherever it may lead. As if to reinforce this point, after Socrates ostensibly won the argument by proving that the soul is immortal, he immediately admonished Simmias and Cebes to go over his arguments after he was dead to check for subtle flaws which the group may have missed.

So far as the nature of the soul is concerned, the *Phaedo* begins with Socrates trying to figure out the sources of generation and corruption, that is, how things come to be and pass away. In his view, the generation of a thing is caused by the parts out of which it is initially composed coming together; its corruption is caused by the parts out of which it is finally composed coming apart. Apparently the bearing of this on the discussion of immortality in the dialogue is to suggest that each person has (or is) a "simple" soul, that is, something that is not composed of parts.

In Plato's view, the soul is what a person essentially is. Its simplicity ensures both personal survival of bodily death and each person's "preexistence" prior to incarnation into a body. In the *Meno*, Plato claimed that this preexistence explains one's ability to acquire knowledge, as in mathematics, that is not derived from sense experience. One's seemingly discovering such knowledge is actually a form of remembering what one saw intellectually prior to birth. The soul's simplicity and its being what a person essentially is also ensure personal survival of changes undergone while one is alive and embodied. Since cessation is due only to decomposition, whatever is ultimately simple *has to* persist through changes—forever! Because the soul is simple, it must be immortal.

In ancient times (and still today) almost everyone assumed that if people survive their bodily deaths, then there must be a vehicle (or medium) for their survivals. However, even before anyone had thought of the idea of an immaterial soul, there was a ready vehicle available: fine matter. When Socrates was alive, many Greeks thought that the soul leaves the body when the person who dies expels his last breath. Probably they also thought that at that moment, the soul simply *is* that last breath. As we have seen, Plato, at least in the *Phaedo*, claimed implicitly, through Socrates, that the soul is immaterial and simple, that is, without parts. That in itself is enough to distinguish the soul from breath, which presumably has parts.

As Bishop Butler was to point out in the eighteenth century, Plato's having thought that the soul is without parts is compatible with his having thought that the soul is material. In the physics of Butler's time, an atom was regarded as a simple, material object. There is nothing in Plato to suggest that he actually thought that the soul is a simple material atom, but neither is there anything that decisively rules out this possibility. So, the most one can say about Plato's speculative derring-do is that it was his genius (or perversity) to have *suggested* a radical alternative to the view that the soul is material, including an alternative to its being a simple material thing. Whether Plato himself subscribed to this radical choice is unclear.

Nevertheless, a fairly straightforward way of interpreting what Plato wrote in the *Phaedo* is that the soul is immaterial not only in being without parts but in being *unextended*. This is how Plato was interpreted in the second century c.e. by leading Neoplatonists. It is also the view of the soul to which René Descartes would subscribe toward the beginning of the seventeenth century. If, in fact, Plato intended to suggest that the vehicle for survival is not any sort of physical object, not even breath but, rather, an unextended thing, then this thought was original to him (or to Socrates). Previously, when others had talked of immaterial souls, they usually meant invisible matter. Plato, in the *Phaedo*, does not always distinguish sharply between something's being immaterial and its being invisible. But, then, sometimes he does seem to distinguish between these two, at least to the extent of insisting that the soul is not only invisible but simple and akin to the gods. As we shall see, in the third century c.e., Plotinus, a pagan Neoplatonist, developed Plato's idea that essentially each of us is (or has) an immaterial, unextended soul. It was this version of Plato's view that turned out to be most influential.

Assuming, for the sake of argument, that Plato did arrive at the idea of an immaterial, unextended soul, how might he have arrived at this idea? Although one can only speculate, there is a natural line of reasoning that would have brought him to this conclusion. He may have reasoned, as the good student of geometry that he was, that any extended thing, merely by virtue of its being extended, is potentially divisible and, hence, potentially corruptible. So, if the self is immortal not only by accident but necessarily, then it has to be unextended. But why did Plato suppose that the self is immortal? While Plato's arguments for immortality in the *Phaedo* are obscure, the central idea behind the most important of them seems to be his conviction that the soul is *essentially* alive. He reasoned that since the soul is essentially alive it could not die. To Plato, this meant that at the approach of death, rather than perishing, the soul would simply withdraw. In any case, it was not Plato's *arguments* for immortality but rather his *conception* of the soul as immaterial, simple, and thereby naturally immortal that turned out to be so enormously influential.

The *Phaedo*, whether or not it faithfully reports Socrates' views, seems to represent an early stage in Plato's thinking about soul and self. Yet even in that early stage, although the soul is said to be wholly immaterial, a unity, without parts, and immune to change (like the transcendent Forms), it is described also as a natural vehicle for psychological continuity, complete with all the complexity and change that go with cognition, desire, decision making, pains, and pleasures. In this light, the part of the soul that would survive bodily death is portrayed as imprisoned for an earthly lifetime in a physical body that is an impediment to its true happiness and interests, which lie in a bodiless, immaterial existence elsewhere. Yet the soul is also portrayed as a life principle, whose essential function is to animate the physical.

As we have seen, it is tempting to suppose, as some commentators have, that Plato's notion of an immaterial soul that can leave its body has its roots in shamanism, particularly as this influence was preserved in the Pythagorean movement. In this interpretation, what Plato did, in effect, was to reinterpret traditional Greek magico-religious ideas within the framework of a newly emerging rationalism. So far as the soul is concerned, he did this by casting the occult self of shamanism into the role of the rational soul. The shaman, through a magical power that gets expressed in trance, detaches the occult self from the body; the philosopher, through the power of reason, which gets expressed in mental concentration, frees the rational soul from bodily contamination. In shamanism, the soul, detached from the body, remembers past lives and acquires occult knowledge; in Plato's view, the soul, detached from the body, remembers past lives and the knowledge of necessary truths, or the Forms, that it acquired when released from bodily contamination. Reincarnation finds a place in both views.[8]

In the *Republic,* Socrates claims that souls are divided into rational, spirited, and appetitive parts. It is the interaction among these parts that explains how people behave. In earlier writings, Plato had stressed that only the rational part of the soul is immortal, the other two parts perishing with the body. As he matured, he struggled to integrate this rather austere a priori *philosophy* of the self as an "immaterial" thing with a more complicated empirical *psychology* of human mentality. Even so, in the *Republic* his discussion of divisions *within* the soul was not primarily meant to propose an empirical psychology but to make the normative point that it is in each person's self-interest that his or her soul be harmonious. In Plato's view, harmony of the soul requires that reason, rather than spirit or appetite, rules. Yet while he thought that it is in one's *self-interest* for reason to rule, reason dictates that a person act not selfishly but in ways that promote the welfare of others. Thus, in Plato's view, the self-regarding impetus of self-interest coincides with the other-regarding concerns of morality.

The details of Plato's normative theories of self-interest and morality need not concern us. For present purposes, it is more important that in explaining these normative theories, Plato launched an empirical psychology, the first of its kind in the West. Others, prior to Plato, tended to make proposals about what sort of matter the soul is made of—air, earth, fire, or water. No one had proposed a theory about how the different parts of a human personality work together to produce human behavior. This sort of thing is what today is called a *faculty* psychology. It is called this because it posits separate mechanisms—or faculties—in the mind (or body) whose function it is to control different aspects of human mentality. Faculty psychologies are contrasted with *functional* psychologies, which explain different aspects of human mentality not by assigning them to different mechanisms in the mind or brain but rather to different ways in which a single organ of mentality functions. Aristotle, and then various thirteenth- and fourteenth-century thinkers, wavered between these two views. Recently, with the advent in cognitive psychology of modular theories of human mentality, a modern descendant of Plato's faculty psychology has come back into fashion.

In the *Timaeus*, which was written after the *Republic*, Plato returned to the question of how to integrate the soul. However, this time he approached the question through a curious creation myth, which for all its speculative flair reveals a newfound physiological dimension to his empirical psychology. In this myth, he began by noting that in creating order out of disorder, "God created in each thing in relation to itself, and in all things in relation to each other, all the measures and harmonies which they could possibly receive." Prior to this divine act, any order or proportion that occurred was an accident. Subsequently, order was part of the scheme of things in which the universe is portrayed as "a single animal comprehending in itself all other animals, mortal and immortal." God's offspring, the demigods, were responsible for completing the design of mortal creatures:

And they, imitating him, received from him the immortal principle of the soul; and around this they proceeded to fashion a mortal body, and made it to be the vehicle of the soul and constructed within the body a soul of another nature which was mortal, subject to terrible and irresistible affections—first of all, pleasure, the greatest incitement to evil; then, pain, which deters from good; also rashness and fear, two foolish counsellors, anger hard to be appeased, and hope easily led astray—these they mingled with irrational sense and with all-daring love according to necessary laws, and so framed man.

Fearing to pollute the divine in humankind any more than was necessary, the demigods physically situated the immortal part of humans above the neck and the mortal part below, placing the neck between them "to keep them apart."

And in the breast, and in what is termed the thorax, they encased the mortal soul; and as the one part of this was superior and the other inferior they divided the cavity of the thorax into two parts, as the women's and men's apartments are divided in houses, and placed the midriff to be a wall of partition between them.

The part of "the inferior soul which is endowed with courage and passion and loves contention" they located "nearer the head, midway between the midriff and the neck, in order that it might more easily join with reason in controlling and restraining desire.[9]

In this curious passage, Plato seems to portray humans as having, in effect, two souls, one independent of the body and wholly rational, the other bodily and passionate but capable to some extent of joining with reason. The passage suggests that Plato had seen that in having previously made the soul so otherworldly in order to insure its immortality, he had deprived himself of the ability to appeal to it to explain human behavior. So he postulated another, this-worldly soul to take up the slack. That move must have made some—Aristotle?—wonder whether there had been any need to postulate an immaterial soul in the first place. Perhaps, though, the immaterial soul is needed to explain either how one comes to have knowledge of the Forms or to explain what is often assumed to be each person's unity of consciousness. How, say, could a material soul—a composite thing—explain unity? That question would haunt philosophers of personal identity into the modern era.

Whatever Plato's motives in the passage just quoted, such empirical, physiological theorizing was startlingly original (though it may have had its basis in Hippocrates [circa 400 B.C.E.]). Yet, as we have seen, by supposing that one's essence—reason—is immaterial, and the rest of one's mentality material, the problem arose of explaining the relationship of this essence—one's true self—to the body. A similar problem plagues Plato's view of reality more generally. His dualism seems to have been motivated by the conviction that only what is immaterial and either itself rational or capable of being grasped rationally is fully real, everything else deriving whatever reality it has from its "participation" in the fully real.[10]

Even so, as we shall see, the view that the soul is an immaterial substance would prove to be remarkably persistent, mainly because it would be endorsed by Christianity. But another reason for its persistence is that it has seemed to many thinkers that each of us has a kind of mental unity that could not be explained if we were wholly material. When, in the twentieth century, personal-identity thinkers en masse finally did embrace materialism, the question of how unified we are mentally and how whatever mental unity we have might be explained has come to the fore.

Returning to Plato, his division of the soul, together with his suggestion that its lower functions are bodily and beastlike, may be the ultimate theoretical origin of the idea of the unconscious. In Augustine, the view became one of true and false selves. In the twelfth century, through the medium of Augustine, it spawned the notion of self-deception. Subsequently, in the sixteenth and seventeenth centuries, the view that the soul is divided and in conflict with itself resurfaced in an army of thinkers, including Montaigne, Shaftesbury, and Rousseau, until in the nineteenth century, first in Schopenhauer, then in Nietzsche, and then finally in Freud, the lower parts of the soul were relegated to "the unconscious."[11]

In the *Phaedrus*, which is one of Plato's relatively late dialogues, and in the *Laws*, which is usually thought to be the latest, Plato introduced what seems to be an entirely different conception of soul. In these dialogues, he defines the soul as a self-moving thing and says that it is this attribute that makes it immortal: "All soul is immortal, for that which is ever in motion is immortal." Things that impart motion to other things but are themselves "moved by something else," he continued, are soulless; they "can cease to be in motion, and therefore can cease to live." Something self-moving, and only something self-moving, cannot "abandon its own nature." Hence, only self-movers are immortal. So, we should "feel no scruple in affirming that precisely that [that is, being self-moving] is the essence and definition of soul."[12]

In these dialogues, the soul is said to be co-eternal with the gods. There is an obvious connection between these reflections and Plato's earlier thoughts in the *Phaedo*, in which he stressed that the soul is essentially alive, as well as a connection with Aristotle's views. Yet Plato's emphasis here on the importance of self-motion raises questions about corporeal souls in humans, animals, and plants. Did he think that these corporeal souls, because they are not "self-moving," are not really souls at all but merely aspects of biological mechanisms, or did he think that even these corporeal souls are immortal?

Whatever Plato's ultimate view, in the surviving literature from the West in which views of the self are expressed, nothing even remotely like Plato's intellectual sensitivity and sophistication, not to mention his imaginative and literary flair, had appeared previously. He represents a new beginning. The view of the self that he expressed in the *Phaedo* was in the West destined to become one of the most influential theories of the self of all time. Even so, it was not the only influential theory of the self spawned by Greek culture. Within 150 years of Socrates' death two other rival theories of the self were expressed, each of which ultimately would become as influential as Plato's. One of these came from Aristotle, the other from several Greek materialists, who became known collectively as the *atomists*.

Aristotelianism

According to Aristotle (384–322 B.C.E.) the soul has parts, which account for its various functions. Early in his career, Aristotle seems to have followed Plato in assuming that the part of the soul that accounts for its ability to think rationally, which he called *nous*, is immortal.[13] Later, in *De anima* (On the life-force, or On the soul) and elsewhere, his statements about the persistence of *nous* are enigmatic. Nevertheless, it is surely true that unlike Plato in the *Phaedo,* Aristotle's main theoretical concern with the soul had little to do with survival of bodily death. Neither did he follow Plato in developing a normative theory of morality based on self-interest. Rather, so far as the soul is concerned, Aristotle was preoccupied with two other problems: the place of humans in the larger scheme of things and the soul's relationship to the body.

As we have seen, in Plato's view there was one main division in reality, that between the material and visible, on the one hand, and the "immaterial" and invisible, on the other. The former became real by "participating" in the latter. The more it participated, the more real it was. Plato's dualism is often called a *two-worlds view*. According to Aristotle, though with some exceptions—such as "the Unmoved Mover," which is responsible for moving the planets—there is only one world, every item of which is a union of matter and form, and therefore, material. Even so, in his view, not all material objects are equally real. There is a gradation of being, at the lowest end of which is inorganic matter and at the highest the Unmoved Mover. Vegetable life is above inorganic matter; nonreasoning animals are above vegetable life; and humans are above nonreasoning animals. Aristotle thought of the Unmoved Mover as pure form. Later generations of Christian theologians cast it in the role of God.

In Aristotle's view, except for inorganic matter, everything has a psyche, or soul, which is its vital principle—that is, what it is about it that accounts for its being alive. Most of the soul is inseparable from the body that it informs. Apparently the soul's rational part—*nous*—is separable, although some scholars dispute whether Aristotle really held this view. On the assumption that Aristotle did hold it, it is not clear whether it was also part of his view that *nous* can retain *personal* individuality when it is separate from a body or whether *nous* is one entity, which is on loan to all individual humans while they are engaged in rational thinking and hence not something that belongs specifically to any individual human. Aristotle didn't explicitly answer this question, perhaps because he wasn't interested in it or, perhaps, because he was uncertain how to answer it. When, in the late Middle Ages and early Renaissance, Aristotle achieved among Christian scholars an authoritative status almost equal to Divine Revelation, the implications of his view of the psyche for personal survival of bodily death became a contentious issue, with some thinkers even suggesting that his true view must have been that no parts of the soul, not even *nous*, are separable from the body.

As for the rest of Aristotle's view of psyche, at the bottom of the scale of souls is the nutritive or vegetative soul, which accounts for assimilation and reproduction. It is found only in plants. Next is the sensitive soul, which includes all of the powers of the vegetative soul plus the additional powers of sensation, which gives rise to imagination, memory, desire, and local motion. Aristotle thought that of the senses, touch and taste are the most important, for just as nutrition is necessary for the preservation of any sort of life, so touch and taste are necessary for the preservation of animal life. Other senses, such as sight, while not strictly necessary to the preservation of animal life, nevertheless contribute to its well-being. The sensitive soul is found only in nonhuman animals. Finally, higher than all of the other souls is the rational soul, which possesses all of the powers of the lower souls but also possesses *nous*, which is reason or intellect. *Nous* is responsible for scientific thought, which has as its object truth for its own sake. It is also responsible for deliberation, which has as its object truth for the sake of some practical or prudential objective.

In Aristotle's view, with the possible exception of *nous*, the psyche and all of its parts come into being (potentially) at the same time as their associated body and are inseparable from it. Hence, with the possible exception of *nous*, the psyche perishes when the body perishes. Throughout most of *De anima*, the psyche is considered to be the form of the body, the two constituting a single living substance. Aristotle defined psyche, or soul, as the first "perfection" of a natural organic body having the potentiality for life. This, his most general definition of soul implies that the soul perishes at bodily death. This is how Alexander of Aphrodisias, one of Aristotle's most important early commentators, later understood him. However, Aristotle muddied this picture.

In *De anima*, Aristotle wrote that the intellect "seems to be a substance that comes about in a thing and is not corrupted." He added:

> Therefore, it is necessary that in [the soul] there be an intellect capable of becoming all things, and an intellect capable of making itself understand all things. And the intellect which is capable of understanding all things is ... separated, not mixed or passible

[i.e., perishable], and, in its substance, is action.... And in its separated state, it is just what it is, and this alone is always immortal. And there is no memory, because [this agent intellect] is not passible, and the passible intellect is corruptible, and without it [i.e., the agent intellect] nothing is understood.[14]

In another work, in the context of discussing conception and fetal development, Aristotle noted that the vegetative soul, having existed potentially in semen, comes into being actually when it provides the vital heat to matter supplied by the mother.[15] He there wrote that the sensitive soul, having existed potentially in the vegetative soul, comes into being actually in a similar way. He ended by noting that the intellective or rational soul cannot have been generated internally. "It remains," he said, "that the intellect alone should come from without, and that it alone be divine." In the rational soul, he claimed, there is a power of acting and a power of being acted upon, the former of which—the agent or active intellect—is ungenerated and incorruptible.

Thus, in many interpretations of Aristotle, the agent-intellect, or *nous*, preexists its associated body and is immortal.[16] Yet, even if *nous* is immortal, it is not a good vehicle for personal immortality. This is because, in Aristotle's view, matter is what distinguishes one thing from another of the same kind. Thus, although the rational part of every individual human soul may be immortal, individual humans may not thereby themselves be immortal, and not just because their bodies die but because there is only one *nous*, which all humans share. Hence, in Aristotle's view, it may be that only what we have in common, and not what distinguishes us from one another, survives the grave. In his words, "All things which are many in number have matter; for many individuals have one and the same intelligible structure, for example, man, whereas Socrates is one."[17] Once the *material* human being is gone, along with his or her memories, only the form, which is the same for all human beings, remains.

In a passage in *On Generation and Corruption* that would become especially important in the thirteenth century when medieval philosophers were trying to rework Christian theology through the lens of Aristotelian metaphysics, Aristotle seems to deny the possibility of personal survival of bodily death. He began by asking why "men and animals do not 'return upon themselves' so that the same individual comes-to-be a second time?" He answered by distinguishing between those things whose substance is imperishable and those whose substance is perishable. In the case of things whose substance is perishable, which he thought to include humans and animals, although *the same kind of thing* can recur, *the very same thing* cannot recur. As we shall see, the failure of Saint Paul and the earliest church fathers to be clear on this point is the basis for a doubt about whether some of them even believed in personal survival of bodily death, in the sense in which we would understand personal survival today.[18]

In addition to the question of whether people survive bodily death, there are the further questions: first, of whether it matters whether they survive it and, second, if it does matter, why it matters. In general, Plato had an easier time explaining why it matters whether people survive their bodily deaths. Apparently he thought that people would be helped in discovering eternal truths if they could get away from bodily distractions. In addition, he tells us that Socrates, in one of his last thoughts, mused about the joys of conversing with the dead. Apparently, then, Plato (or Socrates) thought that since people in the afterlife can converse about earthly events, their souls retain their premortem memories and other mental dispositions. If Plato looked forward to conversing with the dead, he must have thought that people are entitled to anticipate having the experiences of their postmortem selves. It is not clear what Aristotle's views were on any of these topics. In general, Plato had a more unified way than Aristotle of insuring the immortality of each individual's soul, but Aristotle had a more unified way of explaining the soul's relationship to the body.

After Aristotle died, many commentators on his work arose. One of the most important historically was Alexander of Aphrodisias (fl. 200 c.e.), who became head of the Lyceum at Athens. In antiquity, he became famous for writing commentaries on Aristotle that were intended to reestablish Aristotle's views in their pure form. In the Middle Ages, he also became well known for his original writings, including *On the Soul*, in which he argued that human mentality is a mixture of "mortal" and "active" intellects. Only the active intellect, he claimed, which is the same in all humans and in God, survives bodily death. Needless to add, its surviving bodily death is not a way to insure any particular human person's individual personal survival.

Materialistic Atomism

In addition to the tradition in Greek thought that went through Plato and Aristotle, then to Plotinus, and afterwards to the church fathers, there was a perhaps equally influential tradition of materialistic atomism. Thinkers in this tradition included the atomists Leucippus (fl. 440 b.c.e.) and Democritus (460?–370? b.c.e.), who were responsible for the original formulation of the idea that the world is composed of material atoms but who had nothing to say, so far as we know, about the self and personal identity. That task was left especially to the Epicureans and the Stoics, whose schools would become especially influential during the Hellenistic period, when the political center of Europe shifted from Greece to Rome.

Epicurus (341–270 B.C.E.) not only espoused an atomist metaphysics but integrated it into a philosophy of life according to which pleasure is the only good, pain the only evil, and fear of death a needless source of human distress. "God presents no fears," he wrote, and "death no worries. And while good is readily attainable, evil is readily endurable."[19] The problem, he claimed, is not death but the fear of death. And the way to conquer that fear is to accept death for exactly what it is, the physical coming apart of the complex of atoms that is one's soul, resulting in the cessation of any subject that could experience pleasure or pain. "The correct understanding that death is nothing to us," he wrote, "makes our mortality enjoyable, not by adding infinite time, but by taking away the yearning for immortality."[20] Unlike other atomists who went before him, Epicurus denied determinism in order to allow free will. He was not only intellectually but also socially radical. In the community that he founded, men, women, children, slaves, and even prostitutes participated on equal terms.

Stoicism was founded by Zeno of Citium (335–263 B.C.E.). According to his view, the world as a whole, which is divinely planned and permeated by reason (logos), is the best possible organization of matter. His most celebrated disciple, Chrysippus (280–206 B.C.E.), is credited with developing this philosophy into a comprehensive system. A cardinal tenet of this system is that the world is an ideally good organism, the behavior of which is completely determined and whose rational soul governs it for the best. Ultimately, the world is composed of earth, water, air, and fire, the latter two of which constitute a pervasive life force, called pneuma (or "breath"). This life force constitutes the souls of all living things. The world as a whole is evolving inexorably toward a great, all-consuming fire, after which the entire sequence of world events repeats itself in every detail, over and over, without end. Individual humans are thus fated to do everything they do. Nevertheless, they are responsible for their actions. What allows them to be responsible is that the causal determination of their actions works through their agency.

Stoics also thought about the psychological construction of the self, that is, about how conscious beings, especially humans, originally arrive at the view that "I am this self." Their interest in this issue can perhaps be traced to an extension by them of the idea of property ownership to that of a human individual's relationship to him- or herself.[21] And this extension may in turn have been related to their rejection of the commonly held Greek idea of natural slavery. That is, since the Stoics regarded all human beings as equal, regardless of race, class, or gender, it was a short step to the view that each person owns him- or herself. All humans share equally in the world-governing reason. Thus, all share equally in the responsibilities of membership in the universal human community, especially in the responsibility of attuning one's life and character to the *logos*, serenely indifferent to the vagaries of external events. The idea of self-possession is thus linked to that of responsibility for oneself, which is linked to responsibility to the human community, all of which are based on the individual's psychological relationship to him- or herself.

Chrysippus, in what is thought to be the first use *ever* of the word *consciousness*, wrote that every animal appropriates (*oikeiosis*) not only "its own constitution," but "its consciousness" of its own constitution. In making animals, he wrote, nature ensures that each one "appropriates" itself "to itself" so that it will behave in self-interested ways, that is, will reject things that hurt it and pursue things that help it:[22] Later, Roman Stoics elaborated this view. Seneca (4 B.C.E.–65 C.E.), for instance, wrote that every animal instinctively appropriates its own body: "Nature cares for its own products, and because the safest protection is the closest, each product of nature has been entrusted to itself";[23] and Hierocles (fl. 100 C.E.) wrote that "as soon as an animal is born, it perceives itself" so that henceforth it can "be pleased with itself," for "an animal, having got its first conception of itself is at once appropriated to itself and its own constitution."[24] Hierocles then went on to suggest that "each one of us is, as it were, entirely encompassed by many circles, some smaller, others larger." In the "first and closest" of these circles, "the individual has drawn as though around a center, his own mind." This first circle also "encloses the body and anything taken for the sake of the body; for it is a circle of virtually minimal radius, and almost touches the center itself." The second circle, "further removed from the center, but enclosing the first circle" includes "parents, siblings, wife, and children." The "outermost and largest circle" encompasses "the whole human race."[25]

Explicitly accounting for the psychological construction of the self was not a central, high-visibility concern during the classical period, or even during the Middle Ages. Nevertheless, it would emerge again, at the end of the seventeenth century, as one of John Locke's most important preoccupations, and again toward the end of the nineteenth century, in the thought of William James. Chrysippus, it should be noted, anticipated an idea that would be central to Locke's view, namely that humans are both "lumps of matter" and also "persons" and that their identities as lumps of matter may be determined on a different basis than their identities as persons.

In Chrysippus's view, whereas any change may make one a different lump of matter, it does not thereby make one a different person. Instead, he held the view, common among Stoics, that each individual had some unique property, or essence, that remained unchanged throughout the life of the individual, and by which, despite other radical changes, the individual could be identified.[26] Such ideas, which might have led to what we think of as a modern, relational view of personal identity, were overshadowed in the Roman period by the ascendancy of Neoplatonism, which through the influence primarily of Augustine provided the framework for Christian theology from the fourth to the thirteenth centuries.

Related to these earlier Greek materialistic atomistic philosophies, but with a more practical focus, were the medical materialists. The earliest Greek physicians, whose medical works were collectively attributed to Hippocrates, worked under the assumption that both mental (*psyche*) and physical (*soma*) illnesses had their basis in the physical constitution of humans (*physis*). For instance, Hippocrates' *On the Sacred Disease* begins: "It [epilepsy] appears to me to be nowise more divine nor more sacred than other diseases, but has a natural cause from which it originates like other affections." He goes on to describe the similarity of this "sacred" disease with other maladies involving insanity, after which he explains why some forms of mental illness are said to be sacred: "They who first referred this malady to the gods appear to me to have been just such persons as the conjurors, purificators, mountebanks, and charlatans now are, who give themselves out for being excessively religious, and as knowing more than other people." These people, he continued, use "divinity as a pretext and screen" for their own ignorance. Hippocrates' own view was that "the brain," which is "the primary seat of sense and of the spirits" and "perceives whatever occurs in the body," is "the cause of [these] afflictions." Some of these disturbances affect the brain itself and lead to mental illness. Thus, in his view, the way to treat this illness is to treat the brain.[27]

Subsequently anatomical investigations by Herophilus and Erasistratus (c. 330–250 B.C.E.) established the role that nerves play in connecting the brain to the rest of the body. This discovery, apparently, had a great impact on Epicurean and Stoic philosophers of the time, including physicians, since it provided a clear means of explaining in a physical way how mind and body might interact. If the brain were the seat of the mind and could communicate through the nerves to the rest of the body, the activities of the body could be known. The body, then, would not require an immaterial mind that operates, in some unknowable fashion, on all parts of the body. Instead, the mind itself could be some kind of "spiritual matter" (*pneuma*) of a thin and rapidly moving sort. It could have the brain as its center but through the nerves grow tendrils to the rest of the body and in this way both feel and control distant parts of the body.[28]

Such ideas originated early in the views of Greek medical research and are important in providing the beginnings of a naturalistic account of mental phenomena. However, they lost ground in late antiquity as increasingly the dualistic theory of Plato gained favor not only among religiously oriented thinkers but even among physicians.[29]

Finally, at about the same time, other schools of philosophy, especially the Cyreniacs (c. 400– c. 200 B.C.E.) and the Skeptics (c. 360–c. 225 B.C.E.) raised questions about the limits of human knowledge of the external world and of other minds.[30] In the seventeenth century, this sort of skeptical thinking would join forces with a materialist conception of an external world composed of corpuscular mechanisms and become the vehicle for the rise of modern science. It would also, through Descartes's influence, become the vehicle for the development of a new form of mind/body dualism.[31]

II

INDIVIDUALISM AND SUBJECTIVITY

Aristotle's student, Alexander the Great, conquered most of the known world, in the process spreading Greek culture and language from Egypt to India and creating vital centers of learning, such as Alexandria. However, soon after his early death his empire fell apart. There followed in Greece a long period of dynastic fighting from which Rome emerged as the center of a new empire. Although Roman philosophers invariably took Greek philosophical ideas as their point of departure, they often developed these ideas in interesting ways. Nowhere is this more evident than in their theories of the self and personal identity.

Roman Stoicism

The Greek word "*prosopon*" originally meant playing a role in a drama or in a religious ceremony. However, with the rise and democratization of the Greek city-states, the word began to acquire a wholly secular meaning, which had to do with social and legal roles. Certain kinds of citizens were recognized as having rights and duties that distinguished them from others. In earlier Greek thought about people and society, the emphasis was on these roles. Only slight attention was given to the individuals who occupied the roles. People were regarded as little more than placeholders. However, when the Greek city-states declined, there followed a period of pessimism during which the traditional emphasis on harmonious relationships in the polis among essentially replaceable individuals waned. Cynics and Stoics, in particular, emphasized inner resources for adaptation to the general malaise. This gave rise to a new emphasis on individualism. The Latin term "*persona*," from which the English term *person* derives, acquired its modern meaning from within the context of this latter development.

Greek religious myths had earlier given way to Plato's otherworldliness, which then spawned increasingly secular, this-worldly perspectives in the thought of Aristotle, the materialists, and the skeptics. Although Heraclitus had much earlier said that "a man's character is his fate," Aristotle's account of human nature, as in "man is a rational animal," tended to be generic.[1] And when Aristotle did turn to the consideration of character, he was primarily interested in character *types*. Among Roman philosophers, by contrast, a generic approach to human nature was supplemented by consideration of individual character and what distinguishes people. In addition, an earlier focus on biology and behavior was modified to include a heightened interest in human subjectivity.

According to Cicero (106–43 B.C.E.), who was not himself a Stoic but whose thought was pervaded by the spirit of Stoicism, although "character, for man, is destiny," we are invested by Nature with two characters (*personae*). One of these, per the Aristotelian theory of our common human nature, we share with every human being. However, the other distinguishes us from one another. These latter, then, vary from person to person. In Cicero's view, what humans share with one another are the capacity for rationality and the ability to discover their duty. Humans are equipped by nature for these tasks. However, in our "natures and characters," there are "countless" differences among us. These differences, he said, are not necessarily deviations from what is ideal in humanity but rather are potentially good. What is important is that each person "must resolutely hold fast to his own peculiar gifts, in so far as they are peculiar only and not vicious."

As Plato and Aristotle had also done before him, Cicero drew attention to certain intermediary social roles, such as being a wise person, that fall between the generality of our shared human essence and the individuality of who we are as unique people. "Propriety" occurs, he said, "when the actions and words" of an individual are "appropriate to his role." When such propriety is "visibly displayed" in the way we lead our lives, it "elicits the approval" of those who see it. Consistency is key: "How dignified, then, how lofty, how consistent is the character of the wise man [*persona sapientis*]."[2] But Cicero went beyond this sort of recognition of personality types to the recognition of individual uniqueness, even to the point of distinguishing between those of our individual characteristics that merely particularize us from one another and those that express who we really are. In advising people to take possession of their authentic natures, he became the first to express the modern idea that there is such a thing as one's *true self*. Wedding the traditional Greek ideal of realizing *human* excellence with a Roman, and ultimately modern, ideal of realizing *individual* excellence, he claimed that it is not only possible but one's duty to realize one's true self.

This newfound concern with individual character received a remarkable development in the thought of Epictetus (55?–135? c.e.), who began as a student in Rome but returned to Greece to teach. Basic to his view was attention to the distinction between what a person can and cannot control. A person cannot control his initial character or his external circumstances, he said, but can control how he responds to them, in particular, whether he lives in accordance with them. In stressing the importance of playing well the hand that fate has dealt you, he was among the first to highlight the importance of will. "Remember," he wrote, "that you are an actor in a play." You did not write the play or determine your part in it. Your job is to play your part well. If your part is "to act a poor man you must act the part with all your powers; and so if your part be a cripple or a magistrate or a plain man. For your business is to act the character that is given you and act it well."[3] And this only should be the object of your pride, not what you have been given by nature, but how you have responded to whatever you have been given.

To illustrate this point, Epictetus tells with favor the story of Priscus Helvidius, a senator, who was ordered by Emperor Vespasian not to come into the Senate. Priscus answered: "You can forbid me to be a senator; but as long as I am a senator I must come in." Vespasian: "Come in, then, and be silent." Priscus: "Question me not and I will be silent." Vespasian: "But I am bound to question you." Priscus: "And I am bound to say what seems right to me." Exasperated, Vespasian threatened to kill Priscus, if he talked in the Senate. Priscus calmly replied, "When did I tell you, that I am immortal? You will do your part and I mine. It is yours to kill, mine to die without making a fuss: yours to banish, mine to go into exile without groaning."

As in all Stoic philosophy, there is a strong element of resignation in Epictetus's view. In this part of what he wrote, social role is preeminent. However, he also emphasizes individualism by recognizing that because character varies from person to person, what it is to live in accord with nature also varies. For some, he claims, the way to live in accordance with nature is simply to follow the herd, for others to distinguish themselves. If you are the former type, then "you ought to think how you can be like other men," for "just as one thread" in a tunic "does not wish to have something special to distinguish it from the rest," so you too should not wish to have something special. However, if you are the latter type of person, it is as if you wish to be "the purple [thread], that touch of brilliance that gives distinction and beauty to the rest." For such a person, it would be a grave mistake to follow the herd—he would "no longer be the purple." Epictetus concludes,

"That is what I mean by keeping your character: such is its power with those who have acquired the habit of carrying it into every question that arises."[4]

It is sometimes said, though perhaps it is an exaggeration, that in Greek thought there is no idea of an agent's being the *source* of his actions and hence no category of the *will*. In Roman thought and culture, perhaps due in part to the development of a superior legal system, there gradually emerged a vocabulary of the will. As a partial consequence, individual human subjects emerge as agents, the sources of their own actions, which they create and for which they are responsible. Epictetus made an important contribution to this development in the context of advising people to be true to themselves and explaining what he took that to involve. His explanation appealed centrally to the recognition that each of us has a potentially distinctive character, to an awareness of what that character consists in, and to knowing that what a person should do is to act in accordance with his or her character, regardless of the consequences, with the proviso that part of what may be involved in acting in accordance with your character is developing your character. However, he cautions that you should not act out of the character toward which you are developing but only out of the character that you possess at the time.

Marcus Aurelius (121–180 C.E.), a follower of Epictetus who became emperor of Rome, was also concerned with character and individualism. However, Marcus was preoccupied with the spiritual state of his soul. Hence, his thought is distinguished from that of Epictetus by its being religious. It is also distinguished by a heightened interiorization. And, in Marcus's thought, unlike in that of everyone who came earlier and most who would come later, interiorization is fiercely focused in the present moment. He claims, for instance, that since "the present is the same for all" when the moment of death arrives it makes no difference whether one has lived for three years or for thirty thousand years, for "no man loses any other life than this which he now lives." The past is gone. Hence, the person who lives longest "and he who will die soonest lose just the same." The present moment "is the only thing of which a man can be deprived."[5]

And what is one in the present? In Marcus's view, all humans are a combination of form and matter, neither of which "will perish into non-existence, as neither of them came into existence out of non-existence." He said that every part of himself "will be reduced by change into some part of the universe, and that again will change into another part of the universe, and so on forever." He concludes that it is "by consequence of such changes" that he exists, and those who begot him, "and so on forever in the other direction." Typical of his view is the sagelike attitude expressed in his remark on the assumption that souls continue to exist after bodily death: one should suppose that they "are removed into the air and after subsisting for some time there are transformed and diffused, eventually assuming a fiery nature as they enter into the seminal intelligence of the universe, in this way making room for fresh souls which then come to dwell there."

Roman Epicureanism

De Rerum Natura, by Lucretius (95?–54? B.C.E.), is one of the best known products of classical Roman scholarship. In his masterwork, Lucretius denies both the existence of an immaterial soul and personal survival of bodily death. Yet his Epicurean poem is significant less for its effect on his contemporaries than for its effect on medieval and early modern philosophers. It was available and read by philosophers in the Latin West until the ninth century and then again from the Renaissance to modern times. Among Christian thinkers, Lucretius's eloquent arguments for hedonism, materialism, and atheism (actually, a kind of deism) resulted in his being widely regarded, at least until the eighteenth century, as a kind of philosophical Antichrist. However, from the point of view of developments in personal-identity theory in our own times, it is not any of these aspects of his philosophy that is most significant. Rather, it is that he denied Plato's basic assumption that if souls, or minds, continued to exist and have experiences after death, people would be entitled to anticipate *having* the experiences of their postmortem souls. Lucretius, thus, is the first act in a drama that is playing out in our own times—that of figuring out the relative importance of personal identity in the apparently self-interested desire that people have to persist.

In Lucretius's poem, this issue arises indirectly. In the context of his making the point that we have nothing to fear from bodily death, he argues that "if any feeling remains in mind or spirit after it has been torn from body, that is nothing to us, who are brought into being by the wedlock of body and spirit, conjoined and coalesced." He then considers the possibility that "the matter that composes us should be reassembled by time after our death and brought back into its present state." He claims that even if this were to happen to humans—that is, were they, in effect, to be resurrected—it would be of no concern to us "once the chain of our identity had been snapped."

Why of no concern? Lucretius's answer, in effect, seems to be, first, that our persisting—that is, our continuing as the same people we now are—is a precondition of any egoistic concern we might have for the experiences of any *parts* of ourselves that survive our bodily deaths and, second, that whatever *parts* may survive, *we* cease at our bodily deaths: "If the future holds travail and anguish in store, the self must be in existence, when that time comes, in order to experience it." "From this fate," he continues, "we are redeemed by death, which denies existence to the self that might have suffered these tribulations." The moral of these reflections, he thought, is "that we have nothing to fear in death," since "one who no longer is cannot suffer, or differ in any way from one who has never been born, when once this mortal life has been usurped by death the immortal."[6]

Classical scholars differ from each other in their translation of these crucial passages from Lucretius. However, what matters historically is less what Lucretius actually meant than what he was interpreted by later thinkers to have meant.[7] In John Dryden's seventeenth-century translation, which was one of the earliest into English, the passage is translated as follows: "So when our mortal frame shall be disjoin'd, / The lifeless Lump uncoupled from the mind, / From sense of grief and pain we shall be free; / We shall not feel, because we shall not BE.... // Nay, ev'n suppose when we have suffer'd Fate, / The Soul could feel, in her divided state, / What's that to us? for we are only we / While Souls and Bodies in one frame agree.... // We, who are dead and gone, shall bear no part / In all the pleasures, nor shall feel the smart, / Which to that other Mortal shall accrue, / Whom, of our Matter Time shall mould anew."[8]

In sum, in what seems to have been Lucretius's own view, and clearly was a view that some later attributed to Lucretius, even if something that is currently part of us persists and is capable of having experiences and performing actions, if this part of ourselves is not attended by the very bodies we have when we die, then this part is not us and, therefore, is no concern of ours. In order for such a part of ourselves to be attended by the very bodies we have when we die, these bodies would have to exist continuously as integrated, functioning entities, which obviously they do not after bodily death. Lucretius concluded that any such part of ourselves that persists is, therefore, not us. Hence, the experiences and actions of any such part of ourselves that persists are not something that we can look forward to having and performing.

What is impressive in these thoughts is not so much Lucretius's *answer* to the question of what matters in a person's apparently self-interested desire to persist (his view was that what matters presupposes personal identity) but rather his *asking* the question of what matters. No one previously, at least in the West, had asked it. Normally, thinkers simply assumed (as many still do assume) that if at some point in the future they were no longer to exist, but that were they to have continued, their futures would have been bright, then necessarily something of inestimable value, at least from their own egoistic points of view, has been lost. In asking the question of what matters in survival, Lucretius considered the possibility that we might not persist and yet that, even from our own egoistic points of view, not much that matters would be lost—not because our lives were awful or because we did not value ourselves but because personal identity is not what matters in survival.

Unfortunately, Lucretius did not argue for his view that it is identity that matters in survival. Yet, because he was so widely read both during the middle ages and into the modern period, he introduced into the discussion of self and survival the question of what matters in survival. As we shall see, this question resurfaced again in the seventeenth, eighteenth, and early nineteenth centuries and then again in our own times, when it moved to center stage.

Neoplatonism

During the first three centuries c.e., most of Roman philosophy had a this-worldly orientation. Yet there was also a dramatic increase in philosophy with an otherworldly or religious orientation, primarily among marginal groups, such as the Jews and Christians, but also among the Greeks. The most original and influential of these Greek thinkers was Plotinus (204–270 c.e.), who viewed the world hierarchically, with the One at the top of the hierarchy, humans in the middle, and physical objects at the bottom. In this scheme, reality, unity, and intrinsic worth emanate from above and vary directly in proportion to each other. Thus, the One is not only the most real, unified, and intrinsically valuable thing but the source of whatever reality, unity, and intrinsic value other things have that are lower in the hierarchy. Plotinus's development of these ideas marked a new beginning for Platonism.

In Plato's *philosophy* of self and personal identity, in which he put forward his view of the soul, he did not ask what accounts for the unity of the self *at any given time*. Had he raised this question, he might have answered that the soul's imma-teriality and, hence, its indivisibility, accounts for its unity. However, in his *psychology* of self, in the *Republic* and elsewhere, he suggested a different sort of answer. In the context of a discussion in which his concern was on what is conducive to harmony in the soul, he claimed that when the rational part of a person's soul is in charge, the person lives morally and his soul is harmonious.

Six centuries later, Plotinus raised more fine-grained questions about the unity of consciousness. He argued that unity would be impossible if the soul were matter because matter is inherently divisible in a way that would destroy the mind's unity. While conceding that the soul too is divisible, he argued that it is divisible in a way that does not interfere with its unity. "The nature, at once divisible and indivisible, which we affirm to be soul has not the unity of an extended thing: it does not consist of separate sections; its divisibility lies in its presence at every point in the recipient, but it is indivisible as dwelling entire in any part." If the soul "had the nature of body," he continues, "it would consist of isolated members each unaware of the conditions of each other." In that case, "there would be a particular soul—say, a soul of the finger—answering as a distinct and independent entity to every local experience"; hence, "there would be a multiplicity of souls administering each individual." Since the mental lives of such individuals, he points out, would be unlike our own mental lives, each of us cannot be administered by a multiplicity of (equal) souls. "Without a dominant unity," he concludes, our lives would be "meaningless." So far as is known, no one had entertained such thoughts before.[9]

Plotinus's preoccupation with the question of how to account for the unity of consciousness foreshadowed discussions that would reemerge in the eighteenth century and then again in our own times. In the eighteenth century it was also presupposed that each individual human's consciousness is unified. The question was whether matter could account for its unity. In our own times, not only has the unity of each individual human's consciousness been called into question but theoretical fragmentation has raised the prospect that varying accounts of this or that aspect of mentality may not be capable of being integrated into a single coherent account. We shall return to these worries in our final chapter.

In regard to the comparison with the eighteenth century, it is interesting that Plotinus's thoughts about the unity of consciousness are similar to Locke's discussion of what, in our own times, have come to be known as *fission examples*. These are hypothetical examples in which a person's consciousness is supposed to divide into two parts, each of which is mentally complete in itself and neither of which is conscious, from the inside, of the other's mental states. When Locke introduced fission examples, he even used the image of a finger's retaining an independent consciousness after it had been separated from the rest of the body.

Although it is impossible to know whether Locke's reading of Plotinus suggested these ideas to him, it seems highly likely that he had read Plotinus or was at least familiar with his views through the writings of the Cambridge Platonists. In any case, among the questions that eighteenth-century philosophers (but not Locke) soon asked about fission examples, two are crucial: In fission examples, what becomes of the identity of the person (or mind) that divides into two unified wholes—does the prefission person persist? And, if that question were answered in the negative, could the prefission person nevertheless obtain what prior to fission mattered primarily to him or her in survival?

Plotinus's approach to such issues occurred within the context of his view of the soul's concurrent existence at the sensory, intellectual, and mystical levels. At the sensory level, the soul is unified with the body and involved in its life. In this context, the soul uses its powers merely to understand objects of perception or sense. At the intellectual level, the soul contemplates abstract ideas and is conscious of itself as a soul or self fundamentally distinct from the body. This self-consciousness of the soul is its so-called essential level, at which it can move from earthly to celestial existence and, through reincarnation, from one body to another. The third level of the soul is that at which, through mystical contemplation, it fuses with God, in the process losing its individuality. In Plotinus's view, this third level is always present—that is, the human soul is always fused with God, although humans are not always aware of it. In our earthly existence our intellects distract us from this awareness, and rather than being fixed on the eternal, we are bound to sense perception and concrete imagination in time.

As Plotinus describes the human soul, although "our reasoning is our own" and "we ourselves think the thoughts that occupy the understanding," our intellectual capacity is nourished from above and our sensitive capacity from below. Humans, thus, are not only midway between God and the beasts but are partly both. In this view, the sensitive principle is "our scout," the intellectual "our King." We become more kingly by molding ourselves to the intellectual principle, more beastly by becoming preoccupied with the senses. In our earthly existence, it is the intellectual level of the soul that self-remembers. Sense and perception are at an animal level and lack the abstractive powers necessary for self-consciousness and recollection.[10] At death, intellect-based memories are retained for awhile but gradually are forgotten as the soul focuses on higher activities. This is a time when the soul may begin to remember previous lives that were forgotten during its most recent life: "The soul, still a dragged captive, will tell of all the man did and felt; but upon death there will appear, as time passes, memories of the lives lived before, some of the events of the most recent life being dismissed as trivial."[11] However, as the soul turns its attention toward God, even these memories of prior lives are forgotten.

How quickly the soul makes these transitions depends on how it has lived in this life. If in this life an individual has focused on the contemplation of God and led a good life, then in the next life he or she will quickly make the transition to focusing exclusively on God. However, souls bound in this life to a brute existence will not in the next be able to let go of human experiences and, as a consequence, will suffer. "The loftier" part of the soul "must desire to come to a happy forgetfulness of all that has reached it through the lower." Thus "the more urgent the intention towards the Supreme, the more extensive will be the soul's forgetfulness, unless indeed, when the entire living has, even here, been such that memory has nothing but the noblest to deal with."[12] When human contemplation reaches its highest point, one forgets one's self entirely, merging with

God (or shedding the illusion of separateness) and thereafter no longer reenters the process of reincarnation. Instead, one selflessly participates eternally in the contemplation of God. All human memories are lost: "There will not even be memory of the personality; no thought that the contemplator is the self—Socrates, for example—or that it is Intellect or Soul."[13]

In such theoretical interpretations of his mystical visions of the afterlife, Plotinus not only elaborated on Plato's views, but created a new conception of unity with God—one that would transform late Greek Platonism. Through such Christian authors as Augustine, Pseudo-Dionysius, and John Eriugena, as well as indirectly through Islamic and Jewish mysticism, his version of Neoplatonism would deeply influence Christianity, eastern and western, throughout the Middle Ages and into the Renaissance.

As a consequence of the Christian church fathers' eventually selecting the views of Plato and Plotinus as the models for their own theology, they reversed the trend that had been in progress before Plotinus from an otherworldly to a this-worldly orientation. How and why they did this is the next part of our story. In appreciating this story, it is crucial to remember that much of Greek thought was not available generally to Romans, and much of Roman thought was not available to the Latin West until very late in the tradition. For instance, very little of what today we think of as the Aristotelian corpus was available to Romans until about 100 C.E. Before that time, the only Aristotelian works available to those who were not members of Aristotle's school were some of his dialogues, which are now lost. Although Cicero famously called Aristotle "golden throated," he hardly knew Aristotle, whose *De anima* was not generally available until Alexander of Aphrodisias's time. After the fourth century, except for one or two logical works, Aristotle was virtually unknown in the Latin West until the end of the twelfth century. The story of the transmission of Platonic ideas is similar. He survived in only a few works, including the *Phaedo* and the *Timaeus*, and, prior to the Renaissance, hardly any of Plotinus's works survived in the Latin West. Throughout this period, Augustine was the main source of Neoplatonism.

III

PEOPLE OF THE BOOK

Judaism, Christianity, and Islam developed in the same region of the Middle East and have overlapping scriptural traditions.[1] All three are monotheistic, positing a single all-powerful god, who transcends the natural world, which is his creation. All three portray God not only as the god of their particular group or region, but the god of everyone, everywhere. And all three spawned intellectuals who tried to integrate what was handed down in Scripture with pagan philosophy derived from Greece. Because the three religions had so much in common, their intellectuals faced common problems, such as the problem of evil. The theories that they developed to handle these problems were not just narrowly construed theologies but worldviews that incorporated what today we would call philosophy, science, and religion.

Yet, there were important differences between each of these emerging religions and the Greek philosophy on which their intellectuals drew. Chief among these was that Greek philosophy placed a higher premium on secular reason and tended to view its questions ahistorically. By contrast, Jewish, Christian, and Islamic philosophers tended to emphasize revelation as a preeminent source of knowledge and to view their questions within the context of what they took to be the histories of their respective peoples, as related in their holy scriptures.

Judaism

The "Tanakh" (or Hebrew Bible) is the basic Jewish Scripture. It includes the "Torah" (Hebrew for "Law"), the "Prophets," and the "Hagiographa" (Greek for "sacred writings"). The Torah, which is also called the Pentateuch (Greek for "five books"), consists of the first five books of the Hebrew Bible, from Genesis to Deuteronomy. Tradition has it that the Torah was written by Moses under divine inspiration. Parts of the Torah were in use by the Jews by 600 B.C.E., the whole by 400 B.C.E. It contains accounts of how the world and its creatures were created. It also includes a history of the flight of the Jewish people, under the leadership of Moses, from their bondage in Egypt to the Holy Land of Israel, where they settled. And it lays down many "laws," including the Ten Commandments. These laws were intended to govern virtually every aspect of Jewish life.[2]

In addition to the Hebrew Bible, the Jews also wrote commentaries on the Torah, known as the Talmud (literally *teachings*) and commentaries on the Talmud, known as the Mishnah. These consist of biblical interpretation and practical applications of Scripture, as well as parables and stories that present Jewish ethics in more humanistic (less legal) ways. The Mishnah also includes discussion of some topics, such as the immortality of the soul and its superiority to the body, which receive scant treatment in the Hebrew Bible but were taken up later by Jewish philosophers.

The Talmud exists in more than one version. The one completed in Babylon at the end of the fifth century C.E. came to be accepted by subsequent Jews as the basic document fixing Jewish law and ritual. Explicit in this version of the Talmud is the belief both in the immortality of the soul and in the resurrection of the body. For instance, in the *Birkhot Hashahar*, or "Early Morning Benedictions," the following plea occurs: "My God, the soul that You have given me is pure. You created it, You fashioned it, You breathed it into me, You safeguard it within me, and You will eventually take it from me and return it to me in time to come. . . . Praised are You Lord who restores souls to dead bodies."[3]

Jewish philosophy, as opposed to the sort of scriptural commentary and elaboration found in the Talmud, began in the Diaspora community of the Hellenistic world, where beginning in the second century B.C.E. Jewish thinkers produced a philosophical literature in Greek. The point of departure for this philosophy was the attempt to understand the meaning of events related in the Hebrew Bible, especially what these events reveal about the ongoing relationship of the Jewish people and their God. Whereas Greek philosophers went out of their way to divorce their new philosophy from their old religion, Jewish philosophers went out of their way to integrate their old religion with their new philosophy. Christian and Islamic thinkers did the same. This task, then, became a prominent theme in European philosophy to the end of the eighteenth century.

Central to Judaism is the notion of a single God. The new Jewish philosophers were intent on explaining the nature of this God, his relationship to the created world, and his special relationship to the Hebrew people. These explanations begin in Genesis, the first book in the Hebrew Bible, which gives two accounts of the creation. One portrays God as an all-powerful being, who, first, created a "basic" world from nothing and then over a period of six consecutive "days" embellished it, adding the sun, the moon, and the different species of plants and animals. The creation of the world culminated in the creation of man in God's "own image" (Gen. 1:26). The other account tells the familiar story of the first human couple, Adam and Eve, and their ultimate expulsion from the Garden of Eden.

Both of these stories profoundly influenced Western conceptions of human nature and personal identity. The first of them, by stressing the creation of man in the image of God, encouraged philosophers to think about humans as they thought about God, as well as the other way round. The second of them had even greater significance. The idea that humans fell from a previous state of grace in which they were destined for immortality encouraged the search for traces of good and evil in human nature. It also encouraged thinkers to assume that humans are destined to return to their original state.

In Genesis, what led to Adam and Eve's demise was, on the one hand, their desire for heightened knowledge, particularly of good and evil, and, on the other, their disobedient, sinful natures. Prior to their expulsion from the Garden, they had been immortal. The wages of their sin were death, a debt handed down from generation to generation. What, though, is the ultimate significance of death? Is there any way that humans can recapture the immortality that they lost? These questions became central.

In most of the Hebrew Bible prior to the book of Daniel, there is an implicit assumption that bodily death is the end. Individual survival, let alone immortality, is not an option. The exceptions to this rule are intimations of personal survival of bodily death in Wisdom (2:23–24), Ezekiel (e.g., 37), and Isaiah. However, in Daniel (12:2), not only is there commitment to survival of bodily death, but a new idea is introduced: resurrection. For instance, it is written that "many of those that sleep in the dust of the earth will awake, some to eternal life, others to reproaches, to everlasting abhorrence." When Daniel asks for the meaning of these events, he is told, "But you, go on to the end; you shall rest, and arise to your destiny at the end of the days." When ideas such as these appear in Daniel, they appear in an historical context in which the Jews are portrayed as suffering even though they have been good. Resurrection, thus, becomes the means by which God's justice triumphs over injustice, thereby vindicating God and saving human life from being meaningless.

In Asian traditions (and even to some extent in the West), reincarnation, to which everyone was thought to be equally subject, had been used as a technique for achieving cosmic justice. However, in Daniel, only some are expected to survive bodily death, so reward and punishment applies only to them. Nevertheless, at issue is God's justice, which is not fully realized in normal human lifetimes. To remedy this situation, and in sharp contrast to the prevailing message of previous biblical tradition, the earthly lives of some humans, and then eventually all, become just part of the story. The rest of the story concerns life beyond the grave, where God's justice ultimately asserts itself.

Throughout the time that Daniel and earlier books of the Hebrew scriptures were composed, the Jews were materialists. So, when, in Daniel, the idea of resurrection is introduced, it means resurrection of the body, which is resurrection of the whole person. Eventually, in the Talmud, the idea of the resurrection of the body joins hands with the idea, borrowed ultimately from Plato, that humans have an immortal soul. Before this integration would be generally adopted, several sects espoused different views. The Sadducees held the traditional view that there was no afterlife and that reward and punishment occurred only in this life. Not surprisingly, this sect was more popular with the rich than the poor. The Pharisees held the newer and increasingly popular view among the masses that there was something immortal in the soul that, after death, could be eternally punished or rewarded by being resurrected with the body into a new life.

Although there were many previous Jewish commentators on their holy scripture, the first great Jewish philosopher was Philo (fl. 20–40 C.E.), a native of Alexandria. His main project was to harmonize the Hebrew Scriptures and Greek philosophy. However, in doing this he also tried to make the case that whatever good there is in Greek thought ultimately stemmed from Judaism. So far as the creation of the world is concerned, Philo found that the account most compatible with Hebrew Scripture was that of Plato in the *Timaeus*. In the views of both Plato and Philo, God existed from eternity as an immaterial being, without a world, then brought the world into existence. God, then, continued to exist as an immaterial being over and above a material world.

In Plato's view, whereas God is eternal, other things also are eternal, in particular, ideal Forms, such as Beauty and Truth, and unformed matter, the basic stuff out of which the material world would be composed. In Philo's view, by contrast, God alone is eternal. Philo, thus, modified the Platonic account by allowing Forms, which he called *Logos* (Greek, for *word, reason, or plan*), to exist from eternity only as ideas in the mind of God. In his modification of the Platonic view, Philo invented a story of a two-stage creation. First, God created both the Forms, as real beings external to his mind, and unformed matter. Then, God used the Forms and unformed matter to fashion the world as we know it, in the process locating Forms in the thinking part of the human soul, which the Greeks had called *nous*.

Philo accepted Plato's distinction between rational souls, which are created at the beginning of the world, prior to the creation of bodies, and irrational souls, which are created together with bodies, both of humans and animals. In this account, some rational souls remain bodiless. Philo identifies these with the angels of Scripture. Other rational souls are placed in human newborns, whose bodies are already endowed with irrational souls. When the people these newborns become eventually die, their irrational souls die with their bodies, but their rational souls go on. In Plato, the rational soul is indestructible because of the sort of thing it is, that is, "by nature." In Philo, it is indestructible not by nature but by the grace of God.

Although the main influence on Philo's philosophy was Plato, particularly his views in the *Symposium* and the *Timaeus*, Philo was also influenced by other Greek thinkers. From Aristotle, he drew ideas about cosmology and ethics, from neo-Pythagoreans, ideas about the mystic significance of numbers, especially the number seven, and about the importance of self-discipline in preparation for immortality. But Philo did not just borrow and modify. He was also an innovator. Importantly, he was the first to claim that while God's existence can be known, his essence cannot. In contrast to the prevailing Greek philosophical view of a universal Providence subject to unchanging laws of nature, Philo insisted on God's ability to suspend the laws of nature. He saw the world itself as a great chain of being, with Logos just below God and in the role of mediator between God and the world. Foreshadowing Christianity, he called the Logos the first-begotten son of God.

An important point of contrast between Philo and Greek thinkers is that the Greeks, especially the Stoics, tended to view human history as cyclical and pointless. Philo, by contrast, theorized that cyclical changes in human history are actually guided by Logos toward a preconceived goal, to be reached in the course of time. That goal is that "the whole world may become, as it were, one city,"[4] and enjoy the best form of government, which is democracy. His account of this goal is in his interpretation of the messianic prophesies in Isaiah and Micah.

Philo was also innovative in the account that he gave of the human capacity for mystical union with God. In his view, the purpose of this ecstatic union, which he called "sober intoxication," was to lead humans out of the material world and into the eternal world. Like Plato, he regarded the human body as the prison house of the soul. One could argue that it was predominantly Philo's influence that turned what was to become orthodox Christianity toward Platonism.

Christianity

Around the age of thirty, Jesus of Nazareth (c. 4 B.C.E. to 30 C.E.) was baptized by John the Baptist, just prior to John's arrest and execution. Soon after, Jesus began his public career, possibly planning to continue John's work as an apocalyptic prophet. John's basic message was, "Repent, the end is coming." Probably when Jesus was baptized by John, he accepted that message. However, by the time Jesus began his public teaching, he had developed his own distinctive message. Historians disagree about what that message was.[5] According to traditionalists, Jesus was an apocalyptic prophet, in the tradition of John the Baptist. However, traditionalists disagree about whether Jesus regarded himself as the Messiah promised in the Hebrew Scriptures. According to revisionists, Jesus was not an apocalyptic prophet, but a this-worldly social and political reformer. In their view, his main message had to do with promoting social equality and with replacing the Jewish system that stressed holiness and purity with one that stressed compassion.

Aside from the extreme scarcity and ambiguity of the evidence on which historians have had to rely in constructing their accounts, there are two main reasons they have been unable to agree about Jesus' message. First, they disagree about what the evidence should include. The main source of contention here has to do with whether to regard as authentic certain literary evidence that is outside of the New Testament. The most important potential evidence of this sort is the Gnostic Gospel of Thomas, a collection of sayings of Jesus apparently based in part on early sources other than the canonical Gospels. Second, virtually all academic historians, whether conservative or liberal, agree that many of the events depicted in the New Testament are fictitious and that most of the sayings attributed to Jesus are inauthentic. That is, in the views of most academic historians, many of the events that are said to have happened to Jesus, for instance, those depicted in the birth narratives in Matthew and Luke, many of the things that Jesus is said to have done, such as raising Lazarus from the dead and walking on water, and most of the words attributed to Jesus in the New Testament are fictitious. In sum, in the views of most historians, the

Gospels do not primarily represent historical accounts of Jesus, in the modern sense, but rather after-the-fact interpretations of the significance of his life and death by authors who never knew him personally.

All secular (and even most religious) scholars agree that the four New Testament Gospels were not written independently of one another. In their view, when at least two of the four Gospel authors, Matthew and Luke, wrote their accounts, they had before them one or more of the previously written Gospels. That, of course, poses an interesting difficulty, which is known as *the Synoptic Problem*. The difficulty is to figure out the relations of literary dependency among the Gospel of Mark, which is usually regarded as the earliest New Testament Gospel, and the Gospels of Matthew and Luke. According to the solution to this problem that is most widely accepted, Mark was written first, Matthew and Luke were written next and based in part on Mark, and John was written last, perhaps as late as 120 C.E.

The Gospel of John, which is radically different in style and content from the other three Gospels, is all but universally regarded by scholars as the most historically unreliable of the four canonical Gospels. In the other three Gospels, Jesus often teaches in short epigrams (or proverbs), such as, "For to him who has, will more be given; and from him who has not, even what he has will be taken away" (Mark 4:25), and in parables, such as the stories of the Good Samaritan, the Prodigal Son, and the Sower and his Seed. In John, on the other hand, Jesus' teaching style is different. Gone are most of the short, pithy epigrams and parables and in their place are long, abstract discourses:

> Truly, truly, I say to you, he who believes has eternal life. I am the bread of life. Your fathers ate the manna in the wilderness, and they died. This is the bread which comes down from heaven, that a man may eat of it and not die. I am the living bread which came down from heaven; if any one eats of this bread, he will live for ever; and the bread which I shall give for the life of the world is my flesh.
>
> (John 6:47–51)

And again:

> I am the true vine, and my Father is the vinedresser. Every branch of mine that bears no fruit, he takes away, and every branch that does bear fruit he prunes, that it may bear more fruit. You are already made clean by the word which I have spoken to you. Abide in me, and I in you.
>
> (John 15:1–4)

And so on.

While some of the ideas in these passages from John parallel those in the earlier three Gospels, it is obvious that in John the ideas are developed more abstractly. A dramatic symptom of this tendency toward abstraction is that in John, Jesus is identified with the Logos. This identification may show the influence of Philo on John. Some of the early church fathers subsequently developed the idea that Jesus is the Logos. They may have done this in order to express Christian faith in terms that would be intelligible to the Hellenistic world or to impress their hearers with the idea that Christianity, while heir to what was best in pagan philosophy, embodied a higher truth. Be this as it may, there are other dramatic differences in content between the first three Gospels (the Synoptics) and John.

Among these differences are that in the Synoptics, Jesus talks a great deal about the kingdom of God and hardly at all about himself. In John, Jesus talks a great deal about himself and hardly at all about the kingdom of God. For instance, Jesus uses the Greek word for "kingdom" (*basilia*) 18 times in Mark, 47 times in Matthew, 37 times in Luke, and 5 times in John; he uses the Greek word for "I" 9 times in Mark, 17 times in Matthew, 10 times in Luke, and 118 times in John. Such differences are not just statistical. When, in the Synoptics, Jesus uses the word "I," almost all of his self-references are of a conventional kind. In John, by contrast, Jesus regularly makes staggering statements about himself, such as "I am the bread of life" (6:35), "I am the light of the world" (8:12), "I am the way, and the truth and the life" (14:6), and "Before Abraham was, I am" (8:58).[6]

There are possible ways to explain such differences between John and the Synoptics that would preserve for John an early date of origin. Most scholars agree that all such explanations are far-fetched. They conclude that John, who claimed to have been an eye-witness to the events he describes, wrote much later than Matthew and Luke, and elaborated for theological reasons what he claimed Jesus actually said. In other words, in their view, John used Jesus as a spokesperson for his own interpretation of who Jesus was.

For the purpose of recovering the actual words and deeds of the historical Jesus, such issues are crucial. Before historians can even begin to reconstruct Jesus' life, they must separate the authentic wheat from the interpretational chaff. However, for present purposes, it is more important what various New Testament authors thought Jesus said and did than it is what Jesus actually said and did. For it is what New Testament authors attributed to Jesus, and their reflections on what they attributed to him, that have been historically influential. The New Testament authors that matter most in this respect are Paul and John, the earliest and perhaps the latest sources in the New Testament.

Although Paul (10?–67? c.e.) wrote just a few decades after Jesus' death, he had never met Jesus. Based on what he wrote, he seems to have had almost no interest in what the historical (pre-Resurrection) Jesus said or did. John, on the other hand, who presumably wrote last among the authors of the New Testament Gospels, attributed more words and ideas to Jesus than any of the other authors of the Gospels. Moreover, John, partly because he allowed himself the luxury of being inventive but also because he was such a great writer, was able to put into the mouth of Jesus some of the deepest and most gripping teachings in all of the New Testament.

In any case, although Christianity began as a sect of Judaism, only a small fraction of Jews eventually became Christians. The Jews had long awaited a Messiah, but in the first century c.e. most of them were expecting that their Messiah, if he appeared, would be a political leader, who would free Israel from Roman rule and establish Israel as a powerful kingdom in the world; if not that, then they were expecting a spiritual king who at the end of time would appear in glory from the heavens. One thing that they were not looking for was a messiah as apolitical as Jesus in the New Testament accounts seems to have been, especially not someone who would die in humiliation, like a common criminal, on a cross.

Jews believed that their special relation to God would eventually have important consequences for everyone. Nevertheless, they were intensely nationalistic and separatist, almost wholly centered on the people of Israel. Many early Christians who remained in Jerusalem saw Christianity as part of this nationalistic tradition. They continued to worship at the Temple, seeing no conflict between their new beliefs and Jewish ritual. These early Christians, led by Peter and James, continued to require the observance of traditional Jewish regulations, which tended to diminish the appeal of the new religion to non-Jews. Historians tend to think that Peter and James opposed bringing the new religion to gentiles at least until all of Israel had been awakened to its message.

In opposition to this early Christian faction, Paul, who spent most of his life outside of Jerusalem, asserted that the new Christian promise of salvation was available universally, both to gentiles, who were outside of the reach of Judaic Law, as well as to Jews, who lived within it. As we saw in the case of the Stoics especially, but even Philo, one of the ways in which thought in the early centuries of the Christian era differed from thought in classical Greece was in its greater tendency toward egalitarianism and inclusiveness. In Paul's words, for those "baptized into Christ" there is neither Jew nor Greek, slave nor free, male nor female, but all are one.[7]

This difference, in nationalistic instead of universalistic tendencies, was the first important doctrinal controversy within the emerging church. In the end,

Paul's universalism prevailed over James and Peter's Judaic nationalism, thanks in part to the 70 C.E. destruction by the Romans of the Temple in Jerusalem. That event left the Jerusalem Christian community in disarray. Previously, the fledgling movement had been directed and controlled by the Jerusalem community, which was the unique source of authority in faith and discipline. Afterward, Christian life was organized and directed by churches in Rome, Antioch, Ephesus, and Alexandria. The consequences of this shift of power, not only for Christians at the time but for the rest of human history, were momentous.

Paul, a well-educated Hellenistic Jew, had in his early adulthood been an enthusiastic persecutor of Christians. He converted to Christianity on the road to Damascus, when he had a vision of the resurrected Christ. Subsequently he became an equally ardent defender of Christianity. In Paul's view, Jesus was a preexistent divine being sent into the world to rescue humankind from its state of spiritual decay, which Paul thought was due to enslavement by demonic forces that ruled the lower universe. He claimed that it was primarily these demonic forces, rather than the Romans, who were responsible for the death of Jesus, who by his death and resurrection had saved humanity. In addition, Paul believed that Jesus as Christ might return at any moment: "We who are alive, who are left, shall be caught up together with them [that is, the resurrected dead] in the clouds to meet the Lord in the air" so that "we shall always be with the Lord."[8] Although Paul speaks highly of the church as an institution, he thought that the world itself was fast approaching its end and, hence, did not expect the church to last for long.

Paul seems to have known a fair amount of Greek philosophy. Yet he went out of his way to disavow any use of it, declaring that he was not going to adorn his account with "persuasive words of wisdom." He said that his purpose was to implant in his listeners a "faith" that is based not on "human philosophy," but on the "power" and "wisdom of God."[9] A case can be made that the Corinthians to whom Paul was preaching this message were trying to understand his ideas about human survival of bodily death in terms of Plato's ideas and that Paul resisted this Platonic interpretation.[10]

For the Corinthians, as for Plato, the "inward man" (*esōanthrōpos*) was a term used for "reason" (*nous*), the divine and immortal part of humans that should be nourished by education and learning.[11] Paul rejected this idea.[12] In Paul's view, resurrection of the person and resurrection of the body are one and the same: "Before God there is no naked soul, only whole persons: thus the person is called upon to make himself pleasing to God, a task of the whole man."[13] Paul was interested in developing not reason but receptivity, that is, such faculties as conscience and passive understanding. In opposition to Plato, this is what he called the "inward man." This orientation is related to Paul's view that one does not justify oneself before God by deeds but by submission to God's will. Paul's inter-est in inwardness was not due to the soul's being the seat of human reason but based on the potential of God's word to change a person from the inside out. It is from the inside that a person is awakened to a new life and becomes whole. This transformation, Paul thought, is effected by the same spirit of God that awak-ened Jesus from the dead.

Yet despite Paul's antipathy toward philosophy, his words, especially what he had to say about the resurrection, exercised a profound influence on subsequent Christian philosophy. In his account, just as death came through one man—Adam—so also "the resurrection of the dead has come through one man"—Jesus.[14] As we have seen, the idea of bodily resurrection had already arisen within Judaism. At the time of Paul, whether people were resurrected and, if so, how had become a point of contention between Pharisees and Sadducees.[15]

According to the New Testament, some followers of Jesus were convinced that they had seen Jesus alive after his death on the cross and subsequent burial. Most historians of early Christianity believe that whatever the actual experience of these followers of Jesus had been, at least their *thinking* they had seen Jesus after he had died was instrumental in the initial formation of Christianity. When the early church fathers later tried to make sense of the idea that everyone would survive his or her bodily death, most of them felt that it was necessary to under-stand this doctrine of survival in the context of some more-or-less systematic worldview. Their scriptural point of departure in constructing such a view of the resurrection was invariably the words of Paul. Thus, one of Paul's contribu-tions was to elevate the doctrine of the resurrection to one of the central tenets of Christianity: "If Christ has not been raised, your faith is futile and you are still in your sins"; "If the dead are not raised, 'Let us eat and drink, for tomorrow we die.'"[16] Easy enough to say, but from the beginning the doctrine of the resurrec-tion was extremely puzzling, as Paul's pagan critics were quick to point out.

At Corinth, Paul had encountered people who doubted the possibility of res-urrection, and wanted a detailed explanation of how it would come about: "But some one will ask, 'How are the dead raised? With what kind of body do they come?'"[17] Probably Paul accepted from tradition that the resurrected Jesus was able to eat and that his body was solid to the touch. Yet, according to that same tradition, Jesus was able to appear and disappear at will, even passing through locked doors. There was a question, then, about the nature of Jesus' resurrected body. By implication, there was the same question about the nature of anyone's resurrected body.

Paul seems to have concluded that a resurrected body—anyone's—is material but differs in significant ways from the bodies humans have during their earthly lifetimes. He compared the relation of one's earthly body to one's resurrected body, which for him was equivalent to the resurrected person, to a plant that in seeming to die leaves a seed, from which its life continues in another plant of the same sort: "What you sow does not come to life unless it dies. And what you sow is not the body which is to be, but a bare kernel, perhaps of wheat or of some other grain. God gives it a body as he has chosen, and to each kind of seed its own body."[18]

But if this is the model for resurrection, questions about identity quickly arise. Chief among these questions, for those who are sensitive to the distinction between exactly *the same* and exactly *similar* (that is, between *numerical* and *qualitative* identity), is whether the plant that produces a seed and then dies is numerically the same plant as the plant that subsequently grows from that seed or merely one of its ancestors. Ordinarily we suppose that a single plant remains the same plant throughout its life, in spite of changing in various ways, but that plants that grow from its seeds, even if exactly similar to the parent plant, are different plants. So, if the relationship of a person on earth who dies to his resurrection replica is like that of a present plant to future plants that grow from its seeds, then a resurrection replica is not numerically the same person who died but merely a qualitatively similar descendant. Not all of the early church fathers seem to have been sensitive to this distinction.

Another question has to do with whether the bodies people have on earth will be the same as the ones they acquire in the afterlife. Apparently, Paul's answer was that they would not be the same: "There are celestial bodies and there are terrestrial bodies; but the glory of the celestial is one, and the glory of the terrestrial is another"; "So is it with the resurrection of the dead. What is sown is perishable, what is raised is imperishable"; "It is sown a physical body, it is raised a spiritual body"; and, "I tell you this, brethren: flesh and blood cannot inherit the kingdom of God, nor does the perishable inherit the imperishable."[19] But if earthly and resurrected bodies are not the same, that further complicates the project of accounting for the numerical identity of the people on earth with their resurrected counterparts. This is especially true if, as Paul assumed, people are just their bodies.

Early Christian thinkers drew on a variety of images to speak of the transition from earthly life to the afterlife. Some were natural images, derived either from Paul or from their own imaginations: seed to plant, darkness to dawn, one season to another. Some were images that had to do with the making of artifacts: one piece of pottery to another, one statue to another. Some, such as the return of the phoenix, were derived from mythology. Curiously, Christian writers often used images such as these in ways that suggested that they had not yet begun to be worried about *philosophical* questions of personal identity, particularly about questions over which ways of a person's (or thing's) being continued suffice for the before-and-after identity of the person (or thing). For instance, an oft-repeated image these writers used is that of a statue that is melted down and then recast in a form that is qualitatively exactly similar to the original. Most philosophers today would say that the earlier and later statues, while qualitatively similar, are not identical, hence that they are different statues. But if this were true, it would undermine the point of the imagery. Many early Christians failed to see that it would undermine the point of the imagery.[20]

Clement of Rome (c. 30?–100? c.e.), for instance, in a letter of about 90 c.e that he sent to the Christians at Corinth, explained the resurrection primarily in terms of two analogies: that of a seed, which he said dies and decays in the earth before initiating new growth, and that of the phoenix, which he said first dies and then rises as a worm from its own decaying flesh. In the views of many in our own time, the new plant or bird would at best be a qualitatively similar descendent of the original, not the very same plant or bird; hence, it would seem, there would be no personal (or animal) survival, let alone immortality. Clement, it seems, and presumably also his audience, were not perturbed by such niceties.[21] But, then, in their believing in personal survival of bodily death, what exactly were they believing?

Even after this question of identity, as opposed to mere replication, became a matter of explicit philosophical concern, the old images continued to be used, raising questions about how early Christian thinkers understood both bodily identity and personal survival. Bizarre as it may seem, it is possible that many of these early Christian thinkers did not even believe in what we today would regard as personal survival of bodily death. That is, it is possible that to whatever extent *personal survival of bodily death*, in *their* sense of this expression, depended on the resurrection of the body and was not merely ensured by the persistence of the soul, it is not what *we* today would call *personal survival* but, rather, what we would call dying and being replaced by a qualitatively similar replica. When the church fathers later tried to make sense of the idea of personal survival of bodily death, increasingly over time they felt that personal identity does matter—that the individual who rises must be the very same person as the one who died.

Even as Paul wrote, an alternative religious Platonism was spreading in the Greco-Roman world, especially at Alexandria. Philo represented this trend. So too did the Christians at Corinth, whose questions about the resurrection Paul tried to answer. Although Paul, as a materialist, resisted their attempts to understand survival partly in terms of an immaterial soul, their questions encouraged him to adopt some of the language of Platonism, which opened the way for others to reinterpret along dualistic lines what Paul was trying to express in his letters.

As a result, later Christians increasingly interpreted personal survival dualistically. The resurrection, then, came to imply the resurrection of the body—not the resurrection of the person—and the soul, following Plato, was thought to be immaterial and independent of the body. In later developments of this view, Philo became a key source for reinterpreting the doctrine of the resurrection in the Old Testament. Inevitably, then, relying on him as a guide to the theology of the Old Testament encouraged a Platonic interpretation of the New Testament doctrine of the resurrection. In the end, Philo's impact on early Christian beliefs became greater than it had been on Judaism, although Judaism would also move in the direction of distinguishing soul and body, with the soul being immaterial and immortal and the body requiring an independent resurrection.

Islam

The great political and religious unifier in Islamic civilization was Muhammad (570?–632 c.e.), who was born at Mecca into a family of modest means. At the age of twenty-five, he married a wealthy widow but retained his tendency to be critical of materialism and social injustice. At age thirty-five he began to make annual spiritual retreats alone in the desert. In 610, at age forty, he received his first revelation and began to preach. Subsequent revelations came at irregular intervals over a period of twenty years. Muhammad thought that these revelations, which he took to be delivered to him by the angel Gabriel, came directly from God and were perfect transcriptions of an eternal tablet preserved in Heaven. Between 650 and 651, the record of Muhammad's revelations was compiled into the Qur'an, which consists of 114 chapters (surahs) of unequal length. Its basic message is a call to all Arabs to surrender to God's will. The imperative to recognize no God but Allah is reiterated throughout these scriptures.

Muhammad was convinced that God had chosen him to be the final prophet. Abraham, Moses, and Jesus were prophets. But in Muhammad's view, Jesus was not the son of God. Jews and Christians had strayed from the true faith, the one that had been revealed to him. An example of a way they had strayed is that by accepting the doctrine of the Trinity, Christianity had sullied its claim to being monotheistic. Muhammad's task was to convert the Jews and Christians to the true word. In 622, he left Mecca for the northern city of Medina, where he created an Islamic community for which he laid down strict rules. Alcohol, gambling, and usury were prohibited, as was infanticide. His community grew in strength. In 624, he returned to Mecca and made it the center of the new religion. In 632, he died.

Throughout the Qur'an, the pursuit of knowledge is portrayed as an important virtue. Because Allah is all-knowing, humans, in acquiring knowledge, become more godlike. In the eighth and ninth centuries, at a time when learning in Europe had sunk to its lowest point, Muslim culture entered a golden age in which Arabic, Byzantine, Indian, and Persian perspectives and cultural traditions were successfully integrated into a remarkably robust and intellectually vital civilization. Muslim scholars preserved ancient Greek learning, which they had acquired from their contact with Byzantine scholars. They also wrote commentaries and glosses on Greek philosophy, thus augmenting what would become the Western intellectual tradition.

The Qur'an describes humans as God's agents, albeit agents who are ignorant and morally weak. Although humans have the greatest potential of any created being, they alone are capable of evil. This tension is at the heart of the human situation. There is no original sin or redemption. Humans are responsible, both individually and collectively, for their behavior. Although Allah is said to control history, humans are free to accept or reject the Qur'anic teachings. When history ends, each human will face judgment and be held responsible for his or her behavior. The Qur'an provides detailed accounts of the joys of Heaven and the horrors of Hell.

The majority of believers interpret these accounts to mean that the afterlife is just like one's normal life, except that it goes on forever. There is even sex in heaven. But according to some Muslims, one's future existence differs from the earthly one either in being corporeal in a different way or in being spiritual. In any case, immortality is not guaranteed by humans having an indestructible soul but is due entirely to God's mercy. Like the ancient Hebrews, Muslims tend to see humans as an animated body, not as an incarnated soul or an ensouled body. Hence, death is not separation of soul from body, but the dissolution of one's whole being, which is later resurrected whole. Because Islamic scripture places few constraints on how the afterlife is understood philosophically, Arab theologians and philosophers were free to integrate their religious beliefs about the afterlife derived from Scripture with conceptions of the soul and human nature that they acquired from Greek philosophy. They did this within the context of three different sorts of Islamic philosophy: *kalam*, which consisted of scriptural apologetics, especially arguments in defense of monotheism (its opponents included polytheists, members of mystery cults, Neoplatonists, and Christians); *falsafah*, which was pursued relatively independently of scriptural apologetics; and *sufism*, a mystical tradition that originated toward the beginning of the eleventh century, primarily in Spain. In a later chapter, we shall return to consider Islamic philosophy.

Monotheism and Western Conceptions of Self

As we shall see, the three great Western monotheistic religions, with their common origin in the Hebrew Bible, have had an enormous influence on subsequent thinking about the self and personal identity. In each of them, God, the transcendent creator of the universe, is nevertheless personal, with humans created in God's image, thus encouraging philosophical reflection on the personhood of humans. In each, God, though immensely powerful, is yet attentive to the smallest events that occur within the privacy of the human soul, thus encouraging philosophical reflection on human subjectivity. And, most fundamentally, in each, humans are thought not only to survive into an afterlife where what they have done prior to their bodily deaths can be rewarded or punished, but to resurrect, thus encouraging philosophical reflection not only on personal identity over time but on the identity of the body over time. Collectively, the three religions bequeathed to the philosophy of self and personal identity its most enduring preoccupations: personhood, subjectivity, and identity over time.

IV

RESURRECTED SELF

By the middle of the second century C.E, most of the scriptural documents that would later in the century be collected to form the New Testament were well known to Christian thinkers. Attention turned increasingly to the task of interpreting what was novel and puzzling in these scriptures. This task was bequeathed to a group of classically educated pagans, called *apologists*, who had converted to Christianity. Their response was to rationalize Christianity using the resources of Greek philosophy. One of their major preoccupations was the problem of evil. Dealing with it tended to focus their attention on the freedom of the will. However, most in need of rationalization were the deeply puzzling dogmas of the Trinity, the divinity of Christ, and, of course, both the Resurrection of Christ and the resurrection of ordinary humans, each of which concerned the nature of self or person. Their discussion of all of these contributed to the Western conception of a person. But it was their discussion of the resurrection of humans that left a decisive and indelible mark on subsequent attempts to understand the self and personal identity.

The apologists tried to emulate the work of Philo, who had recently harmonized the Hebrew Scriptures and Greek philosophy. As we have seen, Philo's work not only served as a model, but through the Gospel of John may even have influenced the actual content of Christian Scripture. Ironically, Philo had a bigger influence on Christian philosophy than he did on Jewish thought, due to his having been from Alexandria, far removed from the center of Jewish culture, and to his having recently completed for Judaism a task that so closely paralleled the one the apologists felt a pressing need to undertake for Christianity.

Initially some Christian intellectuals resisted the lure of trying to rationalize Christianity by using Greek philosophy. But the project was inevitable. Christian Scripture expressed beliefs but not a philosophy. Educated converts to Christianity could not help but try to understand their newly acquired beliefs, and this meant trying to understand them philosophically. In addition, it was the apologists' self-appointed job to defend Christianity from pagan critics and to stamp out various Christian "heresies." Philosophy was needed for these tasks.

The apologists of the second century and subsequent church fathers (collectively called patristic theologians) faced the twin challenges, first, of deciding what Christian dogma should be and, then, of deciding what it should mean. For the most part, Scripture dictated what dogma should be. But not always. Even in such central concerns as whether each human is endowed by his or her Creator with an immortal soul, Scripture is ambiguous. In any case, external help was needed in figuring out what Scripture meant. Greek philosophy, and its Roman and Jewish derivatives, were the only help available. Thus, throughout the Patristic Period, and as we shall see even into the Middle Ages, pagan philosophy played a seminal role in the formulation of what from that time until our own has remained basic Christian doctrine.

The Resurrection

The discussion among the church fathers of the resurrection of people is the real beginning of the philosophical debate over personal identity. Although the church fathers drew upon pagan theories, there was in classical Greek and Roman philosophy no continuous tradition of discussion of the problem of personal identity. The issue was not a central one for pagan philosophers. It was for the church fathers. Christian dogma was individualistic in a way that pagan philosophy never was. It was critical to early Christian thinkers, and subsequently to all Christian thinkers, both that humans survive their bodily deaths *as individuals* and that *as individuals* they subsequently be held accountable for their earthly lives. Arguably, the promulgation and ultimate widespread acceptance of these doctrines contributed importantly to the emergence of Western individualism. According to St. Paul, Christ, through His Resurrection, had defeated death not only for himself but for everyone, or at least for everyone who heard his message and believed. Not ever ending one's life as the same person one is now was the prize. Spending eternity either in heaven or in hell hung in the balance.

According to Christian Scripture, not only do people survive their bodily deaths, but they survive them in a bodily way. Many pagans found it difficult to believe that the actual bodies that people had on earth would or could be raised or, supposing that they could, that this would be a good thing. After all, many people when they die are old or injured, and all of them are dead! The pagan philosopher Celsus (fl. 175), paraphrasing Heraclitus, questioned why anyone would want to recover his body. Corpses, he said, are more revolting than dung.[1]

Everyone could see for themselves that the human body dies and decays. To pagan critics, and even to many of the apologists, it seemed prima facie that there is no way that the *same* body—not just a *similar* body, but the *very same one*—that dies and decomposes is later raised from the dead. The apologists devoted entire treatises to responding to this worry. Their standard responses claimed that the body that is resurrected is somehow spiritualized, glorified, or at least repaired. Such responses led immediately to two questions: How is the body that dies reassembled to form a new body, especially if the old body had been eaten by animals or its ashes scattered to the winds? And, how is the construction of a new body compatible with its being the very same body as the one that died?

In discussing how the apologists dealt with these issues, it is helpful to distinguish among three views about personal identity: first, that personal identity depends only on the continuation of an immaterial soul; second, that it depends on the continuation both of an immaterial soul and a material body; and third, that it depends only on the continuation of a material body (which was thought by those apologists who were materialists to include a material soul). Some Christian thinkers, such as Origen, who had Platonic views of survival, adopted something like the first of these options; others, like Tertullian, who under the influence of Stoicism became a materialist, adopted something like the third. Eventually, most gravitated toward the second: that personal immortality requires the continuation of the very same immaterial soul and the very same material body.

One of the earliest Christian philosophical accounts of resurrection was that of the apologist Justin Martyr (100?–165?), who was already an enthusiastic Platonist when he converted to Christianity. Justin was eager to point out analogies between Plato's views and Christian dogma. In discussing resurrection, Justin stressed the necessity of bodily purification, but of a sort that preserves personal identity, asserting that what dies and what rises must be the same. He pointed out that even in the views of pagan materialists, the parts into which the body decomposes at death are indestructible and hence available to be reassembled later. He assumed without question, and without argument, that if the parts were reassembled into a body that is qualitatively exactly similar to the original, then that reassembled body would be numerically identical to the original.

Athenagoras (fl. 180), who wrote a little later than Justin and was also a dualist, argued against the Platonic view that a person is simply a soul using a body and for the idea that the body is essential to the person. His view was that personal survival of bodily death requires that the same body be restored to the same soul. In considering the possibility of humans who are eaten by animals, who are then eaten by other humans, with the result that some of the same matter that was once part of the earlier humans became part of the later ones, and also in considering cannibalism, Athenagoras was among the first to face the possibility that the same material stuff might become part of the bodies of more than one *human*.

The fact that Athenagoras brought up these difficulties at all is impressive. However, his response to them left something to be desired. He asserted that human flesh is not "the natural and proper food of men"[2] and hence when eaten cannot be digested and converted into new human flesh. Instead, he said, if one human were to consume matter that was once part of another human, the matter would be expelled or excreted. To illustrate the point, he said that if as a consequence of a shipwreck some humans were eaten by fish, which were then caught and eaten by other humans, the human material that had become part of the flesh of the fish would not become part of the flesh of the humans who ate the fish, but would be excreted by them. This early example of a thinker's using Christian theology to do science nicely illustrates the poverty of the strategy. As we shall see, it was not the last time Christian theorists would employ this strategy. In fact, in one way or another, for the next fifteen hundred years a great deal of the Western discussion of the self and personal identity was an exercise in this dubious practice. Even so, Athenagoras, in spite of the poverty of his answer, made a contribution by drawing everyone's attention to the problem, which others then tried to resolve differently. Scholars refer to the worry that he raised as *the chain-consumption argument*.

About the year 200, there were three major treatments of resurrection, by Irenaeus (130?–203?), Minucius Felix (fl. 200), and Tertullian (160?–230?), the last of the apologists. All three of these thinkers were materialists and so all three tied both personal and bodily identity to material continuity. All three also exhibit that curious property characteristic of so many of the patristics: they insist in their discursive accounts on the importance of the difference between same person (or same body) and mere replica but then in their imagery and examples somehow reveal that they are not fully sensitive to that very issue.

In *Against Heresy*, Irenaeus discusses at length the resurrection of the body, with special attention to the bodies of martyrs. Claiming that resurrection requires that the body that rises is the same as the one that fell, he defended materialism against those who argued for a spiritual understanding of the resurrection of the body. This was not the first time that anyone had considered the continuation of bodily identity (which for Irenaeus was the same as personal identity) through the dissolution of the original body and its reconstitution later. However, when the issue had come up for early classical pagans, for instance in the remarks by Epicharmus and by Plato in the *Symposium*, all that was at issue was the preservation of the same person through the sorts of bodily changes that normally occur to everyone *while* they are alive. That issue was difficult enough. But the challenge that Irenaeus and his fellow apologists faced was of a different order. It was not just normal bodily changes that had to be bridged but the chasm of total bodily dissolution to its subsequent reconstitution.

Surprisingly, that issue had come up in Stoic thought, which may have influenced these particular church fathers, all three of whom were Stoics. Pagan Stoics believed in a kind of eternal recurrence in which the whole world is completely destroyed by a huge conflagration and then reassembled, replete with qualitatively similar individuals. According to Chrysippus these individuals are numerically the same as their preconflagration counterparts. But apparently other Stoics disagreed. This doctrine was also known to Origen, who was not a Stoic but who thought it interesting enough to discuss briefly.[3] In any case, the three earlier church fathers responded in a Christian context to the challenge of whether someone could retain numerical identity through dissolution and reconstitution by addressing issues that continue to echo in the most recent discussions of bodily and personal identity.

For instance, Irenaeus, to illustrate what he meant by the body that rises being the same as the one that fell, uses the example of a statue that melts and then is recast. But as we now would understand it, the recast statue is only a replica of the original, not the same statue, even though it is made from the same material. In Minucius Felix's dialogue *Octavius*, the pagan interlocutor asks the Christian whether Christians "rise again with bodies" and, if so, "whether with the same or with renewed bodies?" He continues, "Without a body? Then, as far as I know, there will neither be mind, nor soul, nor life. With the same body? But this has already been previously destroyed. With another body? Then it is a new man who is born, not the former one restored."[4] In Minucius' discursive account, where it is clear that he understood the pagan's questions and, hence, to that extent was sensitive to the distinction between *same* and *similar*, he answered that God keeps track of the matter, regardless of how it is dispersed, and then reassembles it. But, then, as a way of helping his readers to understand resurrection, he immediately suggested the following analogies: "the sun sinks down and rises, the stars pass away and return, the flowers die and revive again."[5] But while the sun and stars remain the same, this year's flowers are not the same as last year's. Minucius, it seems, was not clear on the distinction between a generational replica and the persistence of the original thing.

Tertullian is famous for having asked, "What has Athens to do with Jerusalem?" From our present vantage point, he is the most highly visible of those who at least at one point in their careers opposed the move to integrate Christianity with pagan philosophy. Later, however, he succumbed to the philosophical urge and drew upon the resources of Stoic materialism. During this period, he wrote *A Treatise on the Soul* and *On the Resurrection of the Flesh*, in both of which he saw the resurrection in terms of the reassembly of the parts into which the body had decomposed, stressing that the very same flesh that sinned must be punished. In his view, everything, including God and the human soul, is corporeal. He pointed out that if a human soul is to suffer in hell, it has to be a bodily substance. He also said that the soul of the infant is derived from the father's seed like a kind of sprout.

In Tertullian's view, "the flesh is the very condition on which salvation hinges." He claimed that "if God raises not men entire, He raises not the dead." But, he said, in the case of the dead, to raise a man entire *is* to repair him if he needs repair, say, by restoring him to some earlier period of his life when he was in better condition: "For what dead man is entire, although he dies entire? Who is without hurt, that is without life? What dead body is uninjured?" For "a dead man to be raised again amounts to nothing short of his being restored to his entire condition."[6]

Even though the materialism of these three early Christian thinkers would be rejected by most subsequent Christian thinkers, their contributions changed personal-identity theory by highlighting the problem of explaining how the body, which decomposes at death, is reconstituted in a way that preserves personal identity. For, if you try to understand survival of bodily death on materialistic grounds, as did Irenaeus, Minucius Felix, and Tertullian, and you admit, as anyone must, that the body decomposes at death, then you have to explain how it can be recomposed in a way that sustains the identity of the person who died. These three did this by proposing what would later be known as a *relational* view of personal identity. What that means, in the case of resurrection, is that what ensures personal persistence is not the persistence of an underlying substance but *the way in which* the body that decomposes and the resurrected body are related to each other. In a full-blown relational account, what ensures the persistence of one's self, or at least of one's body, from moment to moment, day to day, and so on, even during one's earthly life, is the way in which one's constantly changing body is related to earlier and later stages of itself.

Plato's project was simpler, in a way. As a dualist who thought that people are essentially immaterial, unchanging substances, he was not committed to the resurrection of the body. So there was no need for him to give much thought to the mechanics of personal identity. He had to prove that the immaterial soul exists and that the person is essentially the soul (no easy tasks), but after that, so far as personal persistence is concerned, there is nothing left to explain. However, when Christian thinkers subsequently reverted to Platonic dualism, they were not, like Plato had been, in a position to sidestep the thorny issues that are raised by a relational account of identity, for they had accepted the dogma of the resurrection of the body. They, thus, had to account for how the body that falls and the one that subsequently rises are the same. In addition, because in Rome during this period martyred Christians were being eaten by lions, a complication that arose early for most thinkers was the chain-consumption argument, including cannibalism. As a consequence, once bodily identity became an issue of concern, even Christian dualists had to confront issues of identity that went considerably beyond those that Plato had tried to solve. In their sophistication, these Christian theories directly anticipated relational accounts of personal identity that would later come to center stage in the eighteenth century.

The Triumph of Dualism

Origen of Alexandria (185?–254) is regarded by many as the most important Christian intellectual before Augustine. Origen is perhaps most famous for arguing that the souls of angels, human beings, and demons preexisted in a state of perfection before they sinned and fell. Before Jesus Christ became human, all souls which were ever going to exist, including Jesus' soul, existed and had the same nature. That nature was to be a rational being with free choice. No soul is "pure either by essence or by nature, and no one is by nature polluted."[7] There is thus no intrinsic difference between Jesus and any other soul on earth. Whatever differences exist are the contingent consequence of free choices. How badly a soul sinned determined how far it fell. The stars, which are souls, sinned only slightly, and so are only slightly separated from God. Humans, since they sinned more seriously, are entombed in bodies that are subject to death. Demons are even more removed from God. In general, the reason there is a world in the first place is to provide a site for the punishment and rehabilitation of souls, all of whom, once they have reformed, are destined to be restored to a state of perfection.

In Origen's view, some humans are better off than others at birth due to their soul's previous behavior. Otherwise, he argued, it would be impossible to explain why some newborn human babies are born "blind, when they have committed no sin, while others are born with no defect at all."[8] This, of course, is the doctrine of karma, which people tend to associate with Eastern religions, coiled like a worm in the heart of early Christian theology.

Origen's *On First Principles*, the main work in which he expressed his views on personal identity, is preserved mostly in excerpts that were quoted by others who then went on to discuss his views. Most of his critics accused him of being too Platonic, in view of his teaching that people, who begin as incorporeal souls, would return to incorporeality.[9] But some claimed that he brought up the return to incorporeality as a hypothesis only and that he preferred the alternative hypothesis of an ethereal resurrection body. This concession was not enough for his critics. Methodius of Olympus and Jerome, for instance, continued to insist on the resurrection of a genuinely material body.

More significant for personal-identity theory is Origen's explanation of how an improved resurrected body might be the same as the body of a person who had died. Taking his point of departure from scriptural sources in Matthew and Paul, he claimed that after bodily death, when we are in heaven, we will have a spiritual and luminous body that is composed of different stuff than any earthly body. In defense of his claim that such a spiritual body would be numerically the same as a previously existing material body, he pointed out that even before bodily death the material out of which our bodies are composed is constantly changing and is "not the same for even two days." "*River*," he said, "is not a bad name for the body." What then accounts for the fact that before bodily death peoples' bodies, despite these material changes, retain their identity from day to day, month to month, and so on? In Origen's view, what accounts for this is that "the form [*eidos*] characterizing [different temporal stages of these bodies] is the same."[10]

Origen claimed that since the body changes so much in life and yet retains its identity, there is no special problem about its also changing in death and retaining its identity. He reasoned that even if the bits of flesh present at the moment of death *could be* reanimated, there is no particular reason why God *would want* to reanimate them. It is appropriate that the body should change from this life to the afterlife. Just as people would need to have gills if they were destined to live under water, those who are destined to inherit the kingdom of heaven will need spiritual bodies. Yet, in the body's transformation to this "more glorious" state, it retains its "previous form," that is, its *eidos*: "The very thing which was once being characterized in the flesh will be characterized in the spiritual body."[11]

In the light of subsequent developments in personal-identity theory, two things about Origen's views are worth noting. The first has to do with how easy it would have been to object to his solution by raising the possibility of postmortem fission. He stressed that in reconstructing a postmortem spiritual body, God can preserve the body's *eidos* by using matter from any of the previous stages of the person who died. Obviously, then, there is much more matter than would be needed to fashion just one spiritual person. It is easy to imagine a critic suggesting that God, then, could have fashioned out of the old matter *several* qualitatively identical spiritual bodies, each of them replicating the body's *eidos* and hence having an equal claim to being identical with the old body. But there is no record that any critic actually did suggest this. As we shall see, a similar question arose among personal-identity theorists first in the eighteenth century, in the context of trying to understand resurrection, and then again in our own times, in a secular context.

The second issue with Origen's views has to do with the question of whether assimilation time is required to preserve bodily identity. Origen stressed that the matter out of which our bodies are composed is constantly changing. But in the course of everyday life it is not constantly changing all at once. Perhaps, then, the persistence of one's body—its remaining the same body in spite of changes in the matter out of which it is composed—is compatible only with the changes that it undergoes being gradual and organic. Some Christian philosophers who were contemporaries of Origen, as well as some who would come later, seem to have had a worry of this sort. They insisted that in order for God to resurrect someone who had died, God not only had to reuse the very matter out of which the person who died was composed, but God had to use only that matter that was in use at the time of his or her death.

The kind of view for which Origen argued was revived in the eighteenth century by Isaac Watts, Charles Bonnet, and Joseph Priestley, each of whom maintained, first, that in each human, there is a unique "germ" embodied in the constantly changing matter out of which he or she is composed and, second, that it is the persistence of this germ, and only its persistence, that ensures that the later stages of a person are both qualitatively similar to and numerically the same as earlier ones. So far as a person's bodily persistence over time and through various changes is concerned, everything about the matter of which the person is composed other than the persistence of this germ is irrelevant. Both Origen and these later writers seem to be groping toward what today we would call the notion of genetic inheritance, to which they then gave pride of place in their accounts of bodily identity.

For such reasons, Origen's views may seem quite modern to twenty-first-century readers.[12] However, it is not clear that Origen is thinking about bodily identity in the same way that readers today would think of it. For instance, he imagines a case in which our bodies die, "fall into the earth like a grain," become "corrupt," and then are "scattered abroad." Yet, he says, "by the word of God," that "germ which is always safe in the very substance of the body raises them

from the earth and restores and repairs them, as the power which is in the
grain of wheat, after its corruption and death, repairs and restores the grain
into a body having stalk and ear." To readers in our own times, it will sound as
if Origen is here suggesting that the pre- and postmortem person are identical
only to the degree that a stalk of wheat is identical with other stalks that are its
ancestors or descendants. And Origen may indeed be suggesting this! Another
possibility is that what he is trying to convey is that just as in the Platonic conception of personal identity, the vehicle for identity both before and after bodily
death is a person's immortal soul, in his conception of bodily identity the vehicle
for identity is the person's "form": "And so also to those who shall deserve to
obtain an inheritance in the kingdom of heaven, that germ of the body's restoration, which we have before mentioned, by God's command restores out of the
earthly and animal body a spiritual one, capable of inhabiting the heavens."[13]

Origen was the first Christian to champion substance dualism, that is, the
idea that humans are composed of an immaterial soul and a material body. But
the battle would not be won without a fight. Methodius of Olympus (fl. 300), one
of Origen's critics and a materialist, claimed that the body retains all of the same
matter throughout a person's life, neither changing in amount nor in any other
way, except presumably by being rearranged (e.g., in aging). How he accounted
for bodily growth is a mystery. In any case, he claimed that to resurrect the body,
the same material stuff that the person had *throughout* his life had to be used. He
assumed that this stuff was rearranged into the "original form" of the person,
which he took to be a mature form, minus any imperfections. An image he used
to illustrate his view is that of a stone temple within which a "tree of sin" grew.
Eventually, the temple falls and the tree is rooted out. Then, the very same stones
that were part of the original temple are collected and arranged just as before.
Only the tree of sin is missing.

Like others of his time, Methodius, especially in his use of imagery, could be
insensitive to the difference between *same* body and *qualitatively* similar body.
For instance, he imagined that at bodily death, God dissolves each human

into his original materials in order that by remolding, all the blemishes in him might
waste away and disappear. For the melting down of the statue in the former case corresponds to the death and dissolution of the body in the latter, and the remolding of
the material in the former to the resurrection after death in the latter; as also sayeth
the prophet Jeremiah, for he addresses the Jews in these words, "And I went down
to the potter's house; and behold, he wrought a work upon the stones. And the vessel which he made in his hands was broken; and again he made *another* vessel, as it
pleased him to make."

After sliding over the word "another," as if it meant *the same*, Methodius con-cludes, "And the word of the Lord came to me, saying, 'Cannot I do to you as this potter, O house of Israel? Behold, as the clay of the potter are ye in my hands.' "[14]

Yet, elsewhere, and especially in his critique of Origen, Methodius seems to be quite sensitive to the difference between *same* and *similar*:

> If any bronze-artist has destroyed an image made of bronze and wishes to make another out of gold in place of the destroyed one ... anyone would say that it could be similar to the first one, but not that the first image had itself been renewed. Therefore, when a spiritual body is resurrected in the old body's place, so, according to [Origen's] opinion, neither is the form nor the element resurrected; it is not the deceased body, but another similar to it.[15]

In view of Methodius' sometimes being sensitive and sometimes not to the dis-tinction between *same* and *similar*, it is difficult to be sure what his view actually was. It is also curious that he is so sure that Origen's opinion of his example would be that neither the "form" nor the "element" would be resurrected. Although Origen is not as clear about form as he might have been, it would seem that his view of Methodius' example would be that the form would be resurrected.

Origen's ideas had a more sympathetic treatment in the thought of Gregory of Nyssa (335?–395), the brother of Basil of Caesarea; these two, along with Basil's best friend Gregory of Nazianzus, are known collectively as the Cappadocian Fathers. They played an important role in settling the controversy over the Trinity at the Council of Constantinople in 381 and have the status in the East-ern Church that Augustine acquired within the Western. In *On the Soul and the Resurrection*, which is modeled on a Platonic dialogue, Gregory attempted to meet Methodius' objections to Origen, as well as to express his own view. As the dialogue opens, Gregory, grief stricken over the death of his older brother Basil, goes to his sister Macrina for consolation, only to learn that she too has contracted a fatal illness. Macrina is unperturbed, both by Basil's death and by her own impending death. In the dialogue, she plays the role of the sage, con-soling Gregory for what is about to be his double loss. Gregory plays the role of her student.

Particularly interesting is what this dialogue reveals about which objections to Origin's theories of the soul and the resurrection Gregory thinks that he has to answer. His concerns are revealed in the structure of the dialogue itself, which includes ten chapters, each of which highlights a specific issue: survival of the soul; nature of the soul; emotions; condition of the soul after death; how the soul recognizes the elements of its body; purification of the soul; why purification is painful; transmigration of souls; origin of the soul; and resurrection.

Macrina defends the view that the soul, which is immaterial, begins but does not end. Yet, she claims, each person's soul is attached to the elements of his or her body, so that when the elements are scattered at bodily death, the soul continues to be in contact with them. Emotions and desire, while not evil in themselves, are inessential, so they cease at bodily death. Purification of the soul, which begins at bodily death, is painful because the dead person had adhered so closely to what needs to be removed, mainly attachments to the pleasures of the senses. The process of purification ends no later than the conclusion of the present age, when we shall all be restored to our bodies.

Gregory, as a character in the dialogue, defends a materialistic atomism according to which a person *is* his or her body, which is merely a biological machine. He claims that a person's life consists simply in the person's functioning biologically, a view that he says is supported by sensory evidence. Macrina, by contrast, extols the virtues of intellectual intuition to defend a Christianized version of Platonic dualism. However, unlike Plato and some other Christian Platonists, such as Origen, she claims that the soul begins only when the human whose soul it is begins. Late in the dialogue she arrives at her developed view, which is that the soul is "an essence created, and living, and intellectual" which gives to the body both life and the ability to have sensations.[16]

Macrina claims that even though at bodily death the elements out of which the body had been composed may scatter, the soul remains in contact with them, if only intellectually. She points out that this intellectual contact is not unlike the connection that the soul, which is nonspatial, has with the body even before bodily death. Hence, she says, in bodily death the soul and its body never really *separate* since they were never spatially adjacent in the first place. All that happens is that the spatial configuration of the bodily elements changes as the body loses its ability to function. Eventually, the soul gathers the bodily elements together again and refashions out of them a new body, which is purer than the old body, including in its lacking organs of excretion and reproduction and in its no longer causing the person whose body it is to have emotions or desire. The new body is the body one would have had but for the Fall.

Gregory then uses this conception of resurrection to respond to a question that did not arise clearly in the works of his predecessors: why he should even *care* about being resurrected, especially in light of the worry that the resurrected person—because it would not be continuous with, or qualitatively the same as, the person one was—might be someone else: "How, then, will the Resurrection affect myself, when instead of me some one else will come to life? ... for how could I recognize myself when, instead of what was once myself, I see someone not myself? It cannot really be I, unless it is in every respect the same as myself."[17]

Macrina answers that the resurrection matters not because it is a return to the self you were on earth during your state of corruption but because it is a restoration of your true, uncorrupted self. She wards off the objection that without emotions the resurrected self will not be able to experience love by pointing out that love in the afterlife, unlike earthly love, is not born of desire but of an attraction of like for like, and so does not need a corrupted body.

A curious feature of Gregory's view, as expressed in the dialogue by Macrina, is the apparent suggestion that in resurrecting we all return to the same nature. He says that we learn from Paul

> not only that our humanity will be then changed into something nobler, but also that what we have therein to expect is nothing else than that which was at the beginning.... The first man Adam, that is, was the first ear [of wheat]; but with the arrival of evil human nature was diminished into a mere multitude; and, as happens to the grain on the ear, each individual man was denuded of the beauty of that primal ear, and moldered in the soil: but in the Resurrection we are born again in our original splendor; only instead of that single primitive ear we become the countless myriads of ears in the cornfields.[18]

On one interpretation of these remarks, it seems that it is only the qualitatively similar but numerically different matter out of which we are composed at the resurrection that will distinguish among us. Hence, this would be all that is left of our individuality. But in Gregory's view, to preserve the person's identity it is still necessary that the "identical individual" particles out of which the person's body was composed at death be collected and reassembled. If, instead of the identical particles, merely some particles of the same kind are used, then the result "will cease to be a resurrection and will be merely the creation of a new man."[19]

To this view that in the resurrection we will all be returned to an original, more perfect state, Gregory makes an exception. He believed that after much prayer, Macrina was cured miraculously by God of a fatal illness, the cure leaving a scar on one of her breasts. Gregory says that this scar is the handiwork of God and so Macrina will retain it when she is resurrected.

Looking beyond Gregory, the issue of bodily defects underwent an interesting transformation in the first four centuries of the Christian era. In the earliest work of the church fathers, it was assumed that the body that gets resurrected is the same as the body one had at the end of life. Pagans objected that this was a repugnant idea. The example of the martyrs added fuel to the fire since at death their bodies were badly mangled or worse. So, in later thinkers, it tended to be assumed that defects would be repaired. Initially, the new idea was that people are restored to the physical condition they had in the prime of their lives. That emendation, however, took care only of the physical defects of those who had achieved their prime physical condition. What about babies who die young or are born with physical defects? In their cases, it was suggested, they would be restored to the condition they would have achieved had they been able to reach prime physical condition. What, then, of spiritual defects? To correct for them, in Gregory's view, one would have to be restored to the condition that Adam had been in prior to the Fall. So Gregory arrived at the view that everyone is restored to the condition of Adam. However, if he meant that literally, it would seem that all resurrected people wind up having qualitatively identical bodies!

In working out such details, dualists had an easier time than materialists. For materialists, the body was the vehicle for preserving identity, so one had to be careful about suggesting that the body of the resurrected person differed from the body of the person who died. For dualists, such as Origen and Gregory, personal identity had already been secured by the persistence of the soul. The question that remained was merely that of accounting for the resurrection. They still had to be careful to ensure that the body that rose was the same one as the body that fell, but over time they allowed themselves great latitude in satisfying this requirement, to the point where, in what may have been Gregory's view, the body that rises is the "same" as the one that fell by being qualitatively identical to Adam's body.

Such departures from more pristine versions of the resurrection scenario provoked a predictable reaction from critics, including from some dualists. For instance, Jerome (345–420), taking Origen as his target, argued against the preexistence of human souls, claiming that souls are created when their associated bodies are created.[20] On the state of the body after the resurrection, he asserted that in the case of everyone, including Jesus, there is restoration of the flesh as it actually was during the person's lifetime. He also accused Origen of only pretending to adhere to the resurrection of the body: "Mark well that, though he nine times speaks of the resurrection of the body, he has not once introduced the resurrection of the flesh, and you may fairly suspect that he left it out on purpose." In Jerome's view, all flesh is body, but not all body is flesh: "Flesh is properly what is comprised in blood, veins, bones, and sinews." Body may be "ethereal or aerial" and "not subject to touch and sight." In making this point, Jerome distinguished, first, between actual human bodies, which are material in the way flesh is material, and spiritualized or ideal bodies; second, between the "form" of actual, human bodies, which include eyes, teeth, genitals, and so on, and the form of idealized bodies that may lack some of this equipment; and, third, between the very body that one has when one dies and a reconstructed body.

Jerome complained that in Origen's view, rather than God's restoring our actual bodies, God would "transfigure the body of our humiliation and fashion it according to His own glorious body." He said that in Origen's "saying *transfigure*, he affirms *identity* with the members which we now have. But a *different* body, spiritual and ethereal, is promised to us, which is neither tangible, nor perceptible to the eye." Moreover, the changes that one's body "undergoes will be suitable to the difference in its future abode. Otherwise, if there is to be the same flesh and our bodies are to be the same, there will again be males and females, there will again be marriage; men will have the shaggy eyebrow and the flowing beard; women will have their smooth cheeks and narrow chests."[21] Jerome, thus, seemed to have wanted not only that humans keep their same bodies in their afterlife, but that they also maintain the same sorts of social relationships, including the same male and female roles. However, in the cases of infants and old people, he allowed that the bodies they get in heaven will not be the ones they had when they died. Infants will be resurrected as the mature men or women they would have become, old people as they were in their prime. In the end, whereas for Origen dead human bodies would be transformed into new "glorified" bodies, better suited to a heavenly environment, for Jerome, dead human bodies would be restored to their prime human condition.

The Augustinian Synthesis

Augustine (354–430) made seminal contributions to an enormous number of issues that continued to be central sources of concern not only throughout the Middle Ages but into the Reformation and beyond. These included the Trinity, the problem of evil, human freedom, the nature of time, the soul, human psychology, and, of course, resurrection. He is more impressive intellectually than any other church father. In his *Confessions*, he bequeathed to posterity a vivid and compelling portrait of himself, in effect doing for himself what Plato earlier had done for Socrates. In sum, as a consequence of the profundity and depth of his thought and the enduring impression of his personality, on most questions on which he had an opinion he became an authority among Latin Christian thinkers second only to the Bible.

Augustine's *Confessions*, the first Western autobiography of any significance, became the model of that genre for a thousand years. In it, he portrayed himself as one who had progressed from youthful immersion in the world of the flesh to mature concern with the life of the spirit. In telling this story, he opened a door to the exploration of human subjectivity only hinted at in previous writers. Like Socrates, he stressed the importance of caring for one's soul, and he was driven to understand himself as a knower. But the similarities between these two should not blind us to the greater psychological depth and complexity of Augustine's self-analysis or to the novel uses to which he put its results.

Perhaps most importantly, Augustine developed the idea of internal, psychological conflict: "I have become an enigma to myself," he wrote, "and herein lies my sickness." He relates that although he longed to become a Christian, he felt that he could not become one because of his weakness of will and addiction to sensual pleasure. When a person gives into lust, he said, a habit is formed that if unchecked "hardens into compulsion": "The enemy had my power of willing in his clutches, and from it had forged a chain to bind me." The "new will" toward Christianity that had begun to emerge in him "was not yet capable of surmounting that earlier will" toward sensual pleasure. The reason, he said, that his mind "cannot rise with its whole self on the wings of truth" is that "it is heavily burdened by habit." "There are two wills," he said, "and neither is the whole: what one has the other lacks." They fought it out, making of his soul a battlefield in which spirit and lust were locked in mortal combat. He longed for internal peace, but even in his longing for it he was conflicted. "O Lord," he begged, "make me chaste, but please not yet."[22] By thus using himself as a model, Augustine suggested a general theory of internal conflict: "When the mind commands itself to will something, it would not be giving the order if it did not want this thing." Generally, what the mind wants, and therefore wills, immediately translates into action—one wills one's hand to move, and it moves. However, when the mind is conflicted, it "commands itself and meets with resistance." How, Augustine asked, is it possible for a person not to try to do what his mind commands?

One possibility, Augustine claimed, is that in the human person, there are two wills, one of which is one's own and one of which is alien. But a volition that comes from within, Augustine decided, "is not some alien thing" but comes from the mind's one and only self. So, when there is internal conflict, the mind cannot possibly "be giving the order with its whole self." In short, the problem is that the volition does not proceed from a unified mind. In as much as the mind "issues the command, it does will it, but inasmuch as the command is not carried out, it does not will it":

I was the one who wanted to follow that course, and I was the one who wanted not to. I was the only one involved. I neither wanted it wholeheartedly nor turned from it wholeheartedly. I was at odds with myself, and fragmenting myself. This disintegration was occurring without my consent, but what it indicated was not the presence in me of a mind belonging to some alien nature, [but conflict in my own mind].[23]

"If we were to take the number of conflicting urges to signify the number of natures present in us," Augustine observed, "we should have to assume that there are not two, but many" and that the conflicts among them are not just between good and evil but between good and good and between evil and evil. He wrote that "when the joys of eternity call us from above and pleasure in temporal prosperity holds us fast below, our one soul, in no state to embrace either with its entire will, ... is torn apart in its distress."[24] In these remarks Augustine declares a unity of soul, where late-twentieth-century theorists would see a fragmented self.

To find out about the human mind, Augustine urged, "Do not go outward, return to yourself. Truth dwells within."[25] By first going inward, he said, we are led not outward, but upward. By going inward, the first truth that one discovers is one's own existence. The second is that the knowing of this truth does not depend upon the body but on direct self-awareness. Reflecting on this reveals something about our nature: since we know ourselves directly and do not know ourselves as any sort of material object, we are not a material object. In the seventeenth century, Descartes would build on this argument to develop an extreme form of substance dualism—between a thinking, unextended "spiritual" substance and an unthinking, extended, material substance—and declare that the self is essentially a thinking, unextended substance.

Augustine did not go that far. Yet, as a substance dualist, he was among the first to become self-conscious about a problem that would persist in the tradition of Christian dualism at least until the end of the eighteenth century: how to explain the relation of the soul substance to the body. Plato had maintained, in effect, that the soul is related to the body like a pilot to his ship. Augustine's view, in contrast, was that soul and body together form an intimate unit: "A soul in possession of a body does not constitute two persons, but one man."

A man is not a body alone, nor a soul alone, but a being composed of both.... [The soul is] not the whole man, but the better part of man, the body not the whole, but the inferior part of man.... When both are joined, they receive the name of *man*.... [However,] even while a man is alive, and body and soul are united, [Scripture] calls each of them singly by the name, *man*, speaking of the soul as the *inward man*, and of the body as the *outward man*, as if there were two men, though both together are indeed but one.[26]

In Plato's view, the soul at death always leaves forever the specific body with which it had been associated, and when sufficiently purified it eventually leaves body itself forever. In Augustine's view, the dogma of bodily resurrection requires a more intimate relationship between soul and body. Even so, he denied that sensation is an activity of the total psycho-physical organism, insisting instead that in sensation the soul uses the body as its instrument.

Within the realm of spirituality and mentality, Augustine had a penchant for oppositions, which he characterized as inner and outer. The inner is our souls, including reason and will, the outer what we have in common with animals, including our senses and memory images of outer things. This penchant for opposition between the inner and outer reached its most extreme expression in his discussion of memory: "What a great faculty memory is, how awesome a mystery! It is the mind, and this is nothing other than my very self."[27] If we take Augustine literally here, he would hold a position not very different from that attributed to Locke, that personal identity extends only as far as memory. This position would imply that one's identity does not extend to portions of what others might regard as one's own life, such as one's early infancy or to periods of forgetfulness. However, elsewhere and more generally, he held that there is more to self or person than mind or memory.

Augustine justified his view that the human soul is immaterial and immortal by appealing both to Christian Scripture and human psychology. Since Scripture teaches that humans are made in the image of God, whom he took to be immaterial, it follows, he thought, that humans too must be immaterial, at least in part. And since certain objects of intellectual comprehension, as in geometry, are not limited spatially, the soul that contemplates them cannot be limited spatially. Also, our being able to feel when any part of our body is hurt indicates that the soul permeates the body, which it could not do if it was material; nor could acts of willing and thinking be performed by body. However, Augustine rejected the Platonic view that the soul is immutable and imprisoned in the body. In his own view, the soul can be changed either by itself or by the body, and it is not imprisoned.

Augustine credits Ephesians 5:29—"No one hates his own flesh"—with helping him to realize the body's value. Rather than the body being a mere tool, or even worse, a prison, Augustine claimed that it should be regarded as a "temple." He also rejected the Platonic view that the soul yearns to be free of the body. While acknowledging that the soul rules over the body, and hence that the body is subordinate, he claimed that after death, when the soul is separated from the body, the soul yearns to be reunited.

Augustine held that the human soul is created by God, but he had no fixed view about when or how. He toyed with a view, favored by Plato and Origen, that each person's soul existed before its becoming associated with body, but Augustine refused to allow that the soul was put into the body as a punishment for sin. An important question for him was whether God created each individual soul separately or created all souls in Adam's, so that the souls of subsequent people are "handed on" by their parents. An advantage of the latter view is that Original Sin can be explained as a transmitted stain on the soul. A possible disadvantage is that for the soul to be handed down, it would seem that it has to be material. Gregory of Nyssa may have been attracted to the idea that the soul is handed down and hence is material. Augustine insisted that the soul is not material.

When Augustine turned to the topic of resurrection, he struck a compromise between his predecessors, such as Methodius, who emphasized the importance of remaining the same and those, such as Origen, who emphasized transformation, though Augustine leaned toward the former view. He claimed that the body one gets in heaven has to be composed of exactly the same bits as the body one had on earth, presumably at death, but the bits do not have to be used in the same way. For instance, the bits that on earth had composed an arm might in the afterlife be used to compose a leg, and although the number of one's hairs had to be the same, the hairs themselves did not have to be the same. Moreover, the recomposed body, unlike the earthly body which was made of the same stuff, would be unchanging, hence, not subject to development or decay.

Augustine considered the case of people who had become deformed and claimed that, with some exceptions, their deformities would be removed. The exceptions included the martyrs, whose scars were a badge of honor. The afterlife bodies of those who never grew to maturity, such as aborted fetuses, or those who grew to maturity but were always deformed, while composed of the same bits as their earthly bodies, would be beautifully formed and mature.

Although Augustine was horrified by the prospect that some people had been eaten, he denied that it could be claimed "with any show of reason, that all the flesh eaten has been evacuated, and that none of it has been assimilated to the substance of the eater." He pointed out that emaciated animals have become robust by eating flesh, "sufficiently indicating what large deficiencies have been filled up with this food." However, he claimed, the tiny particles out of which consumed and assimilated flesh is composed are eventually released into the air due to evaporation, where God retrieves them. In the case of cannibalism, in particular, he claimed, human flesh "shall be restored to the man in whom it first became human flesh." Human flesh consumed by another "must be looked upon as borrowed by the other person." Like a loan, it must be "returned to the lender." The cannibal's "own flesh, however, which he lost by famine, shall be restored to him" by God.[28]

Augustine held that there would still be a distinction of the sexes in heaven. In a passage in which he considered the debate about whether women would be reconstituted with a female or a male body, he decided that they would be reconstituted with a female body, but one deprived of lust! Both sexes, however, would retain whatever contributed to their physical beauty, which Augustine thought of as harmonious proportionality. In the case of men, retaining what contributed to their beauty meant retaining their beards. Both sexes would retain their genitalia and all of their inner organs. There is the suggestion, though, that since nothing is hidden in heaven, heavenly bodies would be transparent, inner organs exposed to view.[29]

Shortly after Augustine died, the Roman Empire in the West fell to barbarians, and cultural darkness descended over Europe. Augustine, as it were, got the last word, just as the Patristic Period was drawing to a close. Largely because of the importance to Christian thinkers of the dogma of resurrection, the Patristic Period began a discussion of selfhood and personal identity more focused and subtle than any that had taken place previously. In Europe, a comparable intellectual revitalization would await the thirteenth century.

V

THE STREAM DIVIDES

From the end of the Patristic Period to the beginning of the Renaissance, European philosophy divides naturally into two phases: the Early Middle Ages, roughly the sixth through twelfth centuries; and the High Middle Ages, the thirteenth and fourteenth. During the first of these two phases, European philosophers were preoccupied with harmonizing Platonism and Christian revelation. The problem of universals, how a hierarchy of Ideas can be the basis of reality and how the human mind can come to know these Ideas from particulars, were dominant concerns. The metaphysics of personal identity, except in connection with the question of how to individuate one human being from another, was not. The study of psychology was reduced to the investigation of the categories of mystical experience.

During this time, there were few Latin philosophers who could read Greek and there were few Latin translations of important Greek philosophical works.[1] Eventually, the Latin world would regain access to Greek philosophy. Beginning in the second half of the eleventh century and culminating in the thirteenth, a large corpus of work was translated from Arabic and Greek into Latin. This newly translated material, which included some Neoplatonic authors such as Proclus, but most importantly nearly all of Aristotle, did not become widely available until the thirteenth century. Its appearance ushered in the High Middle Ages. This first wave of new translations of Greek philosophy, which focused on Aristotle, was followed in the Renaissance by a second wave, which provided the first Latin translations of many of Plato's works, as well as original translations of other Neoplatonic, Gnostic, and hermetic works.

From the sixth through the eleventh centuries, in the Byzantine East, where Greek continued to be read, the influence of the Cappadocian Fathers—Basil, Gregory of Nyssa, and Gregory Nazianzus—was keenly felt. The writings of the mystical Christian Neoplatonist, pseudo-Dionysius the Areopagite were also important. During this period, there was some interaction between the Latin and Byzantine traditions, most notably through the work of the ninth-century Irish mystic John Scotus Eriugena, one of the few Latins of his age who did read Greek. Eriugena translated the writings of pseudo-Dionysius, who at the time was mistakenly thought to be the Dionysius who had converted to Christianity when he had heard St. Paul preach on the Athenian Areopagus and thus was accorded by Latin philosophers a quasi-scriptural authority. Much later it was discovered that he was not *that* Dionysius but instead had lived in the Near East, probably in the late fifth century, and had written his work under the influence of the Neoplatonist Proclus.

In the Latin West, on the other hand, until the thirteenth century Plato was more influential than Aristotle. Cicero, who had been a student at the Platonic Athenian Academy, reflected in those of his writings that were still available in the Latin West the Skepticism that had come to dominate that school as well as the Middle Platonism that, during his lifetime, was just beginning to replace it. Boethius's influential *Consolation of Philosophy* was Platonic. Of Plato's own works, Latin readers possessed in translation only parts of the *Timaeus*. They did, though, possess some of Plotinus and most importantly Augustine, who acknowledged his debt both to Plato and Plotinus. Augustine's Platonism included acceptance of the eternal presence of Ideas in the mind of God, their immediate comprehension by human reason, and the incorporeality and immortality of the human soul. His repeated assertions that Platonism is closer than any other pagan philosophy to Christian doctrine encouraged later attempts to reconcile them.[2]

The Dark Ages in Europe

In 476, the barbarian Theodoric (454/5–526) defeated the last Roman emperor of the West and inaugurated in Italy the Ostrogothic kingdom. Subsequently, he wanted to maintain diplomatic contact with Constantinople, establishing himself as the chief agent in the West of the Roman emperor in the East. To this end, he enlisted the services of Roman aristocrats who knew both how the Roman bureaucracy worked and how to comport themselves in accordance with Greek court etiquette. In this capacity, Boethius (480–525?) was drafted to became Theodoric's prime minister. Although Boethius seems to have discharged his duties with distinction, Theodoric suspected him of conspiring with the emperor against him. In 524, he imprisoned Boethius and a year or two later put him to death, without a trial.

Before his imprisonment, Boethius had done important work as a theologian and translator. His main theological preoccupation was refuting trinitarian and christological heresies. In his discussion of the Trinity, he introduced Aristotelian categories to differentiate the three persons. His definition of *person*—"a substance that is individual, of a nature that is rational"—became the standard one in medieval philosophy. However, more important than either his theology or his contributions to philosophical terminology was the contribution that he aspired to make, and that he easily could have made, as a translator of Greek philosophy into Latin. No one had yet translated much of Plato or Aristotle, including any of Aristotle's works on metaphysics, natural philosophy, or psychology.[3] So Boethius undertook to translate the complete works of Plato and Aristotle. He intended to show that the philosophies of Plato and Aristotle are compatible.

For some reason that in retrospect is difficult to understand, Boethius decided to begin this massive project by translating Aristotle's elementary logic texts, *Categories* and *On Interpretation* and then, rather than proceeding immediately to Aristotle's more important works, to translate the *Isagoge*, or commentary on *Categories*, by the Neoplatonist Porphyry (233–301). This was supposed to help readers deal with the logic that Boethius had already translated. He then wrote his own commentaries on Porphyry, Cicero, and Aristotle's elementary logic. In the latter, he frequently appealed to theories from Stoic logic and thus preserved this important post-Aristotelian theory for the consideration of medieval logicians. In his commentary on Porphyry, he also nourished interest in the problem of universals. However, due to his untimely death, he got no further in his translations of Plato and Aristotle. As a consequence, his historical import is much greater for what he did not do than for what he did. Had he completed his intended project of translating Plato and Aristotle, or even translated just one of Aristotle's more important contributions to natural philosophy, he might have profoundly changed the face of medieval philosophy.

While in prison awaiting his execution, Boethius wrote *The Consolation of Philosophy*, which became one of the most widely read books in medieval times. In it, he dealt with the issue, as a matter of psychology rather than ethical theory, of how good people to whom bad things happen can nevertheless find meaning in life. Written in a personal style, the argument is Platonic. Philosophy, personified as a woman, nurses the prisoner Boethius to the recollection of the Platonic notion of Good, which "strongly and sweetly" controls and gives order to the universe. Both fortune and misfortune are subordinate to the Good. Evil as something that really exists is excluded. Humans have free will, but their having it is compatible with divine order and foreknowledge. Virtue never goes unre-warded. Boethius found consolation in the expectation of reparation and reward after his death. His book, along with Augustine's *Confessions* and other medita-tive works, cultivated piety and introspective analysis during the hard times in the West of the Early Middle Ages.

During this period, the Eastern church, and Greek philosophy in general, developed independently of the Latin West. East and West would reconnect later, at least to some extent, first through the mediation of the Arabs, who brought, along with their own works, most of Aristotle and commentaries on him.[4] In the East, and later also in the Arab world, Aristotle's chapters in *De anima* on the intellectual soul—in particular book 3, chapter 5—were widely discussed. Alexander of Aphrodisias (fl. 200 c.e.) provided the most authoritative interpre-tation of Aristotle available. His most important contribution was to suggest that the active or productive power of the intellect, what he called the "active (or agent) intellect," is a transcendent singular being, which enters the soul "from without" and is equivalent to Aristotle's transcendent prime mover, or God. He also named the receiver of these ideas, what others would call the potential or possible intellect, the "material intellect" because it served as matter for the active intellect to inform with ideas. In his view, this material intellect was an active power in humans, with the disposition to think the forms, or ideas, brought to it from without, by the active intellect. In thinking these ideas, the material intel-lect becomes "actual" and acquires these ideas, which accumulate as a habitus, a dispositional readiness to use the ideas on subsequent occasions. By suggesting that the material intellect was an active power, he also, in effect, distinguished it from the passible (*pathêtikos*) intellect, which included the irrational powers of the soul, such as imagination and emotion.

Although Alexander saw the active intellect as immortal, he left little room for human personal immortality. He viewed the material intellect, which was the highest part of the human soul, as a power that could become "immortal" while thinking immortal ideas but did not thereby acquire immortality for itself. Rather, it is a power or faculty produced out of a particular organization or mix-ture of the material constituents of the body, and it dies with the body. In taking this position, he followed a trend that developed in Aristotle's immediate succes-sors, Theophrastus and Strato.

Among those who relied heavily on Alexander but who also moved away from him in the direction of an account of personal immortality was Themistius (c. 317–c. 388). He was studied closely by the Arabs and after his work was trans-lated, in the thirteenth century, had a great influence on European philosophers. He is the probable source of the notion of a hierarchy of matter-form relations in the human soul. In contrast to Alexander's notion that the active intellect is equivalent to Aristotle's prime mover, he identified the active intellect with the essential self, of which he wrote, "So just as the animal and what it is to be an animal are distinct, and what it is to be an animal is derived from the soul of the animal, so also the I and what it is to be me are distinct. What it is to be me is, then, derived from the soul, yet from this not in its totality ... [but] from the productive intellect alone." In this passage, Themistius, in effect, introduced in the context of Aristotle's account of the soul a distinction that originated in Plato, and would become very important from John Locke to our own times, between the human organism that one is and one's essential self.[5]

In addition to his thesis that people are their active intellects, Themistius originated a distinction between the potential and the passive intellects that would later be adopted by Aquinas and other Scholastics because it provides a way of reconciling Aristotle's views with the Christian Neoplatonism that Augustine passed down to the Latin West. The substance of this distinction is that the possible or potential intellect is seen as joined to the active intellect as matter to form and that collectively they form a rational soul that is immortal. By contrast, the passive intellect involves those reasoning processes that are related to the emotions, imagination, temporal reasoning, and memory, which are associated with the body and "perish" at death. In Themistius's view, this passive intellect is equivalent to the corporeal soul that Plato posited in the *Timaeus* as the mediator between the rational soul and the body.

However, by connecting the potential intellect to the active intellect and keeping the passive intellect separate and related to the body and emotions, Themistius raised an issue that would prove to be problematic for later Christians, such as Aquinas—whether there is one or many active intellects (or active/potential intellect unities). Themistius suggested that there is only one active intellect but left the issue unresolved.[6]

Returning to the Latin West, after a period of intellectual decline following Boethius's death, philosophical thought was revived again when John Scotus Eriugena (810?–877?) introduced the Greek Christian Neoplatonist tradition, especially as it had been developed by Gregory of Nyssa and the pseudo-Dionysius. Eriugena soon became a controversial figure among Christian theologians, and in the thirteenth century his views were condemned by the Western church. Even so, much of the text of his main work, *On the Divisions of Nature* (*Periphyseon*), continued to be read as an anonymous gloss to his Latin translations of the pseudo-Dionysius. Eriugena thereby influenced both the development of Western mysticism and even thirteenth-century Scholastics, for whom the pseudo-Dionysius remained an authority.

In Eriugena's own view, reality, which emanates from God, first flows through the Platonic Ideas, then through various logical categories, and finally into the realms of number, space, and time, where the Ideas multiply and become subject to change, imperfection, and decay. In the realm of number, the Ideas become pure incorporeal spirits—angels. In that of space and time, they take on the burden of matter, which is the source of suffering, sickness, and sin. Once contaminated by matter, the Ideas are no longer reality but merely its appearance. In human beings, the Idea is the soul, the matter the body. Humans culminate the process of things emanating from God and begin that of things returning to God. They are also a reflection of the Trinity in that in them, being, wisdom, and love are joined.

According to Eriugena, before the Fall, humans were perfect in body and soul. Adam and Eve had been without bodily needs or sexual differentiation, both of which Eriugena took to be a consequence of Original Sin. Human nature, thus, needed to be redeemed. When Christ became human, he took upon himself body, soul, senses, and intellect, and he retained them even when he ascended into heaven, thereby redeeming human nature. Thus began the final return of all things to God.

Building on Origen but going beyond him in the direction of Neoplatonic mysticism, Eriugena claimed that at resurrection the deceased do not exchange their fleshy bodies for spiritual bodies but rather pass completely into pure spirit. In this transformation, ultimately all human individuality, and perhaps individuality altogether, is lost, and differences among humans due to social rank, gender, and even religious accomplishment are dissolved in mystic union with the source.

Two centuries later, Anselm of Canterbury (1033–1109), famous today primarily for his "ontological" proof of the existence of God, also made significant contributions to theology, as well as to the problem of universals. In his theology, he claimed that before the creation of the world from nothing, God possessed in his infinite nature the exemplars of all things that were to be rather than, as in Eriugena's account, creating Ideas after the fact. Anselm also had things to say about what it is to be human. For instance, in his view, since created things, including human beings, subsist more truly as Ideas in God than they do in themselves, humans are participations in, or reflections of, divine reality.

Even so, human psychology was not a topic to which Anselm gave much attention. When he did discuss it, his concern was not so much to illuminate it for its own sake but for the light that it could shed on theology. For instance, he claimed that one must first understand how several men are in species but a single man in order to understand how several persons can be one God and that human nature reflects the Trinity inasmuch as the soul recollects, understands, and loves itself.

Anselm wrote that the soul may be described as "movement toward God." In its attempt to reach God, it goes through three stages: first, from a collection of sensible images it unifies individuals by assembling them into species and genera, ultimately relating them to the unity of God's transcendence. In this ascent, the soul unifies itself as it deepens its identification with God. Humans, composed of body and soul, return to God through the resurrection of their bodies, which are spiritualized or glorified. Anselm agreed that mutable and unspiritualized matter, which Eriugena, following Gregory of Nyssa, viewed as mere appearance, will perish. In the end, everything goes back to God: "For God will be all in all when there is nothing but God."[7] But even though humans, along with everything else, are absorbed into God, in Anselm's view, unlike in Eriugena's, humans, as pure spirits, somehow retain their individual identities. Anselm left the issue of how they manage to do this a mystery.

Other thinkers, influenced by Anselm, tended in their discussions of human nature to keep the focus on universals. William of Champeaux (1070?–1121), for instance, held that human beings are composed of increasingly more specific universals. Socrates, say, is composed, first of substance, then of bodiliness, then of life, then of animality, then of humanity, then of Greekness, and so on. Socrates himself is the sum total of these layered universals. Thus, William claimed that all humans share the same humanity rather than each having his own ontologically distinct humanity. Of course, this view tells us nothing about how humans experience the world or think or behave. In these respects, William's reflections are a far cry from Augustine's and a still farther cry from what was about to come. But before getting to that, it is necessary to trace developments in Middle Eastern thought.

Arab Philosophy

Islam was located just beyond the Latin world, in Spain, Sicily, North Africa, Palestine, Persia, Syria, and Turkey. Between the seventh and twelfth centuries it spawned a brilliant civilization whose scientific, philosophical, and artistic culture absorbed and augmented the heritage of Greece, Rome, Judaism, and Christianity.

When the Arabs translated Greek works, they focused on the most authoritative writers they could find in such fields as mathematics, astronomy, medicine, astrology, alchemy, and philosophy. Initially, these works provided the basic subject matter in these disciplines. Subsequently, Arabs added their own contributions. In philosophy, Arabs acquired almost all of Aristotle's systematic writings, along with several commentaries on them, and some Neoplatonic treatises. They did not acquire nearly as many of the writings of Plato or the major Neoplatonists.

As a consequence, among Arabs Aristotle soon attained an authority beyond what he had possessed in Greek antiquity. But their understandings of Aristotle were colored by Neoplatonic interpretations and accretions, which they were never able to eliminate entirely. Nevertheless, for them the Aristotelian corpus, supplemented by medicine and mathematics, represented a complete encyclopedia of learning. Galen, who had been strongly influenced by Aristotelianism, exercised a profound influence on Arab medicine, and several of the most important Arab thinkers combined philosophy and medicine in their work. The Aristotelianism of the Arabs in turn exercised a powerful influence upon Jewish thought of the later Middle Ages. In the Renaissance, Averroës' response to the question of the soul's immortality became an important impetus to disengage philosophy from theology.

The Persian philosopher al-Kindi (c. 800–866), who was the first to write philosophy (*falsafah*) in Arabic, composed a philosophy of nature, the centerpiece of which was the idea, derived from Aristotle but given a Neoplatonic interpretation, that it is God's mind and causal agency that is manifesting itself in the thought and agency that apparently is generated by humans. Al-Kindi regarded the agent intellect, which is the faculty of the human mind that enables us to formulate abstract ideas and to understand the causes of things, as a separate spiritual entity or intelligence that, in the chain of being, is above mankind. It is due to the presence of the agent intellect in human minds that humans can think theoretically.

Inexplicably, al-Kindi (there is some dispute about whether it really was him) translated parts of the *Enneads* of Plotinus and published them as *The Theology of Aristotle*, thereby creating a cloud of confusion that enveloped Arab philosophy until well beyond its period of greatest creativity in the twelfth century. As a consequence, after al-Kindi no Arab philosopher had a clear conception of what the differences were between the views of Plato, the Neoplatonists, and Aristotle.

The Turkish philosopher al-Farabi (c. 878–950) wrote commentaries on Aristotle in which he tried to harmonize Plato and Aristotle, especially with respect to the issue of creation. He also formulated an influential psychology, based on a Neoplatonic reading of Aristotle, that distinguished human mentality into the *potential intellect* (the mind's capacity to master a body of new knowledge), the *actual intellect* (the mind in the process of acquiring that knowledge and hence actualizing its potential), the *acquired intellect* (the mind considered as having already mastered the knowledge), and the *agent intellect* (a separate intelligence that makes all of this intellectual activity possible). In opposition to al-Kindi and Aristotle, al-Farabi argued that the agent intellect performs the role of the Platonic

Demiurge, imposing form on matter in the creation of the phenomenal world. This view was incompatible with Muslim theology, which denied that God shared creative power with any other being.

In the last half of the twelfth century, as new translations of Aristotle were introduced to Latin philosophers, along with them came translations of the works of several Arabic commentators on Aristotle, the most important of which were Avicenna (Ibn Sina) and Averroës (Ibn Rushd). Although Avicenna (980–1037) influenced Averroës (1126–1198), as well as Latin thought, Averroës' influence was almost exclusively on Jewish and Latin Christian philosophers. Ironically, as a result of religious and political developments in Arab countries, Arab Aristotelianism ceased to be a vital force in the Islamic world at the very time that it began to become a vital force in the Latin Christian West.

In Avicenna's view, the human soul and body are separate substances. Personality resides in the soul, which is neither mixed with the body nor dependent on it nor perishes with it. Rather, the soul, which has vegetative and sensitive, as well as rational powers, animates the body and rules it. However, there are no individual souls until a particular body is animated. Once this happens the soul is then bound to that particular body until bodily death. Two souls never share the same body nor two bodies the same soul. Each soul uses its own unique body for self-actualization, after which it does not need a body to persist.

An individual soul comes into existence because certain matter is especially apt to be animated by soul and used as its "instrument." To perfect itself through attaining theoretical knowledge, an individual soul must completely control the animal passions. Initially, the soul is merely a pure potentiality analogous to prime matter, ready for the reception of intelligibles. Subsequently, it acquires positive dispositions. Its acquisition of theoretical knowledge consists in its reception, in various stages, of intelligibles from the agent intellect, or Giver of Forms, which is the Intelligence of the tenth and lowest celestial sphere. Some of these intelligibles are self-evident truths, which the soul receives independently of sensation, memory, or imagination, faculties that Avicenna assigns to particular regions of the body.

In Avicenna's view, when the body dies the soul continues to exist eternally. There is no bodily resurrection. Like his predecessors al-Kindi and al-Farabi, he saw the agent intellect as an external intelligence that participates in human minds, enabling them to function. Unlike his predecessors, he claimed that the knowledge the individual human mind acquires through this activity becomes its personal intellectual possession, which it then takes with it into the next life. This is how the soul leaves body behind without obliterating its personal individuality. After bodily death, those souls that when animating bodies have led pure lives and actualized their potentialities enter into eternal bliss, contemplating the celestial principles. Those souls that have been tarnished by their association with the body undergo eternal torment, vainly seeking to reunite with their bodies, which once were potential instruments of their perfection.

In support of the idea that the soul in humans is immaterial, Avicenna argued that when one refers to oneself as "I," one cannot be referring to one's body, for if a man were to come into being fully mature and rational but floating suspended in space and totally unaware of his physical attributes or circumstances, he would still be certain of his own existence. This thought experiment, which anticipated Descartes's famous *cogito* argument, was, from the thirteenth century onward, frequently repeated by Latin writers.

Averroës not only understood Aristotle better than anyone up to his time but took himself to be in almost complete agreement with him. He viewed his own project as that of fostering a correct understanding of the master. In his view of Aristotle, the human mind is composed of three intellects: *material*, *agent*, and *speculative*. Adopting from Alexander the term *material intellect* for the potential intellect, Averroës viewed the material intellect as a passive power that humans have to form abstract concepts, with the help of the agent intellect, from the specific and particularized information that originates in sense experience. The material intellect initially is mere potential, containing nothing. All of the content it acquires derives from two sources: the phantasms provided by sense experience and the illumination provided by the agent intellect, which together give rise to abstract ideas. The illumination that the agent intellect provides partially strips the phantasms of their particular material conditions. The fusion of these phantasms in the activity of the agent intellect is the speculative intellect, which is where the products of this fusion—the combination of the phantasms provided by sense experience and the abstract ideas provided by the agent intellect—reside. These concepts in the speculative intellect are, thus, partly material and partly formal.

Most importantly, in Averroës' view there is only one material intellect and only one agent intellect for the entire human race. There *can* be only one of each since these intellects are immaterial and matter is the principle of individuation. The material intellect and the agent intellect originate in the heavens and merely participate in each human's mind, without actually being any human's personal possession. However, since the speculative intellect is material, each human has his or her own speculative intellect. Although the material intellect and the agent intellect are immortal, neither of them is a vehicle for personal human immortality since neither belongs to any human in particular. The speculative intellect dies with the body and, so, is also not a vehicle for personal immortality. In sum, individual humans have no soul of their own that could be a vehicle for personal immortality. Thus, there is no personal survival of bodily death.

Jewish Philosophy

After Philo, Jewish philosophy lay dormant until it flourished again, from the tenth to the thirteenth centuries, as part of a general cultural revival in Islam. During that time Jewish philosophers living in Muslim lands produced a varied philosophical literature in Arabic, in which their approach was either *kalam* or *falsafah*, both of which derived from Arab philosophy. Prominent among philosophers who did *kalam*, which stressed the application of reasoned argument to the Scriptures and challenged rabbinical authority, was Saadia Gaon (882–942), who wrote *The Book of Beliefs and Opinions*. Prominent exponents of *falsafah* included the Neoplatonist Isaac ben Solomon Israeli (c. 855–c. 955) and Solomon Ibn Gabirol (1022?–1060?), who was known in the Latin West primarily as Avicebron (but also as Avencibrol). Of these, Gabriol was the most important for subsequent developments in theories of the self and personal identity.

Gabirol was a Spanish Jew who wrote in Arabic. Many Latins thought he was a Muslim. In *Fountain of Life*, he defended the quasi-materialistic view that with the exception of God, who is not a being but one beyond being, all spiritual as well as corporeal substances are composed of matter and form. What previous philosophers, including Avicenna, had regarded as purely spiritual substances and hence pure form, Gabirol argued are a "hylomorphic" combination of generic matter and form. Humans, in contrast to "spiritual" substances, are composed both of this generic matter and a combination of the four elements of which the lower material world is composed.

Gabirol's view was based, first, on the idea that only God is absolutely simple (noncomposite) and, second, that composition is always a case of indeterminate matter becoming determinate by the presence of a form. It follows that everything other than God has some kind of matter. Physical objects have corporeal matter, but even spiritual creatures, such as angels and the human soul, have some sort of "spiritual matter." Since the human soul has spiritual matter of its own, it is a complete Aristotelian substance in its own right. It does not really reside in the body like an Aristotelian substantial form in unformed matter, producing a single unified substance, for it already is a single unified substance.

This "hylomorphic" view of soul thus supported the Platonic idea that the soul's relation to the body is like that of a captain to his ship. It also supported the more extreme idea that physical objects, all of which are composite, incorporate many different forms, which are "nested together," in a kind of genus-to-species relationship. So, for instance, a given object might be corporeal, animate, and sensate, all of which are ways in which matter can be formed. In objects, these forms are not related to each other haphazardly but rather are "nested." But the human soul, to be immortal, must be a substance in its own right. Since corporeal human beings are composed of a variety of substances—not only soul and body but various sorts of bodily substances—and yet are unified, something has to account for their unity. The idea of "nesting" was introduced in order to account for it. Gabirol's views, which were seen as a step away from Neoplatonism toward a kind of Aristotelian materialism, were translated into Latin and, during the thirteenth and fourteenth centuries, widely debated by Christian Scholastics.

In the second half of the twelfth century, Jewish philosophy, under the influence of al-Farabi, Avicenna, and Avempace (Ibn Bājjah), entered a more rigorously Aristotelian phase. From the point of view of Jewish philosophy, the high point of this phase was reached in the work of Moses Maimonides (1135–1204), who, like Averroës, thought that Aristotle's philosophy represented the highwater mark of human reason. Maimonides agreed with Averroës that Aristotle should be purged of Neoplatonic accretions and embraced systematically, but in a way that would include, rather than ignore, the Jewish theological tradition. In his *Guide to the Perplexed*, which was written in Arabic, Maimonides strongly criticized Jewish *kalam* and pietism, taking instead the view that the essence of Judaism is a speculative understanding of God. He asserted that Jewish theology in its entirety could be understood in Aristotelian terms, without compromising either the theology or the philosophy. Understanding thusly is vital, he claimed, in order to make theology credible to people living in a postbiblical age.

Maimonides believed that humans have immortal souls whose only activity is the pure intellectual contemplation of God. This suggests that in his view, the soul's immortality may not entail personal immortality. In an early work, he seems to have thought that there is no resurrection of the body, but in his *Essay on the Resurrection*, written late in his life, he endorsed the idea. He claimed that resurrection takes place at roughly the time of the return of the Messiah but is not permanent. Rather, it is followed by a second death, which only the "righteous" survive. The form of their survival is as immortal souls, contemplating God.

Maimonides' *Guide to the Perplexed* was translated into Latin and widely read by Christian Scholastics of the thirteenth and fourteenth centuries. It was received with awe and respect, especially by Dominicans, who referred to him simply as "the Rabbi" or "Rabbi Moses." It importantly influenced Aquinas. In it, Maimonides claimed that there are four kinds of perfection that humans can acquire. The first, and lowest, is property. The second is bodily perfection, including psychological balance. The third is moral perfection. The fourth, and highest, is intellectual perfection, including "the possession of such notions which lead to true metaphysical opinions as regards God." With this perfection, he said, humans achieve immortality and, unlike in the case of the other perfections, this last one "is exclusively yours;

no one else owns any part of it."[8] He claimed that "the soul that remains after the death of man, is not the soul that lives in the man when he is born; the latter is a mere faculty, while that which has a separate existence after death, is a reality."[9] He says that this latter soul is what is called "spirit." What he meant by these dark sayings is a matter of dispute, but they would leave their mark. No less a Jewish philosopher than Spinoza would pick up this thread from Maimonides and try to weave it into his own more modern account of human nature.

The Twelfth-Century Renaissance

In the Latin West during the twelfth century, there was a sudden burst of intellectual activity in which individualism and humanism came to the fore. So far as philosophy is concerned, these innovations were due in large measure to the energizing influence of Abelard, the last important philosopher to be unaffected by the translation into Latin of Aristotle's works and the Arab commentaries. Due in part to Abelard's great influence as a teacher, the cathedral schools, which previously had been the main centers of European education, gave place to universities. These then provided a context in which all areas of learning could flourish and scholars as a group began to confront the same key texts. Chief among these, initially, was the *Sentences* of Peter Lombard (c.1100–1160), which is an edited collection of quotations, primarily from Scripture and the church fathers, organized by topic (e.g., God, evil, death).

Later, in the thirteenth century, both Aristotle and his commentators were adopted as core components of university curricula. This resulted in a more scientific approach to natural philosophy due to Aristotle's this-worldly, empirical emphasis. This more scientific approach, as we have seen, centrally involved the reinterpretation of nature in terms of the Aristotelian notions of matter and form, a reinterpretation that severely challenged earlier conceptions of human nature, which tended to be Platonic. At the same time, philosophy became more responsive to its own concerns, rather than simply to those of theology.

In the eleventh and twelfth centuries, several writers independently of one another took an interest in autobiography. The first of these, Otloh of St. Emmeram (1010?–1070?), wrote *On His Temptations and Writings*, in which he surveyed his own life and works. Seemingly motivated to write about himself by his inner distress, he gave lucid descriptions of his dreams and hallucinations, as well as of his chronic depression and recurrent bouts of religious skepticism. He wrote, for instance, that "for a long time I found myself tormented by a compulsion to doubt altogether the reliability of Holy Scripture and even the existence of God himself."

Although "there would be some lucid intervals and some hope of escape," even in these "I was deprived for hours on end of any awareness of solace"; at other times, "I was a good deal strengthened by the proofs of Holy Scripture and fought against the assailing doubts of death with the weapons of faith and hope." But Otloh's misgivings returned: "I was altogether enveloped by complete doubt and darkness of mind, and I thoroughly doubted if there were any truth or profit in the Bible or if Almightily God existed."[10]

Further development of an autobiography genre occurred in the writings of Guibert of Nogent (1053–1124), whose preautobiographical writings had been traditional and stressed the opposition between Flesh and Spirit but whose autobiography, which was written after the style of Augustine, is notable not only for its searching self-examination but for its perceptive and sometimes scathing accounts of the motivations and behaviors of others. In his twenties, Guibert had studied with Anselm, at whose instigation he theorized that human mentality is divided into Reason, Will, and Affection. In Guibert's view, these three are ways to look both toward God and toward the world. Subsequently, he wrote a commentary on Genesis according to this system, which is one of the most sophisticated psychological studies produced in the Middle Ages. Still later, he opened his account of the First Crusade with the searching remark that "it is hardly surprising if we make mistakes in narrating the actions of other people" since "we cannot express in words even our own thoughts and deeds" and "can hardly sort them out in our own minds." He continued, "it is useless to talk about intentions, which, as we know, are often so concealed as scarcely to be discernible to the understanding of the inner man."[11]

Abelard (1079–1142), who initially did not write autobiography, had been a student of William of Champeaux. But Abelard rejected his teacher's preoccupation with abstract metaphysics, putting in its place a philosophical and humanistic concern with human individuality. On metaphysical grounds, Abelard rejected as incoherent William's theory about the ways in which universals of increasing specificity nest "inside" one another in human beings, claiming that each human has his own numerically different humanity. He wrote that even though people say that Socrates and Plato are one in their humanity, it is obvious that they are different from each other both in matter and in form. Abelard's humanism showed up subsequently both in the impetus that he gave to autobiography, which in his hands highlighted the exploration of interpersonal human subjectivity, and in closely related themes that were the centerpiece of his ethical writings.

Abelard's autobiography was a byproduct of personal tragedy. In his late thirties, having acquired a reputation in Paris as a brilliant philosopher and charismatic teacher, he was hired by the uncle of a gifted and beautiful young student, Heloise (1101–1162), to be her tutor. Abelard and Heloise became lovers, Heloise became pregnant, and with the uncle's grudging consent, she and Abelard married. Then, while Heloise was away, the uncle took his revenge on Abelard by hiring several thugs to castrate him. Rather than Abelard's then trying in his condition to play the role of husband and parent, he decided to enter the Abbey of Saint Denis, where he became a monk. Heloise went to a nunnery. The two communicated little for about fifteen years.

Eventually Abelard wrote a long letter, subsequently entitled *The Story of My Misfortunes* (1132?), in which he related in great detail these troubling events. For present purposes, his narration is noteworthy in its describing the emotional responses of various people involved in the tragedy, whose points of view differed, as well as in its speculations about their motivations. Not intended for Heloise's eyes, his letter had been written to console a third party who had recently experienced a grave misfortune. But a friend of Heloise obtained a copy of the letter and sent it to her. Heloise then initiated a remarkable correspondence with Abelard, in which she not only described her own misfortunes but expressed her still burning love for him in language that is at the same time philosophical and erotic—no easy task.

Overall, Heloise's letters may be more nuanced psychologically than anything that had been written previously in the West. For example:

> How can it be called repentance for sins, however great the mortification of the flesh, if the mind still retains the will to sin and is on fire with its old desires? It is easy enough for anyone to … [exhibit an] outward show of penance, but it is very difficult to tear the heart away from hankering after its dearest pleasures…. In my case, the pleasures of lovers which we shared have been too sweet—they can never displease me, and can scarcely be banished from my thoughts. Whenever I turn, they are always there before my eyes, bringing with them awakened longings and fantasies which will not even let me sleep. Even during the celebration of the Mass, when our prayers should be purer, lewd visions of those pleasures [take possession of] … my unhappy soul.

Philosophically also, Heloise pushed the envelope:

> Men call me chaste; they do not know the hypocrite I am. They consider purity of the flesh a virtue, though virtue belongs not to the body, but to the soul. I can win praise in the eyes of men, but deserve none before God, who searches our hearts and loins and sees in our darkness…. Wholly guilty though I am, I am also, as you know, wholly

innocent. It is not the deed but the intention of the doer which makes the crime, and justice should weigh not what was done, but the spirit in which it was done.[12]

Subsequently, Abelard would draw on such thoughts, as well as on the Gospels and Augustine, to craft a subjective approach to ethics.

In his *Ethics, or Know Thyself* (c. 1135), Abelard claimed that sin, which is contempt of God, does not consist in unwholesome desires, say, for forbidden pleasures, but in the intentions and consents that may grow out of such desires. Once intended, the act itself is morally irrelevant. Virtue, on the other hand, consists not in behavior but in living in love with God, while vice consists in living outside of love with God. Personal conscience is binding even when it is mistaken. Abelard even went so far as to argue that those who killed Jesus were not sinning since they thought they were doing the right thing. He thereby horrified many of his contemporaries.

As also in the cases of Otloh and Guibert, Abelard and Heloise's approach strikingly illustrates a new movement in understanding and assessing conduct away from the consideration of external behavior and toward that of inner motivation. One telling symptom of this newfound fascination with exploring the inner space of human subjectivity was the advent, between 1000 and 1200, of private confession as part of the church's normal discipline. Christians were encouraged to identify themselves not just with their public deeds but, as we saw also in the case of Heloise, with their private intentions, desires, fantasies, and dreams. And since what one *really* desires might well be hidden from one's own view, they were encouraged to ferret out their true motivations. For instance, an early confessional manual enjoins Christians to examine "all your thoughts, every word you speak, and all your actions," including "your dreams, to know if, once awakened, you did not give them your consent," being careful not to "think that in so sensitive and perilous a matter as this, there is anything trivial or insignificant."[13]

This newfound fascination with human subjectivity also showed up in other literature of the twelfth century. Crétien de Troyes, whose Arthurian legends were written between 1165 and 1190, went to great lengths to describe not only external actions but also individual points of view. In his stories, individuals are portrayed as having conflicting inner subjective perspectives on the same events, partly due to their different beliefs and previous experiences but also to such things as their differing visual perspectives. In general, he showed greater interest than had others before him in the diversity of peoples' minds. He also stressed the tension between the ideals of his heroes and societal norms.[14] Prior to his work, narratives that told of different people, even of people in conflict with one another, tended not to portray their different points of view or perspectives. Crétien did portray this and so was forced to find new principles of unity for his narratives. This was the beginning of a problem that would become acute in our own times as various kinds of narrators—novelists and historians, for instance— began to lose confidence in their ability to impose unity on diverse events and points of view without distorting what actually happened.[15]

Also in the twelfth century, a medically inspired approach to psychology arose, which would eventually displace the Augustinian/Platonic framework. William of Saint Thierry (c. 1085–1148), in *The Nature of Body and Soul*, written in the 1130s, was among the prime movers of this approach. Although his models were crude, he tried to explain human mentality scientifically, based on the interaction among material systems in the body. This approach then grew throughout the Middle Ages, spurred on by the later appearance of the works of Arab medical philosophers, such as Avicenna. By the beginning of the modern era, such physical-system perspectives had become the dominant approach.

The twelfth century also witnessed the revival and popularization of ideals of friendship and love that were inspired originally by Cicero's *On Friendship* and then given a Christian twist by Augustine, in the *Confessions*. In their twelfth-century versions, two ideas in particular gave rise to these ideals. One was that the essence of friendship is the development of a common mind. The other was that the basis for the common mind that two friends share is participation in the love of Christ. Augustine, perhaps under the influence of Cicero, had given expression to the first of these ideas in writing of a friend who had recently died that it is "well said that a friend is half one's own soul" and that "I felt that my soul and his had been but one soul in two bodies, and I shrank from life with loathing because I could not bear to be only half alive."[16]

Religious contextualizing aside, it is clear that a new ideal of romantic love had emerged. What made it new was that it portrayed love as an affair of the heart at the core of which is service to the beloved. In Europe, before this time, love, especially between husband and wife, tended to be thought of as a practical arrangement. While there may have been no precedent for the new ideal, either in pagan or Christian sources, there is a source: twelfth-century troubadours, especially William of Poitiers, who expressed in his love poems that the lover's happiness is dependent on that of the beloved and that service to the beloved is an important component of a meaningful life.[17]

On a more metaphysical plane, interesting insight into individuality can be seen in Honorius Augustodunensis' grappling with Eriugena's views. A Benedictine monk, Honorius was active from about 1100 to 1135. As we have seen, although Eriugena gave lip service to a spiritualized resurrection, he was not much concerned with the preservation either of a spiritualized body or of individuality. Like Gregory of Nyssa, he saw resurrection as a return to our condition before the Fall. Unlike Gregory, Eriugena endorsed a mystical version of that condition.

In *Elucidarium*, which was written about 1100 under the influence of Anselm, Honorius proposed a materialistic view of resurrection in which he argued that individuals, without losing their individuality, are somehow absorbed into the body of Christ, which on Earth is symbolized by the church. In a later work, *Clavis Physicae* (1120?), he sympathetically summarized Eriugena's view and argued for a more individualistic version of it, one in which he claimed that "the dissolution of flesh which is called *death* should more reasonably be called *the death of death*," since it is the beginning of a growth toward spirit.[18]

Eriugena's views also inspired the pantheism of Amaury of Bena (died c. 1204–7), who held that since God is in all things, Christ is no more in the consecrated bread than in any other object. Amaury denied the resurrection of the body, claiming that heaven and hell are but states of the soul. The sinner carries hell in himself, he wrote, like a bad tooth. The pope, he said, is the Antichrist; the Roman Church, Babylon; the relics of the martyrs, nothing but dust. The spirit within is unaffected by outer rites. It dwells in the heart. He added that every Christian is a member of Christ's body and that to anyone who abides in love, there is no sin. Amaury's Parisian followers inferred that they were allowed whatever license with their bodies they wanted. Their behavior prompted two papal condemnations of Eriugena's works, which were not only a reaction to what was taken to be behavioral impropriety but a sign of the times philosophically. European intellectuals, tiring of Platonic mysticism, were poised to embrace Aristotelian science, which was just beginning to makes its appearance on the stage of European thought.

VI

ARISTOTELIAN SYNTHESIS

Aristotle's Categories *and* De Interpretatione, *together with Boethius's commentaries* on them, had long been translated and available to Latin philosophers. From the mid-twelfth to the mid-thirteenth centuries, most of the remaining works of Aristotle were translated and became available. Avicenna and Averroës, both of whom commented extensively on Aristotle, also became available in Latin. These new writings, which contained much hitherto unknown natural science, dazzled Latin intellectuals, who were accustomed to the otherworldly speculations of Christian Neoplatonists. Aristotle's wide-ranging, systematic approach to scientific knowledge meshed nicely with the new spirit of secular naturalism that independently had begun to make its appearance. To a whole cadre of Christian intellectuals, hungry for a more scientific approach, Aristotle became known as *the philosopher*, a title that he retained until the seventeenth century.

The newly translated works of Aristotle, which for the next century would stimulate and confuse European intellectuals, provoked novel questions and cast old ones in a new light. So far as the self and personal identity are concerned, the essential problem was that since Origen most Latin philosophers had been used to thinking that each human has just one soul, a simple, incorporeal substance which inhabits the body but does not have much else in common with it. On the views inspired by Aristotle's *De anima*, there is not just one soul per human but several, each of which has a great deal in common with the body. The trick, for Christian European thinkers struggling to assimilate Aristotle, was to explain the relationship of Aristotelian souls to one another and to the body in an account that preserves personal immortality. For the first time in Europe since Christian

Neoplatonism had become the received view, the soul was undergoing a process of naturalization. In the seventeenth and eighteenth centuries, it would happen again, only more radically, until eventually the soul was displaced altogether by the mind/brain.

When Latin philosophers first began to face the task of harmonizing their older, mostly Neoplatonic philosophies with the newly arrived Aristotelian theories, Avicenna's approach seemed the most relevant. Despite the great difficulty of Avicenna's thought, its attraction to the Latin West was that he attempted a grand synthesis of Neoplatonism and Aristotle in which he seemed to many to have retained the insights of both. That was essentially the project that Latin scholars had set for themselves. But as Aristotelianism began more and more to replace Christian Neoplatonism, Averroës, who became known in the West as *the commentator,* began to seem more relevant. He shared with Avicenna the view that Greek thought formed a harmonious unity, but his focus was more purely Aristotelian. He stuck very closely to the actual texts of Aristotle, appending his interpretations directly after the very passages on which he was commenting, as if he were addressing the pedagogical needs of students. To Latin philosophers struggling to understand the large amount of difficult new material that constituted the Aristotelian corpus, his commentaries became essential reading. When he differed from Aristotle, often by his accepting the criticisms or original interpretations of Aristotle made by Alexander of Aphrodisias, Themistius, and later Islamic commentators, his views were then automatically also given serious consideration and remained influential in Latin universities well into the seventeenth century.

Over a period of several centuries, under the guidance of Averroës' commentaries, European philosophers gravitated toward the view that certain conflicts between Plato and Aristotle, particularly with respect to the soul, could not be reconciled and that in these cases Aristotle's view is generally preferable. As this happened, some of them began also to realize that Averroës' interpretation of Aristotle, especially his commentary on *De anima,* was hard to reconcile with Christian dogma about the immortality of the soul. However, at the beginning of the thirteenth century, the realization that Aristotle might not be compatible with Christian dogma was still far into the future.

How Can Soul and Body Form a Unity?

In the early thirteenth century, the key issue was whether the rational soul is the form of the body, a substance in its own right, or both. There were problems with each option. If the rational soul were the form of the body but not a substance in its own right, then it would be difficult to explain how it could survive the death of the body. But it was difficult to see how the rational soul, which is form without matter, could be a substance. And on the assumption that the rational soul were a substance, it was difficult to see how one could then account for the unity of the person. A host of thirteenth-century thinkers—John Blunt, Alexander Nequam, William of Auvergne, Alexander of Hales, Anonymous Vaticanus, and Philip the Chancellor, among others—suggested a variety of "solutions" to this problem, none of which was particularly attractive.[1]

Philip the Chancellor (1170?–1236?), one of the most influential thinkers of the early period in which Christian philosophers were trying to assimilate Aristotle, suggested that the soul, which is compound, is composed of a hierarchy of forms, each of which is a substance. The vegetative soul appears first and then materially determines the subsequent appearance of the sensitive soul. These two, he claimed, are merely preparatory to the later arrival of the rational soul, which alone is the human soul. How, then, to explain each human's unity? The answer, in Philip's view, is that these three souls fuse into one. Philip said that as the light from two temporary fires and from the sun may fuse into one source of light, "thus it is in souls."[2] But the fusion is temporary. The vegetative and sensitive souls die with the body, while the rational soul continues. Philip drew inspiration for his theory of human unity from the dogma of the Trinity.

Robert Grosseteste (c. 1168–1253) drew inspiration for his theory from the dogma of the Incarnation. In his view, just as when God joined with Jesus, the unified person of Christ was formed, so when the human soul joins with the human body, a unified person is formed. But where in the body do soul and matter join? Nowhere, he replied, or everywhere. As God is wholly present everywhere in the universe, without being in any place in particular, so the human soul is wholly present everywhere in the body without being in any place in particular. How can a rational soul that is nowhere in particular move a body? Grosseteste answered that the rational soul, while in the body, operates the processes of human life—the nerves, muscles, and so on—by means of light, the corporeal substance closest to the spiritual.[3] But is light nowhere in particular and, even if it were, how, exactly, would the soul affect light, and light run the body? To answer such questions, as well as many others, Grosseteste provided a physical cosmology and experimental science of light, which had an enormous impact on the development of medieval science. Even so, to the question of how an incorporeal soul could affect a fine corporeal substance such as he took light to be, he could provide no satisfactory answer.

Peter of Spain (1205?–1277), on the other hand, distinguished between two kinds of form. One kind gets all of its powers to act and to be acted upon from its union with matter. Forms of this kind are merely forms, not also substances. A second kind of form "has operations and passions beyond matter, as well as in matter."[4] Forms of this second kind, which includes human souls, are also substances. But how could forms of this second kind be substances? Instead of answering this question, Peter addressed another: On the *assumption* that the human soul is a substance, how could it be the form of its human body? His answer is that the human soul was created specifically to be the form of its human body, which is its matter. A difficulty with this suggestion is that the human body, which is not prime matter, already has a form, prior to the arrival of the human soul. Peter's response to this difficulty was to claim that what informs the human body prior to the arrival of the soul is not any form that the body has on its own—he denied that the developing embryo has a vegetative or a sensitive soul—but, rather, form in the father's sperm, which belongs not to the embryo but to the sperm. This form, which departs as soon as the human soul arrives, ensures that the matter of the embryo is suitably prepared to be informed by the human soul.

By 1240, the scholastics had concluded their initial confrontation with the flood of new Aristotelian literature. Although Christian Neoplatonists still looked to Avicenna, who was a dualist, to point the way, they reached no consensus on what the soul is or how it is related to the body. Each new proposal seemed to raise as many questions as it answered. Without dualism it was difficult to see how human immortality is possible. With dualism it was difficult to account satisfactorily for human unity. With or without dualism, each new attempt to synthesize Neoplatonism and Aristotle raised questions that could not be answered without both knowing more about the human body than anyone then did and also developing a clearer understanding of Aristotle's natural philosophy.

At about this time, Aristotle's *De anima*, along with the recently acquired commentaries, became the subject of regular lectures at Oxford and Paris. As this happened, Averroës' views came to the fore. An initial misconception about Averroës' helped him to win an audience. He was thought to have held that each individual human soul had *its own* agent, or active, intellect. His real view was that there is only one agent intellect, which all humans share. It took another two decades for scholastics to appreciate the implications of his real view for personal immortality. By the time they did so, European thinkers had developed a deep appreciation for Averroës' interpretation of Aristotle, and Neoplatonism was on the wane.

Albert the Great (c. 1206–1280) was too much of an Aristotelian to feel comfortable holding, as Peter of Spain had, that the soul is both a complete substance and the form of the body.[5] Instead, he claimed that the soul, which is a complete substance, is the *act of perfection* of the body. How could the soul be a substance? Albert answered that while the soul lacks matter, it has something analogous to matter, which he called, rather mysteriously, *what is* (*quod est*). Not much of a solution, it would seem. But even if it were a solution, it raised the question of how the unity of each person can be explained. Albert answered that each of the two substances of which people are composed have a natural dependence on the other, by virtue of which they jointly constitute just one substance. Albert claimed that if the soul were merely a substance and not also an "act of perfection" of the body, this would not be possible. To his own satisfaction, he was thereby able to account for personal unity and also ensure personal immortality. Others questioned the obvious tensions in his view. However, few of them, at the time, were able to do much better. To his credit, Albert summed up the tensions in his own view by remarking that "when we consider the soul according to itself, we shall agree with Plato; but when we consider it in accordance with the animation it gives to the body, we shall agree with Aristotle."[6] That, it seems, is not only the key to the tension in Albert's view but also to the tensions in virtually everyone's view during the thirteenth century.

Bonaventure Versus Aquinas

During the 1250s, Bonaventure (1217–1274) and Aquinas (1225–1274) became the dominant theorists of the soul. They both sought to safeguard the immortality of the soul while maintaining the unity of the human being, but they pursued this goal differently. In Bonaventure's approach, Aristotelian elements are embedded in a predominantly Neoplatonic, mystical framework, while in Aquinas's, Platonic elements are embedded in a predominantly Aristotelian, scientific framework. Between their competing views, the thirteenth century was presented with a clear choice.

Bonaventure, an Italian Franciscan who spent the most important part of his career at the University of Paris, claimed that the soul, which is the form of a human, is a substance in its own right. It can be a substance, he claimed, since prime matter is neither corporeal nor spiritual but becomes one or the other depending on the form with which it unites. The human soul combines with prime matter to form a spiritual substance. Of course, the body is also a substance. What, then, of the unity of the person? Bonaventure answered that neither soul nor body is a "complete substance." In complete, unified substances, matter and form mutually exhaust each other's appetite for fulfillment. However, when the soul and body are separated from each other, neither exhausts its appetite for fulfillment. Rather, each has a powerful appetite to be joined to the other, the soul to perfect the body, the body to be perfected by the soul. So, even though the soul can exist after the dissolution of the body, it is fully actualized only when it is united to the body. Hence, the soul is not, as Plato thought, imprisoned in the body. Rather, the soul longs for the body. "The completion of nature," Bonaventure said, requires that humans be composed both "of body and soul, just as of matter and form." This is how body and soul, though two substances, constitute a genuine unity.[7]

Is resurrection, then, a natural or a supernatural event? Bonaventure answered that reconstituting the body after bodily death, which is required for there to be a resurrection, is contrary to nature and hence a supernatural event. Reuniting body and soul in the reconstitution is in accord with nature (*secundum naturam*) and hence a natural event. However, reuniting body and soul *inseparably*, as occurs in the afterlife, is not natural but supernatural. The reason for this is that the body is naturally corruptible. In its being joined to the soul in the resurrection, what had been corruptible—the body—becomes incorruptible—but this supernaturally.

Even though reconstituting the body is contrary to nature, the body reconstituted, Bonaventure said, is still the same body: "If an ark is dismantled and then remade from the same planks, according to the same order, we do not say it is another ark, but the same." Bonaventure said that, in the resurrection, God, "like a good craftsman" uses the stuff into which the human body has dissolved, in the same arrangement, to reform the same human body. Bonaventure may have been the first to point out that certain misleading biological analogies, such as one finds in St. Paul, are not good analogies for the resurrection. But neither, he claimed, is his own ark analogy. In the resurrection, when body particles are brought together, they are not bits of inert stuff but infused with something akin to feeling. So the resurrection should be analogized psychologically, on the model of yearning. In particular, it should be understood by analogy with the love of a man for a woman.[8]

Like Bonaventure, Aquinas was an Italian, but a Dominican who spent the important part of his career at the University of Paris.[9] Following his interpretation of Aristotle, he held that the human soul is a unity in which there are faculties or powers of acting. These faculties are hierarchically arranged: vegetative, sensitive, and then rational. The passive intellect, a power neither wholly sensitive nor wholly rational, is at the lowest level of the rational faculty. It deals only with particular knowledge, not with universals. Above the passive intellect are the active and possible (or potential) intellects, including intellectual memory, which have as their object being in general.

A point that bears on moral issues in our own times has to do with the timing of the arrival of the rational soul in fetal development. Grosseteste had maintained that the rational soul is infused at conception but uses only its lower vegetative and sensitive powers until the body develops. Instead of this, Aquinas claimed that since the generation of one thing necessarily entails the corruption of another, "when a more perfect form arrives, the prior form is corrupted; provided, however, that the succeeding form" can perform all of the functions of the preceding forms. The rational soul can do this. So, in Aquinas's view, prior to the arrival of the rational soul, the growth and organization of the embryo is directed first by the vegetative soul and then subsequently by the sensitive soul, upon whose arrival the vegetative soul is obliterated. Both of these souls are biologically transmitted. The rational soul, by contrast, "is created by God *at the end of human generation.*" When the rational soul arrives on the scene, it is "at once both sensitive and vegetative, the preexisting forms having been corrupted."[10]

What this means is, first, that the rational soul arrives relatively late in the process of the development of the human embryo and that before its arrival, the developing proto-embryo has no human soul, hence no soul of any kind that is capable of surviving bodily death. In other words, in Aquinas's view, what we call the conceptus, that is, the fertilized egg that eventually will develop into an embryo, is not, either at the moment of conception or for quite awhile afterward, endowed with an immortal soul. In fact, technically speaking, it is not even human. All of that happens later.

So far as survival of bodily death is concerned, in Aquinas's view certain powers, such as those belonging to the sensitive and vegetative parts, "are in the composite as their subject" and, hence, perish with the body. Other powers, such as the intellect and the will, inhere only in the soul and thus "must remain in the soul, after the destruction of the body."[11] Nevertheless, what has sensations is neither the soul alone nor the body alone nor, as Augustine and other Neoplatonists thought, the soul using the body, but the human being as a whole; soul and body each play a part in producing sensations, which belong to both in union rather than to either separately.

Some forms are capable of existing independently of matter and some not. The ones that are capable are spiritual, or intelligible, substances. Some of these, such as angels, are complete in that they are purely intelligible and have no functions or activities that require material bodies. What makes them substances is that they are a combination of form and existence. Others, such as human rational souls, are incomplete in that they are not purely intelligible and have functions and activities that require material bodies. But they too are a combination of form and existence. In other words, Aquinas, unlike Bonaventure but quite like Albert, felt that some forms can become substances not by combining with matter but by combining with existence![12]

On this point, the main difference between Bonaventure and Aquinas is that Bonaventure held onto a two-substance view of humans, while Aquinas tried to move to a single-substance view. So, in moving from Bonaventure to Aquinas, the shift is from a fundamentally Neoplatonic to a modified Aristotelian view of the soul, with the important exception, derived from Neoplatonism, that form can combine with existence to make a substance. This exception allows Aquinas to hold on to something like Aristotle's view while preserving the doctrine of personal immortality.

Another of Aquinas's innovations was to hold that each angel is the only member of its own species. He was forced to this view by the reflection that since angels are immaterial and matter is the principle of individuation, there cannot be two angels of the same species. So, either there is just one angel or separate angels are assigned to their own species, of which each is the only member! This drastic solution might have been required for humans as well, if human rational souls had never joined with matter in the first place to form a human being. For then, in accordance with Aristotelian metaphysics, there would be only one human rational soul. In Aquinas's view, what individuates the rational souls of different humans while the humans live is partly the fact that God had created those souls in the first place to be the souls of the particular human bodies they inform and also their actually informing those bodies. After bodily death, when human rational souls separate from the bodies they informed, what makes them different from other disembodied human souls is their having been associated historically with different human bodies. In other words, even though there is in each human just one substantial form, the rational soul, which as a substantial form is the same in all humans, God's intentions and human history differentiate human rational souls after bodily death.

Because Aquinas held that a human being is a whole person or self only when a human body—either naturally generated or resurrected—is informed by a rational soul, he took the view that the soul separated from the body after death is a continuation not of the self, but only of a part of the self. In his commentary on 1 Corinthians he states, "My soul is not I."[13] He also viewed the separated state as radically incomplete in other ways. Because human knowledge of particulars requires sensation, or imagination, and these powers of the rational soul require a living body, this knowledge perishes with the body at death. Thus, the separated soul has only abstract, not concrete, knowledge of its own previous activities and of the life of the individual. Instead, and perhaps in compensation, during this phase of its existence, the soul acquires better knowledge of universals and of other intelligences or intelligibles and can acquire a deeper understanding of God. Only when it is reunited with a body at resurrection does the soul reacquire concrete knowledge of the whole person's life. But the resurrected person retains powers that the soul acquired during its period of separation from the body.

Like Bonaventure, Aquinas rejected the Platonic idea that the rational soul is related to the body as a pilot to his ship in favor of the view that the connection is more intimate. Aquinas held that the soul's uniting with the body to form a human is natural and appropriate. It is not, as Origen and then later Eriugena had thought, punishment to the soul for sin in a preceding state. Rather, the soul joins a body because it is its natural destiny to do so. Even so, Aquinas explicitly rejected the idea, which Bonaventure and others had favored, that the particles into which our bodies decompose yearn to be reunited. In his view, the dead particles are inert. The body into which they are reunited is not only free from sinful desire, that is, from "noxious passions, internal and external," but from desire altogether. There is no yearning in heaven, let alone lust or sex. The goal is a stasis that marks the end of human yearning.[14]

Toward the end of his life, Aquinas wrote that St. Paul's seed metaphor might seem to imply both that resurrection is natural—an unfolding of a preordained pattern from within the organism—and that the second organism in question— the sheaf—is different from the first. Aquinas wrote that the resurrection is not natural since nature reproduces species, not number, that is, it produces the same kind of thing, not the very same thing. Thus, the very same body returns not naturally but only by divine power. So, as far as the qualities of the risen body itself are concerned, Aquinas, this time in the tradition of Origen, interprets Scripture to mean that the body returns lighter, or more subtle, as a consequence of the beatification of the soul. Yet, he claimed, not all bodies rise the same.

In response to the chain-consumption argument, Aquinas said that human flesh will rise to be reformed into the body of the human whose flesh it first was. So, in the case of a cannibal who ate both human flesh and other food as well, "only that will rise in him which came to him materially from the other food, and which will be necessary to restore the quantity to his body." In the case of a cannibal who "ate human flesh only, what rises in him will be that which he drew from those who generated him, and what is wanting will be supplied by the creator's omnipotence." But suppose that "the parents too have eaten only human flesh." In that case, "the seed, indeed, will rise in him who was generated from the seed, and in its place there will be supplied in him, whose flesh was eaten, something from another source."[15] So, Aquinas concluded, "if something was materially present in many men," in the resurrection "it will rise in him to whose perfection it belonged more intimately."[16]

Reason Versus Faith: The Challenge of Personal Immortality

The effect of an ongoing increased focus on Aristotle was that some philosophers were moving in the direction of a naturalistic account of the soul, forging ahead into more experiential and scientific theorizing that was divorced from religious belief. The ensuing conflict between naturalistic and religious approaches to the soul led to the formation, in the 1260s, of the "double-truth" theory of the relation between reason and faith, according to which philosophy and religion should pursue truth independently of each other in spite of apparent conflicts in what they might find. This theory affected all of late Scholastic, as well as Renaissance thought, and foreshadowed the more radical divorce between science and religion that would begin in the seventeenth century.

A case in point is Siger of Brabant (1240–1284), whose book *In Tertium de Anima* was completed around 1269 and posed a challenge to the doctrine of personal immortality. Although Siger borrowed from several of the Scholastics who preceded him, he was more of a disciple of Averroës than he was a follower of any of them. In his view, each human has a vegetative and sensitive soul that is biologically transmitted; however, the rational soul (the "intellective soul"), which is neither rooted in the vegetative and sensitive souls nor has any vegetative and sensitive functions, is not biologically transmitted but comes "from without" and is the same in every human. When the rational soul makes its presence felt in a particular human, it does not corrupt the vegetative and sensitive souls but unites with them. However, what results is not "one simple soul" but a "composite soul."[17]

This composite soul is not a compound of matter and form but of hierarchically arranged forms, with those that are lower in the hierarchy acting as a kind of "matter" to those that are above. The rational soul is not the substantial form of the body but rather its perfection. It perfects the body not through its substance but through its power, which is responsible for human understanding. Siger thus emphasized the operational, rather than the substantial, relation of the rational soul to the human body. Aquinas, by contrast, argued that if this view were true, it would be impossible to show that a single individual understands. For a person's understanding would not be *his* but only that of *the intellect* that uses his body. "The action of a part," Aquinas concluded, "is the action of the whole only when the whole is one being."[18]

On the question of immortality, Siger adopted Averroës' interpretation of Aristotle's view of the rational soul, or agent intellect, according to which it must be free of matter in order to perform its function, and if free of matter, it cannot be individuated. As a consequence, he claimed, the rational soul is unavailable as a vehicle for personal immortality.[19] In a futile attempt to make his view more palatable to the ecclesiastical authorities, Siger appealed to a principle interpreted by some as involving the double-truth theory, according to which something could be apparently true according to rational philosophy but false religiously. Aquinas, by contrast, felt that rational philosophy should not produce any apparent truths that conflict with religious faith. His attack on the Latin followers of Averroës who thought otherwise, including Siger, may have played a part, as did the church's official censures, in motivating Siger to change his view. But once it arose, the double-truth theory was not so easily expunged from Scholastic and Renaissance thought.

Late Scholastic Philosophy

John Duns Scotus (1265–1308), from the town of Duns, in Scotland, became a Franciscan while he was at Oxford. He then went to the University of Paris, where he argued against Aquinas's views. A follower of Augustine, Scotus was sympathetic to Neoplatonism. He claimed that not all substances are composed of matter and form. Angels and human souls, whose existence he accepted partly on faith, are simple incorporeal substances. In opposition to Aristotle and Aquinas, he denied that matter is a principle of individuation: "In the order of nature, the soul [whether or not it unites with matter] is an individual in virtue of its own singularity."[20] But what accounts for the "soul's singularity"? Scotus's answer was that an individual person—Socrates, for example—is individuated from its species—human—by a purely formal "individual difference": *thisness* (*haecceitas*). The same, he said, is true of souls.

But Scotus was not entirely opposed to Aquinas. According to Scotus, matter must be a positive entity, quite apart from its form. It follows that God could have created matter without form, and had God done so, it would have existed in a way analogous to that in which Aquinas thought that angels or human souls exist without matter—that is, it could have merged with existence.

In retrospect, one can see that over the years theological Scholastic philosophers, in order to maintain Christian Platonic commitments, tended to get more and more permissive in their Aristotelian ontologies: Bonaventure could not conceive of form existing without matter, and so felt required to postulate spiritual matter in order to accommodate the idea that there are disembodied souls. Aquinas could conceive of form existing on its own without matter but not of matter existing on its own without form. Scotus could conceive of either form or matter existing on its own, without the other.

Scotus claimed that since human intellectual cognition transcends the power of the senses it is not an organic function and, hence, probably resides in something, the human soul, that is not itself extended. Moreover, since humans have free will, they can transcend organic appetite, which they probably could not do if they were wholly material. It is likely then, he thought, that humans have an immaterial soul, which must be the specific form of humans that separates them from the brutes. In addition, he claimed, since humans are a composite of soul and body, the soul by itself is not a human (or person). Thus, human death is the death of humans, which are composite entities, but not the death of the soul. Only what is composite can die. The soul, which is simple, cannot die.

However, contrary to Aquinas, Scotus argued that the human soul without its body is as perfect as when it is joined with its body. Even according to Aquinas, he said, the soul possesses the same being separate from the body as it possesses in union with the body. In Scotus's view, the union of soul and body is for the perfection of the human, not of the soul. He elaborated that the tendency of the intellect to think of material things, and its de facto dependence on the senses, is due not so much to its nature as to its union with the body, which union may well be a consequence of sin.

Finally, in agreement with the growing tide of Latin Averröeist and double-truth theorists but contrary to Aquinas, Scotus thought that neither the immortality of the soul nor the resurrection of the body can be demonstrated. Rather, both can be shown only by probable arguments. Scotus also claimed, contrary to Aquinas and others, that it is not clear what Aristotle's view on immortality was, or even if he believed in it. While Aristotle continued to provide the terminology and the method and continued to nourish the increasingly empiricist spirit of Scholastic philosophy, the careful, energetic attempt by philosophers such as Scotus to synthesize science with Christian revelation brought forth a critical intelligence on the part of philosophers that would ultimately undermine the authority of Aristotle.

In this regard, consider, for instance, the views of William of Ockham (1285–1349), an Oxford-educated Franciscan who, at the University of Paris, was initially a student and then a colleague of Scotus. The central principle of Ockham's thought, and the most consequential, is his claim that only individuals exist—that is, that except as mental concepts, there are no universals. He reasoned that if a distinct and independent universal were in a thing in the normal way in which one thing may be in another, then the so-called universal would be a part of the thing or else identical with the thing. In either case, the so-called universal would not be a universal but a particular. In his view, things are completely particular, and only things exist.

Ockham held that although there are in individual humans a plurality of sub-stances, these substances are unified. He claimed that the human person is the total being of man, not the rational soul alone, which is spiritual and unextended. Nevertheless, it is because humans have such a soul that they are capable of intel-lectual endeavors. Since such a soul is simple, it not only lacks parts but even distinct faculties. So, for instance, what is called the intellect, and is considered by some to be a faculty of the rational soul, is simply the rational soul's power to understand, and what is called the will is simply the rational soul's power to will. Although the importance of this move would not be appreciated until much later, by virtue of such thoughts Ockham was among the first to make the transi-tion from a faculty to a functional psychology.

Ockham defined *person* as an intellectual, complete being that is neither sup-ported by anything else nor able to join with anything else to form a complete being. Since the human soul joins with the body to form a complete being, he agreed with Aquinas that the human soul in a separated form after death is not a person. Ockham also claimed that although humans experience in themselves acts of understanding and willing, there is no reason to attribute these to an immaterial soul (or form). So far as can be determined either from argument or experience, he said, understanding and willing may simply be bodily activities. He dismissed Aristotle's views to the contrary as too ambiguous to be worth considering. Finally, like Scotus but unlike Aquinas, Ockham maintained that neither the existence of God nor the immortality of the human soul can be dem-onstrated. If either is accepted, he said, it must be accepted on faith.

Nicholas de Autrecourt (1300?–1350?), who was associated with the Ockhamist movement, went even further, developing an empirical account of the self much like the one for which David Hume would later became famous. According to Nicholas, individual things are isolated in the sense that neither their existence nor nonexistence can be inferred from the existence or nonexistence of any-thing else. He claimed that this truth by itself is enough to destroy all Scholastic philosophy. Moreover, in his view, substances neither appear to the senses nor can be inferred to exist by appeal to anything that does appear to the senses. Nevertheless, he believed, based on revelation, that each human has a soul, which is immortal. This belief could not be inferred from experience, he claimed, which presented not the substance of the soul but only mental states and acts.

Although Nicholas's skeptical views were similar in many ways to those of the Ockhamists, he used skepticism for a different purpose than they had used it, or than Hume would use it later. The Ockhamists used skepticism to propose a new empirical basis for science. For Nicholas, the point of skepticism was to show the poverty of philosophy and science as intellectual activities. He felt that instead of wasting one's time studying philosophy or science, intellectuals should focus on revelation, develop theories of morality, and lead good lives.

Portrait of an Age

Aquinas's *Summa Theologica* is generally considered the greatest synthesis of philosophy and theology in the High Middle Ages. But it is dry as dust, even in its account of such potentially juicy topics as the afterlife. It took Dante Alighieri (1265–1321), in the *Divine Comedy*, to depict poetically the implications of Aquinas's view and thereby to nourish the imaginations of educated Christians.

The events Dante depicts are supposed to take place on Good Friday, in the year 1300. On that day, in his poem, he travels through hell, purgatory, and heaven, at first guided by Virgil, the great Latin poet, and then by Beatrice, a Florentine woman for whom he wrote the love poems presented in his *Vita Nuova* and whose seemingly meaningless early death led him to think deeply about the afterlife. Virgil resides in limbo, the outer circle of hell, where virtuous pagans and innocent unbaptized infants reside. He guides Dante not only through limbo and hell but also through purgatory, all of which are within or on the earth. Beatrice, depicted as an exalted saint, then guides Dante through heaven itself, which is located above the earth, in concentric circles, consistent with Aquinas's synthesis of Aristotelian cosmology and Christian theology.

Like Aquinas, Dante believed that philosophy and theology, though independent of each other, should reach the same truths. Unlike Aquinas, he did not believe that they should reach these truths in common pursuit, with theology the more foundational science and religious faith the final arbiter. More like Siger than Aquinas, Dante felt that philosophy must pursue truth using its own methods, independent of those used by theologians, for whom the truths of philosophy must be made consistent with Christian revelation.

Dante's views on this issue were determined in part by his views on the ideal relation of political authority and the church presented in his *De Monarchia*. Based on his own experience of being an outcast from his home in Florence, which was under papal authority, he insisted that earthly political authority resided in the emperor, not the pope, whose role should be restricted entirely to revelation and to individual salvation. Probably because of his strong views on the independence of church and state, as well as of philosophy and religion, Dante, in his poem, places Siger next to Aquinas, with Albert, Aquinas's teacher, on the other side, in the fourth circle of heaven.

Bonaventure, like Albert and Siger, is placed in the same circle of knowledge as Aquinas, though on a separate ring representing a loving approach to knowledge, as contrasted with the philosophic approach of Aquinas. Augustine, on the other hand, is placed at the highest human level, in a mystic ring above the empirium, where, along with the Apostles, Beatrice, Mary, and others, he has a clear vision of the Trinity.

Non-Christian philosophers are treated differently. Because most of them were pagans, they could not be placed in heaven, or even purgatory, both of which required baptism. As a result, Dante placed them in the depths of hell, depicted as within the earth, or in limbo, with unbaptized infants, just below the surface. In limbo, souls could experience natural joy but would always feel deprived of the love of God. Since ancient pagan philosophers like Aristotle did not know of God during their own lives, Dante's picture of them is not unlike their own view of natural happiness. Avicenna and Averroës are allowed to join this company of philosophers, despite their having been aware of Christianity yet believers in Islam. Dante's toleration of virtuous non-Christians even went so far as to give the Islamic military leader Saladin, who had defeated crusading Christians, a place in limbo!

By contrast, Epicurus is placed in the sixth circle of hell, the circle of the heretics, not because he did not believe in Christ, since he lived before the birth of Jesus, but because he did not believe in the immortality of the soul. Dante felt that the immortality of the soul is so certain a truth that even pagans should have believed in it. In his *Convivo*, written before the *Divine Comedy*, where, curiously enough, Epicurus is seen in a positive light, Dante goes into a tirade on the issue of immortality of the soul: "I say then that of all the basely stupid opinions the belief that after this life there is no other life is the stupidest, the vilest, and the most pernicious."[21] By the time he wrote the *Comedy*, he had learned of Epicurus's views on the mortality of the soul but apparently had failed to notice that Democritus and Hippocrates had the same view. Dante was not offended that Averroës did not believe in personal immortality apparently because Averroës allowed for immortality of the human intellect.[22]

Dante's conception of eternal justice is well illustrated by his treatment of heretics. In canto 10 of the *Inferno*, he describes the "shades" of Epicurus and others who denied the immortality of the soul. All that can be seen of them is their open tombs. Virgil tells him that because they failed to believe in immortality they remain entombed even in hell. However, after the last judgment, when tombs on earth will open and everyone's body will be resurrected and joined to their souls, disbelievers in immortality, like Epicurus, will have their bodies joined to their souls in hell and their tombs there closed for eternity.

In his poetic description of the process of earthly generation, including the arrival of the immortal soul and its effect on human development, Dante followed Aquinas. The natural course of generation is Aristotelian, with the active part of one's matter coming from the father and the passive part from the mother. The fetus first develops through the vegetative soul, then through the sensitive soul, until, finally, when the brain is sufficiently developed, the rational soul arrives to replace the lower-level souls and unify the human being. In describing this process, Dante explicitly points out Averroës' error in viewing the intellect as external to the human being.

Dante goes on to indicate that after death, souls have the personality they developed during life but their lower capacities can no longer function without a body. So, in agreement with some Scholastics, he posits that an ethereal body gets organized around the soul, though not intimately connected to it in the way its natural body had been. In hell, ethereal bodies are pure shades, without apparent substance; in purgatory, they are substantial enough to produce a shadow in sunlight; in heaven, they are pure light—the closer to God, the brighter the light. Ethereal bodies allow for the experience of pleasure and pain.

Each separated soul is where it is through its own free choice. The sinners are in hell because of their guilt; those in purgatory, because they avoided mortal sin and wish to be cleansed and made pure; those in heaven, because they desire to be close to God. In several cantos, Dante argues strongly against mechanistic determinism in any form. Even though humans have natural inclinations, which guide their activities from infancy onward, and are affected by other influences, ultimately they are personally responsible for their acts and, hence, for their fates in the afterlife. What makes them responsible is that they have rational souls, with the capacity for reflection, and a conscience.

The Divine Comedy is the culmination of Scholastic thought, including in its synthesis not only philosophy and theology but cosmology and poetry. In Western culture, an intellectual and cultural synthesis of this order happened only once. Even as Dante wrote, forces were on the rise which would destroy the unity of Christianity and shatter the central place of religion in intellectual life. One era in human history was about to give way to another.

VII

CARE OF THE SOUL

By his own account, Petrarch (1304–1374) was overwhelmed by the view on the summit of Mont Ventoux as he opened his copy of Augustine's *Confessions*, intent on meditating on the first passage that struck his eyes. It was this one: "Men go to admire the heights of mountains, the great floods of the sea, the courses of rivers, the shores of the ocean, and the orbits of the stars, and neglect themselves." Stunned, Petrarch became angry with himself for "still admiring earthly things." Long ago, he mused, he should have learned from the ancients that "nothing is admirable but the soul" and that "compared to its greatness, nothing is great."[1]

Subsequently, Renaissance philosophers of Petrarch's sort—*humanists*—tended in the fourteenth and early fifteenth centuries to look to classical Greek and Latin literature, with an eye to remaking themselves on the models of great men of antiquity. It was a period of growing secularism and prosperity, due importantly to the expansion of trade, in which well-to-do Christians, more concerned with culture and literature than with philosophy proper, were encouraged by a newfound interest in luxury to seek out pagan writers who had similar values.

In the High Middle Ages, classical Latin literature had been studied. Renaissance humanists added the study of classical Greek literature, which in the early fourteenth century was beginning to appear in Italy. They edited, translated, and commented on the texts that came into their possession, while also writing on grammar, philology, ethics, and history and raising the standards of literary style and historical criticism. In the process, they celebrated humanity.[2]

In the view of humanists, Greek and Roman antiquity was an intellectual and cultural highpoint that had been followed by a long period of decline, the Dark

Ages. Fourteenth-century Italian humanists saw classical civilization as a golden age of creative genius and sought to bring about a rebirth, or renaissance, of this genius. In place of an increasingly arid and arcane Scholastic concern with logic and science, with its deadening obsession to Christianize Aristotle, they accepted classical authors as a source not just of ideas but of spiritual replenishment. In contrast to medievals whose work, inspired by God, was often performed in a spirit of humble submission, the humanists tended to see their own study of classical culture—*studia humanitas*—as a way of celebrating human excellence and aesthetic beauty.[3]

Fifty years earlier, Dante had praised Aristotle as first among the philosophers. Petrarch, who ranked philosophers not according to their scientific merit but their literary prowess and spiritual depth, gave that honor to Plato, whom he took to be a thinker who came near to being a Christian and undoubtedly would have become one had he lived in a Christian age. On Petrarch's scale of values, Aristotle emerged as a source of a sterile intellectualism that endangered faith and undermined literary style. Nevertheless, at Italian universities, Aristotle's natural philosophy continued to be taught. In the fifteenth century, most Italian philosophers were Aristotelians in the tradition of Aquinas and Scotus. But Averroëism also flourished, especially at the Universities of Padua and Bologna.

Platonism

In the thirteenth century, although Aristotelianism dominated philosophy and theology in the universities, Augustinianism survived among the friars and in popular religious literature. In the fourteenth century, a Byzantine tradition of Platonism, along with many previously untranslated works of Plato, arrived in Italy. Lacking the institutional support that Aristotelianism enjoyed, Platonism owed its influence to the appeal of Plato himself, as well as to the personality and power of his Renaissance disciples.

Ironically, Petrarch's knowledge of Plato had been formed not through reading him directly but through Latin authors, such as Cicero and Augustine. Although Petrarch often referred to the *Timaeus*, he was limited, as had been most medieval scholars, to an initial part of the dialogue that had been translated into Latin. The complete Greek text was available in his time—he even possessed a copy. However, lacking a tutor who could teach him how to read Greek, he could behold only the hidden visage of his heart's desire, unable to lift the veil. So far as the authors that he could read in the original are concerned, his hero was Augustine, who had been revered continuously throughout the Middle

Ages, though not often for his personality. But when Petrarch read the *Confessions*, he did not so much encounter Augustine's theories as hear his voice, which spoke to the passionate spiritual yearning of his own soul.

Even though Petrarch was not well acquainted with Plato's works or with his philosophy, he invoked his name in attacking the authority of Aristotle among philosophers of his own time. Later in the Renaissance, Petrarch's successors studied Plato in Greek, and during the first half of the fifteenth century, they translated many Platonic dialogues into Latin, including the *Republic*, *Laws*, *Gorgias*, and part of the *Phaedrus*. Engagement with the Platonic corpus reached its high point in the thought of Marsilio Ficino (1433–1499), the leader of the Florentine Platonic Academy, and in his friend and student, Giovanni Pico della Mirandola (1463–1494). However, Ficino and Pico, both of whom had embraced humanistic values, had been profoundly influenced not only by Petrarch but also by Aristotelianism. As a consequence, they abandoned the superficial polemics of earlier humanists and acknowledged their indebtedness to Aristotle and to medieval thinkers.

Ficino was the most influential Renaissance Platonist. He produced the first complete Latin translations of Plato and Plotinus, as well as other Neoplatonic writings. He also translated works attributed to Pythagoras and Hermes Trismegistus. His Platonic Academy was for decades an intellectual center whose influence spread throughout Europe. In his *Platonic Theology*, he not only gave to his contemporaries a forceful statement of Neoplatonism, in which he tried to counter the appeal of Averroëism, but celebrated the excellence and dignity of humans.

Ficino conceived of a universal hierarchy. The human soul is at the center, with God and the angels above it and the bodily below. Due to its central position, the human soul mediates between the upper and the lower half of reality—between the intelligible and the corporeal—and hence participates both in time and in eternity. Ficino wrote that the soul is "the center of nature, the middle term of all things, the series of the world, the face of all, the bond and juncture of the universe," in sum, "the greatest of all miracles in nature."[4] However, in spite of the soul's almost godlike status, it is intertwined with the body in a harmonious whole: "Every work constructed of many elements, is most perfect when all its members are closely bound together, so that it becomes one in all respects, firm in order and harmony within itself, and not easily dissolved."[5] Ficino echoed Plotinus in writing that the soul "is at once divisible and indivisible"—divisible in that it communicates itself to every part of the body; indivisible in that in each of these parts "it is simultaneously present as a whole and simple entity."[6] To his credit Ficino then tried to explain how the soul communicates with the body by noting that spirit is "formed from the more subtle blood by the heat of the heart, flies to the brain, and there the soul carefully employs it for the exercise both of the interior and exterior senses."[7]

Ficino needed for the soul to be immortal in order to justify his view that the main purpose of human existence is contemplation, which he took to be a developmental process. By contemplation, he meant a spiritual discipline that begins in detaching one's mind from the outside world, then progresses through various stages of knowledge and desire to an ecstatic, experiential union with God. In Ficino's view, the way toward this union with the incorporeal "is to make oneself incorporeal, that is, to separate the mind from corporeal movement, sensation, passion, and imagination." In this way, he thought, it will "become clear by experience" what "a pure soul is: reason living with itself and circulating around the very light of truth."[8]

Since this final union with God is so rarely attained during earthly life, without immortality human existence might be rendered pointless. Ficino thus postulated an afterlife in which the final union would be attained permanently by those who made the necessary effort prior to bodily death. He linked immortality with human dignity by arguing that the human "soul by means of the intellect and will, as by those twin Platonic wings, flies toward God, since by means of them it flies toward all things," and thus "begins to become God." The soul, with every movement toward God "makes progress through the same power through which it was increased" and "is perfected through the same power through which it made progress." In this way, one's soul may in time even "become a god."[9]

Contemplation is a solitary activity. Ficino also recognized the importance of human relationships. It is not enough to be biologically human, he claimed; one must also be morally human. One does this by being humane, which involves loving other humans as equals. Cruel people remove themselves from the human community and thereby forfeit their dignity: "Nero was, so to speak, not a man, but a monster, being akin to man only by his skin." Those who are truly men, Ficino claimed, love and help "all men as brothers."[10]

Ficino's ideal of love and friendship, for which he coined the term *Platonic love*, had its roots in classical and Christian conceptions of spiritual fellowship, as well as in medieval conceptions of courtly love. But Ficino went beyond these to articulate an ideal spiritual relationship for people who are participating together in the contemplative life. In such a relationship, he claimed, there are always at least three partners: two human beings and God, the ground of human friendship. He thus linked the highest form of human relationship to the mostly solitary experience of contemplation. He believed that friendship understood in this sense is the spiritual tie that would unite the members of his Platonic Academy.

Throughout the sixteenth century, his theory of friendship appealed not only to members of his school but to many others and was celebrated repeatedly in prose and verse.

Pico della Mirandola, who was closely associated with Ficino's Florentine Academy, read Hebrew and Arabic and was one of the first Western scholars to be acquainted with the Jewish Cabala. In tending to see similarities where others saw differences, one of Pico's great aims was to synthesize philosophical and spiritual thought. Another was to convince people that they are the authors of their own being. In his *Oration*, which became the most famous expression of the humanist ideals of human dignity and the freedom to choose one's own destiny, he wrote that God said to Adam that he had given Adam no fixed abode, no form of his own, no gift peculiarly his, in order that he might possess as his own whatever abode, form, and gifts he desired: "In conformity with your free will, in whose hands I have placed you, you are confined by no bonds, and you will fix the limits of your nature for yourself." Pico wrote that God even told Adam that He had made him "neither heavenly nor earthly, nor mortal, nor immortal" in order that Adam might mold himself: "You may fashion yourself in whatever shape you prefer. You can degenerate into the lower natures which are brutes or out of your soul's judgment grow upward into the higher natures which are divine."[11] Humans, thus, do not occupy a fixed place in the universal hierarchy but fashion their own destinies. Pico's view prefigured Sartre's famous dictum that existence precedes essence.

For the Florentine Platonists, the concept of human dignity was universal rather than sectarian or personal. Ficino had maintained that while Christianity is the most perfect religion, religion as such is natural to humans and part of what distinguishes them from the brutes. He celebrated religious diversity, maintaining that each religion is somehow in the service of the one, true God. Pico went even further, emphasizing that in spite of contradictions among religious and philosophical traditions, each has had its own true insights. In 1486, he published his nine hundred theses, in which he invited all scholars to a public disputation. Included among his theses were those of a variety of philosophers and traditions, which in his view provided a deep motivation for religious and philosophical tolerance.

The church hierarchy, however, was not in an ecumenical frame of mind. In 1513, the Lateran Council condemned Averroës' doctrine of the unity of the intellect, which implied that the intellectual soul is the same in all men. It also condemned Alexander of Aphrodisias's view that the human soul is mortal. In place of these, it promulgated as official church dogma the personal immortality of the soul. A few years later, in 1517, when Martin Luther (1483–1546) nailed his ninety-five propositions to the door of All Saints' church in Wittenberg, he also nailed all hope for ecumenicalism onto a cross of Catholic and Protestant sectarianism. After this, in Europe, for hundreds of years, religious sects and thinkers of all stripes would vie with each other to see who could be most intolerant. To most of these Christians, the idea that different religions are paths to the same truth would not prove to be as appealing as the idea that only one's own group is on the right track.

Aristotelianism

Pietro Pomponazzi (1462–1525) was the most important of the Renaissance Aristotelians. Trained at Padua, where he also taught, he spent his later, more productive years at Bologna. With the Averroëists, he taught that the pursuit of knowledge, insofar as it is acquired by reason rather than faith, should not make concessions to theology. When he formed his views, original Greek texts by Aristotle and his Greek interpreters, especially Alexander of Aphrodisias, had recently become available. So, there was not as much need as before to rely so heavily on Averroës. Nevertheless, in studying the humanists' newly minted Latin translations of Greek sources, Pomponazzi discovered a naturalistic Aristotle who denied personal immortality but believed that the human soul could participate in the divine.

Pomponazzi, following Alexander of Aphrodisias, held that even the human intellect is a power or function of the corporeal human soul and so is itself corporeal and mortal. However, with this power the soul can understand and thereby participate in eternal ideas. To him this meant that the rational soul is essentially natural and only accidentally eternal—hence, that it is essentially mortal and only accidentally immortal. He thus agreed with the Renaissance Platonists, though for somewhat different reasons, that the human soul occupies a middle place in the universe "between mortal and immortal things" and that it participates both in time and eternity. But, against the Platonists, he insisted that by reason alone one could show that the human soul is mortal. Only by faith and revelation, he claimed, could one know that the rational part of the human soul is immortal.

In stressing the mortality of humans, Pomponazzi was moved to replace Ficino's elitist and otherworldly ideal of contemplation, which finds its necessary fulfillment in a future life, with the much more democratic idea that morality is its own reward, which comes, if at all, in the present life. "There are two kinds of reward and punishment: one is essential and inseparable, the other accidental and separable." The essential reward of moral virtue, Pomponazzi claimed, is virtue itself. It is what makes humans happy.

Pomponazzi's focus on virtue, which emphasized the importance of individual conduct, lay side by side in his thought with a Ficino-like celebration of human solidarity, in which each person, through right actions, contributes to the universal good: "The whole human race is like one body composed of various members which have different functions, but which are suited for the common usefulness of mankind."[12] While relatively few humans can be philosophers, mathematicians, and the like, every human can and must be virtuous. Our talents divide us, he said, but our common capacity for virtue unites us.

Two later Aristotelians of note, Francesco Piccolomini (c. 1523–1607) and Jacopo Zabarella (1533–1589), taught at the same time at the University of Padua and were adversaries. Both had acquired a full command of Greek and so were able to read Aristotle and his ancient commentators in their own words. Piccolomini argued that the immateriality of the intellective soul can be shown from its operations and its objects. In an argument that would appeal to subsequent generations of philosophers, he claimed that faculties that are spatially extended are not able to "turn on themselves"; for instance, an eye, which is spatially extended, can see objects in the world but not see itself. Human minds, on the other hand, are able to turn on themselves. In other words, whereas sense organs can sense objects but not sensation itself, minds can not only think but think about thinking. Whatever has the capacity to turn on itself, such as the human mind, is thus not spatially extended and hence is not material: "Mind, when it understands itself, turns on itself; therefore, it is free from matter."[13] So, in addition to an extended, organic soul, humans must have another unextended, inorganic soul, which because it is inorganic is whole and complete wherever it is. This inorganic, intellectual soul must be immortal.

Zabarella built on the work of Pomponazzi and others, together with his own original research, in order to contribute to the development of an emerging scientific methodology that, while Aristotelian, was independent of theology. According to him, natural knowledge proceeds through analysis of observed phenomena to their inferred causes and returns through synthesis from the latter to the former. Zabarella's Aristotelian approach extended to his conception of the soul. With Ockham and Pomponazzi, and against Piccolomini, he claimed that from the standpoint of natural philosophy, the intellectual soul could be understood only as mortal. He left it to theologians to argue for its immortality.

Averroës had held that the agent (active) intellect, or God, is the source of all purely intellectual ideas. Zabarella agreed. However, he held that intellectual ideas are not merely passively received by the human intellect, which has an individual form for each person, but actively used by it in judgments. In his view, that human judgment is an order above the powers of the organic soul does not imply that the intellectual soul is distinct from matter but only that it has access to the pure conceptions (intelligibility) of things. He wrote that "the body is not the act of the soul, but the soul is the act of the body"—that is, the rational soul is a bodily function, not a separate immaterial and immortal substance.[14]

Zabarella, thus, took Pomponazzi's natural Aristotelianism to its limit, producing a conception of human beings as entirely material, even in their highest intellectual activities. He would have no traffic with notions of immaterial and immortal substances. This aspect of his philosophy interested the Inquisition but was not found to be heretical. Apparently, in contrast to the early Scholastic period, when Aristotelian doctrines were often viewed as heretical, during this period, so long as Aristotle remained "the philosopher," faith and reason were allowed to follow separate paths. It was only those who rejected Aristotle, like Galileo and Bruno, whose ideas were found heretical.

Zabarella died a few years before Galileo arrived at the University of Padua. Scholars disagree about how much he influenced Galileo. What is certain is that although Zabarella anticipated much of the scientific methodology later developed by Galileo and his followers, he did not realize, as Galileo did, how important mathematics would be in understanding nature. Instead, following an Aristotelian tradition, he adopted biology as his primary model for understanding nature. Substantial forms, rather than shape and motion, dominated his conception of nature.

Late Renaissance Natural Philosophy

In the sixteenth century, the humanism, Platonism, and Aristotelianism of the earlier Renaissance continued but increasingly had to compete for attention, first, with theological controversies growing out of the Reformation and, later, with developments that led to the rise of modern science. The natural philosophers of the time who are best known for their original contributions are Paracelsus, Telesio, and Bruno.

In Paracelsus's (1493–1541) view, humans consist of three parts: an "elemental body," which is a corporeal natural being; an "astral body," which is not enclosed within the organism but sends out signals to and receives them from the whole universe; and a soul, which is the seat of a human's highest spiritual activity. Due to the way in which humans are organized corporeally and spiritually, the unity in and of everything ordinarily appears to humans as a plurality.

It is by means of the soul that humans can mystically experience the ground of being and thereby overcome the illusion of separation: "God, who is in Heaven, is in man."[15]

Paracelsus ascribed to humans a corporeal constitution consisting of two sorts of flesh. One of these, the elemental body, has its "origin in Adam" and is "coarse," "earthly," and "nothing but flesh." It is inherited biologically and may be "grasped like wood and stone." It is also mortal. The other flesh, the astral body, is not from Adam. It is "subtle" and not capable of being "bound or grasped, for it is not made of earth."[16] It is what makes humans capable of spiritual activities, but it has not been in humans from the beginning. This flesh is eternal.

Humans, Paracelsus wrote, are the divine in a state of becoming. Nature requires completing, and the work of humans in this process is alchemy, which includes such mundane activities as baking bread and weaving cloth: "the third pillar of medicine is alchemy, for the preparation of remedies cannot take place without it, because nature cannot be put to use without art." He held that human beings are "microcosms" that mirror the "macrocosm" but that they have power over the macrocosm through natural magic. "God did not create the planets and stars with the intention that they should dominate" humans but that the stars, like animals, should obey and serve humans. While the "animal man" is "swayed backwards and forwards by the stars like a reed in the waters," the wise individual can gain power over the stars.[17] This would not be possible if humans, like animals, had only elemental and astral bodies. But, because humans have a soul, they can rise above the stars and free themselves from them, first, by understanding natural laws and using them to their advantage and, second, by cultivating spiritual powers that go beyond natural laws.

At bodily death, humans, as microcosms, separate from the macrocosm. "The elemental body decays and becomes consumed. It becomes a putrid corpse, which being buried in the earth, never again comes forth or appears." The astral body "does not decay, is not buried, [and] occupies no place" but continues to exist and appears as "specters, visions, and supernatural apparitions."[18] The astral body is naturally eternal. It is the astral body that rises from "death" at the resurrection to join the spirit or soul, which has already returned to the "aerial chaos"—God.

Paracelsus, thus, combined inductive natural philosophy; Neoplatonic, hermetic philosophy; Christian faith; and mystical experience in an original mix. In many ways far ahead of his times, he was also a man of the Renaissance, ultimately preferring a holistic, supernaturally based philosophy over pure naturalism. Later thinkers, attempting to free modern science from religion and mysticism, would try in his work to separate the wheat from the chaff.

It was Paracelsus's purpose to replace all classical and Scholastic medicine with knowledge gained not from books but from immediate experience. In an act of disrespect for past learning, in front of his students, he threw the medical works of Galen and Avicenna into a fire, telling them that practicing medicine is more important than book learning. A true intellectual revolutionary, during his own lifetime he became known as the "Luther of Medicine."

Paracelsus addressed a great number of medical, philosophical, and chemical issues, including venereal disease and the plague, as well as the question of how to administer and use medicines properly. Not only did he originate medical ideas well in advance of their adoption in succeeding centuries, but he introduced the use of metallic elements and compounds into the chemical treatment of disease. Although he wrote voluminous works in many other areas, he is especially noted for his alchemical works and hermetic medicine. Today, he is considered by many to be the father of medical chemistry.

At a time when other physicians were still attributing mental illness to demonic possession, Paracelsus attributed it to physiology. He wrote that such diseases "develop out of man's disposition," specifically from an "abuse of the natural strength of reason."[19] He said that humans who lack knowledge may be "thrown into a confused state of mind," which "leads them to doubt and to great preoccupation, together with intense fantasies (daydreaming) and eventually insanity." He attributed some forms of mental disturbance to the disruption of humors caused by powers of attraction from the moon. He may also have been the first to use the word "unconscious."

In *De Rerum Natura*, Bernardino Telesio (1509–1588) taught that in humans there is a biologically inherited material soul, composed of the subtlest form of matter, which is located primarily in the brain but diffuses throughout the body. This material soul, which differs only in degree from the souls in animals, accounts for most of human mentality. To this soul, he assigned ordinary psychological functions and activities, such as perception, emotions, and memory, all of which he tried to explain physiologically.

In addition to this material soul, there is in humans a divine, noncorporeal soul implanted directly by God, which somehow is joined to the material soul and possesses a faculty of thinking and desiring peculiar to it. Thus humans, unlike animals, have two souls, one divine and one corporeal, each with its own intellect and desire. That humans have a nonmaterial soul is what allows them to have free will.

Giordano Bruno (1548–1600) was probably the most original philosopher of the late Renaissance. The impact of his ideas can be felt not only in the Cambridge Platonists and in Spinoza, Leibniz, Bonnet and others but also in the romantic idealism of Goethe, Lessing, Schelling, and Coleridge. While influenced by Neoplatonism, Hermetic philosophy, and Lucretius's atomism, by Bruno's own account it was Pythagoras and his followers who animated his philosophy.[20] Perhaps as a result, he believed in reincarnation and metempsychosis.

Bruno's most fundamental idea is that God is not only transcendent, but immanent—above Nature but also in Nature, as the world soul. A great admirer of Copernicus, he went beyond him in proposing that just as God is infinite with no particular locus, so also the universe, which is a unity of infinite proportion, has no center. He believed that the universe is an animated whole, permeated throughout by the infinite power of God. He thought that all matter—even stone—is infused with living souls (monads), which appear animated only in what we call living beings but which are actually animated in everything. At some time or other, each monad will come to express itself in an overtly animated being, sometimes playing only a minor role but, at other times, becoming the very soul of the living being. It is with this intellectual, soul-infusing matter as a seminal seed that a human body is formed and maintained:

> There is one thing, an efficient and formative principle from within, from which, through which, and around which the composition [of the body] is formed; and it is exactly like a helmsman in a ship, the father of the family at home, and an artisan who is not external, but fabricates from within, who tempers and preserves the edifice; and in it is the power to keep united the contrary elements, to arrange together, as if in harmony, the discordant qualities, to keep and maintain the composition of an animal.[21]

Although the atomic material out of which the human organism is formed constantly changes, the formative soul, which uses replacement atoms, remains the same. The "dwelling place" of this soul, he said, "in all things said to be animate is formed from the center of the heart." At the time of death, the governing soul "leaves through the same door [the heart] through which it once entered."[22] Having left the human body, it then moves on to other forms of existence, with which it combines, depending on how it lived in its human incarnation. In sum, through reincarnation, involving metempsychosis, each monad moves through all forms of existence, in a system governed by universal justice.

Bruno felt that the unity of the whole universe comes from the immanent power of God, which pervades it, even though, when we attend to its parts, we find it divides into a physical plenum of indivisible material atoms as well as into a metaphysical continuum of immaterial monads. The monads act through the atoms to energize and construct all of the possibilities of nature. The goal of human existence is knowledge—to know God through an understanding of Nature and, thus, to get beneath the surface of things to their physical and metaphysical core. This applies equally to the self. Through intellectual understanding we can come to experience God within ourselves. Ultimately, we can even become one with God.

Bruno's radical ideas did not bode well for his relationship with the church. As a young Dominican priest with heretical ideas, he had to leave his order and escape from Italy. But his impressive knowledge and flamboyant personality guaranteed that he would quickly be noticed wherever he went. He became influential with Henry III, then king of France, and later, in England, with Elizabeth I. But, as he was also quick to make enemies, he had to keep moving. Eventually, he returned to Italy at the request of a Venetian nobleman, who, disappointed when Bruno refused to teach him natural magic, turned him over to the Inquisition. Bruno's philosophical ideas, as well as his denial that Jesus was more God than other humans were found to be opposed to Christian dogma. It was determined that his atomism challenged the doctrine of the Eucharist, which at the Council of Trent became dogmatically interpreted in terms of Aristotelian physics (an interpretation that would also cause problems for Galileo and Descartes).

Although Bruno defended his views by invoking the notion of "double truth," his interrogators, who were generally lenient when Aristotelians, like Zabarella, adopted this defense, were not satisfied when Bruno tried to use it. Since Bruno would not retract his philosophy, he was found guilty of heresy and sentenced to death by fire. He is said to have told the Inquisitors, "It is with far greater fear that you pronounce than that I receive this sentence." On February, 17, 1600, he was burnt at the stake. Subsequently, all of his writings were put on the Catholic index of heretical books.

In sum, during the sixteenth century, thinkers such as Paracelsus, Telesio, Bruno, and others, who were themselves profoundly affected by Aristotelianism, attempted to forge rival systems of natural philosophy. They failed to overthrow Aristotelianism not primarily because they were persecuted or because the authorities were stuck in their ways but because their alternatives to Aristotelianism lacked its scope and unity. A more powerful system, with even greater scope and unity, barely visible on the horizon in the sixteenth century, was about to make its appearance.

The Growth of Subjectivity

In a poem published in 1599 that succinctly expressed a newfound fascination among Renaissance humanists with self-knowledge, Sir John Davies wrote, "My self am centre of my circling thought. Only myself I study, learn, and know."[23] From the twelfth century to the end of the sixteenth, thinkers increasingly became preoccupied with what is individual in their psychologies. Around 1600, several writers, including Francis Bacon, discussed the arts of simulation and dissimulation, that is, the presentation of self to others. At the beginning of the seventeenth century, John Donne wrote that in his time "every man" thinks that there "can be none of that kind of which he is, but he." There was also a newfound interest in being sincere and in being true to oneself.[24] But in the late sixteenth century, the French essayist Michel de Montaigne (1533–1592) became the first great apostle of sincerity (he even invented the word). He was also, in a way, an apostle of individualism: "I live from day to day, and without wishing to be disrespectful, I live only for myself: my purposes go no further."[25]

Montaigne saw his own age as one of corruption, violence, and hypocrisy. This dark assessment led him first to question what his age took to be knowledge, then the possibility of knowing altogether, and finally even the human capacity to seek truth consistently. He carved phrases from the skeptical works of Sextus Empiricus, which had recently become available in Latin, into the rafter beams of his study, so that he would be continuously reminded of them. While writing *The Apologie of Raimond Sebond*, perhaps his most important philosophical essay and, in the view of some, the springboard for skepticism in modern thought, Montaigne tried to come to terms with what was for him the extreme trauma of seeing his entire intellectual world crumble into incoherent and meaningless rubble. His creative response, together with other influences from the new science that was about to make its appearance, helped reorient modern philosophy away from the external world and toward subjective experience.

Against the backdrop of Montaigne's critique of what was accepted in his time as knowledge, there emerged in him a hunger to explore the concrete and the individual. He developed and nurtured a profound distrust of generalizations and abstractions: "The conclusions that we seek to draw from the likenesses of events are unreliable because events are always unlike. There is no quality so universal in the appearance of things as their diversity and variety."[26] In exploring individuality, he resolved to start with himself. In a sentence that could have been the motto for his life, he declared, "I am myself the matter of my book."[27] But he saw himself as a product of his own self-reflection: "I have painted my inward self with colors clearer than my original ones. I have no more made my book than my book has made me—a book consubstantial with its author."[28] His intense self-examination spawned his conviction that the self within him or, as he called it, his "master form," was not whole and constant, but fragmented and changeable.

Montaigne's honest and perceptive recognition and exploration of his inner impermanence became his way of trying to snatch from the jaws of a dissolving skepticism an authentic quest for the truth of his own being. Yet he never surrendered completely to subjectivism and skepticism or conceded that they cut him off from knowledge of God. In struggling to know himself, he redoubled his efforts to discover the permanent in the impermanent, the soul in the body, secure in his conviction that God has the unity and permanence that humans lack.

Montaigne's self-absorption led him to give detailed, candid descriptions of his own experiences and of his bodily functions; to meditate steadfastly on the inevitability of sickness, old age, and death; and to search for personal truth by immersing himself through reading and travel in the diversity of external society. Intrigued by reports of the New World, he was compassionately sympathetic with its aboriginal inhabitants, whose straightforwardness and personal dignity seemed to him far superior to the violence and artificiality of his own countrymen. In every social encounter, he sought a solvent for pretense: "As familiar company at table, I choose the amusing, rather than the wise; in bed I prefer beauty to goodness; and for serious conversation, I like ability, even combined with dishonesty."[29]

A student of classical philosophy, in his essays Montaigne quoted liberally from such authors as Horace, Lucretius, Cicero, Sextus, Seneca, and Plutarch. Like other humanists of his era, he thought that compared to the world of antiquity, his own times were mediocre. Socrates, he said, was "the wisest man" who had ever lived. More generally, he used the ancients as the standard for his searing critique of present theory and practice. His constructive alternative was not a new metaphysical system or even a skeptical epistemology but the development through experiential self-examination of an ethics of authenticity, self-acceptance, and tolerance. In his essays, he juxtaposed a profound skepticism of the abstract, theoretical, and general with the burning conviction that truth is within and that there is no greater achievement than honest, informed, realistic self-acceptance.

In Montaigne's approach, the point of his self-examination was not primarily to learn about human nature but about himself. Yet, since every person bears "the whole stamp of the human condition," by self-examination, he felt, one inevitably does learn about human nature. Self-examination does not yield a new theory: "We grasp at everything, but catch nothing except wind."[30] Rather, to learn about oneself is to dissipate through inner attention, rather than through scientific investigation, the cloud of self-delusion in which each of us is ensconced. Montaigne's preoccupation with subjective experience was the final achievement of Renaissance humanism. As we shall see, his approach to subjectivity contrasted sharply with that which René Descartes was about to employ in inaugurating the modern era.[31]

VIII

MECHANIZATION OF NATURE

Even for the purposes of constructing a narrative about theories of the self, the main issue in the seventeenth century was not the self but the emergence of a new approach to science, ushered in by a new theory of the physical world. This approach regarded natural objects as machines and on that basis sought to figure out how they work. The theory was *corpuscularism* (or, *corpuscular mechanism*). The transition from old to new took an entire century. However, once the goal of mechanizing nature had taken hold, there would be no turning back. Henceforth, the entire natural world, eventually including humans, would be portrayed in a new way.

There were two notions at the heart of Aristotelian physics: substantial forms, which combine with prime matter to make each thing the sort of thing it is; and teleology, specifically the issue of what things of various sorts are trying to become, their so-called entelechies. From the perspective of a physics that rests on these two notions, the universe as a whole, as well as many of its parts, can seem like a conscious mind trying to attain some goal.

In the world according to corpuscularism, there is no place either for substantial forms or teleology. Instead, the universe and its parts are conceptualized as if they were clocks, pushed along by springs and pulleys, which—as efficient causes—have no prevision of the ends they might achieve. Corpuscularism removed talk of ends from the science of nature and consigned it to theology and to theories of human consciousness.

But what is the relation of human consciousness to the rest of nature? This question arose in a new light. How it was answered had profound implications not just for what today we would call science but for metaphysics, epistemology, and religion. Prior to the introduction of corpuscularism, metaphysics, epistemology, and religion tended to be viewed as different aspects of one scientific mode of inquiry. Afterward, they were viewed as separate from science.

Objectivity and Subjectivity in a Scientific Mold

From ordinary experience we know that grass is green; water, wet; and snow, cold. From modern science we know that the greenness of grass, the wetness of water, and the coldness of snow are not the familiar greenness, wetness, and coldness of our experience but something entirely different. A blind person can understand the physics of color. Only a sighted person can understand what it's like to experience the greenness of grass.

According to common sense, when an observer seems to himself to be directly observing the greenness of grass, he is directly observing it. According to modern science, when an observer seems to himself to be directly observing the greenness of grass, what's happening is that light is reflected off the grass, hits the retinas of his eyes, and then triggers electrochemical signals that travel up his optic nerves to his brain. It is in the observer's brain, if anywhere in physical space, that the experience of greenness takes place.

How and when did we, as a culture, make the transition from the common-sense view of what happens in ordinary experience to the view suggested by modern science? The change happened toward the beginning of the seventeenth century, as we began to attend to what eventually became known as the distinction between primary and secondary qualities. Although there had been intimations of this distinction in earlier thinkers, it was Galileo Galilei (1564–1642) who first drew attention to it clearly. He explained that primary qualities (weight, texture, and so on) are inherent in bodies, while secondary qualities (taste, perceived color, and so on) are not in the external world but in the minds of observers. In other words, Galileo claimed that primary qualities are *objective* and secondary ones *subjective*.

Galileo motivated his version of the distinction between objective and subjective by means of two thought experiments. In the first, he pointed out that while we can conceive of a material object that is devoid of any secondary quality—one, say, that is without taste or color—we cannot conceive of a material object that lacks primary qualities—one, say, without shape or texture. In the second, he asked the reader to imagine the difference between tickling a marble statue and a human being. So far as the motion of one's fingers is concerned, he claimed, the two ticklings might be identical. What distinguishes them takes place on the side of what gets "tickled." On that side, there is a subjective sensation. There is no such sensation in the statue. As a consequence, the secondary qualities of things should be understood as the effects of the primary qualities of those things on the sensory mechanisms of sentient beings. In the absence of such effects, secondary qualities would not even exist. In Galileo's view, natural philosophy—what today we call *physical science*—could make progress only by attending to primary qualities and ignoring secondary ones.

In Aristotelian science, in which mathematics had little role, the focus was on a world populated by macroscopic objects composed of matter and form. The main goal was to systematically classify different kinds of objects, in the process identifying their so-called substantial forms, which were expressed not mathematically but in a natural language such as Greek or Latin.

Modern science, as Galileo envisaged it, would be different. It would rest metaphysically not on macroscopic objects but on the tiny impenetrable atoms out of which macroscopic objects are composed. And its results would be expressed mathematically. We cannot read the Book of Nature, Galileo wrote, unless we understand the language in which it is written. The symbols of this language are "triangles, circles, and other geometrical figures." Without these, he said, "it is impossible to comprehend a word," and "one wanders in vain through a dark labyrinth."[1]

For the purpose of advancing scientific inquiry into the external physical world, Galileo was wise to sweep troublesome secondary qualities under the rug of the mind. But for philosophers who soon would seek a more comprehensive view of reality that encompassed not only the external physical world but everything, this strategy created as many problems as it solved.

As we have seen, subjectivity had already come to the fore in the sixteenth century, through Montaigne. Its reemergence in the seventeenth, through Galileo, was not a case of two thinkers independently hitting upon the same idea. The kinds of subjectivity with which each was concerned, and their reasons for being concerned with it, differed. Montaigne's preoccupation with subjectivity was born of skepticism and a negative assessment of the European culture in which he was enmeshed. Galileo's was born of optimism and reflection not on culture but on the implications of the new science. Montaigne's investigations were fueled by the quest for qualitative knowledge of self; Galileo's, for quantified knowledge of nature. Montaigne, who eschewed any reliance on generalizations and laws of nature, entered the realm of the subjective by immersing himself in what is individual and particular. Galileo segregated subjectivity by abstracting away from the individual and particular in order to discern the regularity of lawful connections.

Montaigne's approach was intensely first-personal. Galileo's was rigorously third-personal. The obstacles that worried Montaigne in his quest for self-knowledge were passion and spiritual pride. Galileo worried about neither of these. His interest in subjectivity was not to know himself but to clear the debris of the subjective from the path of natural philosophy.

Close on Galileo's heels, René Descartes (1596–1650) was about to enter the fray. Unlike Galileo, who was unbothered by Montaigne's existential crisis and seems even to have sought to marginalize inquiry into skeptical epistemology and human psychology, Descartes had one foot firmly planted in the tradition out of which Montaigne's pessimism had sprung and the other in the new initiatives that spawned Galileo's optimism. To deal with the differences in these two approaches, he refocused Montaigne's dilemmas through the lens of Galileo's conception of subjectivity, but with this difference: unlike Galileo, Descartes had no intention of marginalizing subjectivity, and, unlike Montaigne, he had no intention of dealing with it nonscientifically. Instead, Descartes proposed the certain knowledge of one's own existence as the basis for all knowledge, thereby relocating subjectivity at the epistemological foundations of modern physical science.

The Soul in a Mechanized World

Descartes freed the Platonic view of the soul from its Aristotelian accretions. In doing so, he inadvertently exposed its scientific irrelevance, a consequence that would not become apparent to most philosophers until the end of the eighteenth century. Even so, the main question for Descartes, insofar as the soul is concerned, was also the main question that worried his critics: How could the soul fit into an otherwise wholly material world governed by mechanistic laws?

The metaphysical view at which Descartes ultimately arrived marked the end of Renaissance science and the beginning of a new era in which the main project was the complete and total mechanization of nature.[2] There were two major shifts in perspective: first, the physical world lost its spirituality and became a machine—that is, it became a world in which everything was moved along not by purposes but by the motion of inanimate objects that mindlessly passed on momentum; second, the subjective world lost its physicality—it seemed unlikely, on the new paradigm, that the world as it appears in our immediate experience closely resembles external physical objects.[3]

Descartes was the first major thinker to start using the word *mind* (Latin, *mens*) as an alternative to the word *soul* (*anima*). He declared that the "I" is the mind, which is unextended, and that the essence of mind is thinking. In other words, all thinking is done by mental (unextended) substances, and mental substances are always thinking. His main argument that there are such mental substances is epistemological. He reasoned that each of us can be certain that he or she exists as a thinking thing but not (as immediately) certain that there are material objects. From this, he seemed to infer, erroneously, that we cannot be material objects, an inference that, as we have seen, may well have been inspired by Augustine or Avicenna or both.[4]

Nevertheless, in Descartes's view, everything in the physical world, including the bodies of humans, is composed of matter in various configurations. How this matter moves is governed by laws of motion that have remained unchanged since the origin of the universe. So far as living things are concerned, nonhuman animals are simply complex automata, lacking consciousness. According to this view, in contrast to Aristotle and even Plato, neither plants nor nonhuman animals have a soul, and soul is not required for life. Instead, life is merely an apparent property of complex mechanisms. Humans differ from other living things only in having nonmaterial, immortal souls, which are conscious. Except for the concession that humans have an immaterial soul, Descartes viewed the entire human body and brain as a machine.

Descartes assumed that independently of the activity of the nonmaterial soul, the neural organization of the brain accounts for sensation, perception, and imagination, and that in animals this entirely mechanical system is all that there is. He assumed that during the experience of sensation, "animal spirits" in the sense organs of nonhuman animals are stimulated mechanically by the sizes, shapes, and motions of the matter impinging on their organs. He claimed that this matter carries decodable information about objects external to the organism. This information, he said, is then transmitted physiologically to the brain and eventually to the pineal gland in the brain, where it results in a redirected signal to some other region of the brain or body. In the case of humans, the process works much the same, with some important exceptions. Chief among these is that thoughts are mental acts of the rational soul that remain in the soul and are not coded in the brain at all. Nevertheless, through the pineal gland they do sometimes causally affect the motion of the animal spirits and hence the behavior of the organism. In addition, agreeing with Augustine's claims, Descartes said that what humans sense and imagine, in addition to having bodily concomitants, is directly experienced by the immaterial soul.

Even so, Descartes's mature view of the relationship between humans and other animals is somewhat unsettled. He distinguished sharply, though not always consistently, between those psychological processes that involve the thought of the nonmaterial soul and those other processes involved in sensation, perception, imagination, emotion, learning, and so on that he assumed could be brought about mechanically by the body and brain outside of the realm of consciousness. He is notorious for having suggested that animals are no different than clocks and hence have no qualitative experiences at all. However, in some letters written toward the end of his life, he suggested that animals have sensations and might even have something like thoughts, although they lack anything like human rational thought.[5] On the whole, though, what he seems to have wanted to say is, first, that only beings with nonmaterial souls have consciousness in the full sense, which involves self-awareness, and, second, that lower organisms might have something like consciousness, but of a lower order that lacks self-awareness.

Descartes made an additional proposal that was enormously influential and relevant to many of the main problems that plagued his metaphysical views. This was that all thought is necessarily reflexive. What this means is that if a person is aware, then necessarily he is also aware that he is aware. This view surfaced, among other places, in the seventh set of objections to the *Meditations* (1642; the first edition of the *Meditations* was published in 1641 with six objections and replies), in which the Jesuit Bourdin complained that by holding that it is "not sufficient for [mental substance] to think" and that it "is further required that it should think that it is thinking by means of a reflexive act," Descartes was multiplying entities beyond necessity. Descartes replied that "the initial thought by means of which we become aware of something *does not differ from* the second thought by means of which we become aware that we are aware of it, anymore than this second thought differs from a third thought by which we become aware that we are aware that we are aware." Thus, in his view, each thought not only encapsulates perhaps infinitely many reflexive mental acts but necessarily incorporates a self-reference. Subsequently, this view may have inhibited the emergence of a developmental psychology of the acquisition of self-concepts. For if a person cannot think at all without also thinking *that* he or she thinks, then it is impossible to trace in the pattern of the ways people learn to think the gradual development of their ability to think of themselves.[6]

However, just as importantly, Descartes's view that all thinking is necessarily self-referential suggested to some later thinkers, who were more materialist than Descartes, a way of explaining what it is about consciousness that makes it special. What makes it special, they suggested, is not its immateriality but its being self-reflective. John Locke, who was officially a dualist but often sounds as if he were a closet materialist, was among the first to pick up on Descartes's suggestion that what is called consciousness might be understood simply as a capacity for self-reflection.

Substance

Descartes defined substance as something that is capable of existing by itself, without dependence on any other thing. In his view, it follows that, strictly speaking, there is only one substance: God. However, he allowed that, in a looser sense of the word *substance*, mind and body are also substances and that, in a still looser sense, individual humans, which are a combination of mind and body, are substances. God, who is unique, is a mental substance. Angels, of which presumably there are many, are mental substances. Individual human minds, of which there is one per human, are also mental substances. Human bodies, animal bodies, plants, and inanimate objects are material substances.

Descartes never addressed the question of what individuates mental substances, that is, what makes one mental substance, one angel for instance, different from another. As we have seen, this was a problem in the High Middle Ages that Aquinas solved in part by making every angel the only member of its own species. Descartes's way with this issue was simply to ignore it.

In the case of body—material substance—Descartes's view was that since God is the only substance and God is nonmaterial, *strictly speaking* there are no material substances. However, in the same looser sense of *substance* in which individual minds are mental substances, individual material substances also exist. But curiously, whereas for Descartes there are many mental substances, there may be only one material substance. This would be the case if for there to be two material substances, they have to be separated by empty space. For empty space, if it were to exist, would be extended, in which case it would not be empty, for whatever has extension is material. So, either there is a way to distinguish among material substances other than by their being separated by empty space or else the entire material world is just one thing. There is no record that Descartes ever spoke to the question of which of these alternatives he favored.

Descartes's view of how bodies are individuated caused a split among corpuscular mechanists between those, such as himself, who denied the existence of the void (empty space) and those, such as Pierre Gassendi, Robert Boyle, Isaac Newton, and John Locke, who insisted on it. A closely related issue is whether material substances even have essential properties in any but a pragmatic sense. Descartes claimed that they do but that, unlike Aristotelian forms, material substances have only one essential property: extension. Others, such as Boyle, denied that things have genuine essences, while allowing that for some theoretical purposes, we can talk as if they do.

As we have seen, in addition to thinking that God, angels, and human souls are mental substances and that bodies are material substances, Descartes held that each human soul, or mind, is so intimately connected to its own body as to form with it a separate substance of a third sort. What impressed Descartes about the union of mind and body was that each can bring about changes in the other. But how could two things that have almost nothing in common interact? Descartes answered that mind and body influence each other through the pineal gland, a small organ located in the brain at the meeting point of the symmetries between the left and right hemispheres. He may have selected this organ as the point of interaction because it is the only organ in the brain of which he had knowledge that is not bilaterally duplicated. However, even were he right about the pineal gland, that would not have solved the big mystery about his view, which is not about *where* but *how*, a point that was not lost on his contemporary critics.[7] How two things that have almost nothing in common could interact thus became a question that plagued thinkers at the time, and into modern times, who were otherwise drawn toward substance dualism.

Personal Unity

Descartes rejected the idea, which was congenial to Plato, that the soul's relation to the body is merely instrumental—like that of a pilot to his ship. According to Descartes, Nature teaches each of us by "sensations of pain, hunger, thirst and so on, that I am not merely present in my body as a sailor is present in a ship but that I am very closely joined and, as it were, intermingled with it, so that I and the body form a unit." Otherwise, he reasoned, "I, who am nothing but a thinking thing, would not feel pain when the body was hurt, but would perceive the damage purely by the intellect, just as a sailor perceives by sight if anything in his ship is broken." By the same token, he continued, if I were not one with my body, then "when the body needed food or drink, I should have an explicit understanding of the fact, instead of having confused sensations of hunger and thirst," which are "nothing but confused modes of thinking which arise from the union and, as it were, intermingling of the mind with the body."[8]

The idea for which Descartes seems to be groping in such remarks is that self-concern for our bodies is expressed phenomenologically by a kind of identification we make with the content of our sensations. As a consequence of this identification, when we are aware that our bodies are being stimulated, we *feel* that something has happened to *us*, rather than merely *think* that it has happened to *our bodies*. Nevertheless, in his view, that mind and body form a substance is not an illusion but a real insight, even though mind and body together are not as deeply real a substance as are mind and body individually.

It seemed to some of Descartes's critics that in his view, the mind *should* be related to the body as a pilot to his ship. His response to these critics is unclear and problematic. What he sometimes seems to have been trying to say is that individual nonmaterial minds and their associated bodies form one substance in virtue of their unity as a causal mechanism. In other words, they systematically affect each other, but not other things, in ways that make the two of them together function as if they were one.

As we shall see, Locke would elevate the theme of a human's identification with the content of his or her sensations to a central position in his own theory of personal identity. Perhaps influenced by the Stoics, his word for the form of identification that interested him was *appropriation*, a notion he employed to put together the first phenomenological account of self-constitution both at-a-time and over-time. This aspect of his view was mostly ignored by subsequent eighteenth-century philosophers. However, Bishop Butler, one of his keenest critics, picked up on this aspect of his account. In claiming that if Locke's account of self-constitution were correct, then the self would be fictional, Butler reasserted the pre-Cartesian, Platonic view that a self's relation to its body is like those of a pilot to his ship.

In sum, in a narrow sense, Descartes's main contributions to theorizing about the self and personal identity were, first, to lend the tremendous weight of his authority to a Platonic view of the self, which would eventually be recognized as scientifically useless, and, second, to introduce the idea of the reflexive nature of consciousness, which seems to have inhibited the emergence of developmental accounts of the acquisition of self-concepts. In a larger sense, however, he championed the new mechanistic view of nature that in the hands of others would eventually undo even his own theories of the self. He also provided a naturalistic framework for the development of what by the end of the eighteenth century would become an empirical science of psychology.

Alternatives to Descartes's Dualistic Interactionism

The new science provided philosophers with a powerful motive to be materialists. Christianity provided them with a powerful motive to resist materialism. Among those who responded sympathetically, though not always consistently, to the lure of materialism were the French Catholic Pierre Gassendi (1592–1655) and the English Protestant Thomas Hobbes (1588–1679), both contemporaries of Descartes.

When Gassendi was in a materialistic frame of mind, he basically followed Epicurean atomism, arguing that the soul, or mind, is corporeal on the grounds that it produces corporeal effects, like sensation, reproduction, and digestion. To do this, he reasoned, the soul itself has to be corporeal. However, in his less materialistic moments, which may have been inspired by the Lateran Council's instruction to Christian philosophers to prove the existence of the immaterial soul, he maintained that one could know that dualism is true—that, in addition to a corporeal soul, humans must have an incorporeal soul. Otherwise, he said, humans would not be able to be self-conscious. Imagination, for instance, which is corporeal, cannot itself perceive its own imaginings or be conscious that it imagines. To self-reflect, one must have an incorporeal soul. In addition, humans know universals, and corporeal souls could not know universals. Humans must then have two souls, one corporeal and one noncorporeal.

In Gassendi's view, the human incorporeal soul is an unextended substance, somehow joined to the body, but without density or figure, and whole and complete in all parts of the body. With no organic function, its only activity is to think, including to reflect upon itself. In contrast to the corporeal soul, which is produced biologically, each human's incorporeal soul is created directly by God. Since it is simple and unextended, it cannot be decomposed or divided and is, thus, immortal.

Hobbes made no such concessions. His view was that human bodies, like all bodies, are pushed from behind by forces that have no prevision of their ends. He claimed that these forces wholly account for human mentality. He even went so far as to claim that the very idea of an immaterial substance is a contradiction. Thus, in his view, human souls, angels, and even God, all of which he thought existed, are material.

The potential threat to Christianity posed by Hobbes's materialism was blunted by the crudity of his physiological explanations of mental phenomena. Few were willing to follow his lead, especially since Descartes had recently shown philosophers how they could accommodate the new scientific developments while remaining dualists. But there were obvious problems with Descartes's views too, especially in connection with his account of substance and the influence of mind and body on each other.

As these problems were discussed by dualists, materialism waited in the background. But at the time few were able to embrace materialism wholeheartedly. An interesting case in point is Thomas Willis (1621–1675), who, as an English follower of Gassendi, focused his attention on the "animal soul," which he held to be material, though capable of thought. This is the only soul that nonhuman animals have. Humans have an additional immaterial soul, which controls their animal souls but is not itself open to empirical investigation.

Willis wrote a book on the animal soul in which he described his anatomical studies of animal and human brains, as well as psychophysiological speculations. Nevertheless, he insisted on the special nature of the human rational soul, which fell outside of these speculations. His major contribution to neuroscience was to argue that various brain regions have different functions. For instance, he concluded, based on comparative studies in brain size among different species and on clinical studies of humans, that the cerebral cortex is involved in higher intellectual functions like memory while the cerebellum is involved in more primitive reflexive motor activities. He denied any importance to the ventricles, which from the time of the early church fathers had been taken to be centers of mental function. Willis was one of Locke's teachers at Oxford and, along with Boyle, a major source for Locke's later views on thinking matter.

One of the most imaginative and enduring attempts to resolve the problems in Descartes's approach was that of the Jewish thinker Benedictus (Baruch) de Spinoza (1632–1677). In Spinoza's masterpiece, *Ethics* (1677), which was published in the year of his death, he agreed with Descartes that mental properties and physical properties are qualitatively distinct. However, Spinoza rejected the Cartesian view that each is an attribute of a different sort of finite substance. Instead, he claimed that, in spite of appearances, each mental event is identical to a physical event and vice versa; he also claimed that each is an attribute of the one and only substance, which is infinite and the essence of everything that exists. Conceived under the attribute of thought, this one substance is God; conceived under the attribute of extension, it is Nature.

In his own time, Spinoza was mistakenly denounced as a materialist. He was, rather, what is today called a *neutral monist*. In his view, unlike in the view of Descartes, a human being is not a substance, let alone a mysterious union of two different substances, but an organized collection of attributes of God, who manifests infinitely many different kinds of attributes. Humans, because of the way they are constituted, can be aware only of God's mental and material attributes. But these are two only from a human perspective—that is, they are not different sorts of attributes but only different ways in which humans perceive the same attributes.

Spinoza, unlike Descartes, thus did away with causal relations between minds and bodies. He thereby avoided the embarrassment of not being able to explain how a mental event could cause a bodily event and vice versa. But he did not stop there. In his view, all causal relations are disguised logical relations. This aspect of his view won few followers, but it was symptomatic of a growing unease with the idea of causal relationships in general, which Spinoza, like many who would come after him, found too mysterious to accept at face value, quite apart from the special problems that causality posed for dualism.

Nevertheless, according to Spinoza, everything behaves in accordance with strictly deterministic laws. Hence, he thought, all human choices and actions are determined (in the end, logically) by prior events over which, ultimately, the people whose choices and actions they are have no control. So, in his view, people have no more free will than do trees or stones, which is to say, they have no free will at all. In his view, the closest one can get to freedom—and getting there is the goal of human life—is to accept one's place in the infinite deterministic system. This does not free one from the web of causality, but from anxiety and ignorance. Philosophical understanding brings equanimity in its wake, which is itself the supreme form of human freedom.

Another notable attempt to resolve the problems in Descartes's dualism was that of the Catholic priest Nicolas Malebranche (1638–1715), who subscribed to a view called *occasionalism*. In *The Search After Truth* (1674), Malebranche argued that God is the one and only true cause. When it seems that something other than God has been a cause, there has been in reality only the appearance of causation, due to God's having arranged a co-occurrence of mental and physical events. Thus, for example, if in normal circumstances a person were to will to move his finger, that would serve as the occasion for God to move the person's finger; and were an object in normal circumstances suddenly to appear in someone's field of view, that would serve as the occasion for God to produce a visual perception of the object in the person's mind.

Still another alternative to Cartesian interactionism is the view called *psychophysical parallelism*, whose most famous proponent was Gottfried Wilhelm Leibniz (1646–1716). In his view, at the level of perception it seems that mind differs from body and that natural causal relations are real. But ultimately, he claimed, everything is mind, and there are no genuine causal relationships in nature. In comparing the series of mental and physical events to two clocks that agree perfectly, Leibniz argued that the agreement can be explained in only one of three ways: through mutual influence (dualistic interactionism); through the continual intervention of a skilled craftsman who keeps the clocks in agreement (occasionalism); or due to the clocks having been constructed originally so that their future agreement is assured (parallelism). He rejected dualistic interactionism on the grounds that it is impossible to conceive of how it could work. He rejected occasionalism as invoking constant miracles interrupting the regular course of nature. There remains just psychophysical parallelism—mind and body exist in a harmony that was preestablished by God at the moment of creation. Thus Leibniz, like Spinoza, held that dualism of mind and body is an illusion and that both are really the same thing. However, whereas Spinoza held that this thing is neither mind nor body, Leibniz held that it is mind.

Why did Leibniz suppose that ultimately everything is mind? Refusing, as Descartes had done, to take extension as primitive and unanalyzable, he analyzed extended objects into infinite series of points, which are like mathematical points except that they are real. These "points" cannot be physical, he thought, because they lack extension, which he accepted from Descartes as the essence of matter. So, they must be mental, that is, souls (what else is there left for them to be?). He called them *monads*. Today, when people use the word *soul*, they tend to mean something that is conscious. So did Leibniz, in speaking of monads. He held that each of the infinitesimal monads of which each material thing is composed is conscious. However, the consciousness of most of these monads is quite inferior to human consciousness, consisting only in their "mirroring" the rest of the universe, that is, in their being related to other things in whatever ways they are related.

Personal Identity and Immortality

As we suggested at the outset, in the seventeenth century the main event intellectually, even so far as self and personal-identity theory was concerned, was not self and personal identity theory per se, but science. Nevertheless, each of the philosophers we considered expressed a view about the nature of personal identity and its implications for survival of bodily death. In the case of Descartes, although it was an announced goal of his *Meditations* to prove the immortality of the soul, it was as if he forgot to do it, which puzzled some of his critics. In response to them, he claimed that by proving that the mind is an immaterial substance distinct from the body he had, in effect, done the main work. Apparently, his target had been contemporary Aristotelians. Some, following Averroës, claimed that nothing that belongs specifically to the individual survives bodily death. Others, in the tradition of Pomponazzi and Zabarella, took the more extreme view that soul, wherever it occurs, is simply the form of the body and hence souls decompose, and so end, at bodily death.

In the *Meditations*, Descartes imagined that he held a lump of wax in his hand and then brought it close to a lighted candle, which rapidly caused all of the sensible properties of the wax to change. "Does the same wax remain?" he asked, answering that "no one thinks otherwise." But then, he continued, "What was it in the wax that I understood with such distinctness? Evidently none of the features which I arrived at by means of the senses; for whatever came under taste, smell, sight, touch, or hearing has now altered—yet the wax remains."[9] He answered that in spite of these changes, he nevertheless knew that it is the same lump of wax at the end as it was at the beginning. He used this example to make the point that we learn of the identity of external things over time not through the senses but through understanding, that is, through rational intuition. Later he suggested that we know our own identities in the same way.[10]

In spite of Descartes's far greater influence, it was Hobbes, the materialist, not Descartes, the dualist, who laid the foundations for modern theories of personal identity. In *Leviathan* (1651), Hobbes distinguished between man (human) and person. In *De corpore* (1665), he then raised the problem of identity over time, to which he considered three possible solutions: that the answer lies in "the unity of matter"; that it lies "in the unity of form"; and that it lies "in the unity of the aggregate of all the accidents together."[11]

After discussing the pros and cons of these three answers, Hobbes concluded that "when we inquire concerning the identity" of something, "we must consider by what name" it is called. "For it is one thing to ask concerning Socrates, whether he be the same man [human], and another to ask whether he be the same body; for his body, when he is old, cannot be the same it was when he was an infant, by reason of the difference in magnitude; yet nevertheless he may be the same man."[12] Men (humans), as opposed to their bodies, can change the parts out of which they are composed and still remain the same men:

> Also, if the name be given for such form as is the beginning of motion, then as long as that motion remains, it will be the same individual thing; as that man will always be the same, whose actions and thoughts all proceed from the same beginning of motion, namely that which was in his generation; and that will be the same river which flows from one and the same fountain, whether the same water, or other water, or something else than water, flow from thence; and that the same city, whose acts proceed continually from the same institution, whether the men be the same or no.[13]

Hobbes, thus, had what is called a relational, rather than a substance, view of personal identity.

In Hobbes's time, European philosophy was not yet ready either for his materialism or for a relational view of personal identity, even though neither were new ideas. As we have seen, toward the end of the second century, Irenaeus,

Minucius Felix, and Tertullian had all been materialists and had each proposed a relational view of personal identity. But, after Origen, as dualists within the church gained ascendancy, subsequent Christian thinkers held to a substance view of the identity of the soul and proposed a relational theory only of the identity of the body. After Hobbes, but still in the seventeenth century, Spinoza, Boyle, and Locke also proposed relational views of the identity of the body, and Spinoza and Locke relational views of personal identity. To thinkers in earlier centuries, a relational theory of personal identity had not suggested that the self might be a fiction. To eighteenth century thinkers, it did.

Hobbes was also ahead of his time in his distinguishing between the identity conditions of humans and human bodies. While he was mistaken in thinking of the identity conditions of human bodies as if they were the same as those of inanimate objects, such as a pile of sand, his idea that different sorts of things may have different identity conditions is one that would be endorsed by Locke and most subsequent philosophers. Locke, for instance, ensconced his account of *personal* identity in a more general account of the identity conditions for all objects that change over time. In this more general account, Locke distinguished among the identity conditions for inanimate objects, plants and animals (including human animals), and people.

After Hobbes but before Locke, it may seem as if Spinoza had left no room in his account for the possibility of personal survival of bodily death. His view that mind and body are just two perspectives on the same thing precluded the mind's outliving the body. Yet, he claimed, inconsistently it would seem, that "the human mind cannot be absolutely destroyed with the body" and that "something of it remains which is eternal," something that "we feel and know [to be so] by experience."[14] However, he added, presumably because memory is dependent on the body, that this immortal remnant cannot remember anything of its prior existence.[15]

Spinoza claimed that not everyone enjoys the same postmortem fate. The ignorant man, who is driven by his appetites and is constantly distracted, ceases to be "as soon as he ceases to be acted on," whereas the wise man "is hardly troubled in spirit, but being, by a certain eternal necessity, conscious of himself, and of God, and of things, he never ceases to be."[16] By means of the superior sort of knowledge the wise man acquires, he experiences the intellectual love of God and hence knows this love intuitively. This intuitive knowledge, which is indestructible, makes him immortal. So, in the case of the wise man, what remains after the death of his body is simply the divine idea of him and the personality it expresses, which is perhaps best conceived as a thought or memory of God, or Nature. So long as a human is alive, whether he is wise or foolish, he exists as a body and also as an idea in the mind of God. At bodily death, for reasons that in Spinoza's more general philosophy are unclear, God, or Nature, continues to think the idea of the wise man but not that of the ignorant man. In this sense, the wise man persists as an individual.

Such aberrations in Spinoza's thoughts about the self are remarkably similar to, and probably dependent on, medieval Jewish philosophical speculations. His more consistent view was that what we call individual human beings are not substances, let alone combinations of two different sorts of substances, but rather modes of God. A consequence of this view, but one which he never paused to develop, is that personal identity has to be understood not as the persistence of a substance, since individual people are not substances, but as a relation among qualitative states. In any case, in Spinoza's view, "a free man thinks of nothing less than of death."[17]

In sum, so far as theories of identity in general and personal identity in particular are concerned, Hobbes and Spinoza, while less influential overall than Descartes, were more progressive. Both Hobbes and Spinoza, by embracing relational views of personal identity, set the stage for Locke's relational view. Of the two, Hobbes was more influential, primarily for introducing the idea that the organizational structure of something over time, rather than the stuff of which that thing is composed, can be used as a criterion of the thing's identity. In Locke's hands, this idea would be used to construct a powerful rival to the Platonic conception of the person.

Prior to his late reading of and response to Locke, Leibniz's unpublished reflections on personal identity were on two separate, but closely related issues: what accounts for personal identity and what matters in survival. So far as the first issue is concerned, while wavering somewhat, particularly with respect to the question of whether the self is ever separated from body, Leibniz basically took the view that the self is an immaterial substance whose persistence is assured by its being unextended. However, his early work is progressive in connection with two other issues. One of these is his anticipations of what today we would call *the question of what matters in survival*, the other in his anticipations of what today we would call *a four-dimensional view of persons*.

So far as the question of what matters in survival is concerned, Leibniz remarked, "But the intelligent soul, knowing what it is—having the ability to utter the word 'I,' a word so full of meaning—does not merely remain and subsist metaphysically, which it does to a greater degree than the others, but also remains the same morally, and constitutes the same person. For it is memory or the knowledge of this self that renders it capable of punishment or reward."[18] Leibniz then distinguished between what is required for the soul to persist metaphysically and what it would take for it to matter to the individual whose soul it is whether it persists: "Thus the immortality required in morality and religion does not consist merely in this perpetual subsistence common to all substances, for without the memory of what one has been, there would be nothing desirable about it." As we shall see, his thought here is similar to Locke's later thought that "forensic" concerns involving this life, as well as any future life, do not depend on mere substance but on memory.

However, Leibniz continued the remarks just quoted with thoughts that are more reminiscent of Lucretius (who may have been his source): "Suppose that some person all of a sudden becomes the king of China, but only on the condition that he forgets what he has been, as if he were born anew; practically, or as far as the effects could be perceived, wouldn't that be the same as if he were annihilated and a king of China created at the same instant in his place? That is something this individual would have no reason to desire."[19] Leibniz supposed that without memory, even a reconstituted "self" would not really be oneself, at least with respect to self-concern, and that this would be so even if the reconstituted self were a continuation (or reconstitution) of one's substance.

Leibniz's anticipations of what today we would call a four-dimensional view of persons appears in his early unpublished writing and correspondence. The topic comes up against the backdrop of Leibniz's distinction between the a priori and a posteriori ground of the identity over time of any object, including persons. Here Leibniz has two noteworthy ideas. One is that one cannot tell from experience what individuates one person from another: "It is not enough that I sense myself to be a substance that thinks; I must distinctly conceive what distinguishes me from all other minds, and I have only a confused experience of this."[20] The other is that while a posteriori we attempt to arrive at a true view about the identity of things and persons by comparing their characteristics at different times, it is a separate question, to be answered a priori, what identity over time consists in.

Leibniz's answer to the question of what identity over time consists in, together with his main reason for that answer, is that "since from the very time that I began to exist it could be said of me truly that this or that would happen to me, we must grant that these predicates were principles involved in the subject or in my complete concept, which constitutes the so-called me, and which is the basis of the interconnection of all my different states," which predicates "God has known perfectly from all eternity."[21] A subject's complete concept will include his or her states not just at a given time but throughout his or her entire existence. The view that Leibniz seems to be anticipating here is that the stage (that is, time slice) of a thing or person that exists at any moment or short interval of time is not the whole person but only part of the person and that the whole person consists of an aggregate of such stages that begin whenever the person begins, presumably at bodily birth, and ends whenever the person ends—which in the view of a naturalist would be at bodily death. In Leibniz's view, people are immortal; hence, they never end.

In the *New Essays*, which were written later in response to Locke's *Essay Concerning Human Understanding* and published posthumously, Leibniz discussed a different example that also anticipates developments in philosophy in our own time:

> It may be that in another place in the universe or at another time a globe may be found which does not differ sensibly from this earthly globe, in which we live, and that each of the men who inhabit it does not differ sensibly from each of us who corresponds to him. Thus, there are at once more than a hundred million pairs of similar persons, i.e. of two persons with the same appearances and consciousnesses; and God might transfer spirits alone or with their bodies from one globe to the other without their perceiving it; but be they transferred or let alone, what will you say of their person or self according to your authors? Are they two persons or the same since the consciousness and the internal and external appearance of the men of these globes cannot make the distinction?

Leibniz answered that God and certain spirits could distinguish them. But then asked:

> But according to your hypotheses consciousness alone discerning the persons without being obliged to trouble itself with the real identity or diversity of the substance, or even of that which would appear to others, how is it prevented from saying that these two persons who are at the same time in these two similar globes, but separated from each other by an inexpressible distance, are only one and the same person; which is however, a manifest absurdity?[22]

This "twin-earth" example never found a home in the eighteenth or nineteenth century debates over personal identity, but it found a different one, in our own times, in formal semantics.[23] In any case, none of Leibniz's later reflections, which were not published until 1765, well after Leibniz's death, had any effect on theory in the seventeenth or early eighteenth centuries.

Summary

The seventeenth century began with the revolutionary theoretical innovations of Kepler and Galileo. It ended with the dazzling theories of Newton, who showed once and for all that there could be a natural philosophy of the external world. Yet to most European thinkers of the seventeenth century, the self remained an anomaly. On the eve of the eighteenth century, with the appearance of Locke's *Essay*, the focus was put back on the self. Subsequently, progressive eighteenth-century thinkers were intent on showing that whereas Newton had shown that there could be a natural philosophy of the external world, their job was to show that there could be a natural philosophy of the internal world. By the end of the eighteenth century, leading theorists tended either to marginalize or reject theories that depended for their understanding of the self, or person, on the persistence of an immaterial substance. In place of these, they substituted the view that our minds are dynamic natural systems subject to general laws of growth and development. There would be no transition in the history of Western discussions of the self and personal identity more consequential than this one.

IX

NATURALIZING THE SOUL

God said, "Let there be light"
—Genesis (c. 700 B.C.E.)

God said, Let Newton be, *and all was light*.
—Alexander Pope (1688–1744)

In 1687, Isaac Newton (1642–1727) published his Principia, *perhaps the greatest scientific book* ever written. An immediate consequence among thinkers at the forefront of progressive developments was an unprecedented confidence in human reason. These thinkers then wanted to do for "moral philosophy," which eventually they would call the *science of human nature*, what Newton had done for "natural philosophy." In the early seventeenth century, rationalists, such as Descartes, were at the forefront of progressive developments in the investigation of the mind. By the end of the century empiricism's time had arrived, nowhere more consequentially than in the work of Newton's contemporary, John Locke (1632–1704), who proclaimed its foundational principle: There is nothing in the mind that was not previously in the senses.[1] So far as the self and personal identity are concerned, Locke, following Hobbes, took the decisive step away from substance accounts, according to which the self is a simple immaterial thing, toward relational accounts, according to which it is composed of physical and mental elements.

The Birth of Modern Personal-Identity Theory

In the *Essay Concerning Human Understanding* (1690–94), Locke's most controversial claim, which he slipped into book 4 almost as an aside, was that matter might think.[2] Either because he was genuinely pious, which he was, or because he was clever, which he also was, Locke tied the denial of matter's ability to think to the claim that God's powers are limited, thus attempting to disarm his critics. It did not work. Bishop Stillingfleet and others were outraged. If matter can think, they countered, then for explanatory purposes the immaterial soul might be dispensable. Locke's critics were right. The soul is dispensable. What had always made the soul so handy for proving immortality—that it is simple, static, and inaccessible to empirical examination—is also what made it so useless for investigating human nature. Early in the eighteenth century, as we shall see, Samuel Clarke might take the high road and resist descent into the merely probable and contingent, but when it came to investigating people, the emerging empirical science of human nature was the only game in town. One either played it or took oneself out of the action.

In regard to the identity of persons, Locke had two main ideas, one negative and one positive. The negative idea was that the persistence of persons cannot be understood as parasitic upon the persistence of any underlying substance, or substances, out of which persons might be composed. The positive idea was that the persistence of persons can be understood only in terms of the unifying role of consciousness.

Most of the time when Locke talked about consciousness in the context of talking about personal identity, he meant *memory*. His eighteenth-century critics invariably took him to mean this. They thus attributed to him the view that a person at two different times will have the same consciousness and hence will be the same person, just in case the person at the later time remembers having experienced and done what the person at the earlier time experienced and did. This may not have been Locke's view. In his account of personal identity over time, he may not have been trying to present a noncircular analysis but to do something entirely different—to give a constructive account of the origins of self-constitution. That is, he may not have been trying to say what's meant by *personal identity* but to explain how *selves* arise. And, even if he was trying to present a noncircular analysis of personal identity, one cannot on this memory interpretation explain something that is central to his view, namely, that consciousness, which is reflexive, plays a *dual* role in self-constitution, unifying persons both *over* time and also *at* a time. Memory has to do only with the unification of persons *over* time.

Locke's eighteenth-century critics were right in thinking that the memory analysis of personal identity that they attributed to him is vulnerable to decisive objections. However, almost all of them wanted to defeat the memory analysis in order to retain the view that personal identity depends on the persistence of an immaterial soul. Locke claimed that one can determine empirically whether someone retains the same consciousness over time but not whether someone retains the same immaterial soul. As a consequence, he thought, the soul view is not only a wrong account of personal identity but the wrong *kind* of account, whereas his own view, by contrast, is at least the right kind.

Early in the century, Locke's critics failed to see that even the memory view that they attributed to him was riding the crest of a wave of naturalization that was about to engulf them. Later in the century their vision improved. Thus, Clarke's bravado toward the beginning of the century contrasts nicely with the subsequent defensiveness of George Berkeley and Joseph Butler a few decades later and with the reluctance of most soul theorists, after David Hume, even to do battle on the issue. Toward the beginning of the century, it was enough for Locke's critics simply to defend the immateriality of the soul and related a priori doctrines, such as the reflexivity of consciousness, without also contributing to the emerging science of human nature. But soon even soul theorists—including Berkeley, David Hartley, Thomas Reid, and Abraham Tucker—tended to bracket their commitment to the soul in order to conduct meaningful empirical research.

As the century wore on, in debates among theorists about human nature it tended to matter less and less what one's view was of the immaterial soul. Toward the end of the century, Hartley, a dualist, was an ally of Joseph Priestley, a materialist, while Reid, a dualist, attacked both. And while the main influences on Tucker, a dualist, were Locke, Clarke, and Hartley, it was not Locke and Hartley's dualism that most impressed Tucker but their more scientific pursuits. It is only a slight exaggeration, if an exaggeration at all, to suggest that Priestley could have put forth the very same views he did even if, like Hartley, he had been a dualist. And Reid could have put forth most of his views even if he had been a materialist.

Locke, in the *Essay*, sometimes used the words *person* and *self* interchangeably. But he tended to use *self* to refer to a momentary entity and *person* to refer to a temporally extended one. Seemingly for other reasons, he defined the two terms differently.[3] His definition of *person* highlighted that people are thinkers and, as such, have reason, reflection, intelligence, and whatever else may be required for transtemporal self-reference. His definition of *self* highlighted that selves are sensors and as such feel pleasure and pain and are capable of happiness, misery, and self-concern. These differences in his definitions reflect disparate concerns that he expressed throughout his discussion of personal identity.

Obviously, humans come into being via a biological process. How, in Locke's view, do selves (or persons) come into being? His answer was, via a psychological process that involves five steps. It begins with a human organism's experience of pleasure and pain, which gives rise, first, to the idea of a self—its own self—that is the experiencer of pleasure and pain, and then to concern with the quality of that self's experience (each of us wants more pleasure, less pain). Next, the momentary self thus constituted (or perhaps the organism) thinks of itself (or its self) as extended over brief periods of time (say, the specious present); finally, through memory and the appropriation ingredient in self-consciousness, it thinks of itself as extended over longer periods of time.[4] Locke may have thought that the prior phases of this ordered, multistep process *temporally* precede the subsequent phases, or he may have thought that all five steps happen simultaneously.

Whatever Locke's view on this question of timing, he clearly thought that self-constitution involves appropriation and that appropriation and accountability go hand in hand. A person, he said, is "justly accountable for any Action" just if it is appropriated to him by his self-consciousness.[5] He regarded this appropriation as a natural relation between the organism and its present and past, which then is the basis for a nonnatural relation of moral ownership. It is primarily this view—not, as some have suggested, a vague association between consciousness and conscience, or an equivocation on the notion of ownership—that connects the natural appropriation that is part of human psychology with the nonnatural appropriation that is the concern of both ethics and the law.[6]

One of the most puzzling aspects of Locke's account of personal identity is his view of the ontological status of persons (or selves). There are two aspects to the puzzle: his view of the status of *humans* and his view of the status of *persons*. Commentators often assume that in Locke's view humans are substances and that the puzzle consists in determining whether persons are also substances. However, in his chapter on identity, Locke may have used the term *substance* in a more restricted sense than he did in the rest of the *Essay*. In this more restricted sense, only God, immaterial thinking things, and individual atoms would be particular substances. Other things, such as lumps of gold, oak trees, horses, and persons, would in this restricted sense of *substance* be collections of substances.[7] If this interpretation is correct, then Locke was at least ambivalent about the substantial status of living things, including humans, and perhaps also of inanimate, macroscopic objects such as rocks and chairs.

For this and other reasons, mainly having to do with his failure to adequately explain how the idea of self emerges from experience, Locke encouraged the view, perhaps unintentionally, that persons (or selves) are fictions, thereby laying the groundwork for others to question their substantiality, which then became a major issue. Of course, it is easier to make the case that Locke thought that persons (or selves) are fictions than that he thought that living things or inanimate objects are fictions. But even if he did think that the self is a fiction, he clearly did not mean to suggest that the self is fictional because it is an artifact of legal or ethical theory. In his view, selves are created implicitly by human mentality via processes of appropriation and the application of self-concepts that are ingredients of reflexive consciousness.[8]

In his chapter on identity, Locke was preoccupied with the implications of fissionlike examples. He asked, for instance, "Could we suppose two distinct incommunicable consciousnesses acting the same Body, the one constantly by Day, the other by Night; and on the other side the same consciousness, acting by Intervals two distinct Bodies." He considered a case in which one's little finger is cut off and consciousness, rather than staying with the main part of the body, goes with the little finger. He concluded that in such a case, "the little Finger would be the Person, the same Person; and self then would have nothing to do with the rest of the Body." Later he returned to this example, remarking that "though if the same Body should still live, and immediately from the separation of the little Finger have its own peculiar consciousness, whereof the little Finger knew nothing, it would not at all be concerned for it, as a part of it self, or could own any of its Actions, or have any of them imputed to him."[9] In this latter version of his example, Locke seems to be suggesting that the original consciousness splits, part of it going to the little finger and part remaining in the rest of the body, each part then constituting a whole consciousness qualitatively identical to the original. On this reading, his example is what philosophers in our own times would call a *fission example*, the first one to be considered explicitly in the context of personal-identity theory. Since Locke did not explore the implications of his example, it is impossible to know exactly what he had in mind. But once he published his new theory, the fission-example cat was out of the bag.

The Clarke-Collins Debate

Between 1706 and 1709, Samuel Clarke (1675–1729) and Anthony Collins (1676–1729) confronted each other in a six-part written debate that was well known throughout the century.[10] Their point of departure was the question of whether souls are naturally immortal, where by *soul* they agreed to mean "Substance with a Power of Thinking" or "Individual Consciousness."[11] Clarke defended the traditional Platonic idea that souls are immaterial, hence indivisible, hence naturally immortal. Collins countered that the soul is material. Both agreed that individual atoms are not conscious. Their dispute turned on the question of whether it is possible for a *system* of mere matter to think. Clarke argued that it is not possible, Collins that matter does think.

Throughout their debate Clarke played the part of the traditional metaphysician, arguing largely on a priori grounds that the soul is indivisible, even though, in his view, it is extended. Collins, though not always consistently, played the role of the empirical psychologist. His faltering but often successful attempts to reformulate traditional metaphysical issues empirically embodied the birth pangs of a new approach, one that grew steadily throughout the century. Their debate is, thus, a poignant record of two thinkers' struggles to cope with a rapidly changing intellectual climate, Clarke by hanging onto the old, Collins by groping for the new.

In Collins's view, the basic problem with Clarke's account is that he was trying to settle by verbal fiat what could be settled only empirically.[12] His own approach was the progressive side of Locke's, of whom he had been a close personal friend and disciple. Yet he went beyond Locke in two ways: first, methodologically, if not also ontologically, he was unabashedly materialist; second, he replaced Locke's metaphysically awkward same-consciousness view of personal identity with a more defensible connected-consciousness view.

In response to Collins's call for an empirical analysis of consciousness, Clarke countered by reiterating a priori metaphysics. He claimed, for instance, that strictly speaking, consciousness is neither a capacity for thinking nor actual thinking, "but the Reflex Act by which I know that I think, and that my Thoughts and Actions are my own and not Another's." He claimed that "it would necessarily imply a plain and direct Contradiction, for any power which is really One and not Many ... to inhere in or result from a divisible Substance."[13] In Clarke's view, then, the self is unified, that is, a single thing, and it could not be a single thing if it were material, hence, divisible. This is an expression of the same tension that had emerged as early as Plato's view. The self as immaterial soul was thought to explain something that could not otherwise be explained: the unity of the self. Even so, Clarke conceded that his own "affirming Consciousness to be an individual Power," was neither "giving an Account of what Consciousness is" nor "intended to be so." It is enough, he said, that "every Man feels and knows by Experience what Consciousness is, better than any Man can explain it."[14] In Collins's point of view, Clarke, in effect, was inviting him to explain how on an empirical view consciousness could be understood. This he tried to do.

It seems, then, that in the end their dispute came down to a clash between intuition and science. As those who are familiar with contemporary philosophy of mind will know from similar debates in our own times, this particular conflict may be unresolvable. However, even in the eighteenth century, it became clear that while intuition might be a sufficient basis to resist the reduction of the mental to the material, it was impotent as a source of explanations of mental phenomena. Collins returned to this point again and again.[15] In the case of remembering, for instance, he claimed that he could explain how consciousness could be transferred from a material system of the brain initially composed of certain particles to one composed of other particles, without changing the individual subject of consciousness whose brain is involved.[16] By our current standards, his explanation is crude, but it was a genuine scientific explanation, and Clarke had nothing comparable to offer.

What Clarke did instead was to accuse Collins of "begging the Question by, assuming the impossible Hypothesis" that the subject consisting of a brain that originally had an experience and a subject that subsequently remembered it might be the same. Clarke declared that in Collins's view, consciousness, rather than being a real individual quality, would be a "fleeting transferrable Mode or Power," and hence that the self would be a fiction.[17] Clarke assumed that pointing this out refuted Collins's view. Collins, for his part, appealed to an analogy between consciousness and the property of roundness to blunt the force of Clarke's claim that emergent properties cannot be "real," pointing out that the arches out of which a circle is composed, while not round individually, may be round collectively. Roundness, as even Clarke admitted, is a real property. But neither Clarke nor Collins had a principled, non-question-begging way of showing whether the comparison of consciousness and roundness is a good analogy.[18]

On the way to this inconclusive end, Clarke introduced fission examples as a way of objecting to Collins's (and Locke's) relational view of personal identity. Clarke pointed out that if God in the afterlife can make one being with the same consciousness as someone who had lived on Earth, then God could make many such beings, which in Collins's view, would be the same person. Clarke took it as obvious that such multiple fission descendants would be different people.[19] Subsequently, Clarke and Collins discussed fission examples several times. Because their debate was well known, both fission examples and the idea that they have implications for personal-identity theory were brought to the attention of eighteenth-century theorists.

Scriblerus

Early in the eighteenth century, fissionlike examples seem to have been on the minds of other thinkers who were interested in personal identity. Much of this interest, including some in the popular press, was stimulated by Locke's new account of personal identity.[20] It was also nourished by a fascination with the phenomenon of conjoined, or Siamese twins. In 1694, Richard Burthogge (1638?–1694?) had reported on the phenomenon of a "*Child*" who had a double body, that is, "a double Breast and double Head, and *proper* feelings of all parts."[21] In 1708, Hungarian conjoined-twin sisters toured Europe and captured the imagination of London. Subsequently, in 1714, the twins phenomenon inspired a humorous commentary of sorts on Locke's theory of personal identity. Written by members of the Scriblerus Club (Alexander Pope, John Arbuthnot, Jonathan Swift, John Gay, Thomas Parnell, Robert Harley, and perhaps others), *The Memoirs of the Extraordinary Life, Works, and Discoveries of Martinus Scriblerus* revisited the topic of conjoined twins in the context of a satirical critique of current debates over the metaphysics of soul, consciousness, and personal identity.[22]

As the story begins, Scriblerus is seeking the location of the soul in the body. Not finding it, he hits on the idea that there may be two persons in one body. A chapter then rehearses, from Collins's point of view, the debate between Clarke and Collins over thinking matter. Finally, several chapters deal with Scriblerus's falling in love with and marrying a pair of conjoined twins who share a single "organ of generation." After this marriage, someone else marries just one of the twins. Understandably, this development provokes a controversy. In court, Scriblerus argues that the twins are one person and share one soul since the organ of generation is obviously the "seat of the soul." The other husband argues that in marrying both twins, Scriblerus committed bigamy, and then in consummating his marriage, committed incest. Several judges work out the solution, the result of which is that both the marriages of Scriblerus and of the new husband are dissolved since "two persons [the explicit reference is to the husbands, but must also playfully be to the twins] could not have a Right to the entire possession of the same thing, at the same time."

Although not dealing with fission per se, the identity problems associated with the case of these conjoined twins expresses in concrete form a sort of puzzlement and amusement that Clarke and Collins's discussion of fission must have produced in sophisticated readers of their debate, not the least the members of the Scriblerus Club. There is some evidence that the *Memoirs* were widely read not only for their humor but also as philosophy.[23]

Relational Theories and the Fiction of Self

In antiquity, relational theories of personal identity had not encouraged the view that the self is a fiction—the question did not even arise. In the eighteenth century, as soon as relational theories appeared, the question of whether the self is a fiction was raised. Why later, rather than earlier?

One reason is that the success of corpuscular mechanism had accustomed people to the idea—Clarke is a premier example—that in the material world only atoms and properties that are derivable from atoms "by addition" are real.

Another is that in earlier times, there was not a clear idea of nature as a whole being a machine. By the seventeenth century, this idea was unavoidable. To Galileo and Kepler, through Hobbes, Descartes, and Gassendi, to Newton, Boyle, and Locke, it began to look like one could, in principle, explain all processes in nature either through micromechanical "primary qualities" or through "secondary qualities" associated with human subjectivity.

Descartes had developed a "science" of nature that was strictly mechanical and a new "first philosophy" that posited only the basic mechanical elements and the human soul. In his view, humans are special in being the only organisms with a soul, which, for him, was an immaterial mind, or self, whose essential attribute is thinking or consciousness. Everything else in the physical world is merely a machine, and even humans are mostly machines. But, so far as personal identity was concerned, the body's matter carries no importance. It could eternally replace itself without affecting personal identity, which depends only on the immaterial mind. But when the relational account of antiquity (via Hobbes) reappeared in Locke, consciousness was the main focus. And if consciousness was not a property of a separate immaterial self but of matter, then the reality of the self, as well as the motivation for self-concern, became tenuous.

More than any other eighteenth century critic of Locke, Joseph Butler (1692–1752) took Locke's observations about the role of appropriation in self-constitution seriously. It is "easy to conceive," he said, "how matter, which is no part of ourselves, may be appropriated to us in the manner which our present bodies are."[24] But, he continued, where there is appropriation, there must be an appropriator. Locke had an appropriator in "man," which he distinguished from "person" and allowed might be merely a material organism. Butler thought that he (Butler) had already shown that the appropriator, which he assumed is who one truly is, must be something simple and indivisible and, hence, could not possibly be a material organism. And what this being appropriates, he went on to explain, is not thereby part of itself but, rather, something it owns. Butler had learned from Locke that, for all we know, the thinking principle in us may be material. So Butler astutely conceded that the appropriator might be a simple material entity—it is our simplicity, not our immateriality, that ensures our survival.[25] He thereby adapted the Platonic argument for immortality to the purposes of an age in which materialism was on the rise, recasting the a priori in an empirical mold.

When Butler turned to the topic of personal identity per se, he argued that in a relational view, such as that of Locke or Collins, an individual would have no reason to be concerned for the future life of the person whom he nominally regards as himself.[26] In response to what he saw as the dangers of empirical analysis, he proposed that we take as primitive the idea of personal identity, which, he said, like the notion of equality, defies analysis. He added that we can deter-mine intuitively in "the strict philosophical sense," which requires sameness of substance, that we have persisted. He contrasted this sense of persisting with "a loose and popular sense," such as we might employ in saying of a mature oak that it is the same tree as one that stood in its spot fifty years previously even though it and that former tree have not one atom in common.[27]

Butler said that if selves were to consist only in successive acts of conscious-ness, then it would be a mistake "to charge our present selves with anything we did, or to imagine our present selves interested in anything that befell us yester-day" or that "will befall us to-morrow." Under such circumstances, "our present self is not, in reality, the same with the self of yesterday, but another like self or person coming in its room, and mistaken for it; to which another self will suc-ceed tomorrow."[28] Thus, in Locke's view, each of us would be selves only in a fictitious sense. Butler thought that such a consequence refutes Locke's view but not that it *proves* that Locke's view is false (he admitted that it does not). Rather, "the bare unfolding this notion [that selves are fictitious] and laying it thus naked and open, seems the best confutation of it."[29] Several others, as we shall see, took a different view. Importantly, because they did so, Butler's death marked the end of an era in which religious concerns *dominated* the philosophy of human nature. Henceforth, in the work of the most progressive theorists of human nature, reli-gious concerns would merely be one influence among many—albeit often a very important influence—which shaped the development of theory.

Laying the Foundations for a Science of Human Nature

When Locke published the *Essay*, he dreamt of the emergence of a science of human nature. But he was in the grip of several a priori assumptions that inhib-ited the development of that science. Chief among these was the Cartesian notion that all consciousness is reflexive. And Locke had ulterior religious motives. Nothing is more central to his account of personal identity than his distinction between person and human, but that distinction was an important one for him largely because it allowed him to suggest that matter might think while at the same time accommodating the Christian dogma of resurrection. More than four decades later, when David Hume (1711–1776) published *A Treatise of Human Nature* (1739), he assumed that at least the beginnings of a science of human nature had already emerged.[30] In developing his account of self and personal identity, Hume had gotten beyond both the a priori assumption that conscious-ness is reflexive and the dogma of resurrection. Yet he too had a dream.

Hume's dream was not of the emergence of an empirical philosophy of human nature but of its assumption of its rightful position among the sciences as the foundation of a mighty edifice of human knowledge. The philosophy of human nature was not fitted for this role. Hume's confusion on this issue was not a peripheral mistake but central to his perspective. It was because he thought that the philosophy of human nature—what today we would call psychology—includes epistemology and metaphysics that he thought that it was not just another science but the foundation of all the sciences. In his view, the science of human nature would not only itself be founded on experience and observation, but—and this is how it would be the foundation of all the sciences—it would explain how all knowledge, including whatever is discovered in any of the other sciences, also is founded on experience and observation.

As it happened, for psychologists to find their feet as scientists they had to abandon such epistemological and metaphysical pretensions and realize that it was not their job to get to the absolute bottom of things. That was a task that they could happily leave to philosophers. As psychologists, it was their job to explain human behavior. To do this, they had to take certain things for granted that in a more philosophical frame of mind could be seen as deeply questionable. Fortunately, Hume did not stick consistently to his idea that the science of human nature would be the foundation of all the sciences. Sometimes, he seemed to see, if only through a glass darkly, that the new science would have a different mission.

The contrast between what we are calling, somewhat anachronistically, phil-osophical and scientific approaches is especially poignant in Hume's account of self and personal identity. In book 1 of the *Treatise*, the heart of his account is his argument that belief in a substantial, persisting self is an illusion. More generally, he was intent on showing that belief in the persistence of anything is an illusion. This is what today we would call philosophy, rather than psychology, and this was Hume, the skeptical metaphysician, at his *destructive* best. However, in the remainder of book 1, Hume addressed the task of explaining why people are so susceptible to the illusion of self. And in book 2 he explained how certain dynamic mentalistic systems in which we represent ourselves to ourselves, as well as to others, actually work, such as those systems in us that generate sympa-thetic responses to others. This was Hume the empirical psychologist at his *con-structive* best.[31] In these more psychological projects, Hume often seems to have taken for granted things that in book 1 he had subjected to withering skeptical criticism.

In Hume's view, since all ideas arise from impressions and there is no impres-sion of a "simple and continu'd" self, there is no idea of such a self. This critique of traditional views led him to formulate his alternative "bundle" conception of the self and also to compare the mind to a kind of theatre. In this theatre, none of the actors—the "perceptions [that] successively make their appearance"—is the traditional self. None is either "simple" at any one time or, strictly speaking, identical over time. Beyond that, Hume claimed, humans do not even have minds, except as fictional constructions. Thus, in his view, a crucial respect in which minds are not analogous to real theatres is that there is no site for the mental performance, at least none of which we have knowledge; rather, there "are the successive perceptions only, that constitute the mind; nor have we the most distant notion of the place, where these scenes are represented, or of the materials, of which it is compos'd."[32]

With these philosophical preliminaries out of the way, Hume turned to the psychological task of explaining how objects that are constantly changing, including the materials out of which we ourselves are constructed, nevertheless seem to persist. To begin, he distinguished "betwixt personal identity, as it regards our thought or imagination, and as it regards our passions or the concern we take in ourselves."[33] The difference that he had in mind is between, on the one hand, explaining why we regard anything that changes, including ourselves, as persisting over time (this is personal identity as it regards our thought or imagination) and, on the other, explaining the role that belief in ourselves as things that persist over time and through changes plays in the ways we represent ourselves to ourselves and to others (this is personal identity as it regards our passions or the concern we take in ourselves). The first of these occupied Hume in most of the remainder of book 1, the second in most of book 2.

When Hume sought to explain personal identity as it regards our thought or imagination, the crucial psychological question for him was that of figuring out what causes us to forge a succession of perceptions into a persisting object. His answer, in one word, is: resemblance. When successive perceptions resemble each other, he said, it is easy to imagine that the first simply persists. In fact, "our propensity to this mistake" is so ubiquitous and strong "that we fall into it before we are aware." And even when we become aware of our error "we cannot long sustain our philosophy, or take off this biass [sic] from the imagination."[34]

In this context, Hume insisted that "the controversy concerning identity is not merely a dispute of words." Usually, when people attribute identity "to variable or interrupted objects," he said, their "mistake" is "attended with a fiction."[35] They believe that the identity, which they have claimed obtains, is not just their (perhaps pragmatically motivated) decision to regard distinct but similar objects as the same, but that those objects really are the same. Often they imagine that what makes them the same is the existence of some unifying substance, such as soul, or some unifying mode, such as life or consciousness. Thus, in Hume's view, normally it is not just that someone, in full knowledge of the facts, innocently chooses to call distinct objects that resemble each other the same object, but rather that the person who chooses to do this is immersed in a cloud of metaphysical confusion. Hume concluded this part of his discussion by comparing "the soul" to "a republic or commonwealth," the seeming persistence of which is guaranteed by the relations among its parts, rather than by the persistence of any of its parts.[36]

In Locke's view, memory played a crucial role in constituting personal identity. In Hume's view, it does so also, but for different reasons: it not only creates resemblances among successive perceptions but also reveals to us that our perceptions are causally linked, information we then use as a basis for extending our identities to periods of our lives that we do not remember.[37] In connection with the topic of forgetfulness, Hume said that in his view, which presumably he intended to contrast with the views of Locke and perhaps also Collins, "memory does not so much produce as discover personal identity, by shewing us the relation of cause and effect among our different perceptions." He added that it is "incumbent on those who affirm that memory produces entirely our personal identity, to give a reason why we can thus extend our identity beyond our memory."[38]

Hume continued his critique by questioning the seriousness of trying to make fine-grained distinctions, presumably especially in the case of specially contrived, hypothetical examples, about whether personal identity obtains. He said, "Identity depends on the relations of ideas; and these relations produce identity, by means of that easy transition they occasion. But as the relations, and the easiness of the transition may diminish by insensible degrees, we have no just standard by which we can decide any dispute concerning the time when they acquire or lose a title to the name of identity." It follows, he said, that all of these sorts of "disputes concerning the identity of connected objects are merely verbal, except so far as the relation of parts gives rise to some fiction or imaginary principle of union."[39] In sum, Hume's view seems to have been that disputes about identity are merely verbal if they are about which relations, were they to obtain, would constitute identity. But the disputes are based on substantive mistakes if the disputants suppose that what is merely successive is really the same. In any case, such disputes are always about fictitious imaginary constructs. In his view, that is all there is to say about identity over time and through changes.

Thus, Hume may have thought that a crucial difference between Locke and himself on the question of personal identity was that whereas Locke thought that there is a fact of the matter about whether a person persists, Hume thought that there is a fact of the matter only about the circumstances under which the illusion of persistence is nourished. In his capacity as a psychologist, Hume tried to explain what those circumstances were. But he did not stop there. As soon as he moved on to the largely psychological concerns that dominate book 2 of the *Treatise*, he became deeply involved in what today we would call social psychology of the self. In doing so, he abandoned, but probably without realizing that he had done so, his project of marching up directly to "the capital or centre of the sciences, to human nature itself." Instead, he returned to "the frontier." Hume, thus, completed a transition from skeptical philosophy, to the most general sorts of associational issues, and then to specific psychological hypotheses about how self-representations function in our mental economy, as for instance in his explanation of how sympathy works.

In discussing personal identity, Hume never discussed fission directly, and he had little to say, and nothing new, about how personal identity might be analyzed in a way that links it to questions of accountability and interestedness. However, in his discussion of the example of a church that burns down and then is rebuilt, it seems that he may have been aware of the special problems for judgments of identity that arise in the case of fission. In claiming that, "without breach of the propriety of language," we might regard the two churches as the same church even if the first was of brick and the second "of free-stone," he added the caveat, "but we must observe, that in these cases the first object is in manner annihilated before the second comes into existence; by which means, we are never presented in any one point of time with the idea of difference and multiplicity; and for that reason are less scrupulous in calling them the same."[40]

In his "Essay on the Immortality of the Soul" (1755/1783), Hume returned briefly to the notion of self-concern, commenting that even if we were to assume that there were a spiritual substance that is "the only inherent subject of thought," its continued existence after our bodily deaths would be irrelevant unless it were attended with consciousness and memory. And even if there were such a spiritual substance, consciousness and memory may well be "dissolved by death." In sum, the supposition that the subject of our thought is a spiritual substance changes nothing: "The most positive asserters of the mortality of the soul never denied the immortality of its substance. And that an immaterial substance, as well as a material, may lose its memory or consciousness, appears in part from experience, if the soul be immaterial."[41]

In sum, in Hume's view, all reason or understanding has to work with are diverse perceptions. So it is the imagination that provides the links upon which our conception of self is ultimately based. This is true even though people all but invariably create the fiction that they are something more than just perceptions imaginatively linked.[42] Then, rather than considering the nature of personal identity per se, Hume turned instead, and almost exclusively, to two other questions: first, that of explaining how the fiction of identity arises not only in the case of people but in that of anything that seems to persist over time and through changes; and, second, that of explaining what role the fictional self plays in our emotions and motivations. He thus shifted the emphasis from conceptually analyzing the notion of personal identity to empirically accounting, first, for how it arises and, second, for its functional role. Finally, he claimed that even supposing that there were a spiritual substance and that it thought one's thoughts, there would be no reason to be concerned about its continued existence unless it were accompanied by consciousness and memory.

Innateness, Agency, and Identity

Étienne Bonnot de Condillac's (1715–1780) *Traité des sensations* (1754) was designed to show that external impressions through the outer senses, by themselves, can account for all ideas and all mental operations. Using what would become a famous example of a statue that is endowed with only a single sense, smell, he attempted to show how attention, memory, judgment, imagination, and the whole of mental life might be developed. His views embodied an extreme version of the tabula rasa perspective.

In contrast to Condillac, Thomas Reid (1710–1796), invoking an elaborate theory of innate faculties of the human mind, argued that we have direct unmediated knowledge both of personal agency and of the external world. Reid criticized Hume for supposing that there is nothing more to mind than a "succession of related ideas and impressions, of which we have an intimate memory and consciousness." He asked "to be farther instructed, whether the impressions remember and are conscious of the ideas, or the ideas remember and are conscious of the impressions, or if both remember and are conscious of both? and whether the ideas remember those that come after them, as well as those that were before them?" His point was that since ideas and impressions are passive, they cannot do anything, whereas Hume implied that the "succession of ideas and impressions not only remembers and is conscious" but also "judges, reasons, affirms, denies," even "eats and drinks, and is sometimes merry and sometimes sad." Reid concluded, "If these things can be ascribed to a succession of ideas and impressions in a consistency of common sense, I should be very glad to know what is nonsense." He concluded that in any view in which substance has no place, agency would have no place either.[43] He thought it would be absurd to deny agency. So substance had to be reintroduced.[44]

In his account of personal identity, Reid began by noting that "the conviction which every man has of his Identity, as far back as his memory reaches, needs no aid of philosophy to strengthen it; and no philosophy can weaken it, without first producing some degree of insanity." Thus, "there can be no memory of what is past without the conviction that we existed at the time remembered." Reid criticized what he took to be Locke's reliance on memory to explain personal identity by arguing that in Locke's view, *a man may be, and at the same time not be, the person that did a particular action.*" Suppose:

> a brave officer to have been flogged when a boy at school for robbing an orchard, to have taken a standard from the enemy in his first campaign, and to have been made a general in advanced life; suppose, also, which must be admitted to be possible, that, when he took the standard, he was conscious of his having been flogged at school, and that, when made a general, he was conscious of his taking the standard, but had absolutely lost the consciousness of his flogging.

It follows from Locke's view, Reid continued, "that he who was flogged at school is the same person who took the standard, and that he who took the standard is the same person who was made a general." From that it follows that "the general is the same person with him who was flogged at school." But since "the general's consciousness does not reach so far back as his flogging," in Locke's view, "he is not the person who was flogged. Therefore the general is, and at the same time is not, the same person with him who was flogged at school."[45] So much for a simple memory criterion of personal identity.

According to Reid, "there may be good arguments to convince me that I existed before the earliest thing I can remember; but to suppose that my memory reaches a moment farther back than my belief and conviction of my existence, is a contradiction."[46] Although he did not specifically say so, he seemed to have supposed that if we are rational, we automatically take ownership of the past thoughts, experiences, and actions that we remember. It seems, then, that Reid's continuing commitment to a reflexive account at least of memory, if not of all consciousness, may have prevented him from extending his new approach to a developmental account of the acquisition of self-concepts.

Materialism Redux

David Hartley (1705–1757) was a methodological, but not a substantive materialist. Differing in this respect from Collins before him and Priestley after, he believed that "man consists of two parts, body and mind," where the mind "is that substance, agent, principle, &c. to which we refer the sensation, ideas, pleasures, pains, and voluntary motions." He accepted Locke's concession that it is possible, for all we know, that matter thinks. He doubted that either problems with materialism or prescientific intuitions we have about unity of consciousness could be used to prove that the soul is immaterial, confessing perceptively that "it is difficult to know [even] what is meant by the Unity of Consciousness." He did say, though, that the main problem with materialism is "that Matter and Motion, however subtly divided, or reasoned upon, yield nothing more than Matter and Motion still." It was, he said, "foreign to [his] Purpose" to pursue the issue.

Hartley's humility about establishing his dualism extended to issues involving the afterlife. In his view, "the Immateriality of the Soul has little or no Connexion with its Immortality" and "we ought to depend upon Him who first breathed into Man the Breath of the present Life, for our Resurrection to a better."[47] He never used his metaphysical and theological views to determine the content of his more scientific views. He was a physico-theologian, in the tradition of Bacon, Boyle, Locke, and Newton before him, and in his scientific work it was the physical side that prevailed. In his case, like Locke's, his epistemological views engendered a deep humility, mixed with true religious piety, about the extent to which, through reason, humans can know metaphysical and religious truths. However, his associationist psychology was boldly speculative. There he claimed that all of human nature is built out of associations of sensations and consequent ideas, whose origins are in physical impressions on the organism. In his view, association was a principle in the service of the first truly general account of human and animal psychology, which, he believed, laid the foundation for a mechanistic physiological psychology.

Joseph Priestley (1733–1804) embraced materialism, with little concern for tradition, so long as he could maintain his own liberal version of Christianity. His theology was so liberal that many Christians—including Reid—looked on him as a pariah, while atheists tended to accept him as one of their own. Yet Priestley, like Hartley, was a paradigm of that fusion of theologian and scientist that flourished in England during the Enlightenment. He faced the facts of science head on and modified his Christianity to make faith consistent with reason.

Like Hartley, Priestley was a gradualist. He saw the differences between humans and other animals as differences of degree rather than kind. He saw human infants as starting off more like other animals and only gradually learning adult human modes of thinking, including even the ability to conceptualize themselves. He never mentioned the doctrine of the reflexive nature of consciousness, which he merely assumed to be wrong, an indication of how far the science of

mind had progressed since Clarke's debate with Collins. From Priestley's supposing that brutes and children differ from adult humans in not having second-order
reflections, and that as a consequence their emotions are "less complex," one can
glean how far the science of mind had progressed even since Hume.[48] Finally,
when Priestley suggested that children only gradually acquire self-concepts, he,
in effect, invited others to explain how the notion of self is developmentally
acquired. His student, Hazlitt, accepted the invitation.

Priestley's rootedness in science, together with the matter-of-factness of his
materialistic approach, differed radically from the epistemologically oriented
approach championed by Locke, Berkeley, and Hume. Although Priestley
accepted "the way of ideas," he did not think that it led to skepticism about the
external world, as Reid had claimed, or, indeed, to skepticism about anything.
Priestley was a realist. He did not argue for the existence of an external world,
beyond simply declaring that its existence is obviously the best explanation of
the fact that different people report having similar experiences in the presence
of a common stimulus. Since realism was so unproblematic for Priestley, he
made a much cleaner separation between philosophy and science than Hume, in
particular, had been able to do.

Priestley's thoughts on personal identity primarily form his attempt, in
response to criticisms from more conservative Christians, to show that his materialism is compatible with the Christian idea of resurrection. As a follower of
Hartley, he thought that the sentient and thinking principle in man must be
"a property of the nervous system or rather of the brain."[49] But he went further
than Hartley in suggesting that the brain was not only necessary for human
mentality but sufficient as well. In Priestley's view, it is scientifically useless to
postulate any immaterial substance to account for human behavior. Of course,
all of this will sound quite modern to readers in our own times. However, what
is truly sophisticated and innovative in Priestley's treatment of personal identity
is the way, in his exploratory discussion of a hypothesis, he downplays the importance of personal identity per se and highlights the functions that belief in our
own identities actually serves.

Priestley begins this part of his discussion by considering an objection that he
says was made to "the primitive Christians, as it may be at present," that "a proper
resurrection is not only, in the highest degree, improbable, but even actually
impossible since, after death, the body putrefies, and the parts that composed it
are dispersed, and form other bodies, which have an equal claim to the same
resurrection." He continued: "And where, they say, can be the propriety of
rewards and punishments, if the man that rises again be not identically the same
with the man that acted and died?" In reply, he first makes it clear that in his

opinion "we shall be identically the same beings after the resurrection that we are at present." Then, "for the sake of those who may entertain a different opinion," he proposes to "speculate a little upon their hypothesis" in order to show that "it is not inconsistent with a state of future rewards and punishments, and that it supplies motives sufficient for the regulation of our conduct here, with a view to it."[50] In the language of our own times, the task that Priestley set himself was to show that even if resurrected selves are not strictly identical to anyone who existed on Earth, it does not make any difference since identity is not what matters primarily in survival.

In arguing on behalf of this radical new idea, Priestley first endorsed Locke's view that so far as personal identity is requisite either for the propriety of rewards and punishments or for the concern that we take in our future selves, "the sameness and continuity of consciousness seems to be the only circumstance attended to by us." Then he made it clear that, in his view, whether identity per se obtains is of no great consequence:

> Admitting, therefore, that the man consists wholly of matter, as much as the river does of water, or the forest of trees, and that this matter should be wholly changed in the interval between death and the resurrection; yet, if, after this state, we shall all know one another again, and converse together as before, we shall be, *to all intents and purposes*, the same persons. Our personal identity will be *sufficiently* preserved, and the expectation of it at present will have a proper influence on our conduct.[51]

By his use of the expressions, "to all intents and purposes" and "sufficiently," he here separated the question of whether we will be identical with someone who exists in the future from that of whether it matters.

In other words, Priestley was saying that on the view under consideration, even if the resurrected person were not strictly identical with the person on Earth, he would be close enough to being identical that the loss of strict identity would not matter. And, in considering whether strict identity does matter, he distinguished three ways in which it might: people's so-called self-interested concerns for their own futures; societal concerns that the prospect of future rewards and punishments motivate people to behave themselves; and theological concerns about the propriety of divine rewards and punishments. Thus, toward the end of the eighteenth century and perhaps without inferring anything from fission examples, Priestley introduced and sympathetically discussed one of the key ideas—that identity is not primarily what matters in survival—that has been central to the revolution in personal identity theory in our own times.[52]

What Matters in Survival

In contrast to Priestley, Thomas Cooper (1759–1839) took the much more radical view, first, that identity is not maintained at all, even in successive stages of earthly life, and, second, that this does not matter. What matters, he said, are the causal consequences of associative connections from each self to temporally successive selves.

Cooper's most important philosophical contribution was his *Tracts, Ethical, Theological, and Political* (1789).[53] In a chapter, "On Identity," he first surveys the important eighteenth-century literature on personal identity, including Locke, Leibniz, Isaac Watts, Clarke, Collins, Butler, Priestley, Price, and Charles Bonnet. Cooper's own view, which he expresses all too briefly after his leisurely survey of the views of others, is, in the language of our own times, that personal identity is not what matters primarily in survival. He argued that there is no evidence that people have immaterial souls and ample evidence that all of the matter out of which they are composed is constantly in the process of being replaced, with nothing remaining constant. He thus rejected the "germ" theory of personal identity to which Watts, Priestley, and Bonnet subscribed, saying that there is no evidence that the germs exist and that even were they to exist it is likely they too would undergo constant replacement of their parts.

In Cooper's view, no one lasts even from moment to moment, let alone year to year. Rather, there is a succession of similar people, each of whom is causally dependent for its existence on its predecessors in the series. This similarity misleads people into supposing that identity is preserved, that is, that someone who will exist in the future is the very same person as someone who exists now. He concluded that personal identity is an illusion—at best a pragmatically useful notion with no adequate support in the nature of things. In response to the objection that "the man at the resurrection will, upon this system, be not the same with, but merely similar to the former," he replied that similarity, rather than identity, is the most that can be got even in this life, which no one regards of any consequence. He concluded that maintaining identity should then be of no consequence in connection with the afterlife.[54]

In response to Butler's contention that, given opinions such as Locke's and Collins's, and Cooper supposes also his own view, there would be no basis for self-concern, Cooper replies, "That as the man of to-morrow, though not in all points the same with, yet depends for his existence on the man of to-day, there is sufficient reason to care about him" in that "possessing a reminiscence of the actions of the man of to-day, and knowing that those actions will be referred to him, both by himself and others," it "cannot be indifferent to the man of to-day who looks forward to the properties of the man of to-morrow." Cooper, thus, is sensitive to the issue of what practices people will endorse in connection with personal persistence, as well as people's anticipations of "their own" futures. He said that "the approximation to identity, i.e., the high degree of similarity between the two men, is sufficient to make the one care about the other: and in fact they do so."[55]

As for morality, Cooper says, "A good man knowing that a future being, whose existence depends upon his, will therefore be punished or rewarded as the actions of the present man (whose habits and associations will be propagated) deserve, will have a sufficient motive to do right and abstain from wrong." As for prudence,

> That the man of a twelvemonth hence, or some more indefinitely long period, depending for his existence or properties on the man of to-day, is nearer to the latter considerably, with respect to the interests the latter has in him, than the children of this man of to-day, and yet the children of a person, though at the utmost only half his, furnish very strong motives to care and anxiety concerning them, and a guard upon a man's present conduct, in consideration of the effect it will have upon their future happiness.[56]

Cooper's views were discussed and rejected by Thomas Belsham, who at Hackney College would teach theology to William Hazlitt. In Belsham's *Elements of the Philosophy of Mind* (1801), which is based on his lecture notes at Hackney, he correctly summarized Cooper's view and replied that if "Cooper's hypothesis were generally admitted and acted upon, it would be very injurious to the cause of virtue: for few would be encouraged to virtue, or deterred from vice, if they had no interest in the reward or punishment consequent upon their moral conduct." Not to worry, Belsham reassured his readers, for "men are so much the creatures of habit, that the most extravagant opinions seldom produce any considerable change in their conduct. And in the present case, the conviction of permanent identity, however acquired, is so firmly fixed in the mind that it is impossible to root it out."[57] No doubt Belsham was right about its being impossible for humans to root out from their minds their commitment to the notion of personal identity. Hazlitt, who must have been aware of Belsham's criticisms of Cooper, decided to give it a go anyway.

The Roots of Egoism

William Hazlitt's (1778–1830) first work, *An Essay on the Principles of Human Action* (1805), published when he was twenty-seven years old, was the culmination of a kind of perspective on personal identity that had begun with Locke and been developed by Collins, Hume, Priestley, and Cooper.[58] Yet with respect to certain questions that would become important in our own times, Hazlitt reads more like one of our own contemporaries than any of his predecessors. He wrote that he was led to his central realizations by wondering "whether it could properly be said to be an act of virtue in anyone to sacrifice his own final happiness to that of any other person or number of persons, if it were possible for the one ever to be made the price of the other?" Suppose that one could save twenty other persons by voluntarily consenting to suffer for them. "Why," he asked, "should I not do a generous thing, and never trouble myself about what might be the consequence to myself the Lord knows when?"

On behalf of common sense, Hazlitt answered that "however insensible" he may be now to his own interest in the future, when the time comes he shall feel differently about it and "shall bitterly regret" his "folly and insensibility." So, he continued, still replying on behalf of common sense, "I ought, as a rational agent, to be determined now by what I shall then wish I had done, when I shall feel the consequences of my actions most deeply and sensibly." He was dissatisfied with this commonsense answer. He claimed that he could not "have a principle of active self-interest arising out of the immediate connection" between his "present and future self" since there neither was nor could be any such connection. "I am what I am in spite of the future," he continued. "My feelings, actions, and interests must be determined by causes already existing and acting, and are absolutely independent of the future." Where there is no "intercommunity of feelings," he concluded, "there can be no identity of interests."[59]

Hazlitt conceded that because we remember only our own past experiences and are directly "conscious" only of our own present experiences, in relation to the past and present people are naturally self-interested.[60] The reasons for this, he said, are physiological. Memories depend on physical traces of prior sensations, and these traces are not communicated among individuals. Present sensations depend on the stimulation of one's nerves, and "there is no communication between my nerves, and another's brain, by means of which he can be affected with my sensations as I am myself." In the case of the future, however, Hazlitt stressed that people are neither "mechanically" nor "exclusively" connected to themselves. They cannot be, he thought, since no one's future yet exists. Instead, people are connected both to their own futures and to the futures of others by anticipation, which unlike memory and sensation is a function of imagination and, thus, does not respect the difference between self and other.[61] He maintained that to feel future-oriented concern for someone, one first must project oneself imaginatively into the feelings of that person, and imagination, functioning "naturally," that is, independently of its having acquired a bias through learning, projects as easily into the feelings of others as into one's own future feelings.

Hazlitt no doubt exaggerated the extent to which memory is independent of imagination and underestimated our mechanical connections to our future selves. For instance, in claiming that "I am what I am in spite of the future," he ignored the possibility that future person-stages of himself are no less person-stages of himself for being future. Even so, he was right in insisting that at any given time there is a crucial difference in our relations to our past and future selves. This difference is that we are already affected by past stages of ourselves and not yet affected by future stages. For this reason, at any given time our imaginations play a greater role in linking current to future stages of ourselves than to past ones. And he may also have been right in insisting that so far as our values are concerned, past, present, and future do not have the same status or, if they do, that they come to have it in different ways. He claimed that to understand what these different ways are, one must investigate two issues that his predecessors had failed to address adequately. One of these issues is the role of the imagination in connecting us to the future generally and, in particular, to ourselves in the future; the other is the role of self-conceptions in possibly masking from ourselves salient differences between past, present, and future.

In Hazlitt's account of the role of self-conceptions in our values and in our views of our own interests, he contrasts most sharply with the eighteenth-century British tradition of which he was the culmination. According to him, people are naturally concerned about whether they are pleased or suffer as a consequence of their actions. This is because "there is something in the very idea of good, or evil, which naturally excites desire or aversion." But, he wrote, before the acquisition of self-concepts, people are indifferent about whether those who may be pleased or suffer are themselves or others: "a child first distinctly wills or pursues his own good," he said, "not because it is his but because it is good." As a consequence, he claimed, "what is personal or selfish in our affections" is due to "time and habit," the rest to "the principle of a disinterested love of good as such, or for it's own sake, without any regard to personal distinctions."[62] He claimed that such considerations provide a basis for founding morality not on self-interest, which he regarded as an "artificial" value, but on the natural concern people have to seek happiness and avoid unhappiness, regardless of whose it is.[63]

Adopting this perspective prompted Hazlitt to ask a question that did not arise as starkly or in the same form for any of his predecessors: If people connect to the future through imagination, which does not respect the difference between self and other, why is the force of habit almost invariably on the side of selfish feelings? In answering, he tried to account for the growth of selfish motives in humans by appealing to their acquisition of self-concepts. In his view, when very young children behave selfishly it is not because they like themselves better but because they know their own wants and pleasures better. In older children and adults, he thought, it is because they have come under the control of their self-concepts, which is something that happens in three stages. First, young children acquire an idea of themselves as beings who are capable of experiencing pleasure and pain. Second, and almost "mechanically" (since physiology insures that children remember only their own pasts), children include their own pasts in their notions of themselves. Finally, imaginatively, they include their own futures.[64] The first two stages may have been suggested to Hazlitt by his reading of Locke. The third, at least in the way he developed it, is original. However, even in the case of the first two, Hazlitt thought of these stages less as a philosopher and more as a psychologist might think of them, in terms of the acquisition of self-concepts, and whereas it was unclear whether Locke meant to distinguish developmental stages in the acquisition of self-concepts, Hazlitt clearly meant to do so.

In the first half of the eighteenth century, the possibility of a developmental account of the acquisition of self-concepts that Locke may have glimpsed was invisible to most of his readers. As commonsensical as the idea of this sort of psychological development may seem to us today, it did not begin to emerge in the views of eighteenth-century thinkers until the middle of the century. Hartley had a developmental, associational account of the mind, but he focused on the development of the passions and did not consider the acquisition of self-concepts. Reid, late in the century, had a developmental psychology, but because of his commitment to the immateriality of the soul and to the reflexive nature of consciousness, he may actually have made an exception in the case of the idea of self. Priestley, largely under the influence of Hartley, did think that a developmental account could be extended to the acquisition of self-concepts, but he did not elaborate. Cooper did elaborate, but his views on this issue were relatively ignored.[65]

In France, Jean-Jacques Rousseau (1712–1778), in *Emile* (1762), was sensitive to developmental concerns. In spite of everyone's possessing an immaterial soul of a Cartesian sort, he regarded infants as having only a limited awareness of their sensations and also themselves because of their bodily immaturity. Were people born with adult bodies, they would even prior to experience have a reflexive notion of their own selves.[66] Most other French thinkers of the time were not particularly concerned with the relationship between bodily or mental development and the acquisition of self-concepts. Denis Diderot (1713–1784) was an exception. Within the context of a relational account of personal identity, he claimed that small children do not think as adults do. Limited psychologically to the present and immediate past, he said, they have no way of establishing themselves as independent entities. To do that, he claimed, they would need a better sense of their remembered pasts and their anticipated futures.[67] But Diderot did not sketch the stages through which children progress on their way to a fully developed self-concept.

Hazlitt, as we have just seen, did distinguish between three developmental stages in the acquisition of self-concepts. He also claimed that to progress through all three of these stages, a child has to differentiate its own mental activities from those of others. He then raised the question of how a child's formation of self-concepts is related to its development of empathy and sympathy. No one previously had asked this question.

In Hume's emotional-contagion model of human sympathy, humans infer from external behavior, facial expressions, and the like that others are in some particular mental state. Then, the resulting idea that humans form of another's state becomes converted in their own minds into an impression, so that now they too are in the same state, though perhaps less vivaciously. In explaining how this conversion from idea to impression occurs, Hume appealed to the idea's "proximity" in one's mind to the impression one has of oneself, which he said is "so lively" that "it is not possible to imagine that any thing can in this particular go beyond it."[68] But, then he added not a word of explanation about how people acquire their super-lively self-impressions. Two decades later, Adam Smith (1723–1790), in his *Theory of Moral Sentiment* (1759), gave an unusually thorough account of the role, in sympathy, of shifts from one's own to another's point of view. Yet Smith never attempted to explain how people acquire their ideas of the distinction between self and other in the first place. Aside from the applications of his ideas to ethical theory, Smith's gaze was fixed on the importance of point of view as a feature of adult minds, not on the psychogenetics of point of view in our mental development. The closest he came to discussing the mentality of children was in his explanations of how adults sympathize with "poor wretches," children, and the dead. In his view, in so sympathizing, adults do not simply replicate the other's state of mind in their own minds but, rather, imagine what they themselves would feel if they were reduced to the other's situation but somehow allowed to keep their own current reason and judgment.

In short, whereas Smith was concerned with explaining how sympathy is possible, it did not occur to him to explain how the conceptual apparatus that makes it possible is acquired. Hazlitt, on the other hand, speculated that young children imaginatively include only their own futures and not the futures of others in their ideas of self because the "greater liveliness and force" with which they can enter into their future feelings "in a manner identifies them" with those feelings. He added that once the notion of one's own personal identity is formed, "the mind makes use of it to strengthen its habitual propensity, by giving to personal motives a reality and absolute truth which they can never have."[69] This happens, he thought, because "we have an indistinct idea of extended consciousness and a community of feelings as essential to the same thinking being," as a consequence of which we assume that whatever "interests [us] at one time must interest [us] or be capable of interesting [us] at other times."[70]

Hazlitt claimed that a bias in favor of ourselves in the future could never "have gained the assent of thinking men" but for "the force" with which a future-oriented idea of self "habitually clings to the mind of every man, binding it as with a spell, deadening its discriminating powers, and spreading the confused associations which belong only to past and present impressions over the whole of our imaginary existence." However, whereas a host of previous thinkers—Descartes, Locke, Berkeley, Butler, and others—thought that people have an intuitive knowledge of their own identities, Hazlitt rejected as "wild and absurd" the idea that we have an "absolute, metaphysical identity" with ourselves in the future, and hence that people have identities that are available to be intuited. We have been misled, he claimed, by language, by "a mere play of words." In his view, both children and adults fail to look beyond the common idioms of personal identity and as a consequence routinely mistake linguistic fictions for metaphysical realities. To say that someone has a "general interest" in whatever concerns his own future welfare "is no more," he insisted, "than affirming that [he] shall have an interest in that welfare, or that [he is] nominally and in certain other respects the same being who will hereafter have a real interest in it." No amount of mere telling "me that I have the same interest in my future sensations as if they were present, because I am the same individual," he claimed, can bridge the gulf between the "real" mechanical connections I have to myself in the past and present and the merely verbal and imaginary connections that I have to myself in the future.[71]

Since people have no mechanical connections to themselves in the future, it follows, Hazlitt thought, that so far as their "real" interests are concerned, their "selves" in the future are essentially others. If you've injured yourself, you may in the present suffer as a consequence. But "the injury that I may do to my future interest will not certainly by any kind of reaction return to punish me for my neglect of my own happiness." Rather, he concluded, "I am always free from the consequences of my actions. The interests of the being who acts, and of the being who suffers are never one." So, it makes no difference "whether [you] pursue [your] own welfare or entirely neglect it."[72] Your suffering in the future is only nominally your suffering.

Hazlitt's consideration of fission examples occurred in the context of his critique of the Lockean idea that one's identity extends as far as one's consciousness extends. What, Hazlitt asked, would a theorist committed to this idea say "if that consciousness should be transferred to some other being?" How would such a person know that he or she had not been "imposed upon by a false claim of identity?" He answered, on behalf of the Lockeans, that the idea of one's consciousness extending to someone else "is ridiculous": a person has "no other self than that which arises from this very consciousness." But, he countered, after our deaths,

> this self may be multiplied in as many different beings as the Deity may think proper to endue with the same consciousness; which if it can be so renewed at will in any one instance, may clearly be so in a hundred others. Am I to regard all these as equally myself? Am I equally interested in the fate of all? Or if I must fix upon some one of them in particular as my representative and other self, how am I to be determined in my choice? Here, then, I saw an end put to my speculations about absolute self-interest and personal identity.[73]

Thus, Hazlitt saw that, hypothetically, psychological continuity might not continue in a single stream but instead might divide. In asking the two questions— "Am I to regard all of these [fission descendants] as equally myself? Am I equally interested in the fate of all?"—he correctly separated the question of whether identity tracks psychological continuity from that of whether self-concern tracks it. And, in direct anticipation of what would not occur again to other philosophers until the 1960s, he concluded that because of the possibility of fission, neither identity nor self-concern necessarily tracks psychological continuity.

Hazlitt also used fission examples to call into question whether, in cases in which there is no fission, a person's present self-interest extends to his or her self in the future. He began by asking,

> How then can this pretended unity of consciousness which is only reflected from the past, which makes me so little acquainted with the future that I cannot even tell for a moment how long it will be continued, whether it will be entirely interrupted by or renewed in me after death, and which might be multiplied in I don't know how many different beings and prolonged by complicated sufferings without my being any the wiser for it, how I say can a principle of this sort identify my present with my future interests, and make me as much a participator in what does not at all affect me as if it were actually impressed on my senses?

Hazlitt's answer was that it cannot.

> It is plain, as this conscious being may be decompounded, entirely destroyed, renewed again, or multiplied in a great number of beings, and as, whichever of these takes place, it cannot produce the least alteration in my present being—that what I am does not depend on what I am to be, and that there is no communication between my future interests and the motives by which my present conduct must be governed.

He concluded:

> I cannot, therefore, have a principle of active self-interest arising out of the immediate connection between my present and future self, for no such connection exists, or is possible.... My personal interest in any thing must refer either to the interest excited by the actual impression of the object which cannot be felt before it exists, and can last no longer than while the impression lasts, or it may refer to the particular manner in which I am mechanically affected by the idea of my own impressions in the absence of the object. I can therefore have no proper personal interest in my future impressions.... The only reason for my preferring my future interest to that of others, must arise from my anticipating it with greater warmth of present imagination.[74]

No one, with the exception of F. H. Bradley, would take such ideas seriously again until the late 1960s. Hazlitt not only conceded but embraced and celebrated the idea that the future self is a fictional construct, which in his view had the further implication that people have no special ("self-interested") reason to value their future selves. At least to his own satisfaction, and in a way that clearly anticipated the work of Derek Parfit and others in our own times, Hazlitt tried to explain how the idea that the self is a fiction, far from being destructive to theories of rationality and ethics, actually made them better. In the process, he sowed the seeds, albeit on barren ground, of a modern psychology of the acquisition of self-concepts and of a modern approach to separating the traditional philosophical problem of personal identity from the question of what matters in survival.

Hazlitt was the last progressive figure in a more or less continuous tradition of discussion of the nature of self and personal identity that began with Locke and that took place in Britain throughout the eighteenth century. Two things were mainly responsible for interrupting this tradition of discussion. One of these was the newly emerging separation of philosophy and psychology, each of which throughout the nineteenth and increasingly into the twentieth centuries tended to go their separate ways. Another was Kant, whose *Critique of Pure Reason* had been published, in German, in 1781, but only began to be felt seriously in Britain at the beginning of the nineteenth century. However, once Kant's influence was felt, it effectively changed the focus of debate about the self.

X

PHILOSOPHY OF SPIRIT

Immanuel Kant (1724–1804) was the most influential philosopher of the modern era and one of the most influential of all time. His views on every topic that he considered, and on metaphysics, epistemology, ethics, and aesthetics especially, set the stage for virtually all subsequent philosophical discussions. In addition, he is often credited with creating the rationale for modern political liberalism, with its commitment to the equal dignity of all human beings. Along the way, he spawned a view of the self that has been a major focus of criticism for a large family of twentieth century cultural theorists, including postmodernists, deconstructionists, feminists, postcolonialists, and ethnic-identity theorists.

Kant published his most important work toward the end of the eighteenth century. As the culmination of Enlightenment thought, he was the right person, at the right time, with the right message. Just as the rationalist and empiricist tendencies in European thought had played themselves out, though in an unsatisfying way that on the rationalist side led to dogmatism and on the empiricist to skepticism, Kant broke the impasse, seemingly synthesizing the best in both traditions. But his synthesis, rather than a compromise, was a bold new initiative, full of novel and suggestive ideas, one of which was that by restricting the scope of reason, he safeguarded faith. An area in which he took himself to have done this successfully is his theory of the self. Whether these various views of his actually were successful is debatable; that they were extremely influential is not.

Without question, Kant was an unusually deep thinker. His extraordinary influence has been due not only to his views but to his having driven the discussion in many central areas of philosophy to levels of profundity hitherto unknown.

Ironically, his influence may have been augmented by puzzlement on the part of those who would interpret his views as to exactly what he meant. While it is hard to read Kant and not believe that he was up to something important, often it is equally hard to be sure what that something was. Nowhere is this truer than in his views of the self, which included his thoughts on the soul, his theory of the noumenal self, his remarks on personal identity over time, his thoughts on the role of self-conceptions in the unity of consciousness (which, borrowing from Leibniz, he called *the transcendental unity of apperception*), and, perhaps most importantly, his view, which he took to be a corollary of his ethical theory, that the self is a source of autonomous agency and meaning.

Kant maintained that in order for us to account for certain features of some judgments, in particular for the universality of so-called synthetic a priori judgments, such as the truths of geometry, we have to suppose that our knowledge of reality is limited to the realm of actual and possible experiences. He called this realm *the phenomenal world*. Not included in it are God, freedom, and immortality, the latter two of which directly implicate the self. In Kant's view, the idea of each of these is meaningful, and even necessary for certain practical purposes, mainly having to do with morality. But, he claimed, we cannot *know* that any of these three ideas corresponds to anything real. He held that the notion of the noumenal self is useful as a *regulative idea*. That is, it is useful as an idea that we need to suppose is true for certain practical purposes, including giving us a motive to be moral. He argued that we are obligated to act morally and that it makes sense to act morally only if we will live forever. So, even though we cannot *know* that there is any reality to the regulative idea of such a self and cannot prove the immortality of the soul, we cannot *act* as if there were no reality to it. Hence, the immaterial substance survives in Kant's view not as something that we can know to exist but as something that we need to assume exists.

Kant's theory of the noumenal world, which is key to his project of making a secure place both for knowledge and for faith, has implications for his theory of the soul. The basic idea behind his theory of the noumenal world is that reality as it is in itself—the noumenal world—is radically different from reality as it is represented in our experience—the phenomenal world. The difference between these two worlds—or, alternatively, between these two visions of the one and only world—is due to how humans structure the objects of their experience in basic ways that do not reflect the intrinsic nature of objects as they are in themselves. In other words, the human mind does not merely receive simple ideas of sensation, as Locke had suggested, but, in the process of receiving them, structures them. Thus, the mind, in sensation, is not merely passive, a tabula rasa (blank tablet) on which experience writes, but active. Spatial and temporal relationships are a fundamental part of this human structuring of experience. The world as it exists in itself—the noumenal world—is neither spatially nor temporally extended, whereas the world of our experience—the phenomenal world—is both.

In one interpretation of Kant's view, there is a phenomenal self that is experienced and a noumenal self that is never experienced. The latter lacks spatial and temporal extension. The phenomenal self is capable of being experienced either subjectively or objectively or both. It is extended temporally and perhaps also spatially. In another interpretation of what Kant meant, there is only one self that is capable of being considered either noumenally or phenomenally. In either of these interpretations of his view, the task of accounting for the phenomenal self is no different in principle from that of accounting for any other object or event that exists in space and time, such as planets or atoms. Thus, the phenomenal self is part of the subject matter of what today we would call the science of *psychology*. However, there is no *knowing* the noumenal self—or no knowing the self noumenally—since the noumenal self is outside of the framework of space and time. Even so, in Kant's view, the noumenal self affects the way the phenomenal self is structured in experience.[1]

So far as personal identity itself is concerned, Kant noted, following Locke, that were our identities to reside in spiritual substances, we would have no way of knowing who was identical with whom—this because over any given span of time we would have no way of knowing whether a single immaterial substance or a series of such substances had been associated with a given human being.[2] So, if personal identity were to depend on sameness of immaterial substance, then we would have no way of knowing empirically whether anyone in the present is the same as anyone who existed previously.

How then can personal identity over time be known? Locke thought that it could be known empirically if it consists in sameness of consciousness. Kant disagreed. He thought that someone's consciousness might now be qualitatively exactly similar to that of someone *else's* consciousness. Delusions of memory, which Locke acknowledged may occur, are an obvious case in point. Kant concluded that if personal identity is to be known, it cannot consist in sameness of consciousness. Rather, it must consist, at least in part, in some sort of physical continuity. Kant thus postulated a more objective criterion of personal identity than had Locke. In sum, whereas Locke and Kant both have a relational, rather than a substance, view of personal identity over time, for Locke the relations that matter are wholly psychological, while for Kant they are at least partly physical. In Kant's view, the requirement that the self be partly physical applies only to the phenomenal self, or as he sometimes called it, *the empirical self*. It does not apply to the noumenal self, which exists beyond the reach of any possible experience.

In what is perhaps the most intriguing dimension of Kant's reflections on the self, the so-called transcendental unity of apperception, he maintained that accompanying each experience is an "I think," which is the logical subject of the experience. In his view, there can be no experience that is not the experience of a subject. To this extent he may seem to have been saying simply that thought requires a thinker, which is more or less the move that Descartes made in attempting to prove the existence of a substantial self. The difference, however, is that by *thinker* Kant does not mean a substantial self but something more intimately connected with experience. He tried to explain what this "something" is by saying that "in the synthetic original unity of apperception, I am conscious of myself, not as I appear to myself, nor as I am in myself, but only that I am. This *representation* is a *thought*, not an *intuition*."³ What Kant meant by these dark remarks is a matter of scholarly dispute.

To explain one thing that Kant may have meant by them, we are going to introduce the notion of an *intentional* object, which we will then use in our explanation of Kant's view, even though Kant in this context did not himself employ the notion of an intentional object. The intentional object of a thought has to do with its *aboutness*. That is, even though every thought exists as an item in the world—a particular pattern of neural activity, perhaps—it is also *about* something. The technical name for the thing that a thought is about is its *intentional object*. So, for instance, if you were to think the thought that there is dog food in Fido's bowl, the thought itself might be a pattern of neural activity in your brain, but the intentional object of the thought would not be that neural activity but *that* there is dog food in Fido's bowl. Unlike the pattern of neural activity, the intentional object is not a real object in the world. That there is dog food in Fido's bowl would remain the intentional object of your thought whether or not there actually is dog food in Fido's bowl, whether or not Fido has a bowl, and even whether or not Fido exists. In other words, you can have a thought about something even if what you think is false, indeed even if the supposed object about which you have the thought does not exist. Yet, for your thought to even be a thought, it has to be about something, that is, it has to have an intentional object. In other words, a putative thought without an intentional object would not even be a thought.

By analogy, we want now to suggest, what is central to Kant's doctrine of the transcendental unity of apperception is that in addition to each thought's having an intentional object, it also has an *intentional subject*, that is, someone whose thought it is. Yet, just as a thought can exist without an actual object corresponding to its intentional object, a thought can exist without an actual subject corresponding to its intentional subject. In a nutshell, what Kant seems to be saying is that in order for thoughts to be thoughts, they have to be both unified and about something. Their intentional subject—what Kant calls *the transcendental ego*—is what unifies them. Their intentional object is what they are about. But neither what unifies them nor what they are about actually has to exist apart from the thought, or, as Kant might have put it, neither has to exist except as a "formal property" of the thought.

A puzzle about Kant's view is that unifying is a causal process. So, to say, as we just have, that the self *causes* the unification of thoughts suggests that the self is something *distinct* from the thoughts. On the other hand, if Kant denies that it is distinct, his only alternative would seem to be to claim that the self consists merely in the fact that the thoughts are unified. But if the self were to consist merely in the fact that certain thoughts are unified, how could the self cause those thoughts to be unified? Some philosophers have supposed that what Kant was really saying is that there has to be an organizational principle in virtue of which thoughts are unified in order for them to constitute a coherent whole. Arguably such an organizational principle may be internal to the thoughts themselves. If that were so, it would be a *necessary* element of coherent thought, without being an *extra* element. It would not be a cause of the thoughts being unified, but neither would it consist merely in the fact that the thoughts are unified. It would be the organizational principle by virtue of which the thoughts are unified.[4]

Before Kant, some philosophers, such as Descartes, had tried to infer from the supposed fact that I am the subject of my thoughts the conclusion that I am a thinking substance. Other philosophers, such as Hume in his more skeptical moments, had suggested that thoughts might exist without a subject who thinks them. The former sort of philosopher often went on to infer (mistakenly) that since one cannot be sure that physical objects exist but can be sure that the self exists, then the self cannot be a physical object, in which case it must be a simple, noncomposite, immaterial substance and, hence, naturally immortal. A problem, from Kant's point of view, with such inferences is that they attempt to infer from a premise that is merely "analytically" true a conclusion that, if it's true at all, is "synthetically" true; that is, they attempt to infer from something like a definition some substantive truth about the world. He remarked that "it would indeed be surprising if what in other cases requires so much labor to determine ... should be thus given me directly as if by revelation in the poorest of all representations."[5]

Although this much of Kant's view, while abstract and perhaps overly speculative, may seem clear enough, real problems arise as soon as one starts to ask more searching questions. One such question is, what is the connection of the noumenal self, or selves, with each of us? Part of what makes this such a difficult question is that when Kant says that in the act of experiencing, the human mind contributes spatial and temporal relations to a source of experience that is not itself extended spatially or temporally, he cannot mean literally that the *human mind* does that, for the human mind already is temporally and probably also spatially extended. In other words, the human mind cannot be the mental source of the structuring since it is part of the output or product of the structuring. What, then, is the mental source of the structuring? Presumably, the noumenal self, or noumenal selves. But what is this self like?

If the noumenal self is neither spatially nor temporally extended, it is difficult to understand what it might be like or to see how there could be many noumenal selves, say, one for each human being. What could the difference between different noumenal selves consist in? This problem is analogous to that which was faced by Christian philosophers, such as Aquinas, who wanted to say that there are many incorporeal angels even though matter is the principle of individuation. In such a view, it is difficult to see what could distinguish two nonmaterial angels. In Kant's view, it is difficult to see what could distinguish two noumenal selves. The difficulty is not due to matter being the principle of individuation but to the fact that noumenal selves, assuming there are more than one, are neither spatially nor temporally extended.

A closely related problem is that, in Kant's view, one of the ways in which the mind structures objects of experience when it thinks about them is by subsuming them under the category of quantity, that is, the category of one, more than one, and so on. In his view, this quantitative aspect of "reality" is like spatial and temporal relations in that it is not something that can be known to be a feature of things in themselves but only of things as they enter into human cognition, this time as objects of thought. But if we cannot know that the category of quantity even applies to things in themselves, then how could we possibly know that there is more than one noumenal self, or for that matter that there is more than one thing-in-itself? The answer, which Kant never acknowledged, has to be that we could not know this. Later philosophers did acknowledge this answer. Schopenhauer, for instance, retained Kant's notion of the thing-in-itself but carefully used the singular, rather than the plural, when referring to it.[6]

A similar problem arises with the concept of causality. Kant says that things in themselves "produce" our experiences, but, in his view, we cannot validly apply the concept of causation to acquire knowledge of things in themselves. So, in saying that things in themselves "produce" experiences, if he is not contradicting himself, then either he is just reporting the results of his speculative reveries or he is understanding the notion of "produce" noncausally (but what then could "produce" possibly mean?). Problems such as these are partly what motivated the post-Kantian German idealists, beginning with Fichte and ending with Hegel, to jettison the noumenal world.

Despite such problems, among Kant's contemporaries his distinction between the noumenal and phenomenal world sometimes had a wholesome effect. A case in point is Karl C. E. Schmid (1761–1812), who, in the second edition of his *Empirical Psychology* (1796), followed Kant in setting strict methodological limits to empirical psychology. Schmid relegated all questions about the substantiality, simplicity, or immutability of the soul, including any about its causal relationship to the body, beyond these limits, in a domain he called "dogmatic metaphysics."[7]

In addition to Kant's response to a tradition of thought about the self that began in Britain with Locke and Hume, there is another side to his thoughts about the self. This other side, which has to do with the self as a source of autonomous agency and meaning, is his response to a tradition that began in France. To understand the influence of this other tradition on Kant's thinking, it will be helpful to briefly revisit an earlier tradition of romanticism.

French Romanticism

Jean-Jacques Rousseau (1712–1778) was for Kant an object of dangerous fascination. A model of obsessively routine punctuality, Kant is said to have blinked just once, on the day that he came into possession of a copy of Rousseau's *Emile* (1762). He became so absorbed in reading *Emile* that he forgot to take his daily walk. Later, Kant wrote that before reading Rousseau, he had "despised the common man who knows nothing." After reading Rousseau: "This blind prejudice vanished: I learned to respect human nature." But Kant's respect did not erase his distrust of romantic enthusiasm: "I must read Rousseau until his beauty of expression no longer distracts me," for "only then can I survey him with reason."[8] Nevertheless Kant's fascination with Rousseau was such that in Kant's purposefully austere study, otherwise undecorated, there was on the wall just one ornament: a portrait of Rousseau.

Rousseau was the greatest of the modern romantics. As much as Montaigne, he was an apostle of subjective feeling. Subsequent to Rousseau, especially in Germany, romanticism regathered its strength to erupt again, with unprecedented force and splendor both in poetry and in philosophy. However, before this would happen, there would be, in Kant's metaphysics, an immersion in philosophical theory more complete, more penetrating, and more abstract than anything the world had previously known. And there would be, in Kant's practical and moral philosophy, the most powerful expression of classical liberalism. Yet there is a tension at the heart of Kant's celebration of liberalism that derives from the contrast between his emphasis on what all rational beings have in common and Rousseau's emphasis on individuality. This tension would exercise a continuing influence on thought about the self throughout the nineteenth and twentieth centuries.

At the age of fifty-three, Rousseau, in his *Confessions* (written 1765–70), had turned to autobiographical reflection. Ten years later, during the last two years of his emotionally turbulent life, he began his *Reveries of the Solitary Walker* (written 1776–78) by returning to a theme that had been the central issue in his intellectual life—the clash between the innocent, morally pure individual in isolation from society and the inhuman, alienating, and corrupting influence of society:

> Now I am alone in the world, with no brother, neighbor or friend, nor any company left me but my own.... I would have loved my fellow-men in spite of themselves. It was only by ceasing to be human that they could forfeit my affection.... But I, detached as I am from them and from the whole world, what am I? This must now be the object of my inquiry.[9]

Rousseau gave two heartfelt answers to this question.

One of these grew out of his reflection on a time in his youth when he met Madame de Warens and first tasted the freedom and bondage of satisfying his deepest desires. "She was twenty-eight," he related, and "I was not yet seventeen." During those few years, "I was myself, completely myself, unmixed and unimpeded." Only then, he continued, when "I lived only for her, and my whole life was in hers," can I "genuinely claim to have lived."

> Loved by a gentle and indulgent woman, I did what I wanted, I was what I wanted, and by the use I made of my hours of leisure ... , I succeeded in imparting to my still simple and naive soul the form which best suited it and which it has retained ever since.... I needed a female friend after my own heart, and I had one. I had longed for the country, and my wish was granted. I could not bear subjection, and I was perfectly free, or better than free because I was subject only to my own affections and did only what I wanted to do. All my hours were filled with loving cares and country pursuits. I wanted nothing except that such a sweet state should never cease.[10]

But it did cease. And when it ceased the dominant motif of Rousseau's social world turned from love to cruelty.

More than forty years later, Rousseau discovered himself again, but this time he discovered a more spiritual self. It happened, over a period of several months, on the island of Saint-Pierre, to which Rousseau had fled following the stoning of his house by his neighbors in the village of Môtiers. There, the Protestant minister, Montmollin, who had earlier tried unsuccessfully to have Rousseau excommunicated, provoked Rousseau's neighbors into hateful violence. Safe again, in a tranquil new setting, Rousseau rediscovered peace:

> But if there is a state where the soul can find a resting place secure enough to establish itself and concentrate its entire being there, with no need to remember the past or reach into the future, where time is nothing to it, where the present runs on indefinitely, but this duration goes unnoticed, with no sign of the passing of time, and no other feeling of depravation or enjoyment, pleasure or pain, desire or fear, than the simple feeling of existence, a feeling that fills our soul entirely, as long as this state lasts, we can call ourselves happy, not with a poor, incomplete and relative happiness, such as we find in the pleasures of life, but with a sufficient, complete and perfect happiness which leaves no emptiness to be filled in the soul.[11]

In his youth, Rousseau sought his identity not in abstract philosophical theories but in revelations born of the fulfillment of wild, passionate desires. In his maturity, he rediscovered his identity in the spiritual serenity of release from desire, a state born of total absorption in the present.

Rousseau brought to his experience an unshakeable faith both in God's existence and in the immortality of his soul—in spite of his inclination to get his ideas from his experience rather than interpreting his experience in terms of ideas. As a philosophical backdrop for his faith, he seems to have presupposed that the soul is a Cartesian spiritual substance to which things happen without its thereby being changed in any way, other than its remembering what happened. Rousseau thought that remembering one's life before bodily death is necessary if survival of bodily death is to have any value. He also insisted that humans are responsible for everything they do. The mind can free itself from both dependence on the past and sensation in the present. He thought that the inner certainty of the existence of such a self undergirds ethics, which in turn tends to support belief in God, the only completely free being in the universe.

Wherever Rousseau got such convictions, in the part of his thought that was most influential on Kant and the subsequent tradition, he wedded his convictions to his trust in subjectivity and distrust of cultural elaboration. In practice, this took the form of his regarding the frail voice of conscience in him as the word of

God, a source of moral authority that overrode both Scripture and philosophical theory. Kant too would hear such a voice, but whereas for Rousseau it emanated from his inner self, in Kant it emanated from reason.

So far as theories of the self and personal identity, narrowly construed, are concerned, Rousseau influenced the tradition not in his thinking of the self metaphysically along Cartesian lines, but in his quasi-ethical conceptions—in particular, in his thinking of the self, first, as uniquely individual, second, as the innocent source of human benevolence and, third, as something that stands in a reciprocal relationship with a corrupting society. In Hobbes, man in a state of nature is a brute, motivated to enter into community with society, which is a civilizing influence, solely by considerations of self-preservation. Rousseau tamed Hobbes's brute: "Savage man," he wrote, "is at peace with nature, and the friend of all his fellow creatures." However:

> The case is quite different with man in the state of society, for whom first necessities have to be provided, and then superfluities; delicacies follow next, then immense wealth, then subjects, then slaves. He enjoys not a moment's relaxation; and what is yet stranger, the less natural and pressing his wants, the more headstrong are his passions, and still worse, the more he has it in his power to gratify them; so that after a long course of prosperity, after having swallowed up treasures and ruined multitudes, the hero ends up by cutting every throat until he finds himself, at last, sole master of the world. Such is in miniature the moral picture, if not of human life, at least of the secret aspirations in the heart of every civilized man.[12]

Yet, Rousseau reasoned, all of us have been socialized, not just the man of wealth and privilege. So no matter how strenuously we try to recover our pristine innocence, it is gone. We are already the product of a reciprocal dialogue between individual and society.

The socialized self, already lurking furtively in the shadows of Montaigne's essays, is in Rousseau's writing brought into full view. This idea, stripped of its romantic nostalgia, was developed particularly by post-Kantian German philosophers so as to give birth to a conception of the self as a social entity, an idea that contrasted sharply with the atomistic, encapsulated, and possessive individualism of theories of the self from Descartes to the end of the eighteenth century. Yet, unlike Rousseau, the German romantics sought a socialized self that is edifying. But before these developments could unfold, Kant had to set the stage.

The ethical dimension of Kant's view of the self marks the final transition from the ideology of premodern, aristocratic societies, in which the highest value is honor, to modern societies, in which values are more democratic. Making this transition required the collapse of social hierarchies, the traditional basis for honor. It also required a new articulation of the equal dignity of all human beings. Kant would be the source and spokesperson for this basic tenet of liberalism.

In Kant's view of human nature, the inherent equality of every human person is paramount. Theoretically, in a society based on Kant's notion of equality, the innate, inalienable dignity of every human person would be recognized. However, what Kant failed to take into account, and this is where Rousseau enters the picture, is that each human being is not just equal, but unique. That is, for each individual, there is a certain way of being human that is specifically his or her own way. In this romantic view, an important part of the point of life is to be true to oneself. In Kant's distillation of pure reason, there is no place for the celebration of difference.

The inherently irresolvable tensions between these conflicting views of human nature is central to modern liberalism. According to many postmodern critics of Kant, an overemphasis on the equal dignity of all human beings obscured Kant's recognition of the value in what distinguishes individuals and groups from one another. For some of those, like Kant, who see value in everyone, including the members of marginalized groups, it is what people—*everyone*—has in common that is important, not what distinguishes people from each other. But in the view of individuals and groups who have been overlooked and marginalized, this humanistic celebration of equality leaves what is distinctively valuable about *them* unacknowledged. If they were not different, they say, they would not have been marginalized in the first place. Kantians, of course, would not approve of any group's being marginalized, but neither—as Kantians—would they celebrate any group's differences. So, if the members of marginalized groups, and those sympathetic to their cause, do not themselves celebrate their differences, it seems that no one will. Hence, *the politics of difference*.

German and English Romanticism

In his *Critique of Pure Reason*, Kant crafted his philosophy of self largely as a response to Hume. Even so, he agreed with Hume's opposition to speculative metaphysics, which both men regarded as a pretension of reason. But whereas Hume opposed metaphysics on the grounds of a general skepticism that extended even to science and merely probable knowledge, Kant emphasized that knowledge in science is not only possible but includes, at its core, beliefs that are absolutely certain. He thus saw his own view as a way of transcending Humean skepticism and repositioning the knowledge enterprise on foundations too weak for speculative metaphysics but strong enough to support science.

Ironically, those German philosophers who followed immediately in Kant's wake and were among his most ardent admirers reinstated the spirit of speculative metaphysics that both Hume and Kant had tried so hard to vanquish. These German romantics, as they were called, partly under the influence of Rousseau, celebrated subjectivity and the empirical self. They also left behind the Enlightenment preoccupation with science and put in its place a newfound appreciation of religion. In the world according to post-Kantian German romanticism, Reality, rather than a stream of impressions or even a structured phenomenal world, is nothing so much as a cosmic Self. Yet, in spite of themselves, these thinkers contributed to the scientific investigation of consciousness. They did this by eliminating some of the tensions in Kant's two-worlds view and insisting on what they took to be the harmonious systematization of what remained. Unfortunately what remained was not always capable of being harmoniously systematized. Nevertheless, as a happy byproduct of their attempts to systematize it, they substituted for the extreme atomism of eighteenth-century British and French accounts of the self a heightened appreciation of its social dimensions.

Johann Wolfgang von Goethe (1749–1832), who was primarily a poet and playwright rather than a philosopher, conveyed the romanticism of Rousseau to the German-speaking world, in the process animating it with the spirit of *Sturm und Drang* (storm and stress). His *Sorrows of Young Werther* (1774), in which he expressed his philosophy of life, was so emotionally wrenching that its publication, in Germany, precipitated an epidemic of suicides. Central to Goethe's message was his view that humans are hopelessly alone in an immense universe of opposing forces: life and death, light and dark, love and hate. Amid these forces, torn by the stresses of life, some humans may not find themselves at all. But those who do, find themselves only in their own activities, which, so far as value is concerned, are everything. There is no goal of life beyond the mere living of it, which through love and passion may lead to an expansive personal evolution.

Friedrich von Schiller (1759–1805), Goethe's best friend, was also primarily a poet and playwright. Yet, as one of the first important thinkers to be profoundly influenced by Kant, in his person he bridged the gap between the Enlightenment (Kant) and romanticism (Goethe). To some extent he also bridged this gap in his views, which highlighted the romantic quest for a harmonious integration of the self. However, in Schiller, the motivations for this quest are less individualistic and introspective than they are social and historical. Like Rousseau, he stressed the idea that the rise of civilization had fragmented the individual.

However, unlike Rousseau, he claimed that the main cause of this fragmentation was the extraordinary "increase of empirical knowledge, and the more exact modes of thought." These, he claimed, had produced "sharper divisions between the sciences" and "a more rigorous separation of ranks and occupations."[13] Still, there might be a cure. In society as a whole, the cure would spring from art, particularly the contribution that "aesthetic education" could make to a happier, more humane social order. In individuals, the cure would consist in an inward freedom of the soul that enabled people to achieve wholeness and harmony in the midst of internal and external conflict.

Although Kant and his German followers would eventually have an enormous impact on philosophy in the English-speaking world, it would take time because of the density of Kant's thought and the difficulty of translating it into English. However, some German philosophy would fairly quickly make its way into England. The conduit for this influence was Samuel Taylor Coleridge (1772–1834), the leading intellectual of English romanticism. In his autobiographical work *Biographia Literaria* (1817), which would become standard reading at English-speaking universities throughout the nineteenth century, Coleridge desperately tried to maintain his belief in an immortal soul while also keeping up with advances in science, including the science of human nature. In struggling with the question of how the self, which is free, could possibly fit into a mechanically determined natural world, he remarked that in the mechanistic view of Hartley and Priestley, his words "may be as truly said to be written by" the universe as by himself, for "the whole universe co-operates to produce the minutest stroke of every letter, save only that I myself, and I alone, have nothing to do with it, but merely the causeless and *effectless* beholding of it when it is done." But, he continued, it is too much even to call it "a beholding; for it is neither an act nor an effect; but an impossible creation of a *something-nothing* out of its very contrary! It is a mere quick-silver plating behind a looking-glass; and in this alone consists the poor worthless I!"[14] Yet, this I, he insisted, in contradiction to this fatalistic picture, "is essentially vital, even as all objects (as objects) are essentially fixed and dead."[15]

In trying to explain this vital essence, Coleridge distinguished three levels of self-consciousness. The first is that of "those who exist to themselves only in moments"; the second that of "those who are conscious of *a* continuousness" but are unable to think about it. Both of these levels can be attributed to animals. The third level is that of "those who tho' not conscious of the whole of their continuousness, are yet conscious of *a* continuousness, and make that the object of a reflex consciousness." Coleridge said that "of this third Class the Species are infinite; and the first and lowest, as far as we know, is Man, or the human Soul."[16]

In Coleridge's only recently published *Opus Maximum*, he explains his main ideas on the origins of self-consciousness:

> The first dawnings of a baby's humanity will break forth in the Eye that connects the Mother's face with the warmth of the mother's bosom, the support of the mother's Arms. A thousand tender kisses excite a finer life in its lips, and there first language is imitated from the mother's smiles. Ere yet a conscious self exists, the love begins; and the first love is love of another. The Babe acknowledges a self in the Mother's form years before it can recognize a self in its own.[17]

This observation by Coleridge, that the first understanding of a self comes not from immediate reflection on one's own mind but on the personality exhibited in the loving face of the mother, is one of the earliest expressions of the view that self-consciousness follows the discovery of self *in the other*. In the 1890s, James Baldwin, the father of developmental psychology, would make this idea the cornerstone of his own theories.

Coleridge also considered how an infant, through emotional deprivation and attention to mere objects, rather than through interaction with its mother, might become an object to itself. With the loving mother there, the infant enters into an "I-thou" rather than an "I-it" relationship and comes to know itself as an "I-am." Coleridge relates how his own three-year-old child awoke during the night, pleading to his mother, "Touch me, only touch me with your finger." Why? the mother asked. "I am not here, touch me, Mother so that I may be here."[18] Subsequently, the child moves on from requiring the mother to affirm his own existence: "It becomes a person; it is and speaks of itself as "I," and from that moment it has acquired what, in the following stages it may quarrel with, what it may loosen and deform, but can never eradicate—a sense of an alterity in itself, which no eye can see, neither his own nor others."[19]

Having thus provided a remarkably modern explanation of the social origins of self-consciousness, Coleridge found the basis of human personality and self-consciousness in the powers of reason and will. These, he claimed, distinguish humans from beasts and, at personality's highest level, bring us closest to God, or the infinite I Am, the ultimate source and ground of all self-consciousness and personality. In developing this theory, he followed in the footsteps of Kant and the German idealists but also provided a developmental account of pathologies of the self as well as of healthy development. According to this account, some, by becoming alienated from their higher selves through emotional deprivation early in life, are turned downward to an animal nature, while others, through love in the first instance and most importantly between infant and mother, are raised to their highest nature.

Absolute Idealism

Johann Fichte (1762–1814), a professor of philosophy first at Jena and then at Berlin, taught that the goal of philosophy is "the clarification of consciousness." He denied the existence of the noumenal world and also resolved what he took to be a tension in Kant between the theoretical and the practical in favor of the latter, which for him was supreme. He hoped to show that the clarification of consciousness involves, at its core, acknowledging the supreme importance of the self. He distinguished the self from a substantial soul, which he vehemently rejected as "a bad invention." Rather, the self is pure spiritual activity, free from divisions and limitations. In this activity, oppositions between subject and object, action and result, do not exist. However, one cannot know this activity directly, through introspection, but only through reflection and abstraction. The human will is free. Its freedom, he claimed, settles once and for all the question of whether there can be a science of psychology: there cannot. Instead, the mind can know itself by reflecting on itself and deducing the terms of its unity. It is, he thought, because the truth about the self—that it is free, unfettered, and purely active—is so difficult and unsettling that people are drawn to thinking of them-selves as objects, whether spiritual or material. This idea would resonate in the next century in the thoughts of Heidegger and Sartre.

Like Hume before him and John Stuart Mill after, Fichte, by analyzing con-sciousness, hoped to achieve a "science of all sciences" and the "absolute" basis of all knowledge. He also hoped to show how speculative and practical reason are not disparate faculties, as they had been for Kant, but two interrelated activities of a self-posited subject of consciousness. But how, in Fichte's view, does this subject of consciousness arise? His answer is that it posits itself: "The I is what it itself posits, and it is nothing else but this." In explaining what he meant, Fichte shifted from talk of the I to talk of the concept of the I, and from talk of thought to talk of action: "The concept of the I arises through my own act of self-positing, by virtue of the fact that I act in a way that reverts back upon myself."[20]

Fichte elaborated that in *thinking* about an object—a wall, for instance—"the freely thinking subject, forgets about itself and pays no attention to its own free activity"; in thinking, one "disappears into the object."[21] However, in acting, including in the act of thinking, there is an aspect of consciousness that always at least involves self-awareness and self-positing.[22] That is, although one may in thinking about the wall mentally "disappear into the object," in acting with regard to it, there is a self-posited I distinct from the wall. In other words, just as Kant had claimed that accompanying every *thought* is an "I think," Fichte claimed that accompanying every *action* is an "I think." However, whereas in Kant, the "I think" is a logical presupposition of thought but not something that necessarily involves self-awareness, in Fichte, the "I think" does involve self-awareness. What is confusing, though, is that in Fichte, the self-awareness seems to be the product of a retrospective positing; what comes after seems to determine the nature of what came before.[23] How exactly this happens is a mystery that Fichte does little to explain. What is not mysterious, though, and seems a genuine advance, is that Fichte turned a spotlight onto the self-referential dimension of self-awareness, which he regarded as a developmental phenomenon. This aspect of his thought, together with Kant's earlier ruminations on the transcendental unity of apperception, originated the kind of phenomenology that would later come into fruition in Husserl.

There is another aspect of Fichte's thought that would also bear fruit later. In his basic scheme, he distinguished fundamentally between "I" and "not-I." I is the self-posited, the creative source of everything. It does not have a *nature*. Not-I is the world. It does have a nature. However, part of what the world contains is an *objective self*, which is different from the original I in having a nature, which is itself determined through subjective choice. In freely choosing, he said, we determine *our own natures* as rational beings: "A free being must exist before it is determined—it must have an existence independent of its determinacy."[24] Essence comes later. Everyone creates his own essence through acting freely. Thus, our existence as subjects precedes our self-determination as objective selves in the world. In other words, existence precedes essence.

In his later work, Fichte defined God as infinite moral will which becomes conscious of itself in individuals. He declared that the knowledge and love of God, which requires the knowledge and love of self, is the goal of human life. In Fichte's view, God is everything and undivided. The world, which is illusory and merely seems to consist of separate objects, is produced by thought. What we call *human knowledge* is thus a distorted picture of infinite, undivided, pure activity. The point of human life, in the context of time, is to see through the distortions and realize complete spiritual freedom.

F. W. J. von Schelling (1775–1854) was, at age fifteen, admitted to the theological seminary in Tübingen, where he became captivated by the philosophies of Kant, Fichte, and Spinoza. At age nineteen, he began writing philosophy, the core of which was his account of the Absolute, which he took to be not only an eternal, timeless ego but the real ego of each individual human. Schelling maintained that the Absolute can be apprehended only in a direct, intellectual, as opposed to sensory, intuition. Later, he decided that Fichte had erred in giving an inadequate account of nature, which Schelling claimed exhibits active development toward spirit. He saw precursors of this spirit in such natural phenomena as light, gravity, magnetism, and electricity, but especially in organisms that unconsciously unify their parts into a harmonious whole. Schelling's objective became to integrate this new developmental view of nature into what was basically Fichte's philosophy. Schelling believed that this required a bridge between nature and spirit. He found the bridge he was looking for in artistic creation, in which the natural, which is unconscious, and the spiritual, which is conscious, become one. He then tried to show that in all beings, not just in artistic creation, the Absolute expresses itself as the unity of the subjective and the objective. Subsequently, he retired into relative inactivity until his wife's death, in 1809, provoked a religious turn in his thought. This led him to write a book on immortality, according to which God, in becoming self-conscious, projects ideas of himself, thereby creating the world.

Georg Wilhelm Friedrich Hegel (1770–1831), who was Fichte's successor at the University of Berlin, claimed that the point of philosophy is to discover the place of reason in the world. That place, he thought, is not only central but constitutive: "the rational is the real." Hegel reified reason as the Absolute, which he said was dynamic, developing over time. He called the development of the Absolute *the dialectical process*. In his view of this process, reason itself is not eternal but "historical." By its being historical, he meant that its manifestations at many levels of culture and social life evolve over time. He thereby gave new meaning and relevance to human history. With the notable exceptions of G. B. Vico (1668–1744), J. G. Herder (1744–1803), and Kant, other modern philosophers writing before Hegel had tended to neglect history.

Hegel's stress on the two themes of reason and history is what is most distinctive and original in his philosophy. Much of the rest is derivative, especially from Rousseau, Kant, Fichte, and Schelling, the latter of whom complained that Hegel had become famous by stealing his ideas (Schelling and the poet Hölderlin were Hegel's college roommates at Tübingen). Whatever the truth in this accusation, in Hegel's view the Absolute or *world-spirit*, is embedded in the progressive evolution of human life and culture, stages of which are its unfolding as it moves toward its goal of complete self-realization. In each stage, he elaborated, there are certain facts of human psychology (habit, appetite, judgment) that reveal the progress of *subjective spirit*; there are certain laws, social arrangements, and political institutions (the family, civil society, the state) that reveal the progress of *objective spirit*; and art, religion, and philosophy reveal the progress of *absolute spirit*.

According to Hegel, in the development of the Absolute, movement from one stage to another involves intense struggle. Thus, what began in post-Kantian idealism as an all but static metaphysics of the Absolute became in Hegel a dynamic philosophy of human culture.

For present purposes, the most important and also most novel aspect of Hegel's view is his emphasis on the social aspect of reality. This emphasis shows up at the higher levels of world history, and at these levels even acquires an ominous tone, for instance, in his elevating the universal and social over the individual with the remark that in his own time, the "mere individual aspect has become, as it should be, a matter of indifference."[25] But Hegel's emphasis on the social also shows up in other ways, such as in his insistence that because an embryo lacks social relationships it is not yet human, and in his analysis of lower-level phenomena of consciousness.

One of the most innovative and consequential of Hegel's analyses of the relations between the individual and the social is his famous account, in *Phenomenology of Spirit*, of the master-slave relationship.[26] In this account, he bypasses the traditional problem of solipsism by simply taking it for granted that others exist and are known. He argues that self-consciousness realizes itself only through the recognition of others, that self and other develop interactively, and that while interpersonal harmony is possible, it must be preceded by a period of domination and struggle. Specifically, Hegel claimed that self-consciousness arises in an individual not through an act of introspection and not in isolation from others but by means of a dynamic process of reciprocal relationships in which each recognizes the other as a self-conscious being, becomes aware of that recognition of himself in the other, and ultimately becomes dependent on the other for his self-consciousness. In other words, if there were just two individuals, A and B, involved in an interaction, then A would become self-conscious by recognizing not only that B is self-conscious but also that B recognizes that A is self-conscious, and the same would be true of B. According to Hegel, this would happen even if A were B's master and B were A's slave. In such a situation, Hegel thought, the master, so far as his attempt to become self-conscious is concerned, would wind up becoming the slave of his slave.

In Hegel's account of this process, these developments occur in the context of a "life-and-death struggle," presumably in a state of nature like the one Hobbes described, in which each individual strives to self-assert his or her own independence by negating dependence on the other. Yet in this struggle, the "winners" ultimately must realize that they cannot kill the losers since their getting the losers to recognize them as independent self-conscious beings is the whole point of their own activity.

Hegel's analysis of the master-slave relationship is more complicated and phenomenologically subtle than our brief sketch of it. And commentators disagree on exactly what Hegel had in mind. For present purposes, what matters are not so much these subtleties but noticing that the social dimension of his analysis is in sharp contrast to the approach taken by Enlightenment thinkers, such as Descartes, Hobbes, and Locke, and even by many of the romantics, such as Rousseau. Descartes, for instance, in addition to having no respect for history, found no role in his philosophy for the social (unless the individual's relationship to God counts as social!). He explained how knowledge is possible by considering the individual in isolation not only from other people but even from the material world, to which the individual has only indirect access though the medium of his private subjectivity. Hobbes, even in his political thought, characterized humans in a state of nature as being presocial, where, he said, the life of each is "solitary, poor, nasty, brutish, and short." Individuals in a state of nature are willing to enter into genuine social relations with others only from considerations of self-interest. Even Rousseau, for all his romanticism, celebrated the purity of the individual in isolation from corrupting social influences.

Hegel is at the other end of the spectrum. In almost every aspect of his thought, he emphasized the social, but nowhere more consequentially than in his account of self-consciousness. Subsequent theorists influenced by German idealism, including not only philosophers but also many of the earliest and most influential psychologists, followed him in regarding the self as essentially social. As we shall see, whether the self is regarded as individual or social may profoundly affect how reasonable it is to hope for some sort of theoretical convergence among the many accounts of the self that would proliferate in the twentieth century.

The basic idea of those philosophers in the tradition of German idealism who pushed a conception of the self as dynamic and social is that what we take as the real world is pervaded by activity, or "spirit." Fichte, in his pre-Schelling writings, emphasized conscious human activity, both in self-knowledge and free action. In Schelling, nature is the source of the dynamic activity of spirit, which comes to "know itself" in human self-consciousness and human freedom, which together are the acme of nature's spiritual activity. Hegel develops this idea in his theory of how spirit comes to know its own activities in nature, culture, and human consciousness. In his view, not only is Absolute Spirit God, but, in the upper limits of our consciousness, we are God as well. In explaining these ideas, Hegel gave a dynamic account of the development of the human mind from unconsciousness, to consciousness, to self-consciousness. He expressed this theory in terms of the development both of history and the individual. Yet, because his main focus was on history, his psychological theory of individual development is thin. The slave metaphor, although it concerns only one phase of the growth of mind, the part dealing with self-consciousness, is the most interesting part of his analysis, and the most influential, not only because it brought in the social but because of its reliance on the idea of reciprocity.

Reactions to German Idealism

Hegel had many admirers, among them Marx, as well as many critics and detractors. Of these critics, Arthur Schopenhauer (1788–1860), Søren Kierkegaard (1813–1855), and Friedrich Nietzsche (1844–1900) are most worth mentioning. Whereas Hegel stressed the primacy of reason, objectivity, and rationality, Schopenhauer substituted will for reason, Kierkegaard subjectivity for objectivity, and Nietzsche irrationality for rationality.

In his most important work, *The World as Will and Idea* (1818), Schopenhauer accepted Kant's distinction between the noumenal and phenomenal worlds and his claim that the existence and nature of the phenomenal world depends on its being experienced.[27] But, in contrast to Kant, he claimed that through intuition the noumenal world can be known. Its nature is will, a nonrational, blind, ceaselessly desiring, meaningless striving after existence. He argued that this will is what each human being is essentially—one's true nature. The phenomenal properties of humans—their intellects, preferences, and even their bodies—are objectifications of will. Since will is amoral, humans, at bottom, are horrible creatures. A key purpose of civilization is to break and tame them. Except for art, humans have few sources of pleasure. In sharp contrast to Hegel, Schopenhauer claimed that human history, far from being a progressive manifestation of spirit, is without purpose and essentially pointless.

Schopenhauer was among the first Western philosophers to have access to translations of Hindu and Buddhist scripture, by which he was profoundly affected. He claimed that while humans tend to see themselves as independent, self-sufficient beings, on the noumenal level there is neither unity nor plurality. The subject, which is the knower, rather than lying within the forms of space, time, and quantity, is presupposed by these very forms, which is why the subject is neither one nor many. When humans know something, it is this noumenal subject that knows, but this subject is never itself known.

Schopenhauer wrote a dialogue to express these ideas.[28] Ostensibly devoted to the immortality of the soul, the real issue under discussion is not so much whether people survive their bodily deaths—that is, preserve their individuality—as what matters in human survival. Philalethes, who represents Schopenhauer, argues that personal identity, or, as he puts it, the preservation of individuality, does not matter— that is, that even from an egoist point of view, the preservation of individuality is not all that important. His antagonist, Thrasymachos, holds to the commonsensical view that the preservation of individuality is what matters primarily.

Philalethes assumes that people do not survive their bodily deaths as the individuals they were while alive. But, he argues, nothing of great value has been lost since a person's individuality is not his or her "true and inmost being," but only its "outward manifestation." "Your real being," he says, is eternal and unbounded. "So when death comes, on the one hand you are annihilated as an individual; on the other, you are and remain everything. Your life is in time, and the immortal part of you in eternity."

Thrasymachos is not impressed by this view. So, to convince him, Philalethes asks him to consider how he would feel if someone were to guarantee him that after his death he shall "remain an individual," but only on condition that he "first spend three months of complete unconsciousness." Thrasymachos replies that this would be fine. Philalethes continues: "But remember, if people are completely unconscious, they take no account of time. So, when you are dead, it's all the same to you whether three months pass in the world of consciousness, or ten thousand years." Thrasymachos agrees. Then, Philalethes says, "If by chance, after those ten thousand years have gone by, no one ever thinks of awaking you," that would be no cause for concern either: if "you knew that the mysterious power which keeps you in your present state of life had never once ceased in those ten thousand years to bring forth other phenomena like yourself, and to endow them with life, it would fully console you." No, Thrasymachos replies. You must think, then, Philalethes continues, "that your individuality is such a delightful thing" that "you can't imagine anything better." That's right, Thrasymachos answers, my individuality is "my very self. To me it is the most important thing in the world. . . . I want to exist, I, I. That's the main thing. I don't care about an existence which has to be proved to be mine, before I can believe it."

In reply, Philalethes wheels out his heavy artillery: Schopenhauer's philosophy of will:

When you say I, I, I want to exist, it is not you alone that says this. Everything says it, absolutely everything that has the faintest trace of consciousness. It follows, then, that this desire of yours is just the part of you that is not individual—the part that is common to all things without distinction. It is the cry, not of the individual, but of existence itself; it is the intrinsic element in everything that exists, nay, it is the cause of anything existing at all. This desire craves for, and so is satisfied with, nothing less than existence in general—not any definite individual existence. No! that is not its aim. It seems to be so only because this desire—this Will—attains consciousness only in the individual, and therefore looks as though it were concerned with nothing but the individual. There lies the illusion—an illusion, it is true, in which the individual is held fast: but, if he reflects, he can break the fetters and set himself free. It is only indirectly I say, that the individual has this violent craving for existence. It is the Will to Live which is the real and direct aspirant—alike and identical in all things.

But people, mired in illusion, see the Will only in themselves. Hence,

individuality is not a form of perfection, but rather of limitation; and so to be freed from it is not loss but gain. Trouble yourself no more about the matter. Once thoroughly recognize what you are, what your existence really is, namely, the universal will to live, and the whole question will seem to you childish, and most ridiculous!

Thrasymachos answers that rather than his own desire for individual survival seeming to him to be childish, it is Philalethes who seems to be "childish" and "ridiculous—like all philosophers!" At this point, the dialogue ends.

But Schopenhauer continues: If our individual selves are at bottom an illusion, how can people overcome their egoistic concerns? Up to a point, he says, by developing the human capacity for sympathy and thereby becoming more virtuous. But what is really needed to overcome our self-centeredness is not mere sympathy but a "transition from virtue to asceticism," in which the individual ceases to feel any concern for earthly things. In this "state of voluntary renunciation," individuals experience "resignation, true indifference, and perfect will-lessness," which lead to a "denial of the will to live." Only then, when humans have become "saints," are they released from insatiable Will.

The Danish philosopher Søren Kierkegaard, regarded by many as the founder of existentialism, is famous for his rejection of abstract philosophy, particularly Hegel's theories, on the grounds that life cannot be represented adequately within a conceptual system. The core of human existence is passion, which implies that human existence is not primarily thinking, but living. Most important, passion involves living in a condition of extreme inwardness in which a person embraces all of the contradictions in his or her being. The speculative or objective thinker may also embrace all views, but he or she lives none of them. The existing or subjective thinker strives to realize or live out a single idea. Like

Kant and Schopenhauer, Kierkegaard believed that humans are both in- and outside of time and hence that time and timelessness are two contradictory sides of human existence. The human project is to embrace both sides of this contradiction not as abstractions but as concrete, lived reality.

"Man is spirit," Kierkegaard proclaimed, and "spirit is the self." And what is the self? He answered, "A relation that relates itself to itself."[29] Which means? In part, that the self is the passionate embracing of both sides of man's contradictory nature; that is, "the self is freedom." In other words, "the self is the conscious synthesis of infinitude and finitude that relates itself to itself." But "to become oneself is to become concrete." This involves "an infinite moving-away from itself in the infinitizing of the self, and an infinite coming-back to itself in the finitizing process."[30] Kierkegaard claimed that the objective thinker, such as Hegel, does not fully exist because he ignores this task. Instead, in roaming indifferently from idea to idea, he considers ideas in relation to one another but not in relation to himself. The subjective thinker, on the other hand, such as Socrates, always aware of the either/or of ethical choice, joins idea and existence.

Ethical choice always proceeds from a subjective, individual point of view, which is the only one available to humans. Modern rationalists, Kierkegaard claimed, in expressing themselves as if from an absolute point of view, have forgotten this elemental fact. They have thereby confused a self-forgetful excursion into philosophical imagination with real transcendence. Authentic existence requires real transcendence. This requires attention to the details of one's own life, to the "how" of each lived moment. In sum, the subjective thinker, infinitely interested not in pure thought but in his or her own existence, elevates reality above possibility.

Friedrich Nietzsche, German classicist, philologist, philosopher, and critic of culture, had his greatest *immediate* influence not on philosophy proper but on culture and depth psychology (eventually, of course, he had a profound influence on philosophy). In a passage that for both its immodesty and its secularism could not have been written by Kierkegaard, Nietzsche asked, "Why do I know more things than other people? Why, in fact, am I so clever? I have never pondered over questions that are not questions. I have never squandered my strength. Of actual religious difficulties, for instance, I have no experience."[31] He asked, "Who among philosophers was a psychologist at all before me?" He answered that no one was. "Out of my writings," he continued, "there speaks a psychologist who has not his equal."[32] There are many today who would agree.

A difference between the psychological style of Kierkegaard and that of Nietzsche is that whereas Kierkegaard plumbed the depths of the ego through a penetrating self-examination that sought truth through subjectivity, Nietzsche was perennially suspect of subjectivity and sought the truth of his being not in personal self-examination but in an impersonal and historical analysis of subjectivity. "Direct self-observation," he wrote, "is not nearly sufficient for us to know *ourselves*." Instead, "we require history, for the past continues to flow within us in a hundred waves; we ourselves are, indeed, nothing but that which at every moment we experience of this continued flowing." Nietzsche continued, "It may even be said that here too, when we desire to descend into the river of what seems to be our own most intimate and personal being, there applies the dictum of Heraclitus: we cannot step into the same river twice."[33] But even going to history—any form of self-examination—can be misleading. The danger, he said, "of the direct questioning of the subject about the subject and of all self-reflection of the spirit lies in this, that it could be useful and important for one's activity to interpret oneself falsely."[34]

Neitzsche is famous for having proclaimed that the rise of Enlightenment secularism meant that "God is dead." He is virtually unknown for having uncovered, in his personal reflections, the perhaps deeper truth that the self is dead. He did this by unmasking the notions of substance and subject. "The concept of substance," he said, "is a consequence of the concept of the subject: not the reverse! If we relinquish the soul, 'the subject,' the precondition for 'substance' in general disappears. One acquires degrees of being, one loses that which has being."[35] The subject, he said, is but a "term for our belief in a unity underlying all the different impulses of the highest feeling of reality." But, he claimed, there is no such unity, only "the fiction that many similar states in us are the effect of one substratum: but it is we who first created the 'similarity' of these states; our adjusting them and making them similar is the fact, not their similarity, which ought rather to be denied."[36] There is neither subject nor object, he concluded. Both are fictions.

Moreover, he claimed, the subject is a useless fiction. Souls or spirits, even were we to suppose that they exist, could not reasonably be thought to be the cause of anything. The reason for this is that an immaterial soul has no interior structure on the basis of which we could understand its causal power: "there is no ground whatever for ascribing to spirit the properties of organization and systematization. The nervous system has a much more extensive domain; the world of consciousness is added to it."[37] There is no point in postulating a cause if we cannot understand how it could possibly bring about its supposed effect. We can understand how the nervous system could bring about certain effects. We cannot understand how spirit or soul or consciousness could bring about any effect.

To the objection, but what then explains unity of consciousness, Nietzsche answered, what unity of consciousness? "Everything that enters consciousness as 'unity,' " he said, "is already tremendously complex." Rather than unity of consciousness, we have "only a semblance of Unity."[38] To explain this semblance, rather than a single subject, we could do as well by postulating "a multiplicity of subjects, whose interaction and struggle is the basis of our thought and our consciousness in general." We do not have any reason to believe that in there is a dominant subject overseeing this multiplicity. "The subject is multiplicity."[39] Philosophers have bought into the fiction of self, he continued, by supposing that if there is thinking, there must be something that thinks. But the idea that "when there is thought there has to be something 'that thinks' is simply a formulation of our grammatical custom that adds a doer to every deed."[40] By following Descartes's line of reasoning, he announced, "one does not come upon something absolutely certain but only upon the fact of a very strong belief."

Intellectual culture, Neitzsche claimed, has made several "tremendous blunders." These include: an "absurd overestimation of consciousness," in which it has been transformed "into a unity, an entity: 'spirit,' 'soul,' something that feels, thinks, wills"; spirit has been postulated "as cause, especially wherever purposiveness, system, co-ordination appear"; "consciousness" has been regarded as "the highest achievable form," a "supreme kind of being, as 'God' "; "will" has been "introduced wherever there are effects"; "the 'real world' " has been regarded as "a spiritual world, as accessible through the facts of consciousness"; and "knowledge" has been regarded "as uniquely the faculty of consciousness."[41] And the "consequences" of these blunders—the mistaken ideas that they have spawned? They are the ideas that "every advance lies in an advance in becoming conscious; every regression in becoming unconscious"; that "one approaches reality, 'real being,' through dialectic; that one distances oneself from it through the instincts, senses, mechanism"; that "all good must proceed from spirituality, must be a fact of consciousness; that any advance toward the better can only be an advance in becoming conscious."[42]

Nietzsche concluded that we have been victimized by our language, that is, by

our bad habit ... of taking a mnemonic, an abbreviative formula, to be an entity, finally as a cause, e.g., to say of lightning "it flashes." Or the little word "I." To make a kind of perspective in seeing the cause of seeing: that was what happened in the invention of the "subject," the "I"![43]

In other words, we have imposed our thoughts and concepts on a reality that we have falsely assumed is similarly structured: " 'Subject,' 'object,' 'attribute'— these distinctions are fabricated and are now imposed as a schematism upon all the apparent facts. The fundamental false observation is that I believe it is I who do something, suffer something, 'have' something, 'have' a quality."[44]

Nietzsche, in this latter period of his life, held that life neither possesses nor lacks intrinsic value. Yet evaluations are always being made. These, he claimed, must be symptomatic of the condition of the evaluator. In the West, most basic cultural values of philosophy, religion, and morality are expressions of an ascetic ideal that came into being when suffering became endowed with ultimate significance. Traditional philosophy, he said, gave birth to this ideal by valuing the soul over the body, the intellect over the senses, duty over desire, reality over appearance, and what is timeless over the temporal. Christianity added to this an emphasis on personal immortality, by means of which each individual's life and death acquire cosmic significance. Common to both traditions was the powerful assumption that existence requires explanation. Both denigrated experience in favor of some other, "true" world. Both, he claimed, may be read as symptoms of decline, that is, of life in distress. He characterized the age in which he lived as an age of passive nihilism, that is, one not yet aware that its religious and philosophical absolutes had been rendered groundless. With the growing awareness that the metaphysical and theological foundations for traditional morality had collapsed, there would come a pervasive sense of purposelessness and meaninglessness, that is, the triumph of nihilism. Since most people would not be able to accept this result, they would seek a surrogate god, such as the nation-state, with which to invest life with meaning.

Hermeneutics

Wilhelm Dilthey (1833–1911) sought the philosophical foundations of what came to be known as the "human sciences" (*Geisteswissenschaften*), which included history, philosophy, religion, psychology, art, literature, law, politics, and economics. He opposed the idea that the methodology of the human sciences should approximate as closely as possible to that of the natural sciences (*Naturwissenschaften*). "Nature we explain," he wrote, "psychic life we understand." In inner experience, unlike in nature, the elements "are given as a whole." Initially, there "is the experienced unity." Only afterward does one distinguish the elements of this unity. Dilthey claimed that this fact "brings about a very great difference between the methods through which we study psychic life, history, and society, and those through which the knowledge of nature is achieved."[45]

In place of the positivist ideal of trying to make historical studies scientific, Dilthey tried to establish historical studies, and more generally the humanities, as interpretative disciplines whose subject matter is the human mind. However, it is the human mind not as it is revealed subjectively, in immediate experience, or as it is analyzed in psychological theory, but as it manifests or "objectifies" itself in action, particularly as expressed historically, in language, literature, and institutions.

> What the human spirit is can only be revealed through historical consciousness of that which the mind has lived through and brought forth. It is this historical consciousness of mind which alone can make it possible to arrive gradually at a scientific and systematic knowledge of man.... What man is only history can say.... The rejection of historical inquiry is tantamount to forswearing knowledge of man himself—it is the regression of knowledge back to a merely genial and fragmentary subjectivity. [46]

Dilthey claimed that an interpretive or hermeneutic methodology is the only avenue to reconstructing the internal cognitive processes that motivate and give meaning to human actions.

But that meaning can never be fully grasped. For one thing, history is constantly being rewritten as new events unfold and new interpretations are constructed. For another, the "fluidity" of human life ensures that it will never be captured in a mere account. "It is," Dilthey wrote, "as if lines have to be drawn in a continually flowing stream, figures drawn which hold fast." But "between this reality of life and the scientific intellect there appears to be no possibility of comprehension, for the concept sunders what is to be unified in the flow of life." One cannot represent truths about human behavior "scientifically," as "universally and eternally valid, independent of the mind which propounds" them. Rather, "the flow of life is at all points unique, every wave in it arises and passes."[47] Thus, he thought, there is no such thing, even in principle, as a completed science of human beings. Rather, an understanding of humans, to whatever extent it occurs, will be the product of increasingly adequate interpretive traditions and can never be complete. Historical consciousness, by undermining confidence in absolute principles, sets people free to understand and appreciate the diverse possibilities of human experience.

Dilthey's most important contribution was his attempt to demonstrate the primacy of interpretation to the project of understanding humans. In this attempt he used hermeneutics, which previously had been important only to biblical interpretation. From his own immersion in the issues of interpretation, he urged the idea that interdependent coherences of feeling and meaning are constitutive of the life-world of human culture. He rejected the idea that consciousness resides in separate egos from which the social world is excluded.

Rather, reflective self-experience has been extracted from its dynamic role in social meanings and so cannot be a starting point or basis for knowing.

Absolute Idealism at the End of the Century

Hegel gets most of the credit for pushing the philosophy and psychology of the self in a social direction. So far as philosophy is concerned, at the end of the nineteenth century the leading light in the United States was Josiah Royce (1855–1916) and in England, F. H. Bradley (1846–1924). Royce, who was an absolute idealist in the tradition of Hegel, stressed the unity of human thought with the external world. His idealism also extended to religion, the basis of which he conceived to be human loyalty. Yet he also had strong empirical inclinations. In his study on self-consciousness, he claimed that his goal, rather than abstract metaphysics, was to provide an explanation for variations in consciousness that may be found empirically, especially in abnormal psychology. In his view, abnormalities of self-consciousness typically are *"maladies of social consciousness,"* that is, have to do with a patient's views of his relations with others.[48]

In *The World and the Individual* (1901–13), Royce described, in words strongly reminiscent of Hazlitt but almost certainly inspired by Hegel, what he took to be a fundamental fact at the root of the social origin of self-consciousness: "Were no difference observed between the contents which constitute the observed presence of my neighbor, and the contents which constitute my own life in the same moment, then my sense of my neighbor's presence, and my idea of myself, would blend in my consciousness, and there would be so far neither Alter nor Ego observed."[49] In other words, he claimed that people would never have conceived of themselves were it not for reflecting on the relationship between self and other. As he put it elsewhere:

> Self-conscious functions are all of them, in their finite, human and primary aspect, social functions, due to habits of social intercourse. They involve the presentation of some contrast between Ego and non-Ego. This psychological contrast is primarily that between the subject's own conscious act, idea, intent, or other experience, and an experience which is regarded by him as representing the state of another's mind.[50]

Although self-consciousness begins only in social relations to others, Royce argued that it eventually comes to include other aspects of the physical world. "By means of habits gradually acquired, this contrast [between self and other] early comes to be extended to include that between one's inner states and the represented realities that make up the physical world."

The English philosopher F. H. Bradley, who was also an absolute idealist in the tradition of Hegel, considered mind to be the basis of the universe. In his most ambitious work, *Appearance and Reality: A Metaphysical Essay* (1893), he claimed that personal identity is conventional, that it is best regarded as a matter of degree, and that how we think of it should be determined pragmatically, in ways that permit us to think of it differently for different purposes. He even used a fission example to criticize Locke's simple memory view of personal identity:

> If the self remembers because and according as it is *now*, might not another self be made of a quality the same and hence possessing the same past in present recollection? And if *one* could be made thus, why not also two or three? These might be made distinct at the present time, through their differing quality, and again through outward relations, and yet be like enough for each to remember the same past, and so, of course to *be* the same.[51]

Bradley concluded from this example "that a self is not thought to be the same because of bare memory, but only so when that memory is considered not to be deceptive." He claimed that it follows that:

> Identity must depend in the end upon past experience, and not solely upon mere present thinking. And continuity in some degree, and in some unintelligible sense, is by the popular view required for personal identity. He who is risen from the dead may really be the same, though we can say nothing intelligible of his ambiguous eclipse or his phase of half-existence. But a man wholly like the first, but created fresh after the same lapse of time, we might feel was too much to be one, if not quite enough to be two. Thus it is evident that, for personal identity, some continuity is requisite, but how much no one seems to know.[52]

He concluded: "If we are not satisfied with vague phrases and meaningless generalities, we soon discover that the best way is not to ask questions."

But what if we do persist in asking questions? Then, Bradley said, we will be left with this result:

> Personal identity is mainly a matter of degree. The question has a meaning if confined to certain aspects of the self, though even here it can be made definite in each

case only by the arbitrary selection of points of view. And in each case there will be a limit fixed in the end by no clear principle. But in what the *general* sameness of one self consists is a problem insoluble because it is meaningless. This question, I repeat it, is sheer nonsense until we have got some clear idea as to what the self is to stand for. If you ask me whether a man is identical in this or that respect, and for one purpose or another purpose, then, if we do not understand one another, we are on the road to an understanding. In my opinion, even then we shall reach our end only by more or less of convention and arrangement. But to seek an answer in general to the question asked at large is to pursue a chimera.[53]

In these remarks, Bradley anticipated views that would come to the fore toward the end of the twentieth century. According to these more recent ideas, while personal identity is not a matter of degree, the relations of physical and psychological continuity on which personal identity supervenes are matters of degree, and these relations all but exhaust what matters, or at least what should matter, to people in their egoistic concern for their own survivals.

XI

SCIENCE OF HUMAN NATURE

At the beginning of the nineteenth century, most progressive intellectuals still held that humans had been made in the image of God. By the end of the century—due primarily to the influence of Charles Darwin and Karl Marx—most held that humans had been made in the image of biology and society. Even earlier in the century, naturalizing tendencies had made an appearance in the guise of physiological inquiry into the brain and psychological inquiry into the development of self concepts. It would take some time for these momentous changes to be fully assimilated into intellectual culture. But when they were finally assimilated, the process of naturalizing the soul, and with it humans beings, would be all but complete.

Biological Materialism and the Origins of Experimental Psychology

In the West, materialism had its origins in classical Greece. But once the church opted for Platonic dualism, it was not until the seventeenth century that a physical science emerged that could make materialism all but irresistible. That happened primarily through Isaac Newton, whose work gave great impetus not only to materialism but also to mechanism—the idea that the world of inorganic matter runs like a clock.[1]

Earlier, Descartes had suggested that animals are, in effect, automata, but he made an exception in the case of human animals. Hobbes had been a thoroughgoing materialist, but he did not make significant contributions to physical science. Spinoza had been the most consistent, and perhaps even the most influential materialist of the modern era, but because he was widely regarded as an atheist, Christian thinkers avoided positive discussion of his views.[2]

In *Man the Machine* (1748), Julien Offray de la Mettrie (1709–1751) extended Descartes's automata theory from nonhuman to human animals, in the process giving vivid expression to an idea, which had already been endorsed by Anthony Collins and other less-influential materialists, that the conscious and voluntary actions of humans differ from instinctual and involuntary actions not in being composed of a different sort of stuff but only in being more complex.[3] In making this point, La Mettrie replaced Descartes's rather simplistic, clocklike mechanisms with more sophisticated conceptions that better accounted for human autonomy. Among those whom he influenced was Paul-Henri d'Holbach (1723–1789), who in *System of Nature* (1770) defended secular materialism. In it, d'Holbach argued, at the time sensationally, that humans are a product entirely of nature, that their moral and intellectual abilities are simply machinelike operations, that the soul and free will are illusions, that religion and priestcraft are the source of most manmade evil, and that atheism promotes good morality.

In 1795, Pierre Cabanis (1757–1808) argued that the brain is the organ of consciousness in the same sense in which the stomach is the organ of digestion. Subsequently, he proposed that since consciousness and sensibility are material mechanistic processes, it must be possible to formulate a physiologically grounded, developmental account of self-consciousness.[4] He concluded that the immaterial soul is superfluous. However, unequipped with d'Holbach's mental steadfastness, he could not sustain this vision. By the end of his life, he had retreated to the view that the ego is immaterial and immortal.

Despite such backsliding, theoretical development along materialistic lines continued. In the first half of the nineteenth century, the empirical doctrine of functional localization—the notion that specific mental processes are correlated with discrete regions of the brain—had been proposed.[5] The first important steps toward confirming this hypothesis were taken by Franz Josef Gall (1758–1828), whose phrenology was based on three principles: that the brain is the organ of the mind; that it is composed of parts, each of which serves a distinct, task-specific mental "faculty," such as hope or self-esteem; and that the size of different parts of the brain is directly proportional to the strength of the faculties that they sustain. In Gall's view, mental faculties tend to operate independently of each other; that is, the brain, rather than a single unified system, is composed of a community of systems, which ordinarily work in tandem but sometimes oppose each other.

Toward midcentury several brain physiologists advanced a more radical view: that the brain, rather than a single organ, is a pair of organs, in much the same sense that human kidneys and lungs are each pairs of organs. This view had surfaced before, in antiquity, when Hippocrates had written that "the human brain, as in the case of [the brains of] all other animals, is double."[6] In the nineteenth century, the view was championed by the English physician A. L. Wigan in *The Duality of the Mind* (1844). Wigan claimed that "a separate and distinct process of thinking or ratiocination may be carried on in each cerebrum simultaneously."[7]

Others argued for the unity of brain activity. Of these, the French physiologist Jean-Pierre-Marie Flourens conducted experiments on animals in which he excised various portions of the brain and noted the resulting behavioral deficiencies. What he tended to find was that while particular functions were weakened, they were rarely totally lost. He took this to confirm Descartes's view of the unity of mind.[8] Much later in the century, in this same tradition, Hughlings Jackson proposed a unified functional organization of the entire nervous system, in which he tried to accommodate the duality thesis within the context of a higher-order unity of the mind. The duality view then fell into relative obscurity until it was revived in the 1970s to account for the strange consequences of split-brain operations on epileptics.[9]

Throughout the first half of the nineteenth century, many thinkers, and most of the general public, were unaware of the rather esoteric work that had been going on in brain physiology.[10] All of this changed with the appearance of Charles Darwin (1809–1882), who was to the project of naturalizing human nature what in an earlier century Newton had been to the project of naturalizing physical nature. As is well known, from 1831 to 1836, Darwin traveled as an unpaid naturalist on the H.M.S. *Beagle* to the east and west coasts of South America and on to the Pacific islands. Upon his return, he became preoccupied with an issue he called *the species problem*. Solving it required finding a mechanism that could explain why the species that are present differ from place to place and from era to era. In 1838, Darwin read the British economist Thomas Malthus (1776–1834), who, in *An Essay on the Principle of Population* (1803), had argued that human population growth is always kept in check by a limited food supply. This led Darwin to realize that in the struggle for survival, "favourable variations would tend to be preserved, and unfavourable ones to be destroyed," resulting in "the formation of new species."[11] Among nineteenth-century thinkers, this idea was not new. But earlier theorists, such as Jean-Baptiste de Lamarck (1744–1829), had failed to discover a mechanism for the process. In his newfound theory of natural selection, Darwin had found a mechanism: competition over scarce resources, which only the most fit would survive.

For decades, Darwin refrained from publishing his views. Then, in 1858, he received from Alfred Russel Wallace (1823–1913), a naturalist working in the Malay Archipelago, a paper in which Wallace had arrived at a theory like his own. Wallace too had been led to his ideas by reflecting on Malthus's book.

Darwin's friends, Charles Lyell and Sir Joseph Hooker, then arranged for a joint paper by Darwin and Wallace to be presented on July 1, 1858, to the Linnean Society of London. Meanwhile, Darwin hurriedly finished *On the Origin of Species by Means of Natural Selection, or The Preservation of Favoured Races in the Struggle for Life* (1859).

Ironically, among those skeptical of Darwin's theory, so far as its application to humans is concerned, were his mentor, Lyell, and his codiscoverer of evolution by natural selection, Wallace. Both maintained that humans had a special status, different from other organisms in nature. Nevertheless, among most scientists Darwin's views quickly prevailed. Subsequently, his principal opposition came from the clergy, who were outraged both that his views were inconsistent with a literal reading of Genesis and that they erased a metaphysical gap between "man and the brutes."

Darwin continued to write quietly, allowing his friends to defend his theory in public, especially Thomas H. Huxley (1825–1895), who in debating with clergy and theologians promulgated what was basically a gospel of evolution. In *The Descent of Man, and Selection in Relation to Sex* (1871), Darwin elaborated on the controversial subject of human evolution, which he had only alluded to in *Origin*, expanding the reach of evolution to include moral and spiritual traits of humans. In *The Expression of the Emotions in Man and Animals* (1872), Darwin compared the connections between behavioral symptoms and their corresponding emotional states in humans and nonhuman animals, arguing that expression of emotions such as anger, despair, hatred, and love are common in nonhuman animals. In both of these latter works, Darwin's goal was to emphasize the continuity between humans and other animals.

One important and immediate consequence of evolutionary theory for the philosophy of human nature was that it established once and for all that humans are animals. Another was that it provided a mechanism for the appearance of different species on Earth that explained how they might have evolved from lower forms of life in a wholly natural way, with no conscious prevision of the ends to be achieved. In an earlier era, most thinkers, including even progressive ones such as Boyle, looked toward the skies and compared humans with angels. By the end of the nineteenth century, virtually all progressive thinkers looked toward the earth and compared humans with apes. The person most responsible for this change was Darwin. So far as the science of human nature is concerned, he was not only the most influential thinker of the nineteenth century but arguably the most influential of all time. But great as was his contribution to the process of naturalizing human beings, the theory of evolution was not the only theoretical initiative that had this effect.

As the century progressed, physiological research not only continued unabated but, together with evolutionary theory, stimulated more global hypotheses. For instance, the English philosopher S. H. Hodgson (1832–1912), in *The Theory of Practice* (1870), argued for a view that he called *epiphenomenalism*, according to which thoughts and feelings, regardless of how intense they may be, have no causal power. He compared mental states to the colors laid on the surface of a stone mosaic and neural events to the supporting stones. Subsequently, Huxley, in his widely read "On the Hypothesis that Animals are Automata, and Its History" (1874), claimed that states of consciousness are the effect of molecular activity in the brain. It follows, he said, that animals are "conscious automata." Like Hodgson, he claimed that states of consciousness are *effects*, but not *causes*, of brain activity.

Also in 1874, the British physician W. B. Carpenter (1813–1885), in *Principles of Mental Physiology* (1874), introduced the idea that the brain-mind complex is divided between conscious and unconscious states and processes, employing the notion of "unconscious cerebration" for the latter. He then strongly, but perhaps inconsistently advocated Cartesian dualistic interactionism. Unfortunately for his view, in the two and a half centuries since Descartes, little progress had been made in explaining how there could be causal influence either way. John Tyndall (1820–1893), who called dualistic interactionism "unthinkable," said that while "a definite thought, and a definite molecular action in the brain [may] occur simultaneously, we do not possess the intellectual organ, nor apparently any rudiment of the organ, which would enable us to pass, by a process of reasoning, from the one to the other."[12]

In the face of such an overwhelming difficulty, neutral monism, which in the seventeenth century had been championed by Spinoza, was reinvented in the nineteenth century by G. T. Fechner (1801–1887), who was also responsible for the formal beginnings of experimental psychology. Fechner sketched out a dual-aspect view of the relation between mind and body, according to which the two are simply different ways of conceiving of the same reality. This view was adopted by G. H. Lewes (1817–1878), whose *Physiology of Common Life* (1859/1860) enticed the young Pavlov to study physiology. In *Optik*, Hermann von Helmholtz (1821–1894) proposed a comprehensive physiological theory of color vision and an unconscious-inference theory of perception. Finally, in the last quarter of the nineteenth century, Wilhelm Wundt (1832–1920) argued for the need to transcend, through the use of experimental methods, the limitations of what was then the direct, introspective study of consciousness. Experimental psychology, which had been born with Fechner and nurtured by Helmholtz, was raised to maturity by Wundt, who then served as the guardian of the "new psychology." Students from around the world, but especially from the United States, traveled to Leipzig to study experimental technique and returned home imbued with the spirit of the new approach.[13]

The Psychopathology of Self

In the eighteenth century, Franz Anton Mesmer (1734–1815) had demonstrated what he called *animal magnetism*, later to be called *hypnotism*. He claimed that everything in the universe, including everything within a human body, is connected by a physical, magnetic fluid, which is polarized, conductible, and capable of being discharged and accumulated. It is a disequilibrium of this fluid within the body that leads to disease. To cure this disease, a physician would redirect the fluid by serving as a conduit by which animal magnetism is channeled from the universe at large into the patient's body by means of "magnetic passes" of the physician's hands. Patients who received this treatment would experience a magnetic "crisis," like an electric shock, after which they would be cured. In 1785, an official inquiry headed by Benjamin Franklin, the American ambassador to France at the time, discredited Mesmer's views. Mesmer then left Paris and lived the rest of his life in relative obscurity. He died in 1815, but his ideas persisted.

Mesmer's most important disciple was the Marquis de Puységur (1751–1825), who many regard as the founder of modern psychotherapy. The discoverer of what today we call *hypnotic suggestion*, he claimed that "magnetic effects" depend on the effect of the therapist's personality and beliefs and on his rapport with patients. His techniques, often together with Mesmer's explanation of why they worked, spread rapidly.[14]

In England, James Braid (1795–1860) published *Neurypnology; or, the Rationale of Nervous Sleep, Considered in Relation with Animal Magnetism* (1843), in which he claimed that the magnetic effects of Mesmer are produced not as a consequence of any agent passing from the body of the therapist to that of the patient but by "a peculiar condition of the nervous system, induced by a fixed and abstracted attention."[15] He named this state *neurohypnosis*, later shortened to *hypnosis*, and explored its use in relieving pain during surgery.[16] By claiming a link between hypnotic phenomena and brain physiology and then introducing a terminology that was more palatable to the medical and scientific establishment, Braid was instrumental in preparing the way for the eventual use of hypnosis in psychotherapy.

Counterbalancing the movement toward greater respectability, between 1848 and 1875 hypnotism became increasingly tarnished by its association with mediumistic spiritualism, on the one hand, and stage demonstrations, on the other. As a consequence, before hypnotism could be accepted as a respectable research and therapeutic tool, it had to be brought back from the realm of pseudoscience to which it had been consigned. Charles Richet (1850–1935), a young French physiologist whose work revived interest in the scientific use of hypnosis, gets much of the credit for doing this. Richet's work attracted the attention of Jean-Martin Charcot (1825–1893), who created at the Salpêtrière hospital in Paris what eventually became the most influential center for research in neurology. In charge of a ward containing women suffering from convulsions, Charcot discovered that, under hypnosis, he could replicate not only convulsions but other symptoms of hysteria as well, such as paralysis. This led him to try to distinguish symptoms that were organic in origin from others that are mental and to suggest that there are "ideas" split off from normal consciousness at the core of certain neuroses. His theories exerted a profound influence on two of his students, Pierre Janet (1859–1947) and Sigmund Freud (1856–1939).

Janet employed automatic writing and hypnosis to investigate the nature of a variety of automatisms, including what subsequently came to be known as multiple-personality disorder and the experience of possession. In developing an analytical framework to conceptualize these and related phenomena, he paved the way for his own and Freud's later approaches to therapy. In 1893, Josef Breuer (1842–1925) and Freud published a paper in which they gave an account of Breuer's initial discovery of a new therapeutic method, based on Breuer's work with Anna O, who under hypnosis provided Breuer, in reverse chronological order, with information about the circumstances under which each of her symptoms appeared, as well as the trauma that originated them. As she did this, her symptoms went away. Her cure by what Breuer and Freud called *the cathartic method* is often regarded as the origin of psychoanalysis.

Theodule Ribot (1839–1916), the "father" of the French school of psychopathology, was one of the first scientific psychologists to take a brain-oriented view of the dissociation of personality. In his *Diseases of Personality* (1885), he claimed that "experimental psychology" cannot rest content with the traditional assumption that each human possesses an "ego" that is "absolutely one, simple, and identical," which results only in "an illusive clearness and a semblance of a solution." For a genuine explanation, he claimed, it will be necessary to explain how the ego "is born, and from what lower form it proceeds."[17] He added that the traditional view cannot explain the "unconscious life of the mind," whereas the more scientific view "expresses the unconscious in physiological terms." This is important, he said, because "nervous activity is far more extensive than psychic activity" and consciousness needs to be explained in terms of its concrete physiological conditions of appearance. He claimed that "all manifestations of psychic life, sensations, desires, feelings, volitions, memories, reasonings, inventions, etc., may be alternately conscious and unconscious."[18]

Ribot went on to characterize numerous diseases of the personality, including physical abnormalities such as "double monsters" (for instance, the Hungarian twins that were parodied in *Scriblerus*), as well as cases of multiple-personality disorder. He claimed that "the organism and the brain, as its highest representation, constitute the real personality, containing in itself all that we have been and the possibilities of all that we shall be." In the brain, "the whole individual character is inscribed," together "with all its active and passive aptitudes, sympathies, and antipathies; its genius, talents, or stupidity; its virtues, vices, torpor, or activity." "What emerges and reaches consciousness," he said, "is little compared with what lies buried below, albeit still active. Conscious personality is never more than a feeble portion of physical personality."[19]

Ribot further claimed that the unity of the ego is "the cohesion, during a given period, of states of consciousness" and unconscious physiological states. He concluded that "unity means co-ordination" and that with consciousness subordinate to the organism, "the problem of the unity of the ego is, in its ultimate form, a biological problem." So, "to biology belongs the task of explaining, if it can, the genesis of organisms and the solidarity of their component parts." "Psychological interpretation," he said, "can only follow in its wake," appealing to the theory of evolution to support his view that biology is the ultimate ground upon which psychology—even human personality—is built.[20] Subsequently, psychologists began to divide up mental functions and investigate them separately. This divide-and-conquer strategy would lead in our own times to a tremendous growth of knowledge, the price of which was serious theoretical fragmentation. Whether the pieces can be put back together is an issue to which we shall return.

The Birth of Sociology

The revolution in thinking about human nature that by the mid-nineteenth century was well underway did not simply involve understanding humans as belonging with the rest of nature. Almost as fundamentally, it involved contextualizing them in their cultural and social environments. Earlier thinkers had anticipated this new approach, but it was not until the nineteenth century, in the work of Auguste Comte (1798–1857), that the new science acquired visibility. From 1830 to 1842, Comte published his great philosophical history of science, the six-volume *Course of Positive Philosophy*, in which he tried to synthesize what he took to be the most important intellectual developments of his time. In it, he also provided criteria for a scientific approach to the historical study of society, for which he invented the label *sociology*. Best known now as the father of French positivism, Comte attempted to reconcile science and religion in order to promote his view of how society ought to be organized.[21]

Comte's constructive theory emanated from his historical study of the progress of the sciences, especially astronomy, physics, chemistry, and biology. In his view, every science goes through three stages, each of which corresponds to a specific form of mental and material development: the theological, the metaphysical, and, finally, the positive. In the theological stage, which is further broken down into the substages of animism, polytheism, and monotheism, humans view nature as having will. In animism, objects have their own will; in polytheism, many divine wills impose themselves on objects; and in monotheism, the will of one great God imposes itself on objects. In the second, metaphysical, stage, causes and forces replace will, and Nature is viewed as one great naturalistic system, put in motion by a First Cause. Finally, in the third, positive, stage, the search for absolute knowledge is abandoned, as is the First Cause. In their place, the quest becomes that of discovering laws "of relations of succession and resemblance." Comte believed that this developmental transformation of science is headed toward the perfection of thought and that progress through the stages and substages is both inevitable and irreversible. Each successive science is necessarily dependent on a previous one, for instance, biology on chemistry. Further, as the phenomena under consideration become more complex, so do the methods with which scientists investigate them.

In contrast to Descartes, who thought that the geometrical method was the one right method of inquiry, Comte believed that each science has its own distinctive logic, which is revealed in the historical study of that science. The final science that he claimed to have discovered, which he thought had not yet entered its most mature stage, was sociology, which would give meaning to all of the other sciences by delineating their historical development. Through this science, he claimed, humans will finally understand the true logic of mind.

Comte divided sociology itself into social statics, that is, the study of sociopolitical systems in their unique historical contexts, and social dynamics, the study of developmental progress. As Thomas Kuhn would also famously do in the 1960s in accounting for scientific development, Comte distinguished between stable periods of order and unstable ones of progress.[22] He claimed that what was needed in his own time was a new synthesis of order and progress, which would lead to a new, higher form of social and intellectual stability. In this regard, he claimed that while the French Revolution had been a progressive development, in that the ancien régime had been based on obsolete theological knowledge, the revolution was negative in that it yielded no rationale for the reorganization of society. This, he said, would be provided by a new religion and a new faith, in which the Catholic clergy would be replaced by a scientific-industrial elite. For his "positivist religion," he created a pantheon of secular saints, which included Adam Smith, Dante, and Shakespeare, and he appointed himself as high priest!

So far as the self is concerned, Comte tried to explode what he regarded as a prejudice in favor of there being a unified, indivisible *I*. He began by noting that metaphysicians of Descartes's time and earlier were expected, by theologians and others, to preserve "the unity of what they called the *I*, that it might correspond with the unity of the soul." But, he said, now that researchers no longer labor under that expectation, "the famous theory of the *I* is essentially without a scientific object, since it is destined to represent a purely fictional state." Nevertheless, he continued, there are phenomena to which the word, *I* refers. Those who wish to study these phenomena will find that they consist only in "the equilibrium of various animal functions," something that is present in all animals. It is the "harmony" among these animal functions that gives rise to the illusion of a unified *I*. Hence, what philosophers and psychologists have attempted in vain to make an attribute of humanity exclusively "must belong to all animals, whether they are able to discourse upon it or not."[23]

Comte's reputation was ably promoted by the unflagging efforts of his ardent disciple, Emile Littré (1801–1881), a French lexicographer and philosopher. Littré rejected Comte's positivist religion, which he considered a product of Comte's tired, disturbed mind. Sticking to the high ground, Littré claimed that positivism afforded the best hope for the development of society along rational lines.

Karl Marx (1818–1883), the other great social theorist of the age, was also something of a spiritual idealist. Against the backdrop of the Industrial Revolution, with its attendant and unprecedented specialization of labor, he urged that people should not be restricted to one monotonous form of work, which can result only in alienation. Ideally, a person could and should do many things, say, be a philosopher in the morning, a gardener in the afternoon, and a poet in the evening. With Friedrich Engels (1820–1895), Marx published *The Communist Manifesto* (1848), a landmark event in the history of socialism. He also wrote *Capital* (1859), one of the most important economic treatises ever written. Revolutionary to the core, Marx wrote that the main point of philosophy is not to understand the world but to change it. Yet, one of the most important ways he changed it was by revolutionizing the ways in which social scientists subsequently understood it.

In his early twenties, Marx was captivated by Ludwig Feuerbach's (1804–1872), *The Essence of Christianity* (1841), in which Feuerbach argued that the ways in which people conceive of God are projections of their own natures, so the worship of God is actually worship of an idealized self. Feuerbach made a similar point about the ways in which idealist philosophers, particularly Hegel, conceive of Spirit. The young Marx initially agreed but soon decided that while Feuerbach was right in his criticism, he had failed to track the problem to its roots: "Feuerbach resolves the religious essence into the *human* essence. But the human essence is no abstraction inherent in each single individual. In its reality it is the ensemble of the social relations."[24] What Marx meant is that the conscious life of human beings, including not only mundane, day-to-day reflections, but law, morality, religion, and philosophy, is but a reflection of underlying social relations, which are wholly material. Soon he would progress to the idea, which would become so potent in the philosophies of the last half of the twentieth century, that not only had Feuerbach not properly identified the essence of humans but that humans have no essence.

Marx's idea that mental production is merely a reflection of underlying social and economic realities did not explain the evolution of consciousness. So, to complete his theory, he adapted Hegel's idea that historical processes evolve dialectically, spurred on by conflicts among their contradictory aspects. However, unlike Hegel, Marx located the sources of the conflicts in basic social and economic realities. In *The German Ideology* (1846), Marx and Engels reiterated these themes, adding that "in direct contrast to German philosophy which descends from heaven to earth, here it is a matter of ascending from earth to heaven." That is, the correct approach is not to set out from what men say, imagine, and conceive "in order to arrive at men in the flesh," but to set out from real, active men. "Morality, religion, metaphysics, and all the rest of ideology as well as the forms of consciousness corresponding to these," they said, "no longer retain the semblance of independence." "It is not consciousness that determines life, but life that determines consciousness."[25]

Thirteen years later, in his autobiographical preface to *A Contribution to the Critique of Political Economy* (1859), Marx reflected on "the general result" at which he had arrived and that "served as a guiding thread" for his thought. He said that it "can be briefly formulated as follows":

> In the social production of their life, men enter into definite relations that are indispensable and independent of their will, relations of production which correspond to a definite stage of development of their material productive forces. The sum total of these relations of production constitutes the economic structure of society, the real foundation, on which rises a legal and political superstructure and to which correspond definite forms of social consciousness.

Marx then summed up this "general result" by remarking that "it is not the consciousness of men that determines their being, but, on the contrary, their social being that determines their consciousness."[26]

Although Marx's direct contributions to self- and personal-identity theory were few, his effect on the theorizing of others was enormous. He drew attention to what he took to be the sociohistorical determinants of self and personal identity. Twentieth-century Marxists and other social constructivists would try to explain the link between these determinants and individual psychology.

British Theories of the Self

As we have seen, in Britain, by the end of the eighteenth century, discussion of fission examples in connection with personal-identity theory, as well as consideration of the thesis that personal identity is not what matters primarily in survival, had been introduced into debate. And toward the beginning of the nineteenth century, in the writings of Hazlitt, the debate over personal identity was proceeding along a trajectory that may seem quite up to date to students of analytic personal-identity theory in our own times. Hazlitt had even provided a rudimentary developmental account of the acquisition of self-concepts. However, subsequently in Britain, theorists of personal identity tended to be less progressive.

Thomas Brown's *Lectures on the Philosophy of the Human Mind* (1820) was much more psychological than philosophical, though he believed that mental philosophy had implications for epistemology. Nevertheless, for the most part he studied phenomena of mind from a realist perspective. Among his contributions was an important critique of introspection based on what he took to be the absurdity of the idea that one indivisible mind could be both subject and object of the same observation.

When Brown dealt with the issue of personal identity, or what he preferred to call *mental identity*, he became preoccupied with the question of how we come to suppose that the self that remembers is the same one that is remembered. Viewing all conscious mental states as "feeling," or experiential states of various kinds, he suggested that "the belief of our mental identity" is "founded on an essential principle of our constitution," in consequence of which, "it is *impossible* for us to consider *our* successive feelings, without regarding them as truly *our* successive feelings," that is, as "states, or affections of one thinking substance."[27] From such intuitions of the substantial identity underlying proximate experiences, one readily goes on to view more distant remembered experiences as one's own as well, thus conceiving an identical self underlying the stream of conscious experiences.

James Mill (1773–1836) built on Brown's observations but tried to reduce all mental phenomena to associations. When Mill considered the problem of identity, he first dealt with the notion of identity of objects, which he accounted for in terms of associated resemblances over time. In the case of people, he supposed that necessarily when one remembers having some experience, one believes that it was oneself who had it. In such cases, he maintained, "the Evidence" of one's own existence, and "the Belief" in it "are not different things, but the same thing."[28] In the case of times that one does not remember, but when one nevertheless believes one existed, one relies on verbal evidence from others, which is itself based on observations that others have made of one's bodily and psychological continuity and resemblances among person stages. He, thus, focused less on mental identity than on a body-based personal identity.[29]

John Stuart Mill (1806–1873), although an enthusiastic follower of Comte, criticized his negative attitude toward psychology, primarily on the grounds that he "rejects totally, as an invalid process, psychological observation properly so called, or in other words, internal consciousness, at least as regards our intellectual operations." In Comte's scheme, Mill continued, there is "no place" for "the science of Psychology," which he always speaks of "with contempt." In its place, "the study of mental phenomena, or as he [Comte] expresses it, of moral and intellectual functions," comes "under the head of Biology, but only as a branch of physiology. Our knowledge of the human mind must, he thinks, be acquired by observing other people."[30]

Mill's self-avowed "psychology" was primarily epistemology. By 1865, when he wrote his *Examination of Sir William Hamilton's Philosophy,* it had been thirty-five years since his father's book was first published, and much had changed in the relations between philosophy and psychology. Kantian philosophy had come to Britain, which Hamilton had tried unsuccessfully to integrate with the Scottish commonsense approach. In 1856, James Ferrier, who opposed Hamilton as much as Mill later would, published *Institutes of Metaphysic*, in which he made a disciplinary distinction between metaphysics and psychology, declaring that metaphysics, which belongs to philosophy, has to be purified of all naturalistic reasoning. An apostate of the Scottish school, Ferrier asserted that metaphysics is composed of "Epistemology" and "Ontology," thus introducing the term "epistemology" into the English language. He viciously attacked Reid, declaring him philosophically incompetent, while rejecting as failed epistemology the naturalistic and psychological approach to the mind that Reid had tried so hard to promote.

Mill, who followed a similar line in criticizing Reid's intuitionism, thought that his own phenomenalist project, which he called *the psychological theory*, was a kind of foundational psychology. But, rather than an anticipation of what was to come, it was psychology in the sense in which Hume's main focus in book 1of the *Treatise* was psychology. In Mill's view, material objects are "permanent possibilities of sensation," and other minds are inferred to exist based on an analogy with one's own case, which Mill presumed one knows directly. Like objects in the external world, Mill supposed that minds too are just actual and possible sensations. Since the ego or self is not given in experience, accounting for self-knowledge was a problem for his theory. He responded that self-knowledge must be based on an intuitive belief in our own continued existence that comes with our ability to remember past states of mind as our own. Self and memory, he said, are "merely two sides of the same fact, or two different modes of viewing the same fact."[31]

Mill explained that when a person—I—remembers something, "in addition" to the belief that I have "that the idea I now have was derived from a previous sensation," there is "the further conviction that this sensation" was "my own; that it happened to my self." "In other words," Mill continued, "I am aware of a long and uninterrupted succession of past feelings, going back as far as memory reaches, and terminating with the sensations I have at the present moment, all of which are connected by an inexplicable tie, that distinguishes them not only from any succession or combination in mere thought, but also from the parallel succession of feelings" that are had by others. "This succession of feelings, which I call my memory of the past, is that by which I distinguish my Self. Myself is the person who had that series of feelings, and I know nothing of myself, by direct knowledge, except that I had them. But there is a bond of some sort among all the parts of the series, which makes me say that they were feelings of a person who was the same person throughout and a different person from those who had any of the parallel successions of feelings; and this bond, to me, constitutes my Ego."[32] .

William James later criticized Mill for having fallen back "upon something perilously near to the Soul," quoting as evidence Mill's remark that it is "indubitable" that "that there is something real" in the tie which is revealed in memory when one recognizes a sensation's having been felt before, and thereby "connects the present consciousness with the past one of which it reminds me." This tie, Mill said, "is the Ego, or Self." Hence, "I ascribe a reality to the Ego—to my own mind—different from that real existence as a Permanent Possibility, which is the only reality I acknowledge in Matter." This ego, he concluded, "is a permanent element." James remarked that "this 'something in common' by which they [remembered feelings] are linked and which is not the passing feelings themselves, but something 'permanent,' of which we can 'affirm nothing' save its attributes and its permanence, what is it but metaphysical Substance come again to life?"[33] James concluded that Mill here makes "the same blunder" that Hume had earlier made: "the sensations per se, he thinks, have no 'tie.' The tie of resemblance and continuity which the remembering Thought finds among them is not a 'real tie' but 'a mere product of the laws of thought;' and the fact that the present Thought 'appropriates' them is also no real tie." But, James continued, whereas Hume was content "to say that there might after all be no 'real tie,' Mill, unwilling to admit this possibility, is driven, like any scholastic, to place it in a non-phenomenal world." James concluded that "Mill's concessions may be regarded as the definitive bankruptcy of the associationist description of the consciousness of self."[34]

James's alternative is basically to stay with the phenomena of consciousness but to concede that

> the knowledge the present feeling has of the past ones is a real tie between them, so is their resemblance; so is their continuity; so is the one's 'appropriation' of the other: all are real ties, realized in the judging Thought of every moment, the only place where disconnections could be realized, did they exist. Hume and Mill both imply that a disconnection can be realized there, whilst a tie cannot. But the ties and the disconnections are exactly on a par, in this matter of self-consciousness.

In anticipation of what in the late twentieth century would come to be known as *the closest continuer view*, James continued:

> The way in which the present Thought appropriates the past is a real way, so long as no other owner appropriates it in a more real way, and so long as the Thought has no grounds for repudiating it stronger than those which lead to its appropriation. But no other owner ever does in point of fact present himself for my past; and the grounds which I perceive for appropriating it—viz., continuity and resemblance with the present—outweigh those I perceive for disowning it—viz., distance in time.

James concluded that "my present Thought stands thus in the plenitude of ownership of the train of my past selves, is owner not only de facto, but de jure, the most real owner there can be, and all without the supposition of any 'inexplicable tie'—in a perfectly verifiable and phenomenal way."[35]

It was not just J. S. Mill for whom the idea of the immaterial soul exerted a lingering attraction. In a passage reminiscent of Hazlitt and one that may in our own times have influenced Derek Parfit, Henry Sidgwick (1838–1900) mused, "It must surely be admissible to ask the Egoist, 'Why should I sacrifice a present pleasure for a greater one in the future? Why should I concern myself about my own future feelings any more than about the feelings of other persons?'" He persisted: "Grant that the Ego is merely a system of coherent phenomena, that the permanent identical 'I' is not a fact but a fiction, as Hume and his followers maintain; why, then, should one part of the series of feelings into which the Ego is resolved be concerned with another part of the same series, any more than with any other series?"[36] Sidgwick's question is one that Priestley, Cooper, and Hazlitt had previously raised and answered in somewhat different ways. However, Sidgwick, without the prod of fission examples and with substance accounts of identity still a respectable option, managed to set the question aside.

In 1805, when Hazlitt published his *Essay*, what at the time was called *mental philosophy* was well on its way to spawning psychology, an empirical science that would, by the end of the century, emerge as a discipline separate from philosophy. However, the emergence of the two as distinct disciplines would take most of the century to achieve. The same mixing of metaphysical and empirical issues that was so prevalent in the eighteenth century would continue to infect the thinking of major nineteenth-century British theorists, such as Thomas Brown, James Mill, and J.S. Mill. And, while religious dogma would no longer dominate discussions of the mind, the presuppositions of an indivisible soul continued to work in the background of many discussions of the ego, even among progressive thinkers.

In a more scientific vein, in *The Senses and the Intellect* (1855) and *The Emotions and the Will* (1859), the Scottish psychologist Alexander Bain (1818–1903) worked out a sensory-motor associationism that became a turning point in the evolution of associationist psychology. Before Bain, associationists, like Hume and Mill, were committed to experience as the primary source of knowledge and so neglected the possibility that movement and social interaction were sources of self-attributions. Bain, in a more realist mode, accepted movement and social interaction as primary and then drew upon them to explain higher mental functions. He claimed, for instance, that when attention is turned inward upon oneself as a personality "we are putting forth towards ourselves the kind of exercise that properly accompanies our contemplation of other persons":

We are accustomed to scrutinize the actions and conduct of those about us, to set a higher value upon one man than upon another, by comparing the two; to pity one in distress; to feel complacency towards a particular individual; to congratulate a man on some good fortune that it pleases us to see him gain; to admire greatness or excellence as displayed by any of our fellows. All these exercises are intrinsically social, like Love and Resentment; an isolated individual could never attain to them, nor exercise them. By what means, then, through what fiction can we turn round and play them off upon self? Or how comes it that we obtain any satisfaction by putting self in the place of the other party? Perhaps the simplest form of the reflected act is that expressed by Self-worth and Self-estimation, based and begun upon observation of the ways and conduct of our fellow-beings. We soon make comparisons among the individuals about us.

For instance, we see that some do more work than others and so receive more pay, that some are kinder than others and so receive more love, that some surpass others in "astonishing feats" and so attract "the gaze and admiration of a crowd."

> Having thus once learned to look at other persons as performing labors, greater or less, and as realizing fruits to accord; being, moreover, in all respects like our fellows;—we find it an exercise neither difficult nor unmeaning to contemplate self as doing work and receiving the reward.... As we decide between one man and another,—which is worthier, ... so we decide between self and all other men; being, however, in this decision under the bias of our own desires.[37]

When compared with the tactics of someone like Mill, Bain's approach is distinctive, first, for its realism, in that he begins by assuming the existence of the physical world, including as items in it other people and himself; second, by the primacy he gives to social observation, in that we first make judgments about others and only later think of ourselves as one "other" among many; and, third, by his suggestion that this progression from others to self not only explains the origin of the notion of self but also our ability to feel toward the self emotions that originally we felt toward others.

In 1855, the same year in which Bain published *The Senses and the Intellect*, Herbert Spencer (1820–1903) published *The Principles of Psychology*, which grounded psychology in evolutionary biology. William James would later build on both of these contributions to psychology.

Developmental Psychology

At the dawn of the nineteenth century, most British theorists were still torturing themselves trying to find epistemological grounds for personal identity. With the exception of Hazlitt, it was not until Bain, late in the century, that they considered either how self-concepts are actually acquired or the impact of social context on their acquisition. On developmental issues, German and French theorists did better. However, serious interest in the impact of social context on development would await the midcentury appearance of the views of Hegel and Marx.

Early in the century, Johann Friedrich Herbart (1776–1841), who had studied at Jena under Fichte and was the successor at Königsberg to Kant, wrote several works that were primarily psychological, including his *Textbook of Psychology* (1813) and *Psychology as a Science* (1824–25). Independently of Hazlitt, Herbart advocated that one acquires the concept of self in developmental stages, advancing this hypothesis against the backdrop of his view that psychology could be both empirical (but without experiments) and mathematical. He claimed that initially the idea of self comes from humans' experience of their bodily activities, which provides them with information about themselves as well as objects in the world with which they interact. Subsequently, as they more thoughtfully relate past to present thoughts, they come to identify more with their ideas than with their bodies. Thereby, they develop a notion of an ego or subject of their thoughts, which they then generalize as an abstract ego, or identical subject of experience, that persists throughout their lives.

In France, Maine de Biran (1766–1824), who is sometimes regarded as the father of French existentialism, described the human self as developing through a purely sensitive, animal phase, to a phase of will and freedom that finally culminates in spiritual experiences that transcend humanity. As a developmental psychologist, he was concerned especially with the active or voluntary self, which infants first notice in experiencing the resistance of the world to their desires. He claimed that the continuity of voluntary agency provides children with a basis for their concept of themselves as extended over time.

In America, the genetic psychology of James Mark Baldwin (1861–1934) had an enormous influence on subsequent developmentalists, particularly on Piaget. Baldwin, a psychologist, and his friend, Josiah Royce, a philosopher, theorized about the social origins of the self at about the same time, publishing their ideas, in the mid-1890s, in different works. The fundamental principle of Baldwin's theory was that imitation or mimicry was the foundation of social life and the origin of the infant's understanding of the category *person*. This principle had been suggested, in the latter part of the eighteenth century, in theories about the role of mimicry in sympathetic imagination. Adam Smith, in particular, likened imagination to mimicry and connected both to social phenomena through the medium of sympathy. Later, Dugald Stewart (1753–1828), who replaced Smith at Edinburgh, recognized what he called sympathetic imitation as an important social phenomenon. He even postulated that such mimicry was especially powerful in childhood and, as such, at the very foundations of social life. However, with the possible exceptions of Coleridge and Hazlitt, no one in the eighteenth or early nineteenth century seemed to recognize how these phenomena were connected to the development of infants' acquired knowledge of themselves and others as people with minds. Thinkers tended to presuppose an individualistic perspective. Understanding one's own mind was acquired prior to acquiring knowledge of the minds of others.

By the end of the century, James Baldwin and Josiah Royce were able to go beyond this. Baldwin, in particular, had an especially clear grip on the concept of psychological development. In contrasting the old-fashioned soul view ("a fixed substance, with fixed attributes"), he said that it was as if "knowledge of the soul was immediate in consciousness, and adequate." "The mind was best understood where best or most fully manifested; its higher 'faculties' even when not in operation, were still there, but asleep." It was, he said, as if soul theorists assumed that "the man is father of the child," that is, that "if the adult consciousness shows the presence of principles not observable in the child consciousness, we must suppose, nevertheless, that they are really present in the child consciousness beyond the reach of our observation." The proper procedure ("the genetic idea"), Baldwin claimed, is precisely the opposite of this.

> Are there principles in the adult consciousness which do not appear in the child consciousness, then the adult consciousness must, if possible, be interpreted by principles present in the child consciousness; and when this is not possible, the conditions under which later principles take their rise and get their development must still be adequately explored.[38]

No one in the eighteenth century had such a clear grasp of the notion of mental development.

In Baldwin's theory of the origins of self-consciousness, rather than first becoming aware of themselves as persons, children first become aware of others. Later, by becoming aware of their effort to imitate others, they become aware of their own "subjective" activity. Next, they come to understand what others feel by "ejecting" their own inner states onto others: "The subjective becomes *ejective*; that is, other people's bodies, says the child to himself, have experiences *in them* such as mine has. They also have *me's*." In this last phase, Baldwin concludes, "the social self is born."

In *History of Psychology* (1913), Baldwin summarized a mature version of his theory:

> In the personal self, the social is individualized.... A constant give-and-take process—a "social dialectic"—is found between the individual and his social fellows. By this process the materials of self-hood are absorbed and assimilated. The "self" is a gradually forming nucleus in the mind; a mass of feeling, effort, and knowledge. It grows in

feeling by contagion, in knowledge by imitation, in will by opposition and obedience. The outline of the individual gradually appears, and every stage it shows the pattern of the social situation in which it becomes constantly a more and more adequate and competent unit.

He continued:

The consciousness of the self, thus developed, carries with it that of the "alter"-selves, the other "socii," who are also determinations of the same social matter. The bond, there-fore, that binds the members of the group together is reflected in the self-consciousness of each member.... When the self has become a conscious and active person, we may say that the mental individual as such is born. But the individual remains part of the whole out of which he has arisen, a whole that is collective in character and of which he is a specification.[39]

In the twentieth century, this collectivist vision of the origins of self conscious-ness, which was beyond the scope of early thinkers, came to dominate the psy-chology of the self. Yet even as *psychologists* increasingly have found the origins and identity of the individual self within, and only within, a shared social reality, twentieth century analytic *philosophers*, in accounting for personal identity, have maintained an individualistic focus.

The Last Philosopher-Psychologist

Nineteenth-century philosophy of self and personal identity was dominated in the first half of the century by Kant and in the second half by Hegel. Concur-rent with philosophical developments, there was a growing spirit of naturalized science, typified by Darwin and independently including inquiry into the devel-opment of self-concepts and the physiology of the brain. The American philos-opher and psychologist William James (1842–1910) integrated this naturalizing impulse with a scientific philosophy of the self. James, no friend of either Kant or Hegel, remarked, "With Kant, complication both of thought and statement was an inborn infirmity, enhanced by the musty academicism of his Königsberg existence. With Hegel it was a raging fever."[40] James's more straightforward alternative was the philosophical movement known as *pragmatism*, which was based on the principle that the criterion of an idea's merit is its usefulness.

For present purposes, the part of James's work that matters most is not his pragmatism per se, but two chapters from his *Principles of Psychology*. In the first of these—"On the Stream of Consciousness"—he began his "study of the mind from within."[41] In his view, beginning in this way meant that one does not begin, as Hume did, with "sensations, as the simplest mental facts, and proceed synthetically, constructing each higher stage from those below it." Rather, consciousness presents itself as a much more complex phenomenon: "what we call simple sensations are results of discriminative attention, pushed often to a very high degree." When psychologists begin, as they should, with "the fact of thinking itself" and then analyze this fact, they discover, he claimed, that thought tends to be part of a personal consciousness. In other words, they discover that thoughts, as they actually occur, are not separate but belong with certain other thoughts, depending on whose thoughts they are: "My thought belongs with my other thoughts, and your thought with your other thoughts."[42]

James conceded the theoretical possibility that there may be a mere thought that is not anyone's thought, but he said that if there were any such thing, we could not know it: "The only states of consciousness that we naturally deal with are found in personal consciousnesses, minds, selves, concrete particular I's and you's," each of which "keeps its own thoughts to itself." Thoughts are not traded, and each person has direct access only to his or her own thoughts. "Absolute insulation, irreducible pluralism, is the law." No thought of which we have knowledge is "this thought or that thought, but my thought, every thought being owned." This ownership provides a natural barrier between thoughts, preventing one of "the most absolute breaches in nature." As a consequence, James claimed, the "personal self" should be "the immediate datum in psychology." "The universal conscious fact is not 'feelings and thoughts exist,' but 'I think' and 'I feel.'" It follows, he thought, that no psychology that hopes to stand "can question the existence of personal selves." On the contrary, "it is, and must remain, true that the thoughts which psychology studies do continually tend to appear as parts of personal selves."[43]

A problem arises, though, from the fact that dissociative phenomena, such as automatic writing, reveal that there are "buried feelings and thoughts" that are themselves part of "secondary personal selves." These secondary selves "are for the most part very stupid and contracted, and are cut off at ordinary times from communication with the regular and normal self of the individual." Even so, "they still form conscious unities, have continuous memories, speak, write, invent distinct names for themselves, or adopt names that are suggested and, in short, are entirely worthy of that title of secondary personalities which is now commonly given them." As Pierre Janet showed, James wrote, these secondary personalities often "result from the splitting of what ought to be a single complete self into two parts, of which one lurks in the background whilst the other appears on the surface as the only self the man or woman has."[44]

In the second of James's two most relevant chapters—"On the Consciousness of Self"—he began by considering the widest and most empirical issues, then proceeded to the narrower and less empirical, ending with "the pure, Ego." He said that "the Empirical Self" that each of us has is what each of us is most tempted to call *me*. But, he warned, "the line between *me* and *mine* is difficult to draw."

> We feel and act about certain things that are ours very much as we feel and act about ourselves. Our fame, our children, the work of our hands, may be as dear to us as our bodies are, and arouse the same feelings and the same acts of reprisal if attacked. And our bodies themselves, are they simply ours, or are they us?

In James's view, there are no definite answers to such questions. "*In its widest possible sense, a man's Self is the sum total of all that he CAN call his,* not only his body and his psychic powers, but his clothes and his house, his wife and children," and so on. "All these things give him the same emotions. If they wax and prosper, he feels triumphant; if they dwindle and die away, he feels cast down,—not necessarily in the same degree for each thing, but in much the same way for all."[45] James concluded that "the Self" may be divided into the empirical self, on the one hand, which includes the material, social, and spiritual selves, and the pure Ego, on the other.

Our material selves include our bodies, possessions, and families. For instance, if a family member dies, "a part of our very selves is gone. If they do anything wrong, it is our shame. If they are insulted, our anger flashes forth as readily as if we stood in their place." But each of these to different degrees. For instance, some possessions, say our homes, may be more a part of us than others.

Our social selves consist of social recognition: "*a man has as many social selves*" as there are individuals and groups "*who recognize him* and carry an image of him in their mind. To wound any one of these his images is to wound him."

> The most peculiar social self which one is apt to have is in the mind of the person one is in love with. The good or bad fortunes of this self cause the most intense elation and dejection—unreasonable enough as measured by every other standard than that of the organic feeling of the individual.[46]

A person's fame, and his honor, also are among his social selves.

James said that by *the spiritual self*, that is, the empirical spiritual self, he means one's "inner or subjective being." This inner being is a set of "psychic disposi-tions" that "are the most enduring and intimate part of the self," including one's ability "to argue and discriminate," one's "moral sensibility and conscience," and one's "indomitable will." It is "only when these are altered," James said, that a person is said to have been alienated from him or herself. But, of course, not every alteration results in alienation.

This spiritual self may be considered either abstractly—say, by dividing con-sciousness into faculties—or concretely. Considered concretely, it may be consid-ered either as "the entire stream of our personal consciousness" or the "present 'segment' or 'section' of that stream." Either way, James wrote, "our considering the spiritual self at all is a reflective process," the "result of our abandoning the outward-looking point of view" in order to "think ourselves as thinkers." James concluded, "This attention to thought as such, and the identification of ourselves with it rather than with any of the objects which it reveals, is a momentous and in some respects a rather mysterious operation, of which we need here only say that as a matter of fact it exists; and that in everyone, at an early age, the distinc-tion between thought as such, and what it is 'of' or 'about,' has become familiar to the mind."[47]

Considering the spiritual self abstractly, "the stream as a whole is identified with the Self far more than any outward thing" But:

> *a certain portion of the stream abstracted from the rest* is so identified in an altogether peculiar degree, and is felt by all men as a sort of innermost centre within the circle, of sanctuary within the citadel, constituted by the subjective life as a whole. Compared with this element of the stream, the other parts, even of the subjective life, seem tran-sient external possessions, of which each in turn can be disowned, whilst that which disowns them remains.

But, what is "this self of all the other selves"? James answered that most would say that it is "the active element in all consciousness."

> It is what welcomes or rejects. It presides over the perception of sensations, and by giving or withholding its assent it influences the movements they tend to arouse. It is the home of interest,—not the pleasant or the painful, not even pleasure or pain, as such, but that within us to which pleasure and pain, the pleasant and the painful, speak. It is the source of effort and attention, and the place from which appear to emanate the fiats of the will.

A physiologist, James said, would associate the self with "the process by which ideas or incoming sensations are 'reflected' or pass over into outward acts." For it is "a sort of junction at which sensory ideas terminate and from which motor ideas proceed, and forming a kind of link between the two." Moreover, it is "more incessantly there than any other single element of the mental life, the other elements end by seeming to accrete round it and to belong to it. It becomes opposed to them as the permanent is opposed to the changing and inconstant."[48]

So much, James thought, would be a matter of common agreement. But as soon as one tried to go farther, opinions would diverge, some calling this "self of selves" a *simple active substance* or *soul* and others a *fiction*. Yet this self of selves is not merely a object of thought but is also felt: "Just as the body is felt, the feeling of which is also an abstraction, because never is the body felt all alone, but always together with other things."

In what, then, does "the feeling of this central active self" consist? Not, James answers, in the apprehension of a *"purely spiritual element."* Rather, *"whenever my introspective glance succeeds in turning round quickly enough to catch one of these manifestations of spontaneity in the act, all it can ever feel distinctly is some bodily process, for the most part taking place within the head,"* or *"between the head and throat."* James conceded that there may be more to the apprehension of this "spiritual self" but insisted that "these cephalic motions are the portions of my innermost activity of which I am most distinctly aware." If the rest, "which I cannot yet define should prove to be like unto these distinct portions in me, and I like other men, *it would follow that our entire feeling of spiritual activity, or what commonly passes by that name, is really a feeling of bodily activities whose exact nature is by most men overlooked."*[49]

Were this hypothesis true, one consequence, James claimed, is that in order to have "a self that I can *care for,* nature must first present me with some *object* interesting enough to make me instinctively wish to appropriate it for its *own* sake," which I would then use as the basis to create a material, social, and spiritual self. The origin of the entire array of self-expressions and behaviors is that "certain *things* appeal to primitive and instinctive impulses of our nature, and that we follow their destinies with an excitement that owes nothing to a reflective source." These are "the primordial constituents" of our *mes.* Whatever else is subsequently "followed with the same sort of interest, form our remoter and more secondary self." Hence, James claimed, the words *me* and *self,* "so far as they arouse feeling and connote emotional worth," mean everything which has "*the power to produce in a stream of consciousness excitement of a certain peculiar sort."*[50]

James said that a human's "most palpable selfishness" is "bodily selfishness," and his "most palpable self," his body. But a human does not love his body because he identifies himself with it; rather, he identifies himself with it because he loves it.[51] This self-love is part of a more general phenomenon. Every creature instinctively "has a certain selective interest in certain portions of the world," where "interest in things means the attention and emotion which the thought of them will excite, and the actions which their presence will evoke." Thus, animals in every species are particularly interested in their own prey or food, enemies, sexual mates, and progeny. These things are intrinsically interesting and "are cared for for their own sakes."

In James's view, individual thoughts are, in effect, agents. Thoughts distinguish on the basis of how they themselves feel those other thoughts which belong to the self from those which are merely conceived: "The former have a warmth and intimacy about them of which the latter are completely devoid." James said that the main question of interest is "what the consciousness may mean when it calls the present self the same with one of the past selves which it has in mind."[52] The key to his answer is "warmth and intimacy," which "in the present self, reduces itself to either of two things—something in the feeling which we have of the thought itself, as thinking, or else the feeling of the body's actual existence at the moment," or both. "We cannot realize our present self without simultaneously feeling one or other of these two things." And "which distant selves do fulfil the condition, when represented? Obviously those, and only those, which fulfilled it when they were alive."

Continuity and similarity importantly affect one's sense of self: "the distant selves appear to our thought as having for hours of time been continuous with each other, and the most recent ones of them continuous with the Self of the present moment, melting into it by slow degrees; and we get a still stronger bond of union":

> Continuity makes us unite what dissimilarity might otherwise separate; similarity makes us unite what discontinuity might hold apart. *The sense of our own personal identity, then, is exactly like any one of our other perceptions of sameness among phenomena.* And it must not be taken to mean more.... The past and present selves compared are the same just so far as they are the same, and no farther. A uniform feeling of 'warmth,' of bodily existence (or an equally uniform feeling of pure psychic energy?) pervades them all; and this is what gives them a generic unity, and makes them the same in kind. But this generic unity coexists with generic differences just as real as the unity. And if from the one point of view they are one self, from others they are as truly not one but many.[53]

James suggested that we think of the self and its unity like we might think of a herd of cattle: The owner gathers the cattle together into one herd because he finds on each of them his brand: "The 'owner' symbolized here that 'section' of consciousness, or pulse of thought, which we have all along represented as the vehicle of the judgment of identity; and the 'brand' symbolizes the characters of warmth and continuity, by reason of which the judgment is made." The brand marks the cattle as belonging together. But "no beast would be so branded unless he belonged to the owner of the herd. They are not his because they are branded; they are branded because they are his."

This account, James said, knocks "the bottom out of" common sense: "For common-sense insists that the unity of all the selves is not a mere appearance of similarity or continuity, ascertained after the fact," but "involves a real belonging to a real Owner, to a pure spiritual entity of some kind." It is thought that it is the relation of the various constituents to this entity that makes them "stick together." But in reality, the unity "is only potential, its centre ideal, like the 'centre of gravity' in physics, until the constituents are collected together." According to common-sense, "there must be a real proprietor in the case of the selves, or else their actual accretion into a 'personal consciousness' would never have taken place." But what actually does the uniting is "the real, present onlooking, remembering, 'judging thought' or identifying 'section' of the stream." This is what "owns" some of what it "surveys, and disowns the rest," thus making "a unity that is actualized and anchored and does not merely float in the blue air of possibility."[54]

Thus, in James's view, unity is not present until the unifying thought creates it: "It is as if wild cattle were lassoed by a newly-created settler and then owned for the first time. But the essence of the matter to common-sense is that the past thoughts never were wild cattle, they were always owned. The Thought does not capture them, but as soon as it comes into existence it finds them already its own." Thus, James said, common sense would have us acknowledge an "Arch-Ego, dominating the entire stream of thought and all the selves that may be represented in it, as the ever self-same and changeless principle implied in their union." The "soul" of traditional metaphysics, as well as "the 'Transcendental Ego' of the Kantian Philosophy," are but misguided "attempts to satisfy this urgent demand of common-sense."[55]

James said that just as "we can imagine a long succession of herdsmen coming rapidly into possession of the same cattle by transmission of an original title by bequest," it is "a patent fact of consciousness" that "the 'title' of a collective self" is passed from one Thought to another in an analogous way:

Each pulse of cognitive consciousness, each Thought, dies away and is replaced by another. The other, among the things it knows, knows its own predecessor, and finding it 'warm,' in the way we have described, greets it, saying: "Thou art mine, and part of the same self with me." Each later Thought, knowing and including thus the Thoughts which went before, is the final receptacle—and appropriating them is the final owner—of all that they contain and own. Each Thought is thus born an owner, and dies owned, transmitting whatever it realized as its Self to its own later proprietor.... Such standing-as-representative, and such adopting, are perfectly clear phenomenal relations. The Thought which, whilst it knows another Thought and the Object of that Other, appropriates the Other and the Object which the Other appropriated, is still a perfectly distinct phenomenon from that Other; it may hardly resemble it; it may be far removed from it in space and time.[56]

James conceded that his account leaves a crucial element unclear: "the *act of appropriation* itself."

The word, *appropriate*, James said, is "meaningless" unless what is appropriated are "objects in the hands of something else":

A thing cannot appropriate itself; it is itself; and still less can it disown itself. There must be an agent of the appropriating and disowning; but that agent we have already named. It is the Thought to whom the various 'constituents' are known. That Thought is a vehicle of choice as well as of cognition; and among the choices it makes are these appropriations, or repudiations, of its 'own.' But the Thought never is an object in its own hands, it never appropriates or disowns itself. It appropriates to itself, it is the actual focus of accretion, the hook from which the chain of past selves dangles, planted firmly in the Present, which alone passes for real, and thus keeping the chain from being a purely ideal thing. Anon the hook itself will drop into the past with all it carries, and then be treated as an object and appropriated by a new Thought in the new present which will serve as living hook in turn.

Thus, James claimed, the present moment of consciousness is "the darkest in the whole series." While "it may feel its own immediate existence," nothing can be known *about* it until it recedes into the past.

Its appropriations are therefore less to *itself* than to the most intimately felt *part of its present Object, the body, and the central adjustments*, which accompany the act of thinking, in the head. *These are the real nucleus of our personal identity*, and it is their actual existence, realized as a solid present fact, which makes us say 'as sure *as I exist*, those past facts were part of myself.' They are the kernel to which the represented parts of the Self are assimilated, accreted, and knit on; and even were Thought entirely unconscious of itself in the act of thinking, these 'warm' parts of its present object would be a firm basis on which the consciousness of personal identity would rest.[57]

Such consciousness, James said, "can be fully described without supposing any other agent than a succession of perishing thoughts, endowed with the functions of appropriation and rejection, and of which some can know and appropriate or reject objects already known, appropriated, or rejected by the rest."

Thus, in James's view, the subjective phenomena of consciousness do not need any reference to "any more simple or substantial agent than the present Thought or 'section' of the stream." The immaterial soul, he said, "explains nothing." But were one to go this route, James added, rather than individual souls, "I find the notion of some sort of an anima mundi thinking in all of us to be a more promising hypothesis."[58]

According to James, the core of personhood is "the incessant presence of two elements, an objective person, known by a passing subjective Thought and recognized as continuing in time."[59] James resolved to use the word *me* for "the empirical person" and *I* for "the judging Thought." Since the "me" is constantly changing: "the identity found by the I in its me is only a loosely construed thing, an identity 'on the whole,' just like that which any outside observer might find in the same assemblage of facts."[60] The I of any given moment is a temporal slice of "a stream of thought," each part of which, as "I," can "remember those which went before, and know the things they knew" and "emphasize and care paramountly for certain ones among them as 'me,' and appropriate to these the rest." The core of what is thought to be the "me" "is always the bodily existence felt to be present at the time." [61]

Remembered past feelings that "resemble this present feeling are deemed to belong to the same me with it." And "whatever other things are perceived to be associated with this feeling are deemed to form part of that me's experience; and of them certain ones (which fluctuate more or less) are reckoned to be themselves constituents of the me in a larger sense," such as one's clothes, material possessions, friends, honors, and so on. But while the "me" is "an empirical aggregate of things objectively known," the "I" that "knows them cannot itself be an aggregate." Rather, "it is a Thought, at each moment different from that of the last moment, but appropriative of the latter, together with all that the latter called its own."[62] In other words, what one calls "the I" is constantly changing. The *I* as a persisting thing is a fiction.

XII

BEFORE THE FALL

The twentieth century began in grand ideologies and ended in narrow specializations.
Between the two there was a long night of two World Wars, in the aftermath of
which theorists put the knife to optimism, modernism, and the hegemony of
Western culture. Many theorists began to think of the self more as a product of
culture than as its creator. The last half of the century witnessed rampant, uninte-
grated scientific specialization; the withering philosophical critiques of deconstruction and postmodernism; the penetrating attack in analytic philosophy on
the very concept and importance of personal identity; novel perspectives spawned
by feminism, postcolonialism, technological development, and a newfound
awareness of gender, sexual, and ethnic identities. As a consequence, the self,
which began the century looking unified—the master of its own house—ended it
looking fragmented—a byproduct of social and psychological conditions. Meanwhile, for almost everybody, at least in industrialized cultures, life became more
complex. As a result, individual experience may itself have changed in ways that
mirrored the growing complexity and fragmentation in theory.

In the late nineteenth century, in the work of psychologists like Wilhelm
Wundt and William James, philosophy and psychology, despite growing dispar-
ity in their interests and approaches, still enjoyed a marriage of convenience.
The divorce came in 1913. In that year, 107 professors of philosophy from
Germany, Austria, and Switzerland signed a petition protesting the filling of
chairs of philosophy with experimental psychologists. They claimed that
although "experimental psychology has long been recognized as an independent
field which demands the full energy of a scholar," professorships of philosophy

were still being filled with experimentalists. The time has long since past, the petitioners concluded, to face up to the reality that philosophy and psychology are separate disciplines and that they should be funded and staffed separately.[1]

Philosophy

For most of the twentieth century, philosophers of all schools, whatever else they disagreed about, and they disagreed about almost everything else, agreed that philosophy had a method distinct from the sciences. To phenomenologists, initially the method was that of unveiling the generic structures that underlie conceptualizations of ourselves and the world in experience and thought; subsequently, the method became that of recovering a more authentic version of experience. To analytic philosophers in the 1920s and 1930s—"logical positivists"—the method was analyzing concepts. To many analytic philosophers in the middle third of the century—"ordinary language philosophers"—it was that of investigating the everyday uses of language in order not to solve but to dissolve philosophical problems.[2]

In both phenomenology and analytic philosophy, from the beginning of the century (after William James) until the 1960s, no important philosopher of the self took the view that philosophy properly done is continuous with empirical science in the sense that it takes scientific results as its point of departure. That idea, which among analytic philosophers is so widespread today, owes its popularity to the ascendency of analytic pragmatism.[3] So, one way of thinking about philosophy of the self in the twentieth century is that during the first half of the century it labored to separate itself from science and in the last half to reintegrate itself with science. The relevant sciences were psychology and sociology.

Also in both phenomenology and analytic philosophy, but earlier in phenomenology, the idea caught on that immediate experience is suspect. Rather than a basis on which a view of the world, but particularly of the relations between self and other, could be securely constructed, it became commonplace to suppose that immediate experience must be understood as a product of social and historical influences and may need to be cleansed of its misleading or enslaving accretions.

In the phenomenological tradition, the influence of Hegel and Marx, together with the demise of foundationalism in epistemology, gave rise to a greatly heightened interest in social conceptions of the self. Max Scheler (1874–1928) began to examine social attitudes, such as empathy and sympathy. Heidegger, and later Sartre, stressed that the idea of an individual isolated from social and worldly involvements is an abstraction. In the analytic tradition, ordinary-language philosophy, inspired by "the later Wittgenstein," stressed such themes as the impossibility of a "private language" and the epistemological significance of collectively shared "forms of life."

Phenomenology

In developing a method for the description and analysis of consciousness, Edmund Husserl (1859–1938) aimed to resolve the opposition between empiricism and rationalism by exposing the origins of each in the interests and structures of experience.[4] In 1901, he wrote that "pure phenomenology represents an area of neutral investigations"—not itself an empirical science, but one "in which different sciences are rooted." Its purpose, he said, is "to prepare the ground for *psychology as an empirical science.*"[5]

In *Ideas: A General Introduction to Pure Phenomenology* (1913), Husserl set himself the goal of establishing a body of knowledge that is not based on any presuppositions. By his slogan, "back to the things themselves," he meant back to what is *given* in experience. His aim was first to intuit and then to describe what is given, which would then become the basic data on which theories could be built. He thought of himself as the first authentic empiricist. To get to the absolute bottom of things, he claimed, we need to purify our intuitions by suspending use of any general concepts as well as belief in physical objects, the world, and even our own existence as bodies, until we can reveal the basis of these in experience. He called this suspension of belief a "phenomenological reduction" and claimed that when pursued to the end, it revealed the indubitable existence of a "transcendental ego" or "pure consciousness," for which everything that exists is an object. The transcendental ego, he said, is not accessible to empirical observation but only to phenomenological description. Whereas other things exist only "relative" to the transcendental ego, it exists "absolutely" and is indestructible. Even if the entire world were destroyed, he said, it would remain. It is the absolute foundation of the experienced world.

By 1935, Husserl had modified his view. He now held that the transcendental ego is not absolute, but "correlative" to the world. He also held that the world is what it is not for any transcendental individual, but for an intersubjective community of individuals. The subject matter of phenomenology, he said, should be collective experience. Thus conceived, phenomenology was now closer to sharing its subject matter with the empirical sciences, but it was still more basic than them in that it focused on revealing the necessary conditions for the coherence and adequacy of experience. Through examining communal experience, it became the study of the lived world and of our experience of it.

Later, Husserl tried to understand the status of the "soul" not as a metaphysical entity but as psychic life that is revealed in our experience in and of the world. Basic to his view was that while the soul is, of course, in the world, it is not in it in the same way that a physical object is in it. This difference in the way in which the soul is in the world derives from the fact that the human body is not only living but self-appropriated; that is, "it is 'my physical body,' which I 'move,' in and through which I 'hold sway,' which I 'animate.'"[6]

In Husserl's view, people experience their own souls but not the souls of others. They experience their souls through their "holding sway" over their own bodily actions, such as "seeing with the eyes, touching with the fingers, . . . striking, lifting, resisting, and so on, objects in the world." In what would seem to be a development of Kant's transcendental unity of apperception, Husserl claimed:

> It is only *my* being-as-ego, as holding sway, that I actually experience as itself, in its own essence; and each person experiences only his own. All such holding-sway occurs in modes of "movement," but the "I move" in holding-sway (I move my hands, touching or pushing something) is not in itself the spatial movement of a physical body, which as such could be perceived by everyone . . . the activity of holding sway, "kinesthesis," which is embodied together with the body's movement, is not itself in space as a spatial movement but is only indirectly co-localized in that movement.[7]

That is, what I experience in my own case are actions, rather than mere bodily movements, and I experience these as my own actions, not the actions of others. Moreover, I experience them as spatial, but in a phenomenological, rather than a physical, sense of spatial since it is only one's bodily movements that are truly physically spatial.

According to Husserl it is only through first experiencing my own actions that I later experience the actions of others, and through their actions their subjectivity:

> Only through my own originally experienced holding sway . . . can I understand another physical body as a living body in which another "I" is embodied and holds sway; this again, then, is a mediation, but one of a quite different sort from the mediation of inauthentic localization upon which it is founded.

In other words, it is not that I first experience an ego—a "soul"—locating it where its body is located. Rather, I first experience my own soul holding sway over my own body, that is, my own *activity*. Then, I experience the activity of others. From these latter observations I posit the souls of others not as substances but as others "holding sway" over their bodily movements that are their own actions: "Only in this way do other ego-subjects firmly belong to 'their' bodies for me and are localized here or there in space-time."[8]

In Husserl's view, physical bodies in space are individual in virtue of their causal relationships with other physical bodies. Souls are individual on a different basis: "For the ego, space and time are not principles of individuation; it knows no natural causality.... Its effectiveness is its holding-sway-as-ego; this occurs immediately through its kinesthesis, as holding-sway in its living body."[9] That is, the ego as such is neither localized in space nor causally related to any bodies that are localized in space in the same sense of "causality" in which bodies in space are causally related to each other. Rather, the ego, which is not a substance in its own right, is causally related to physical bodies in the way appropriate to egos, that is, in its "holding sway" over those of the movements of its own body which are its actions. Thus did Husserl try to avoid Descartes's problem of being unable to explain how the soul causes bodily actions.

Martin Heidegger (1889–1976), who had been a student of Husserl, focused on what he called "the question of Being." His early and most influential work, *Being and Time* (1927), is primarily about *Dasein*, or human being, as the place where the question of Being arises. His aim was to disclose what it means to be a human being. The basic problem, in his view, is that the essential truth about ourselves has been covered over by millennia of cultural and linguistic accretions. He claimed that much of language is *fallen discourse* and that nonphilosophical language is *mere chatter*. In other words, we have become obscure to ourselves not only by inherited intellectual conventions and theories but by our routinized habits of thinking and acting. His project was to remove this obscuring rubbish so that human existence could show itself.

In Heidegger's view, *Dasein*, which includes all of those beings for whom the question of Being—the meaning of their own existences—is an issue, has a temporal structure. His central project was to reveal that structure. To do so, he reconceptualized the self as a dynamic system of interrelationships of meanings or signification. He concluded that human existence, at its most fundamental level, is a making intelligible of the place in which we find ourselves. "Dasein," he said, "*is* its disclosedness." This process of making intelligible—"*Aletheia*," "unconcealment," "disclosing"—is the most primordial form of "truth."[10] In other words, against the Cartesian tradition of thinking of individual humans as thinking subjects and the Kantian one of thinking of them as transcendental unities of apperception, Heidegger understood humans as embedded in a dynamic system of relationships, called *being-in-the-world*, which affords the only true access that we have to ourselves. What it reveals is a being who is not only enmeshed in but constituted of dynamic relationships—physical, social, and historical. We never see ourselves as if from God's point of view or bring ourselves before ourselves as mere objects.

Heidegger claimed that ordinarily we have no experience of ourselves as subjects causing our own activity. One simply copes, in an organized purposive way. One is only occasionally in a deliberate, purposeful, reflective mode in which oneself as a subject is distinguished from the object of one's activities. For example, normally when I enter a room I cope with the furniture, rather than think about it. What enables me to do this is not a set of beliefs about rooms and furniture but behavioral skills that I have developed in walking through many rooms. In such situations, "Self and world are not two entities, like subject and object." Rather, "self and world are the basic determination of Dasein itself in the unity of the structure of being-in-the-world." Yet in the everyday interpretation of ourselves, we tend to understand ourselves "objectively," in terms of the "world" with which we are concerned. "When Dasein has itself in view *ontically*, that is, in this misleading way, it fails *to see* itself in its true nature, which is in terms of temporality and situatedness." Dasein does this because it is essentially "falling." That is, it *"flees* in the face of itself into the 'they.' " The source of Dasein's ordinary "I-talk" is the they-self, which is an inauthentic voice.[11]

To see ourselves for what we are, Heidegger claimed, we need to free ourselves from this inauthenticity:

> In the "natural" ontical way in which the "I" talks, the phenomenal content of the Dasein which one has in view in the "I" gets overlooked. But this gives *no justification in our joining in this overlooking of it*, or for forcing upon the problematic of the Self an inappropriate "categorial" horizon when we interpret the "I" ontologically.[12]

In other words, our being is revealed, to the limited extent that it is, through our use of language, which can articulate the meaning of the situations in which we are involved. However, this process inevitably involves "falling," that is, the covering-over of our essence by interpreting ourselves in the publicly available but distorting language of everyday "ontic" life. Heidegger thus aimed to interpret our everyday ontic experience "ontologically," that is, in terms of what it reveals about the essence of human existence. For example, he argues that our ordinary feelings of *guilt* bear witness to the fact that as we make choices, we are always actualizing one possible self at the expense of others. Our guilty indebtedness to these other possible selves is thus an ineliminable feature of our existence, which is symptomatic of our essential ontological "finitude."

It is in the experience of *anxiety* that our authentic being makes itself felt. A symptom that something has gone terribly wrong, anxiety testifies to the "groundlessness" of human existence and reveals an ineradicable insecurity. This insecurity is due to the fact that our existential trajectories—our life projects, roles, and identities—have "always already" been shaped by a past that we can never get behind and they head off into a future in which they will always be incomplete, cut short by a death we can neither avoid nor control. We exist as a "thrown project." We have no choice but to project our life projects toward the impenetrable horizon of our impending deaths. This gives rise to the "uncanny" feeling that we are not at home in our lives.

According to Heidegger, our "existence" at root is such a standing-out into time, a temporal suspension between birth and death. Because the essential temporal structures of our lives determine how things come to matter to us, he characterized these structures collectively as "care."

> Care does not need to be founded in a Self. But existentiality, as constitutive for care, provides the ontological constitution of Dasein's Self-constancy, to which there belongs, in accordance with the full structural content of care, its Being-fallen factically into non-Self-constancy. When fully conceived the care-structure includes the phenomenon of Selfhood. This phenomenon is clarified by interpreting the meaning of care; and it is as care that Dasein's totality of being has been defined.[13]

The goal of *Being and Time* was to reveal the essential temporal structures of our lives in terms of which we make our own existence intelligible.

According to Heidegger, only when we have become aware of the ontological structures conditioning our existence does an "authentic" life lived in ontic-ontological accord become possible. He claims that in decisive moments of resolution, we discover ways of integrating our newfound existential knowledge into the projects which constitute our lives, thereby appropriating our lives so as to make them our own.

In his later work, Heidegger abandoned the notion that there is any *essential* structure of Dasein. He continued to address what he took to be the question of Being and to characterize the form this question has taken in our Cartesian, technological age, in which scientific results are regarded as the highest type of truth. He criticized technology not only for the now commonly recognized ways in which it damages society and culture but because in a world in which technology is paramount, everything—human relationships, living arrange-ments, art, religion, communication, education, politics, even our very biological and intellectual lives—becomes packaged and put into operation in ways that obscure the authentic nature of our being.

In Jean-Paul Sartre's (1905–1980) first book, *The Transcendence of the Ego* (1936), he held, in opposition to Cartesians and Husserl, that the existence and nature of one's own self is "no more certain for consciousness" than are the selves of others. It is only "more intimate."[14] There is no private self. The self is public—an object in the world. Hence, there is no need to struggle, as had the Cartesians and Husserl, with the question of what would justify transcending one's private self in order to get to the world. We are, as Heidegger had insisted, already and primarily being-in-the-world.

Like Heidegger—and, for that matter, even like the later Husserl—Sartre claimed that lived experience is systematically concealed. It is as if the experi-ences of which we are immediately aware have been filtered through a distort-ing lens of traditional concepts, beliefs, and language. It is possible, as both Husserl and Heidegger also insisted, to unravel these distortions and uncover a more revealing, unfiltered "prereflective experience." In Sartre's view, to approach phenomenology, as Husserl had done, by adopting the transcendental standpoint, obscures the true nature of this prereflective experience. Instead, he tried to recover its true nature by investigating the self within the framework of its worldly connections.

Also like Heidegger, Sartre discovered a fundamental distinction between the mode of being of material objects (being-in-itself) and that of conscious beings (being-for-itself). He claimed that consciousness cannot exist by itself but only by being conscious of something and that consciousness, which is inherently empty, is exhausted in the pure apprehension of its object. Since consciousness isn't anything, its content is provided not by what it is intrinsically but by what it is not.

Prereflective consciousness of an object is consciousness of it with no self-consciousness, that is, no awareness of ourselves as being aware of an object: "When I run after a streetcar, when I look at the time, when I am absorbed in looking at a portrait, no I is present. There is consciousness of the streetcar-having-to-be-caught."[15] However, Sartre claimed that even in prereflective consciousness, there is a kind of indirect awareness of self. While counting cigarettes, he said, I may not be aware of my counting them. Yet if I were asked what I was doing, I would answer that I was counting them. Thus, "losing oneself in the world," which is the defining characteristic of prereflective consciousness, is losing oneself only at the level of consciousness. Outside of consciousness, the organism may still be tracking its activities. By contrast, in reflexive consciousness, one does encounter an ego or I not as an object but as an awareness of objects.

The ego or I emerges through the objectifying "look" of the other, which forces one's own reflection to turn upon itself. For Sartre, it is in the other's "look" directed toward me that I first encounter myself as an in-itself. In my inward life as a for-itself, I am fully immersed in my activities, counting cigarettes, reading a book, and so on. I *am* those activities, not a subject performing them. My for-itself consciousness is no more than the consciousness of such activities. However, with the appearance of "the other," I become aware of myself "engaged in the activities" and thereby become an "I" to myself for the first time. Thus, "the other is the indispensable mediator between myself and me." "By the mere appearance of the other, I am put in a position of passing judgment on myself as an object. For it is as an object that I appear to the other." Before the intrusion of the other, I was only a for-itself. After the intrusion of the other I become an in-itself.[16]

Sartre mentions shame to illustrate his point. While I am engaged prereflectively in a shameful act, I *am* that act. There is no "I" apart from the act itself. But once captured in the look of another, I realize that there is an I who is engaged in a shameful act. I suddenly acquire a self to be ashamed of. "Shame is shame *of oneself before the Other*; these two structures are inseparable. But at the same time I need the Other in order to realize fully all the structures of my being. The For-itself refers to the For-others."[17] Thus, for Sartre, as for Hegel in his account of the master-slave relationship, I and other are interdependent. Every human is both subject and object, for-itself and in-itself, and is brought into being by the relations between them.

In Sartre's view, human existence is the relationship between a person's present and future. The past, which is gone, is no part of one's essence. Either there is no essence of oneself, or if there is, it is ephemeral. What one is in each moment depends on how in that moment one projects oneself into the future. So existence—the activity of projecting oneself into the future—always precedes and determines essence. Humans, thus, are radically free. They are constrained neither by the past nor by their present natures.

Sartre claimed that facing one's radical freedom can be terrifying and is always uncomfortable. Because facing it makes one feel insecure, this act inevitably produces anguish. Yet one must face it to live authentically. Hence, humans are constantly tempted to live inauthentically, which they do by pretending to themselves that they are not free. To maintain this pretense, they try to convince themselves that their actions are determined—by their character, their circumstances, their natures, or whatever. The last thing they want to admit is that their actions are determined only by their free, unconstrained choices. Sartre called this pretense *bad faith*. To illustrate it, he gave the example of a girl sitting next to a man who she knows would like to seduce her. He takes her hand, and there is a moment of truth. She must make a decision. She can leave her hand in his or withdraw it. Either way she conveys a message: she accepts him or she rejects him, at least for the time being. Rather than facing the painful necessity of making this decision and conveying it to him, she "fails to notice" that he has taken her hand. So she leaves her hand in his not as a way of conveying acceptance but because she "doesn't realize" where her hand is or what it means for it to be there. Her pretense is that she is but a passive object, a mere thing, and so not fully conscious, not fully free.

Another illustration Sartre gives is that of a waiter in a café who identifies with his role. He pretends that he is not free—that this role is who he is. He, thus, allows his role as waiter to determine his every action and attitude. To sustain this pretense he avoids facing up to the fact that he has chosen to put himself into the role of a waiter and that he is free to modify the requirements of that role or to give it up altogether, at any time. Instead, he plays the part mechanically, pretending that he is essentially a waiter—that his being a waiter has been thrust upon him and that it determines his being. In refusing to face his freedom, he is in bad faith.

In sum, the evolution of phenomenology from the early Husserl through Heidegger to Sartre is from abstract to embodied phenomenology. Each of these thinkers had as an objective to reveal the self as it truly is behind the distorting veil of culture and language. Heidegger, Sartre, and the late Husserl had the additional objective of showing that the self's way of existing is not as a private inhabitant of consciousness but as an involvement in worldly activities. Finally, Heidegger and Sartre foreshadowed a theme that would be developed later: that there can be no science of human nature because there is no human nature. Realizing one's true nature, they stressed, not as a thing, but as a worldly activity, pointed the way to a more authentic mode of living.

Analytic Philosophy

In the opening decade of the twentieth century, analytic philosophy arose, primarily in England, as a reaction against Hegelianism, which was still the dominant approach. The original analytic philosophers looked for inspiration back over the heads of the German idealists and their descendants to the British empiricists, especially to Hume but also to John Stuart Mill. In a series of papers, the Cambridge classicist G. E. Moore (1873–1958) subjected F. H. Bradley's Hegelian metaphysics to a penetrating analysis, based mostly on the demand that one measure up to higher standards of clarity than those which Bradley himself achieved. The result was that Bradley's claims, and by implication Hegelianism in general, seemed much less compelling than they otherwise might have. Moore was joined by his colleague Bertrand Russell (1872–1970) and shortly afterwards by Russell's brilliant but enigmatic student, Ludwig Wittgenstein (1889–1951). Russell and Wittgenstein aspired to use the resources of modern symbolic logic, as developed in the 1870s by Gottlob Frege, to restate empiricist metaphysics and epistemology in a logically rigorous way. Some such project has been an important hallmark of analytic philosophy ever since.

In the early twentieth century, a theme common both to phenomenology and analytic philosophy was that what is ultimately real is not the "external world" but conscious episodes. Philosophers in both traditions stressed the subjective nature of reality. That is, they took subjectivity to be primary and the external world of physical objects to be a construction out of subjective elements. Yet, when it came to theories of the self and personal identity, there were two major differences between the traditions. The first is that phenomenologists after Husserl simply bypassed the Cartesian epistemological agenda and assumed without argument that there is an external world. Analytic philosophers felt obligated to prove it. The second is that phenomenologists assumed that self and other are intimately and constitutively intertwined. In their view, it is not just that people are social but that the social dimension enters into what it is to be an individual person. Hegel's master-slave example provided a point of departure. Analytic philosophers, on the other hand, took the individual as primary and self-sufficient, assuming that individuals can be fully described without reference to the other. They conceded, of course, that humans live in a social context. But, in their view, in constructing a basic ontology it is not necessary to attend to this context. That job, they thought (and, for the most part, still do think), can be left to sociologists, political scientists, economists, social psychologists, and the like.

Even so, in analytic philosophy, the other did arise as an issue. But it arose in the same way that the external world arose as an issue. Both the other and the external world are not immediately given and so must be known, if at all, on the basis of an inference from what is immediately given. However, in the case of the other there is a problem in addition to any that arises in the case of mere external things. Others are conscious. So, if others are known, their being known must be by means of *two* inferences: first, others as mere external objects and, second, others as conscious beings.

Between the beginning of the twentieth century and World War II, analytic philosophy went through three phases: logical atomism, logical positivism, and ordinary-language philosophy. Logical atomism, which was popular for at most only a few decades, can be dated from the publication of Bertrand Russell's *Our Knowledge of the External World* (1914). One of its sources of inspiration was Wittgenstein, who at the time was a student of Russell's at Cambridge. Some of Wittgenstein's early ideas were subsequently developed in his *Tractatus Logico-Philosophicus*, written during World War I but published in 1921. Another source of inspiration was Russell's *Philosophy of Logical Atomism*, which was based on eight lectures that he gave in 1918. The focus of Russell's logical atomism was on basic metaphysics especially, though also epistemology, and had little to say about the self and personal identity.[18] When, in the last of his lectures, Russell did broach the question of personal identity, he first pointed out that when you identify someone on the street as the same person you had seen before, you do so not on the basis of a persisting metaphysical substance but physical appearances. When in your own case you make the same sort of reidentification, you have more to go on, but it is the same sort of thing: experiences. The main difference between the two is that in the case of oneself, the experiences will be derived not only from external observations of one's own body but from introspection.

Russell claimed that in the case of both reidentifications, those of others and those of oneself,

> it does not matter in the least to what we are concerned with, what exactly is the given empirical relation between two experiences that makes us say, "these are two experiences of the same person" … because the logical formula for the construction of the person is the same whatever that relation may be, and because the mere fact that you can know that two experiences belong to the same person proves that there is such an empirical relation to be ascertained by analysis. Let us call the relation R. We shall say that when two experiences have to each other the relation R, then they are said to be experiences of the same person. That is a definition of what I mean by "experiences of the same person."[19]

In other words, as had Locke, Russell subscribed to a relational analysis of what's meant by *personal identity*, both at-a-time and over-time. But unlike Locke, Russell was interested only in the logical form of the analysis, not in trying to explain what the actual relations are that bind together the different experiences of a continuing person.

With one exception, Russell's sort of formal approach to questions about self and personal identity was typical of logical atomism. The exception is Wittgenstein. At the end of the *Tractatus*, he makes a number of enigmatic remarks about the self: "*The limits of my language* mean the limits of my world"; "I am my world (the microcosm)"; "The subject does not belong to the world; rather it is a limit of the world"; "Death is not an event in life; we do not live to experience death"; and "Our life has no end in just the way in which our visual field has no limits."[20]

In Wittgenstein's view, human persistence would be a puzzle regardless of when it occurred:

> Not only is there no guarantee of temporal immortality of the human soul, that is to say, of its eternal survival after death; but, in any case, this assumption completely fails to accomplish the purpose for which it has always been intended. Or is some riddle solved by my surviving forever? Is not this eternal life as much of a riddle as our present life? The solution of the riddle of life in space and time lies *outside* of space and time.[21]

Other analytic philosophers, rather than trying to apply such remarks of Wittgenstein to our understanding of the self, tended to ignore them.

Logical positivism, which followed quickly on the heals of logical atomism, showed the same pattern of concerns and the same basic indifference to substantive questions about the self and personal identity. Typical is the account provided by A. J. Ayer (1910–1989) in *Language, Truth, and Logic* (1936):

> We know that a self, if it is not to be treated as a metaphysical entity, must be held to be a logical construction out of sense experiences.... Accordingly, if we ask what is the nature of the self, we are asking what is the relationship that must obtain between sense-experiences for them to belong to the sense-history of the same self. And the answer to this question is that for any two sense-experiences to belong to the sense-history of the same self it is necessary and sufficient that they should contain organic sense-contents which are elements of the same body. But, as it is logically impossible for any organic sense-content to be an element of more than one body, ... it follows necessarily that the series of sense-experiences that constitute the sense-histories of different selves cannot have any members in common. And this is tantamount to saying that it is logically impossible for a sense-experience to belong to the sense-history of more than a single self. But if all sense-experiences are subjective, then all sense-contents are subjective. For it is necessary by definition for a sense-content to be contained in a single sense-experience.[22]

If this sort of account gets beyond those of Locke and Hume, it is only by insisting that the relations among person stages on the basis of which personal identity is defined are physical. But this point had been made by Kant. Moreover, Ayer ignored without comment two kinds of examples that were embraced as possibilities by Locke: that of two selves sharing one body and that of one self having two bodies. Ayer's commentary was not a great leap forward.

Ordinary-language philosophy was inspired by the "later Wittgenstein," that is, Wittgenstein between the two World Wars. In 1933 and 1934, he dictated to his class in Cambridge a set of notes that became known as the *Blue Book*, and from 1934 to 1945, he dictated to two of his pupils another set of notes—the *Brown Book*. These two books became the foundation for his subsequent *Philosophical Investigations* (1953).[23]

In Wittgenstein's ordinary-language approach, problems about self and personal identity tend to be introduced in the context of ruminations about the application of terms, such as the first-person pronoun, *I*, and proper names. There is a philosophy-of-language flavor about most of these discussions, which often makes it sound as if the topics of self and personal identity are not really being pursued in their own right but as examples of a certain kind of linguistic issue, such as how to understand demonstrative and self-reflective terms.

Wittgenstein claimed that certain sorts of uses of the first-person pronoun are immune to error through misidentification; for instance, if I say, "I am thinking of taking a vacation in Hawaii," I cannot be mistaken about who is doing the thinking. In the *Blue Book*, he began by making the point that "our actual use of the phrase 'the same person' and of the name of a person is based on the fact that many characteristics which we use as the criteria for identity," such as bodily and psychological criteria, "coincide in the vast majority of cases." He continued:

> I am as a rule recognized by the appearance of my body. My body changes its appearance only gradually and comparatively little, and likewise my voice, characteristic habits, etc. only change slowly and within a narrow range. We are inclined to use personal names in the way we do, only as a consequence of these facts. This can best be seen by imagining unreal cases which show us what different "geometries" we would be inclined to use if facts were different. Imagine, e.g., that all human bodies which exist looked alike, that on the other hand, different sets of characteristics seem, as it were, to change their habitation among these bodies. Such a set of characteristics might be, mildness, together with a high pitched voice, and slow movements, or a choleric temperament, a deep voice, and jerky movements, and such like.

Wittgenstein said that "under such circumstances, although it would be possible to give the bodies names, we should perhaps be as little inclined to do so as we are to give names to the chairs of our dining-room set."[24]

Alternatively, Wittgenstein continued, "it might be useful to give names to the set of characteristics, and the use of these names would now *roughly* correspond to the personal names in our present language."

> Or imagine that it were usual for human beings to have two characters in this way: People's' shape, size, and characteristics of behavior periodically undergo a complete change. It is the usual thing for a man to have two such states, and he lapses suddenly from one into the other. It is very likely that in such a society we should be inclined to christen every man with two names, and perhaps to talk of the pair of persons in his body. Now were Dr. Jekyll and Mr. Hyde two persons or were they the same person who merely changed? We can say whichever we like. We are not forced to talk of a double personality.[25]

The basic idea seems to be that in ordinary language there are criteria for the application of expressions like "same person" but that these criteria do not dictate how the expression is to be applied in very unusual circumstances. Rather, there are a variety of ways in which we could elaborate the criteria so that they do apply in unusual circumstances. Often we are free to choose among these ways since nothing in our linguistic habits dictates which choice we should make:

> There are many uses of the word "personality" which we may feel inclined to adopt, all more or less akin. The same applies when we define the identity of a person by means of his memories. Imagine a man whose memories on the even days of his life comprise the events of all these days, skipping entirely what happened on the odd days. On the other hand, he remembers on an odd day what happened on a previous odd day, but his memory then skips the previous even days without a feeling of discontinuity. If we like, we can also assume that he has alternating appearances and characteristics on odd and even days. Are we bound to say that here two persons are inhabiting the same body? That is, is it right to say that there are, and wrong to say that there aren't, or vice versa? Neither. For the *ordinary* use of the word "person" is what one might call a composite use suitable under the ordinary circumstances. If I assume, as I do, that these circumstances are changed, the application of the term "person" or "personality" has thereby changed; and if I wish to preserve this term and give it a use analogous to its former use, I am at liberty to choose between many uses,

that is, between many different kinds of analogy. One might say in such a case that the term "personality" hasn't got one legitimate heir only.

And so it goes.[26]

When Wittgenstein left Cambridge, the philosophical center of the English-speaking world moved to Oxford, where ordinary-language philosophy took root most influentially in the work of J. L. Austin (1911–1960) and Gilbert Ryle (1900–1976). Austin, in a series of influential papers and later in *Sense and Sensibilia* (1962), used careful attention to ordinary usage to tear apart the sort of talk about sensations and sense data that was prevalent in logical atomism and logical positivism. A central feature of Austin and Ryle's approach was to reinterpret talk about others' seemingly private mental states as talk about their public behavior. For instance, in his paper, "Other Minds" (1961), Austin remarked that "it seems fair to say that 'being angry' is in many respects like 'having mumps.' It is a description of a whole pattern of events, including occasion, symptoms, feeling, and manifestation, and possibly other factors besides."[27] Meanwhile, his colleague, Ryle, attacked not only the Cartesian idea of a self distinct from the body—"the ghost in the machine"—but the very idea of an inner life. In *The Concept of Mind* (1949), he argued that all meaningful talk of mental episodes—"twitches, itches, and twangs," even a person's being angry—was not about anything private to a person's interior life but about bodily "dispositions to behave."[28]

In the 1950s and 1960s, in England, ordinary-language philosophy, whose hallmark was to deny inner life, came into full bloom. Meanwhile, on the continent, phenomenology, whose focus was the examination of inner life, was gathering steam. There was little love lost between proponents of these two approaches. At a conference, the French phenomenologist Maurice Merleau-Ponty, in a conciliatory gesture, remarked to Ryle, "But are we not doing the same thing?" Ryle responded, "I hope not!"[29]

Psychology

In the first half of the twentieth century, psychology became a discipline of its own. As a consequence, philosophy and psychology established their own separate traditions of inquiry that developed more or less independently of each other. In psychology, the main focus has always been on work being done by experimentalists. In the early part of the century, these experimentalists were introspectionists. Chief among them was E. B. Titchener (1867–1927), who disseminated in North America the approach and theories of Wundt. However, from the 1920s until after World War II, the chief experimentalists were behaviorists, initially J. B. Watson (1878–1958) and then later Edward Guthrie (1886–1959), Clark Hull (1884–1952), and B. F. Skinner (1904–1990). In general, introspectionists and behaviorists had little to say about the self and nothing to say about it of lasting importance. That job was left to empirical theorists from three different traditions: depth psychology, humanistic psychology, and social and developmental psychology.

Depth Psychology

Born in the nineteenth century, depth psychology grew to maturity in the work of Sigmund Freud (1856–1939), who proposed a radically new way of understanding human psychological development and of treating mental abnormality, which included new understandings of the unconscious, of infantile sexuality, and repression. His original theory focused on the relationships among conscious and unconscious mental phenomena. Previously, most theorists had understood the self in terms of consciousness, including rationality, free will, and self-reflection. A few—Schopenhauer and Nietzsche, for instance—had claimed that there is an irrational, unconscious part of the mind that dominates the rational. But Freud had a much more elaborate theory of how this happens, for which he claimed support from his psychotherapeutic and historical case studies, as well from his analyses of dreams and mental slips.

Freud claimed that most human behavior is explicable in terms of unconscious causes in the person's mind, a view which he supported by appeal to ingenious interpretations of such things as slips of the tongue, obsessive behavior, and dreams. In short, the mind is like an iceberg, the bulk of which—the unconscious—lies below the surface and exerts a dynamic and controlling influence upon the part which is above the surface—that is, consciousness. It follows from this, together with a general commitment to universal determinism, that whenever humans make a choice, they are governed by mental processes of which they are unaware and over which they have no control. Free will is an illusion. Nevertheless, one can empower the ego by making the unconscious conscious.

Freud's account of the unconscious and his therapeutic innovations are best illustrated by his famous model of the tripartite structure of the mind or personality, his *id*, *ego*, and *superego*. The id is that part of the mind constituted by instinctual drives that require satisfaction, the superego that part constituted by socially acquired but internalized control mechanisms. The ego, or conscious self, is created by the dynamic tensions and interactions between id and superego and has as its function the reconciliation of their conflicting demands in dealing with external reality. All consciousness resides in the ego. The contents of the id are permanently consigned to the unconscious mind. The superego is an unconscious censor that seeks to restrict the blind, typically pleasure-seeking drives of the id. As Plato had done before, Freud saw mental health or psychological well-being as the establishment of a harmonious relationship between the three elements that constitute the mind.

The instincts, for Freud, are the principal motivating forces in the mind, energizing it in all of its functions. There are, he held, a small number of basic instincts, which may be grouped into two broad categories: the life instinct (*eros*), which covers self-preserving and erotic instincts; and the death instinct (*thanatos*), which covers all the instincts towards cruelty, aggression, and self-destruction. Freud gave sexual energy—*libido*—a central importance in human life, arguing that it can be discerned in children from birth and that it is the most important motivating force in adult life.

Freud's most famous disciple, Carl Jung (1875–1961), long admired Freud, who eventually came to see Jung as his heir apparent. The two finally met in 1907. However, in 1909, their relationship cooled, after which Jung went his own independent way, theorizing that the mind has three parts: the ego, the personal unconscious, and the collective unconscious. The ego is the conscious mind. The personal unconscious is any aspect of the mind that is not presently conscious but could be, including, say, suppressed memories. The collective unconscious is the outcome of our experience as a species. Although we can never be conscious of it directly, the contents of the collective unconscious—most often called *archetypes*—affect our experiences and behaviors, especially our emotions, by functioning as unlearned tendencies to experience things in a certain way.

In Jung's taxonomy of archetypes, *the shadow*, which he called the "dark side" of the ego, is a remnant of our prehuman, animal past, during which there was no self-consciousness and concerns were limited to sex and survival. The *persona* is one's public image—the mask one shows to others. It includes one's social sexual identity. The *anima* is feminine energy present in the collective unconscious of men, the *animus* masculine energy present in the collective unconscious of women. The anima is associated with deep emotions and the life force, the animus with logic and rationality. The anima and animus are the archetypes through which humans communicate with the collective unconscious. Like Freud, Jung believed that all humans are bisexual. When we begin our social lives as infants, psychologically we are neither male nor female. Subsequently our sexual identities are determined by our social conditioning.

The most important archetype is *the self*, the ultimate unity of the personality, symbolized by the circle, the cross, and the mandala (a drawing used in meditation to focus and center the mind). Jung called development toward the self *individuation*. In his view, the goal of life is to realize the self, which requires transcending all opposites, so that the various aspects of one's personality are expressed equally. One is then both male and female, ego and shadow, good and bad, conscious and unconscious, an individual and the whole of creation. Jung thought that not before midlife does an individual achieve individuation and fully become a self. His idea of self-realization is similar to what humanistic psychologists would later call *self-actualization*.

Existential and Humanistic Psychology

In the 1930s, what came to be called *existential psychology* tended to look for inspiration not to depth psychologists but to phenomenologists. Whereas Freud had said that the goal of therapy is to make the unconscious conscious, existential, and, later, humanistic, psychologists said that it is to realize one's most developed authentic self.

Ludwig Binswanger (1881–1966) studied under Jung, who introduced him to Freud. In the early 1920s, he cultivated an interest in Husserl, Heidegger, and the Jewish theologian Martin Buber (1878–1965). Inspired by such thinkers, he turned away from a Freudian perspective and toward an existential one. In the early 1930s, he became the first existential therapist. From Heidegger, he adopted the notions of *Dasein* and *thrownness*, as well as the idea that we can choose who we become. Binswanger saw this latter idea, which he called *being-beyond-the-world*, as intrinsic to Dasein. From Buber, he took the idea that we are not "locked away" in ourselves but open to one another. In developing his own therapeutic approach, he made a point of empathizing with his clients in order to enter into their worldviews, thus viewing them not as in depth psychology, from the psychologist's perspective, but so far as he could from his clients' own first-person perspectives. His goal was to understand and interpret their physical (*Umwelt*), social (*Mitwelt*), and personal (*Eigenwelt*) worlds. Instead of viewing his clients as driven by unconscious forces, he emphasized choice. In his view, inauthenticity results from one's allowing a small number of externally imposed or habitually acquired themes to dominate one's concerns, thus restricting one's choices and hence denying one's freedom.

Rollo May (1909–1994), another prominent existential psychologist, together with Ernest Angel and Henri F. Ellenberger, edited the first American book on existential psychology, *Existence* (1958), which greatly influenced the emergence of American humanistic psychology.[30] In May's own contribution to this volume, he argued that a proper existential approach to therapy, rather than forcing clients to conform to the theories of their therapists or to rely on standard therapeutic "techniques," involves "fully engaging" with clients. He distanced himself from Freudian psychotherapy by claiming that therapists ought to "analyze the structure of human existence," as Heidegger had, which, he said, would "yield an understanding of the reality underlying all situations of human beings in crises." May claimed that existentialism provides psychology with the ability to bridge the chasm in the sciences between what is *abstractly true* and what is *existentially real*.[31]

Also in this humanistic tradition, Carl Rogers (1902–1987), in *Client-Centered Therapy* (1951), posited a "life force," which he called *the actualizing tendency*, an in-built tendency in every living thing to develop its potentials to the fullest extent possible. If one does this, then one becomes one's *real self*, which is not a static condition but a fluid process of becoming. One's being unconditionally positively regarded by others promotes one's becoming one's real self. However, if one receives only conditional positive regard, one tends to develop instead an *ideal self*, which is a standard one cannot meet. Rogers called the gap between what an individual actually perceives himself to be and what he feels that he should be *incongruity*. The greater the gap, the more incongruity; the more incongruity, the more suffering. Incongruity is what Rogers means by *neurosis*.

In Rogers's view, an ideally healthy person—a "fully functioning person"—is one who, open to experience, "lives existentially." This means that he or she is self-trusting, experiences freedom, and acts and thinks creatively. Being open to experience, which is the opposite of defensiveness and which involves being able to accept reality, implies the accurate perception of one's experiences, including one's feelings. Being open to one's feelings is a prerequisite to being open to actualization. Fully functioning people experience a feeling of freedom and take responsibility for their own choices. They are more creative. They not only actualize themselves but contribute to the actualization of others.

Finally, Abraham Maslow (1908–1970) claimed that human needs are arranged hierarchically.[32] On the ground floor are physiological needs; above them, needs for safety and security; then needs for love and belonging; then needs for the esteem of others and for self-esteem. He called these four kinds *deficit-needs*. Finally, there is the need to actualize the self, which he called a *being-need*. Humans move through these levels of need in developmental stages. Deficit-needs cease being felt once they are satisfied. Being-need continues to be felt; in fact, it may even become stronger the more it is satisfied. It involves the continuous desire to fulfill potentials and to become the most complete, fullest version of oneself that one can become—hence the term self-actualization.

In order to better explain what he meant by self-actualization, Maslow picked out a group of people whom he felt were self-actualized. They included Spinoza, Lincoln, Gandhi, Einstein, and Eleanor Roosevelt. He also developed a list of qualities that seemed to him to be characteristic of self-actualized people. These included being able to distinguish what is false and dishonest from what is real and genuine, being disposed to treat life's difficulties as problems demanding solutions rather than as personal troubles, and believing that often the journey is as significant as the destination.

Self-actualizers are more comfortable being alone; rely on their own experiences and judgments rather than being overly susceptible to social pressure; treasure ethnic and individual variety; are compassionate; value intimate personal relations with a few rather than more shallow relationships with many; prefer to joke at their own expense, or at the human condition, rather than at others; are more likely to accept people as they are than to try to change them; are spontaneous and simple rather than pretentious or artificial; and so on. They also tend to have more *peak experiences* than others, that is, more experiences that take them out of themselves and make them feel part of the infinite and the eternal.

Toward the end of his life, Maslow inaugurated what he called the *fourth force* in psychology: the first was depth psychology; the second, behaviorism; the third, humanism and existentialism; the fourth, transpersonal psychology. Perhaps the best-known transpersonalists today are Charles Tart and Ken Wilber.

Social and Developmental Psychology

After Hegel, social and developmental psychology had its serious scientific beginnings toward the end of the nineteenth century in the work of J. M. Baldwin. It blossomed in the first half of the twentieth century. However, the label *social psychology* did not appear as the title of a book until 1908, when it was used simultaneously by the sociologist E. A. Ross (1866–1951) and the psychologist William McDougall (1871–1938).

Among sociologists, the leading theory throughout most of the twentieth century was *symbolic interactionism*, which was an outgrowth of American pragmatism and the work of G. H. Mead. By contrast, psychologists, because of their focus on experimentation and individualistic explanation, were not influenced by Mead's work until the latter half of the century. Among them, Floyd Allport's

(1890–1978) *Social Psychology* (1924), which promoted a behavioristic and experimental approach to social phenomena, set the early standard.

George Herbert Mead (1863–1931) studied philosophy at Harvard, where he
was introduced to the views of Josiah Royce and William James. Later, he studied
psychology at Leipzig, where he became acquainted with the work of Wilhelm
Wundt and G. Stanley Hall (1844–1924). Later still, he taught philosophy and
psychology at the University of Michigan, where he met John Dewey (1859–1952),
who secured a position for him in the philosophy department at the University of
Chicago. Mead spent the rest of his life in Chicago.

In *Mind, Self and Society* (1934), Mead's most important work, he describes
how the mind and self arise out of social interaction.[33] Instead of approaching
human experience from the standpoint of individual psychology, he analyzed it
from the "standpoint of communication as essential to the social order." In his
view, the "development of the individual's self, and of his self-consciousness
within the field of his experience" is preeminently social. Viewing mind as a
form of participation in an interpersonal, hence social, process, Mead thus
rejected the traditional view of the mind as a substance separate from the body
and also more recent attempts to account for mind solely in terms of physiology
or neurology. In his view, the physiological organism is necessary but not sufficient for mental behavior. Without interpersonal behavior, there would be no
significant symbols for the individual to internalize. And without this internal-
ization there would be no human mentality as we know it.

Mead claimed that individual selves are products, not preconditions, of social
interaction. Like J. M. Baldwin before him, he argued that "the self is something
which has a development; it is not initially there, at birth, but arises in the process of social experience and activity."[34] Experiences of one's own body are "organized about a self." Although it is possible to see one's own bodily parts without
recognizing them as one's own, ordinarily we experience them as our own, that
is, as belonging to our own self. It is this reflexivity of the self that distinguishes
human from animal consciousness, which does not include a reference to an "I."
There is a form of prereflective human consciousness that does not include self-
consciousness, but most human consciousness is not of this sort.

In self-consciousness, the "individual enters as such into his own experience . . .
as an object."[35] This can be accomplished, in Mead's view, "only on the basis of
social relations and interactions."[36] Individuals attempt to view themselves from
the standpoint of others. Mead stressed the importance of language, play, and
games, which take place by means of shared symbols—words, roles, gestures,
rituals, and so on. These basic social processes render the reflexive objectification
of the self possible. "When the response of the other becomes an essential part in

the experience or conduct of the individual ... the individual appears in his own experience as a self; and until this happens he does not appear as a self."[37]

In Mead's view, it is only in playing a game that an individual attains self-hood. The key is role playing, as in a child's acting as though she were a nurse, in which she internalizes not only the role she is playing but the roles of others who are involved in the game as well. This interplay of roles organized according to rules generates "the generalized other."[38] It is only when individuals view themselves from the standpoint of the generalized other that "self-consciousness in the full sense of the term" can emerge.

The game, in Mead's view, becomes an instrument of social control in which an individual "becomes a something which can function in the organized whole, and thus tends to determine himself in his relationship with the group to which he belongs."[39] Yet, how individuals respond to the social world is not mechanically determined. Rather, individuals decide what to do in the light of others' attitudes. The "me" is the social self, an organized set of attitudes of others that the individual represents to himself, and the "I" is a response of the organism to these attitudes. Mead says that the "me" is "a conventional, habitual individual," and the "I" a "novel reply" of the individual to the generalized other.[40] The "I" is not knowable in immediate experience. It is knowable, but only in memory and then no longer as a subject but as an object. The I's responses in the present are *conditioned* but not determined. Human freedom, though real, is qualified—conditioned freedom.[41]

In sum, the human personality (or self) arises in a social situation. As a consequence of symbolically mediated social interaction (language, gestures, play, games, etc.), the "me" arises. The organism, as it develops, must respond both to its situation and to its "me." Its response is the "I." For Mead, both community and individual are necessary to identity. The "me" is a symbolic representation of social structure, without which the "I" could not act. Yet the "I" breaks through this social structure: "Social control is the expression of the 'me' over against the expression of the 'I.'"[42] Since human society includes many generalized others, individuals are not confined to just one. Rather, individuals may be members of different groups and may therefore relate to different generalized others at different times. In theory, there is no limit to the individual's capacity to incorporate new others into its dynamic self-structure. How individuals do this determines their social identities.

Lev Vygotsky (1896–1934), like Baldwin and even before Mead, provided a developmental account of self-consciousness that required a parallel conception of the other. All three of these thinkers take their point of departure from Hegelian dialectic, though all of them deny their direct dependence on Hegel.

Vygotsky, a Russian, maintained a closer allegiance to Marx. His theory of self-consciousness, like that of Mead, depended more on a theory of communication and the importance of language in human social life than did Baldwin's, who focused on an earlier prelinguistic phase of development involving imitation as the primary means of acquiring self-consciousness.

Vygotsky's theory of self-consciousness starts with the claim that the nature of mind is social and that mental phenomena are to be understood in terms of the signs that mediate both social and mental life. He thought that the reflexology of Pavlov, which applies as readily to animals as to humans, could not deal adequately with complex forms of self-consciousness found only in human social life. For Vygotsky, "the meaningful word is the microcosm of human consciousness."[43] Hence it is not surprising that "the mechanism of knowing oneself (self-awareness) and the mechanism for knowing others are one and the same."[44] Rather than claiming that we know others only because we know ourselves, he claimed that we know ourselves only to the extent that we are another for ourselves.

Consciousness of speech and of social experience emerge at the same time, in an interdependent manner. It is in listening to and repeating words that we become aware of a self. Rather than the child developing egocentric inner speech for self prior to understanding the speech of others, as Jean Piaget (1896–1980) had supposed, Vygotsky claimed that social speech comes first and that it is only through social speech that the child becomes conscious of itself and can describe and control itself. Thus, like Baldwin and Mead, he opposed the reigning paradigm, with its historical basis in Descartes, that knowing one's own mind precedes understanding of the minds of others. Instead, following Hegel, he claimed that consciousness of self and other are codependent and social and depend directly on the social meanings of one's society, particularly as they appear in language.

In sum, during the first half of the twentieth century the goal of most psychoanalytic and personality psychologists, from Freud to Rogers, was to discover deeper recesses of the self hidden below the surface of normal experience. In the case of Freud and other depth psychologists, this search led to the exploration of unconscious motives, rooted in the past and in human biology, that determined present behavior. In the case of existential and humanistic psychologists like Binswanger and Rogers, the focus was not on uncovering historical and biological determinants of behavior but on releasing the experience of an "authentic" or "real" self in the present. These approaches, together with most of the phenomenology which preceded them, tended to share two underlying assumptions: that there is a real self beneath the surface of expressed personality and that to know who one is, is to uncover this real self. In the work of critical theorists, these assumptions, as well as much that was presupposed in social and developmental approaches, came under suspicion.

Critical Theory

The Institute for Social Research, better known as *the Frankfurt School*, was loosely associated with the University of Frankfurt. In the 1920s it became a mecca for German leftists, who, under its auspices could for the first time at the university level study Marxist political economy and the history of the labor movement. Under Max Horkheimer (1895–1973), who became its director in 1930, it helped to create a novel, radical style of philosophical social science known as *critical theory*. Other well-known critical theorists from this early period are Theodor Adorno (1903–1969), Herbert Marcuse (1898–1979), Walter Benjamin (1892–1940), Erich Fromm, and Jürgen Habermas.

Despite diversity in their intellectual disciplines and individual approaches, most Frankfurt School analyses involved reflection on what critical theorists took to be the pathological decline of Western culture in the early twentieth century, dominated as it was by industrial capitalism and the rise of National Socialism. In attempting to diagnose what went wrong and what needed to be done to correct the situation, members of the Frankfurt School turned to avant-garde art, depth psychology, Marxism, and a messianic religious faith. They referred to the interdisciplinary work that emerged from their studies not as philosophy, sociology, aesthetics, or psychology but simply as "theory." It was among the first interdisciplinary approaches to the critique of culture.

In his inaugural lecture as director of the institute, Horkheimer, a philosopher by training, defined the task of the institute as that of organizing philosophically inspired inquires that philosophers, sociologists, economists, historians and psychologists could join together to pursue. As he had intended, the first studies under the institute's name were evenly balanced between theoretical speculation and empirical support. But before the institute could develop this approach, the Nazis came to power. In 1933, members of the school were forced into exile. Many of them relocated to Columbia University, including Horkheimer, Adorno, and Marcuse, who became the main proponents of the institute's work and in whose views a theoretical-philosophical approach began to overshadow the empirical. During this period, their theoretical perspective darkened as the influence of Nietzsche and Freud began to overshadow that of Marx. Critical theorists expressed suspicion that apparently rational and conscious human choices and goals are really the product of dangerous, unconscious, irrational drives. They trashed the Kantian ideal of a rational, autonomous self. They also attacked the idea of historical progress. Even those eras in which humanity seemed most to have liberated itself—the Enlightenment, in particular—were reinterpreted by them as rotten to the core.

This dark viewpoint was most forcefully expressed in Horkheimer and Adorno's *Dialectic of Enlightenment* (1972), in the introduction to which they wrote that although "the Enlightenment has always aimed at liberating men from fear and establishing their sovereignty," the "earth radiates disaster triumphant." "What men want to learn from nature," they continued, "is how to use it in order wholly to dominate it and other men." The book goes on to show the Enlightenment's self-ruination in such literary works as Sade's *Juliette*, in the culture industry, and in modern anti-Semitism.[45] An early essay by Horkheimer, "The Jews and Europe," cautioned that "those who do not wish to speak of capitalism should be silent about fascism."[46]

After the war, with the group now split between Germany and America, contributions to critical theory became, if anything, more pessimistic. Only a few critical theorists, such as Habermas, were oriented toward social action. Erich Fromm, who years earlier had split from the Frankfurt School, distinguished his thought from the others by becoming seriously engaged with theorizing about the differences between men and women, anticipating later attempts to produce a feminist Marxism and a poststructuralist analysis of the socially constructed nature of gender. The influence of the Frankfurt School resonated in the poststructuralism that came to fruition in the period immediately following the war.

XIII

PARADISE LOST

For the modern history of theories of the self, World War II was a watershed.
Before the war, the seeds of dissolution of the self had been sown and had even
begun to sprout, but this new growth was overshadowed by the luxuriant foliage
of expansive theories. In phenomenology especially—but even in analytic philosophy, depth psychology, existential and humanistic psychology, social and
developmental psychology, and even critical theory—the self survived. While
some of these approaches demoted the self, none dismantled it. Across disciplines, the self had fragmented. Within disciplines, it was still intact. As a consequence, by midcentury the self may have been challenged, but it was not
dethroned. That task was left to the second half of the century.

The Decentered Self

The Swiss linguist Ferdinand de Saussure (1857–1913) theorized that language is
a system of signs that are culturally determined and that carry meaning in virtue
of their differences from one another. In a famous analogy, he compared language to pieces in a game of chess. Each linguistic sign connects a *signifier*, which
is a material thing in the world, such as a written mark or spoken sound, with
something *signified*, which is a concept in the mind of a language user. Hence, in
his view, the basic relationships that constitute language are not between words
and the world. They are, rather, among the signs and between signs and concepts
in the mind. Saussure and, independently of him, the American pragmatist

Charles Peirce (1839–1914), proposed extending a theory of signs beyond the linguistic to yield a general science of signs, which became known as *semiotics*. In the 1950s and 1960s, structuralist and semiotic theorists—most notably, Claude Lévi-Strauss (b. 1908) and Roland Barthes (1915–1980)—built upon the theories of Saussure to devise models of human culture generally.[1]

Jacques Lacan (1901–1981)

Also in the 1950s, Jacques Lacan, a practicing psychotherapist, began to develop his own theory of psychoanalysis, based primarily on Freud but also on the linguistics of Saussure and the structural anthropology of Lévi-Strauss. Freud had been a realist about the system of id, ego, and superego. He believed that each component of this system exists and has a biological basis. Lacan rejected Freud's realism and theorized that the self, or subject, rather than a real thing with a basis in biology, is nothing more than "a moment in discourse" and, hence, is based in linguistically mediated relationships. He thought that this insight had the momentous consequence that individual people, rather than being unique and particular are social and general, and rather than being stable are in motion. This vision of a socially and linguistically constituted, destabilized self, he claimed, "decenters" fundamental assumptions in Western thought.

Freud had been interested in the process by which children become civilized, productive adults. He hoped that by bringing the contents of the unconscious into consciousness, repression and neurosis would be minimized, thereby strengthening the ego or self. His goal was the development of an ego that is more autonomous. In Lacan's view, Freud's goal is an impossible dream. Since the ego is an illusion, it can never replace or control anything, let alone the unconscious. Lacan's theoretical interest was not in how children become civilized, productive adults but in how they acquire the illusion of self.[2]

According to Lacan's theory, the components of the unconscious are at least partly constituted by language. But, he claimed, in language, rather than there being relations between signifier and signified, there are only relations among signifiers. The components of the unconscious form *chains of signifiers*, but ones that continually change. If there were signifieds, he thought, the meaning of any particular signifier might be relatively stable. Since there are no signifieds, the chains of signifiers have nothing to tie them down. With these chains constantly sliding and shifting, there is nothing to provide stable meaning. In his view, the impossible dream of becoming a stable "self" would require for its realization stopping the chains of signifiers so that the word *I* acquired a stable meaning. But there is no way, he claimed, that this can be done.

Lacan postulated three phases of development in the transition from infant to adult: the *real*, the *imaginary*, and the *symbolic*. The period of the real lasts about 6 to 18 months from birth. Initially, the infant cannot distinguish itself from any other object, including its mother. It has no sense of self or of individuated identity. It also has no sense of its body as a coherent unified whole. It does, though, have several needs—for food, comfort, security, and so on. It is driven by these needs, which are capable of being satisfied and ideally are satisfied. The real, as a psychic place in which there is this original unity, includes only a sense of completeness. There is no language in the real. However, when the child begins to separate from its mother, it starts to experience loss.

This original "state of nature" has to give way in order for the infant to form a separate identity, which involves separating from the mother. As the infant moves from the real to the imaginary, it tragically loses its primal sense of unity and the security and comfort that goes with it. At some point in this progress of separation, it looks at its reflection in a mirror, then looks at a real person—presumably, its mother—then looks back again at its reflection. In this action, Lacan said, the child acquires the idea that it is an integrated being, a whole person, like its mother. But, he added, in seeing its image in the mirror and thinking, "That's me," the child makes a mistake.

The mistake is that the child thinks that it is its mirror image. To make matters worse, when the child initially makes this mistake, often another person is there to verbally reinforce it: "Look, that's you." This mistake then creates what Lacan called the "armor" of the subject, an illusion of wholeness, integration, and totality that surrounds and protects the child's fragmented sense of its own body. This illusion of wholeness gives birth to the *ego*. That, in essence, is Lacan's famous *mirror theory*. The idea that one is an ego or self, he said, is always a fantasy, based on an identification with an external image.

Whereas the real is a realm of objects, the imaginary, which is prelinguistic and based in visual perception, is a realm of conscious and unconscious images. In this realm, the mirror image, an "ideal ego," becomes internalized as the child builds its sense of self and identity. The fiction of a stable, whole, unified self that the child saw in the mirror becomes compensation for its having lost its original sense of oneness with the mother's body. The child protects itself from the knowledge of this loss by misperceiving itself as not lacking anything. For the rest of its life, the child will misrecognize its self as an illusory other—an "image in a mirror." This misrecognition provides an illusion of self and of mastery.

Once the child has formulated an idea of otherness and of a self born of its own mirror image, it enters the symbolic realm, but without totally leaving the imaginary. The realm of the symbolic is the structure of language itself and is always about loss or absence, since absent objects are the only ones for which one needs words. The child has to enter the symbolic in order to become a speaking subject and to designate itself by the word *I*.

Since the real is incapable of being represented in language, as soon as the child enters the symbolic, the real is irretrievably lost. The child then shifts from having *needs* to having *demands*, which are always for recognition or love from another. The child's awareness of separation—of otherness—creates anxiety and a sense of loss. It then demands a return to that original sense of fullness and nonseparation that it had in the real. But that return is impossible once the child acquires the idea of an other, and it has to acquire this idea in order to become a self or subject, which it needs to do to be a functioning cultural being. Whereas the needs it left behind could be satisfied, its newfound demands cannot be.

The other, which Lacan also called the *phallus*, is a structural position in the symbolic order—its "center." Everyone is trying to merge with the other in order to shed the sense of separation. But since the other is not a person but a position, no one can merge with it. So, the ever-present conception of other creates and sustains a never-ending *lack*. Lacan calls the experience of this lack *desire*. It is, in his view, the desire to be the other. It can never be fulfilled. It is not *need*—the desire for some object. It is not *demand*—the desire for love and another person's recognition of oneself. Rather, it is the desire to be the center of the system, of the symbolic, of language itself, and hence to rule the system. The desire is for an unattainable goal. Paradoxically the other or phallus and the realm of the real are similar in that both are places where things are whole, complete, full, and unified—where there is no lack. They are also places that are inaccessible to the human subject-in-language. Yet the other and the real are opposite in that the real is the maternal—the ground from which we spring, the nature we have to separate from in order to have culture—and the other/phallus is paternal—the patriarchal order of culture, the position from which everything is ruled.

Michel Foucault (1926–1984)

Like others at the time, Michel Foucault was critical of the Cartesian idea of a self-transparent subject and the related Kantian ideal of autonomous agency. In his early work—from *Madness and Civilization* (1961) to *The Archaeology of Knowledge* (1969)—he theorized about how systems of knowledge are creative.

He introduced the term *discourse* for the ways in which academic disciplines discuss and thereby constitute their subject matters, and he then reduced both the knowing subject and the disciplinary subject matter to a function of discourse.

During this period, he claimed that the idea that individual humans are either autonomous agents or lucid transcendental sources of meaning is "warped" and "twisted." What is warped about it is that so much of what the individual is and utilizes—especially his or her biology, language, and desires—are not chosen but given, not understood but opaque. To be lucid transcendental sources of meanings, individuals would have to choose and understand themselves. Yet, the scope of human choices is severely limited, and the understanding that would be necessary for autonomy eludes humans.

The Kantian autonomous agent, Foucault claimed, is an internally contradictory ideal. He thus famously proclaimed "the death of man"—the death of the autonomous subject. He said that the autonomous subject is a recent invention and will soon pass away.[3] The reason it will pass away is that man cannot be, as Kant proposed, both a transcendental source of meaning and an object of empirical knowledge for himself. From Kant to Husserl, this impossible ideal has been pursued. The reality, he claimed, is that man, rather than having a discoverable nature, is constantly being reconstituted as a subject and object for himself.

In his later work—from *Discipline and Punish* (1975) to *The History of Sexuality* (1976–84)—Foucault investigated control, management, surveillance, and policing. Increasingly, he came to see discourses and the styles of subjectivity that they spawn as the product of deeper relationships of power. He also investigated the history of the ways in which individuals have constituted themselves as subjects. Finally, he theorized about the ways in which certain forms of writing opened up clearings of new discursive activity.

Foucault began exploring this later theme in "What Is an Author?" (1969), which was published a few years before this later period. In this essay, he discussed the relationship between an author and a text, theorizing about how a text refers back to its author as a figure who preceded and created it. He suggested that a certain form of writing, which he called *écriture*, is not about reference to a signified but is a play among signifiers. An example of this sort of writing is Samuel Beckett's novels and plays; in one of these, *Texts for Nothing* (1974), he asks, "What does it matter who is speaking?"

Foucault claimed that écriture tends to be self-referential—writing about writing or about language itself—rather than a vehicle for the author's expression of his or her emotions or ideas. It isn't meant to communicate from author to reader, he said, but rather to circulate language itself, regardless of anything specific about the author or reader. "It is a matter," he said, "of depriving the subject (or its substitute) of its role as originator, and of analyzing the subject as a variable and complex function of discourse." The primary concern of this sort of literature is with "creating a space into which the writing subject endlessly disappears." Whereas traditionally in the West, writing has been a vehicle for achieving immortality, écriture "kills" the author.[4]

In Foucault's poststructuralist view, relations among author, text, and reader are replaced by those between a structuring language and subjects, which are positions within the structure of language, that is, within a text. His proclamation that the author is "dead"—compare Nietzsche's that "God is dead"—is his way of saying that the author has been decentered, that is, relegated to linguistic structure—a subject position, not a center. In place of an "author," Foucault discovers a kind of writer who establishes a clearing. He said that such writers— "founders of discursivity"—produce "the possibilities and the rules for the formation of other texts." By setting "up a struggle of interpretations which starts a new line of history," they establish "an endless possibility of discourse."[5]

In his three-volume *History of Sexuality*, Foucault claimed that Christians had appropriated for their own purposes practices of self-examination that the Stoics had used to control disruptive desires and thus gain mastery over them and so constitute their ethical selves. The Christian subject, he claimed, identifies himself not with his public deeds but with his most private desires, which often are hidden. So he has constantly to examine his desires to reveal his *true* motivations. This discipline was encouraged by the gradual development of confessional practices in the West, which produced a stable, unified subject—"the man of desires." An early confessional manual exhorted Christians to examine all of their thoughts, speech, and behavior, even their dreams, to discover their true desires and not to think "that in so sensitive and perilous a matter as this, there is anything trivial or insignificant."[6] This, Foucault claims, is our modern practice. The man of desires is an inner self of sorts—the locus of private wants and intentions. Foucault wrote that not only Christians but also Freud appropriated this self. In seeing humans as subjects who need to recover the repressed truth about themselves—the secret of their sexuality—Freud dressed this self in secular clothing. Foucault rejected Freud's scientific pretensions of having invented a science of the subject.

In Foucault's view, Freud's ideas about the subject "made it possible to group together, in an artificial unity, anatomical elements, biological functions, conducts, sensations, and pleasures." They also enabled him "to make use of this fictitious unity as a causal principle." But, Foucault insisted, the Freudian sexual subject is as much an abstraction as Kant's autonomous subject. It thus has no causal power but is itself the product of power. However, once Freud proposed this self and Western culture accepted it as the truth, it constrained people by bringing them "under the sway of a logic of concupiscence and desire." Foucault added that whenever the question of knowing who we are arises, "it is this logic that henceforth serves as our master key."[7] Freud's successfully analyzed subject was his ideal of human freedom. Foucault said that this idea is illusory—the search for meaning is not liberating but enslaving.

Toward the end of his life, Foucault sought a heightened consciousness of how individuals are embedded in cultural practices, especially in various sorts of power relationships, to enhance individual freedom. In his final interview, he said that he had tried to distinguish "three types of problems: that of truth, that of power, and that of individual conduct," but that he had "hampered" himself by overemphasizing truth and power at the expense of individual conduct.[8] Now, he continued, he hoped to break free of mere subjectivity by reappropriating the ancient practices of care of the self. These, he said, do not include finding a deep, inner truth but, rather, governing "one's own life in order to give it the most beautiful form possible."[9]

In Foucault's view, during the seventeenth century, as seen in particular in Descartes's thought, there was a major shift in Western thought on the self's relation to itself. Before this shift, the focus of this relation was on care of the self. It was presumed that "truth" about the self, and knowledge in general, depended on active concern for and care of the self. Only a person who attended to his or her self and took care of it could be expected to gain truth about the self, or about anything else. In ancient Greece, care for the self had an indirect effect on care of others, for in care of self, one was concerned about one's ethical activity in general, as well as in having truthful knowledge of the psyche's nature and content. In the Roman period, the focus on care of self became less tied to particular social roles but still implied that a healthy relationship to one's self led to healthy relationships with others. In the Christian period, care of the self continued, but concern shifted from cultivation of a healthy self, which involved mastery of the self by reason, to awareness of one's inner desires. This awareness was to be a springboard for cultivating good desires and rooting out evil ones in order to become worthy of heaven. Selfish desires in particular would be eradicated. According to Foucault, this ideal prevailed throughout the Middle Ages and into the Renaissance, though during the latter period interest in cultivating a healthy self was rekindled.

Throughout this early period, it was thought that only a healthy, cared for, and self-knowing self could attain truth. Descartes gave impetus to the view that truth about the self, as well as truth more generally, required only a rational mind, not a healthy one. One's ethical behavior was no longer seen as a necessary condition for knowledge, either of one's self or of anything else. The result was a shift away from the ethics of self to the knowledge of self. Ethics was no longer regarded as a precondition for knowledge of self. As a consequence, there emerged a search for one's "true" self, as if this were an object that could be known, rather than one that had to be created or constructed.

Foucault claimed that in Descartes's thought, knowledge of the true self was thought to be immediate and clear. In later thinkers, it was thought to be less clear but still something that a person could hope to discover, either through detailed self-examination or through the human sciences. Increasingly, our true selves have moved further and further from direct view as our thoughts and behaviors have required interpretation both from the natural sciences of man and sociohistorically. But neither type of interpretation finds a stable "true" self, which Foucault claimed is an impossible ideal.

In the end, Foucault advocated a return to the project of care for the self and to the constructing of an ethical self. But this self-construction, he said, cannot be the same as in ancient times. We are in a different period, with different concerns. In our own time, what is important is to cultivate our freedom to re-create the self by disassembling and reconstructing the habitual selves that we find ourselves to be as we are constituted in social and power relations with one another. He claimed that each of us needs constantly to "release oneself from one self" and reshape and "customize" oneself: "I would like it to be an elaboration of the self by the self, a studious transformation, a slow and arduous transformation through a constant care for the truth."[10]

Jacques Derrida (1930–2004)

A student of Foucault, Derrida also rejected structuralism, stressing that language is unstable and lacks an external reference—"there is nothing outside the text."[11] Texts, he said, are mere "semiotic play." Derrida named his view *deconstruction* and said that even though words and concepts, including *self*, are open to question, we have no choice but to use them. However, once we are aware that they are open to question, we should put them "under erasure," that is, never lose sight of the fact that their meaning is ephemeral.

According to Derrida, in the 1950s structuralists started thinking about "the structurality of structure," that is, about how every system, especially language and philosophy, has a structure. He said that the earliest intimations of such issues began with Nietzsche and marked a major shift or break in Western philosophy. From this point on, philosophers could begin to see their systems not as absolute truth but as constructs or structures. Derrida claimed that all structures seemingly refer to a center, which is what holds the elements in the structure together—for instance, the center of a system of religious belief might be God. Other elements in a structure can be replaced. But if the center is replaced, the structure goes with it. The center is both within the structure and also outside of it. In Derrida-speak, the center "escapes structurality," thus rendering the concept of a centered structure "contradictorily coherent."[12]

In Derrida's view, before the 1950s the history of philosophy comprised the continual substitution of one centered system for another—for instance, Enlightenment thought, the center of which is reason, replaced scholasticism, the center of which was God. That the center of such systems is the foundation of the rest of the system makes the center irreplaceable. The center, thus, is the "transcendental signified"—the seemingly hidden source of meaning, which because it cannot itself be represented in language is always beyond our grasp.

Derrida associated the center of a structure with *desire*. All systems, he claimed, want ultimately to be fixed and totally meaningful. The center is what provides the illusion of fixity and meaning—hence also the illusions of stability, transparency, and self-sufficiency. He called these characteristics, *presence*. Something would be fully present if it were stable, fixed, and self-explanatory. But nothing ever is fully present.

The deconstruction or disruption of the illusion of presence results in *play*, which is what happens when the apparently stable structure of language is destabilized. For instance, if the stability of a structure depends on its use of certain "binary oppositions," such as male/female, rational/irrational, legitimate/illegitimate, nature/culture, and so on, then by revealing the ambiguity and inadequacy of these oppositions, one can put into play all of the elements of the structure. Such a destabilization does not change language, or linguistic structures, but merely removes an illusion. The whole point of deconstruction is to put the elements of linguistic structures into play—that is, to destabilize them—and, thus, to remove an illusion.

Derrida's basic strategy to dispel the illusion of presence is to make use of the logic of *différance*, which, he wrote, "is the systematic play of differences, of the traces of differences, of the spacing by means of which elements are related to each other."[13] *Différance* means that each appearance of a sign *differs* from all of its other appearances; each reappearance of a sign keeps meaning on the go, resulting, ultimately, in a never-ending chain of differences. *Différance* also implies that the meaning of a sign is always *deferred* indefinitely, by intervals of spacing and temporalizing. *Différance* thus functions to block conceptual closure on the meaning of terms, thereby deconstructing the "transcendental signified."

Derrida's objective is to dispel the illusion that language conveys presence by deconstructing language into a "play of differences."[14]

Derrida, thus, talked about deconstruction in terms of *decentering*. He claimed that any sign that is thought to be an absolute center, identical to itself, can be fractured into *différance*. He described decentering as "the stated abandonment of all reference to a center, to a subject, to a privileged reference, to an origin, or to an absolute archia." Yet, he claimed, all absolute centers deconstructed through *différance* reappear as *trace*, that is, as an interplay of presence and absence, or identity and difference. All seemingly fixed metaphysical centers, including God and the self, once placed "under erasure," signify a presence that is at the same time absent and an absence that is at the same time present.[15]

In sum, in Derrida's view, the stability of structures presupposes the adequacy of binary oppositions, which are always inadequate. By revealing their inadequacy, a structure is destabilized, thereby putting its elements into "play." Once this has happened, he said, the theorist is left with two choices. One is to discard the structure and try to build a more stable one (but since there can be no stable structures this objective can never be obtained). The other option is to keep using the structure, but in full awareness of its inadequacy and instability. This latter option involves ceasing to attribute truth to the structure and, instead, seeing it as a construct built around an ultimately flawed and illusory central idea that holds the whole thing in place.

Derrida called this latter option *bricolage* and the person that does it a *bricoleur*, that is, someone who uses a system that he or she knows to be flawed in order to get a particular job done. Bricolage is his alternative to logocentrism— the traditional Western obsession with logic, theory, and the goal of explaining everything. Bricolage is mythopoetic, rather than rational, and a play, rather than a system. It is supposed to provide a way to think and talk about systems without building a new system, that is, without establishing a new center, subject, or privileged point of origin.

In explaining such ideas, Derrida did not provide a separate critique of the notion of self. Rather, his critique of the self falls out of his larger critique of structure and his discussions of the other. What emerges from these is that the self is the center of various structured ways humans have of talking about themselves. As the center of such discourses, the self seems to lie behind and hold together the elements of what it is to be a human. Yet the self, as a kind of organizational and ontological postulate, is to "self talk" what God is to "religious talk"—an absent presence, which because it can never be revealed always promises more than it can deliver. What it promises—what God as a center of religious discourse also promises—is substantiality, permanence, and luminous meaning.

The Politicized Self

The legacy of a host of modern thinkers—particularly Kant, but also Darwin and Freud—was an effort to understand what is common to all selves. Kant tried to do this, in part, by revealing our "transcendental" structures of experience; Darwin, by uncovering our biological nature; and Freud, by bringing into view our psychic origins in unconscious aggression and sexuality. For the purposes of this section, the details of their radically differing views, and of the views of many others who followed in their footsteps, are not so important as what they have in common: the idea that when it comes to the self, one size fits all. None of these thinkers denied differences among selves, but their energy was directed toward discovering similarities. This tendency dovetailed with a dominant strain in modern liberalism, introduced by Kant toward the end of the Enlightenment, according to which the principle of equal respect requires that people be treated equally, in a way that is blind to their differences.

In the twentieth century, but particularly in the latter half of the century, a number of theorists, convinced that an oppressive dominant majority has ignored, overlooked, and repressed what is distinctive about those they oppress, turned their attention to what differentiates people from one another. Various groups—women, gays, lesbians, and ethnic minorities—have tried to articulate their own accounts of what it is to be a self and to have an identity, each of their accounts indexed to a different marginalized group. In taking this line, they came into conflict with traditional liberalism.

According to the new identity politics, society has to recognize and even encourage personal and group differences. Those who favor Enlightenment ideals often accuse advocates of the new identity politics of encouraging discrimination. Advocates of identity politics often retort that Enlightenment ideals, were they ever realized, would, by enforcing homogenization, negate the identities of members of groups that are already marginalized. Against the backdrop of this debate over ideals, theorists of various sorts have tried to fashion accounts of personal and social identity that are congenial to their own ideals and political agendas.

Ethnic and Post-Colonial Studies

W. E. B. DuBois (1868–1963), who was a student of William James, was the first person of African descent to earn a Ph.D. from Harvard. In *The Souls of Black Folk* (1903), a classic in the literature on ethnic identity, DuBois's central question is, "How does it feel to be a problem?" The attempt to understand ethnic or racial identity in terms of consciousness begins with this book. DuBois's answer to his own question was his theory of *double consciousness*. In his view, American society prevented "the American Negro" from developing a "true self-consciousness." Instead, it "only lets him see himself through the revelation of the other world":

> It is a peculiar sensation, this double-consciousness, this sense of always looking at one's self through the eyes of others, of measuring one's soul by the tape of a world that looks on in amused contempt and pity. One ever feels his twoness—an American, a Negro; two warring souls, two thoughts, two unreconciled strivings; two warring ideals in one dark body, whose dogged strength alone keeps it from being torn asunder.

Appreciating Hegel's analysis as a challenge, DuBois said that "master" and "slave" are "locked in a mutually interdependent consciousness they both somehow must move beyond." "The history of the American Negro," he concluded, is the history of psychological strife—"this longing to attain self-conscious manhood, to merge his double self into a better and truer self."[16]

Frantz Fanon (1925–1961), originally from the Antilles, studied medicine and then psychiatry in France before moving to Algeria, where he supported the nationalist movement for independence. In *Black Skin, White Masks* (1967), he developed themes about black identity that complemented and extended those of DuBois and influenced many thinkers and activists, including Malcolm X (1925–1965) and the Black Panthers. In response to questions about the psychological effects of white colonialism on a native black population, he answered: "It is the settler who has brought the native into existence and perpetuates his existence."[17]

Colonialism, Fanon said, is a systematic negation of the native population—a furious determination to deny natives all the attributes of humanity. It forces the people it dominates to ask themselves constantly, "Who am I?"

> Here, in contrast, we observe the desperate struggles of a Negro who is driven to discover the meaning of black identity. White civilization and European culture have forced an existential deviation on the Negro.... What is often called the black soul is a white man's artifact.[18]

Fanon claimed that the effect of colonialism on native speech is paramount: "to speak is to exist absolutely for the other." The native is encouraged to believe that he will become "proportionately whiter—that is, he will come closer to being a real human being—in direct ratio to his mastery" of the language of the colonial masters. To become more "civilized" by adopting French language and customs is to become "whiter"—a process, through language, of self-alienation.[19]

Fanon understood blackness as a product of socialization rather than biology. In developing DuBois, he talked about "third person consciousness"—a three-way split in conscious identity: the body and mind identities assigned to blacks by whites and the identity that blacks assign to themselves. In his view, these identities are complicated by the inevitably doomed quest the black embarks on to become the other—that is, to become white: "I moved toward" the other, and as I did so, "the evanescent other, hostile but not opaque, transparent, not there, disappeared."[20]

Influenced by Sartre, who was himself influenced by Hegel, Fanon emphasized how the movements, attitudes, and "glances of the other fixed" and fragmented his self, the "fragments" then being "put together again by another self."[21] He said that under colonialism, black identity is constructed by the other, the white. There is no place where natives can construct their own identities outside of the colonial gaze of the other. However, he criticized Sartre's account of "the look" for forgetting to notice the importance of imbalances in power between the person who looks and the person who is looked upon. He also criticized Sartre for dismissing consciousness as "nothing," and hence being insensitive to the need for black people to achieve a positive identity. Finally, in response to Sartre's suggestion that blacks in the Algerian resistance movement are just picking up a torch that others had already carried, he accused Sartre of failing to recognize the critical importance of black agency.

Amina Mama obtained her doctorate in psychology from the University of London. Her research interests have centered on bringing gender analysis to bear on subjectivity, social relations and politics. In her most influential book, *Beyond the Masks: Race, Gender, and Subjectivity* (1995), she develops DuBois's and Fanon's accounts of how psychology has been compromised by racial politics. In her view, the hidden purpose of the models of black subjectivity that have been produced by psychology are not meant to garner better and better insights into the true nature of what it is to be black but to facilitate the work of social administrators to manage blacks or to justify the social mission of black radicals to regain control over their own lives. To support this thesis, she analyzes psychological studies of people of African descent living in the United States and the United Kingdom in order to show how supposedly scientific analysis reflects shifts in racial politics going on at the time of the studies.

So far as identity issues themselves are concerned, Mama's fundamental point is that scientific psychologists always insist on understanding black subjectivity as defined by white racism, thus "ignoring the existence of the diverse cultural referents available to many black people." For instance, she says of the original studies of the "Negro" damaged by slavery that nowhere in this work

> is there any acknowledgment of the various collective (cultural) responses to the long black history of oppression, or in fact that they might have had any experience apart from that of racism. Racial oppression itself is inadequately conceptualized as monolithic, total, and homogeneous in its effects. The nuances and intricate set of social etiquette and behavior or betrayal and collusion, or inversion and resistance, that constitute racism as a social process are barely touched upon.[22]

In the spirit of Foucault, Mama analyzes black psychology as a discourse intersecting with social and cultural factors, not as a science gradually clarifying a fixed set of facts.[23]

Feminism and Gender Studies

Most feminist theorists of self and personal identity are united in their opposition to the Enlightenment ideal of the autonomous self on the grounds that it is motivated by a patriarchal political agenda. They have criticized two of the ideal's key tenets: that rationality alone is essential to the self, and that the self is transparent, unified, coherent, and independent. Against the backdrop of this criticism, they have added their own insights into identity to ideas already current in the culture—often ones derived from psychoanalytic theory or poststructuralism—to develop accounts of self and personal identity that support and encourage respect for women. For instance, the poststructuralist Julia Kristeva, after postulating that the self is a speaker who can refer to itself as "I," has claimed that since both the rational orderliness of the symbolic, which is culturally coded masculine, and the affect-laden allure of the semiotic, which is culturally coded feminine, are indispensable to any speaking subject, there is no discourse that is purely masculine or purely feminine. Nancy Chodorow, on the other hand, has appropriated object-relations theory to craft a "relational theory of the self" that reaffirms the value of feminine traits, especially nurturing, and highlights the importance in self-development of emotion, desire, and interpersonal relationships. In her view, the negligible involvement of men in childcare has warped men's self-development, resulting in the formation of selves that are rigidly differentiated, compulsively rational, and overly independent.[24]

In addition to feminist theories, ideas of gender identity arose in the context of gay and lesbian studies and then followed a course similar to the discussion of identity in feminism. In *Gender Trouble* (1990), Judith Butler argued that feminism made a mistake by trying to assert that "women" are a group with common characteristics and interests. She claimed that after feminists rejected the idea that biology is destiny, they developed an account of patriarchal culture that assumed that new masculine and feminine genders would inevitably be built upon "male" and "female" bodies, making a similar destiny equally inescapable. That feminist argument, she added, allowed no room for choice, difference, or resistance, and it resulted in "an unwitting regulation and reification of gender relations"—reinforcing a binary view according to which human beings are divided into two neatly defined groups, men and women. She claimed that feminism has tended to diminish the opportunities for women to choose their own individual identities.[25]

Many current feminist theorists agree with this criticism of earlier feminist theory. One of them, Sandra Bartky, has recently remarked:

> It is by now widely conceded that feminist theories of the Second Wave (not to mention First Wave), whatever their other virtues, have been race and class biased, heterosexist and ethnocentric, that they have often construed as the experience of women generally what was merely the experience of those women who, by virtue of relative race or class privilege, were in a position to theorize their experience in the first place.[26]

Thus, Bartky concluded, "Disadvantaged feminists have charged relatively advantaged feminist theorists with having visited upon many of the world's women what androcentric political theory has visited upon women generally—enforced invisibility or else the distortion and falsification of the substance and texture of their lives."[27]

Butler also argues, inspired by Foucault, that although sex (male, female) is seen to cause gender (masculine, feminine), which is seen to cause desire (toward the other gender), actually gender and desire are flexible, not determined by any stable factors. She concludes that rather than being fixed by biology or anything else, gender should be seen as fluid, shifting and changing in different contexts and at different times, determined, if at all, only by how one acts: "Identity is performatively constituted by the very 'expressions' that are said to be its results."[28]

In other words, gender is what you *do*—a potentially variable performance—not *who you are*—a fixed universal.

Butler argues that all of us stage a gender performance, whether we are in the mainstream or out of it. So it is not a question of whether to *do* a gender performance but which performance to do. By choosing to be different, we might help to change the dominant gender norms and the binary understanding of masculinity and femininity that supports them. She says that although currently certain configurations of gender have come to seem natural in our culture, it does not have to be that way. To smash these dominant cultural configurations, she calls for subversive action—"gender trouble." This action would include the mobilization, upsetting, and proliferation of genders—and therefore of identities. Her idea of identity as free-floating—unconnected to an "essence"—is also foundational to *queer theory*, according to which our identities, gendered and otherwise, do not express an authentic self—an inner "core"—but are instead the dramatic *effect* (rather than cause) of our performances.

Social and Developmental Contributions

During the latter half of the century, in social and developmental psychology, many theorists have focused on the self as an object of knowledge and followed G. H. Mead in conceiving of it through a generalized other. Irving Goffman, in particular, in his classic *The Presentation of Self in Everyday Life* (1959), initiated a "dramaturgical model" in which the self is conceived in terms of social roles that people play in the drama of life. Following his lead, social psychologists have developed *role theory*, in which a whole host of concepts involving self, role playing, self-monitoring, self-role identification, and role conflict have been used to explain how individuals relate to social worlds. Sylvan Tomkins proposed a dramaturgical model called *script theory* to describe how children come to develop knowledge of self and other in social settings. In contrast to role theory, his approach focused not on standard "generalized" roles but on specific individual scripts that get formed from particular social interactions in which children are involved.

While many Anglo-American social psychologists have been studying various social-cognitive notions of self, like self-schema, self-image, and so on, in relative isolation from one's relation to others, continental social psychologists have developed a view according to which social identity is more fundamental than personal identity. That is, according to *social-identity theory*, the ways in which one thinks of oneself in relation to groups with which one is involved is more fundamental in defining who one is than one's individual characteristics. More recently still, and along similar lines, is the incursion into social psychology of social constructivism, which is an extension of poststructuralism. This approach has emphasized the role of language and cultural, ethnic, gender, and lifestyle diversity in self-constitution to form a "multicultural" approach to the social psychology of the self.

In recent years, developmental psychologists have become interested in a new, theory-of-mind approach to the developmental origins of self-consciousness. Initially, this approach was stimulated by studies of the evolution of social cognition. Nicholas Humphrey, for instance, has proposed that human intelligence evolved primarily as social intelligence and that our capacity to become conscious of our own mental states served the function of allowing us to understand the mental states of others.[29] He suggested that by having access to our mental states, we could use our own minds to simulate the minds of others, imagining what we would feel and do in their situations. Such simulation could also help us anticipate our own reactions to imagined situations that do not currently exist but which might occur.

Within a year of Humphrey's article, David Premack and Guy Woodruff published an important paper on whether chimpanzees have a theory of mind.[30] It was thought at the time that although other animals, with the exception of humans, could not recognize themselves in mirrors (soon after it was learned that orangutans and dolphins could), chimpanzees could do so. It was also known that until they were eighteen months old, human infants could not recognize themselves in mirrors. But self-recognition, although it can be taken to imply knowledge of oneself as an independent being, does not imply either that one is reflexively aware of one's own mind or that one is aware that other similar beings also have minds. The Premack and Woodruff paper attempted to provide evidence that chimps have theoretical understanding of the contents of others' minds, which could reflect on their understanding of minds as such, including their own. Premack and Woodruff's conclusions have been hotly debated. It is still in doubt whether chimps appreciate mental states, their own or others. Nevertheless, a burgeoning area of research in comparative and developmental psychology had been spawned.

Although the debate over whether animals are able to understand mental phenomena continues, in the case of humans, developmentalists have succeeded in tracing the origins of consciousness of self and other from infancy. They have discovered that almost from birth, infants are sensitive to the difference between animate and inanimate objects and that infants are able to recognize and contagiously mimic emotional and other facial expressions. These discoveries have provided the basis for attributing to infants a "social self" that participates in feelings and activities with other beings of the same species. Before reflective awareness of such participation occurs, infants have also developed an "ecological self" that can distinguish boundaries between their bodies and the world.

In addition, theorists have discovered that as infants, during their first year of life, acquire greater knowledge of their bodies, they become better able to appreciate parallels between their bodies and the bodies of others. So by the middle of that first year, the infant is beginning, purposely, to imitate the bodily movements of others.[31] Yet it also continues contagiously to mimic emotional expressions. Toward the end of the first year, it is able to participate with others in shared activities and can become aware of the meaning of others' emotional attitudes toward objects. Yet infants, at this time, are still not aware of distinctions between their own mental attitudes toward objects and the attitudes of others with whom they interact. They merely enter into and share such attitudes with significant others. Not until the second year do they become aware of themselves and others as having distinct attitudes toward the same objects or events.

An interesting phenomenon that occurs during this period is the infant's sympathetic responses to others' emotional expressions. In humans, but not in lower animals, emotional contagion is typically a stage on the way toward understanding the point of view of others and sympathizing with them. As M. L. Hoffman, in particular, has shown, there is in humans, from the age of about ten to eighteen months, a gradual development of understanding of the sources of contagiously acquired emotions.[32] For instance, typically infants of ten months respond to the distress (say, crying) of another by becoming distressed themselves, as a consequence of which, ignoring the other, they console only themselves. Later, apparently realizing that they share emotions in common with the other, intermittently they console the other as well as themselves. Eventually, they no longer cry but, apparently recognizing that it is the other who is sad, may simply try to console the other. Subsequently, a normal child's sympathetic responses show an increasing sensitivity to the needs of others not merely by consoling them but by responding more specifically to their mental states and motivations based on a better appreciation of their points of view.

This is one of several phenomena, including mirror self-recognition, that indicate that the eighteen-month- to two-year-old child has begun to differentiate between self and other and to acquire an appreciation of certain mental states of self and other as existing concurrently yet as different from one another. At this time, the child is also acquiring mastery in language, which greatly facilitates its communicating about mental states in self and other. Even so, researchers are convinced that two-year-olds do not yet have what researchers call a (representational) theory of mind. The child at this time is competent in dealing with perceptually available mental states in self and other but is not yet able to represent mental states that may have existed in the past or will exist in the future but are not currently present. Nor at this stage are children able to deal with misrepresentation, that is, with mental states, such as belief, that misrepresent current states of affairs. Since Premack and Woodruff's paper, theorists have called the possession of such capacities the possession of *a theory of mind*. In a classic study by Heinz Wimmer and Josef Perner, it was shown that not until children are four years old are they capable of representing correctly another's false belief.[33] Three-year-olds merely assume that the other knows what they themselves know, even when this could not be the case, say, because the other was not in a position to acquire the knowledge.

The discovery that four-year-olds, but not three-year-olds, are capable of representing false belief sparked an enormous amount of research on what came to be known as *the age-four transition*, and important other findings were made. For instance, it was discovered that besides understanding false belief as it applied to another's mind, some children were also able to distinguish appearance from reality, as well as to appreciate that people might see things differently from their own physical points of view. At this same time, children also learn more about their own mental states. They are able at this age to remember their own past beliefs that are false, as well as to remember previous desires that have changed. They also acquire an understanding of themselves as extended but as transforming through time, and, more generally, acquire "an autobiographical self." There is also evidence that, at this time, they first begin to deal with a future self whose motives differ from their own current motives.

Collectively, these findings suggest that children become generally conscious of their own mental states—past, present, and future—at the same time that they become able to represent abstractly (as opposed to perceiving) the mental states of others. In other words, at this time children become aware of their own minds, as well as of the minds of others. Thus, at this time, children acquire both a "private self" and an "extended self." In effect, it is only at this late date in development that they acquire reflexive consciousness, in the eighteenth-century meaning of that term.

Thus, only after children turn four can they begin to form a concept of themselves as persisting over time. And it is apparently a necessary condition for children to form a concept of their own minds as such, that they be able to form a concept that others also have minds. For without the distinction between mental states in self and other (or between present, past, and future mental states in themselves), children would form no notion of mental states as states of mind at all.

These findings in the developmental psychology of self also suggest that reflexive consciousness, far from being an intrinsic property of mind, may only be a theoretical construct and that the mind itself may be a fiction, that is, a theory that children in Western culture acquire in order to explain human behavior.

The Narrative Self

Although narrative approaches to the self began early in the century, it was not until late in the century that they would come to dominate personality theory. Alfred Adler (1870–1937) had early on suggested that life has a storylike structure. Then Henry Murray (1893–1988), in *Explorations of Personality* (1938), which initiated the study of personality in academic psychology, proposed that the focus of what he called *personology* should be on the whole life of the individual, rather than on the person at any particular time, whether past, present, or future. To emphasize this point, he claimed that what it is to be a person is to have a life history of the sort that persons have: "the history of the organism is the organism."[34]

Murray, who took over the Harvard Psychology Clinic instituted by Morton Prince, had enormous influence on the development of North American personality psychology—as much through his students, collaborators, and followers as through his own work. In the first generation of this influence, one of his collaborators, Erik Erikson, developed his own life-history approach to the person. Others included Sylvan Tomkins, who developed a drama-based, script theory for interpreting lives, and, more recently, Dan McAdams, who developed his own distinctive narrative approach to identity and personality. Subsequently, theorists in this tradition developed "dialogical" theories of self that go beyond the notion of a single narrative self to consider multiple selves within the individual, in dialogue with one another.

Erik Erikson's (1902–1994) most important book, *Childhood and Society* (1950), was soon followed by *Young Man Luther* (1958) and *Identity: Youth and Crisis* (1968), in both of which he enriched and applied his theory of the adolescent identity crisis. He also wrote the psychohistorical *Gandhi's Truth* (1969), which focused on development in maturity. As an ego psychologist, Erikson followed in the footsteps of traditional Freudians such as Anna Freud and Heinz Hartmann, but his work also has similarity to neo-Freudians such as Karen Horney, Erich Fromm, and object-relation theorists such as Ronald Fairbairn and Donald Winnicott. All these theorists shared a common goal of enriching Freud's concept of the ego. However, compared to the rest, Erikson was much more society and culture oriented. He was also more oriented toward ego development throughout the life span.

One of Erikson's main contributions to personality psychology is his proposal of a theory of ego development that involves eight sequential stages. He saw each stage as initiating a developmental task that challenges the individual to acquire new skills, predominantly of a psychosocial nature. The stages, which have optimal times for engagement, can be understood through the opposition of terms that refer to the primary task wherein a balance must be achieved. The eight stages are: infancy—*trust* versus *distrust*; toddler—*autonomy* versus *shame and doubt*; preschool—*initiative* versus *guilt*; school—*industry* versus *inferiority*; adolescence—*ego identity* versus *role diffusion*; young adulthood—*intimacy* versus *isolation*; middle adulthood—*generativity* versus *stagnation*; and late adulthood—*ego integrity* versus *despair*.

While Erikson linked his view of the earlier stages to Freud's theory of psychosexual development, his view of the latter stages are unique to his theory. Most important of these is his account of adolescence as involving a crisis in ego identity in which one either formed an identity of one's own or avoided the task. The cost of avoidance was maintaining conflicting childhood identifications, which led to role confusion and diffusion.

Ego identity requires knowing who you are and how you fit into society. It requires forming for yourself an identity or self that satisfies both your own internal needs and those of society. The task is easier if the society already has a clear role that you are expected to fill and respects you for filling it, and you have good role models. It helps also if there is a clear boundary between childhood and adulthood, supported by "rites of passage." Under such conditions, there is little reason for an adolescent to experience a "crisis" in making the transition from childhood to adulthood. However, without these sources of support, adolescents are likely to experience role confusion or to be uncertain about their place in society. Then they are likely to suffer an identity crisis, coming face to face with the question, "Who am I?"

In some cases, this always uncomfortable experience of not knowing who one is becomes pathological. The adolescent may become totally disoriented, unable any longer to identify with past childhood roles, with no alternative role into which he or she can imagine fitting. It is at this time that adolescents form temporary identifications, often in groups, to unusual, even deviant, identities, but ones that they eventually overcome as they move on to form their own particular identities.

Erikson suggested that adolescence in modern society is allowed a *psychosocial moratorium*, a period in which one takes a "time out" from both childhood and adulthood. It is a kind of extended rite of passage that allows one the time to figure out what one wants to be. During this time, one can "try on" different identities without being required to commit to them, with room to return to childhood identifications or don alternative adult identities. In some cases, adolescents prefer to end the process as quickly as possible, in order to diminish anxiety or because of lack of clarity about the task of this period of life. In such cases, the child moves quickly into an adult role but has engaged in what is called *foreclosure* and may face the same crisis at a later period in adulthood. As depicted by Erikson, identity crisis and identity formation are tasks of late adolescence. As we shall see, McAdams thinks that the task extends beyond this period, to the end of one's life.

Erikson's concept of the identity crisis captured the imagination of many thinkers in the latter part of the twentieth century, not only among personality theorists and life span psychologists but among theorists in many disciplines. Indeed, we can wonder whether this widespread interest tells us more about our era than about the concept's immediate value for use in explaining the challenges of adolescence as a stage of life. Perhaps—like Freud's theories of the unconscious and our sexual nature—its impact on thought in the late twentieth century has a great deal to do with general sociohistorical changes in our experience and conception of self. For just as the concept of self was beginning to be attacked on all sides and many individuals, mainly post–World War II adolescents, were beginning to feel the stresses of what has become known as postmodernity, there emerged a term, *identity crisis*, that captured the very anxiety about the self's existence as the persistent thing that they were feeling, perhaps for the first time as a general phenomenon of Western culture. No longer was it only exceptional people, such as Luther, Kierkegaard, or William James, who faced identity anxiety. Now a whole postwar generation, particularly adolescents trying to adjust to the threat of the cold war and nuclear annihilation, felt it. How were they to anticipate their futures? Where were meaningful identities to be found? Such questions gave an immediacy to Erikson's theory—probably one that would not have been felt to the same extent by adolescents and young adults at other times and places.

Dan McAdams, a leader in using narrative approaches to study human lives, has built on Erikson's views to argue that identity is itself a narrative construction—an internalized and evolving life story that integrates the reconstructed past, perceived present, and imagined future in such a way as to provide a person's life with some semblance of unity and purpose. Typically, such self-defining stories—"personal myths"—are first constructed in late adolescence. However, they are continually updated and revised through one's life.

McAdams treats infancy as a stage that sets the *narrative tone* of one's story. A trusting relationship with one's caretakers makes one optimistic and prepares one to treat one's life as a comedy rather than a tragedy. He sees the young child as being exposed to many stories and playing at being diverse characters. In late adolescence, when the personal myth is formed, it is composed using *nuclear episodes*—memorable high, low, or turning points in one's past that indicate *continuity* or *change* in who one is.

The story that one generates at this time tends to be simple and—at least with respect to the future—unrealistic. The character that one portrays as one's self is usually one-sided and ideal. Later, alternative sides of one's character or personality have to be taken into account. So, in narratives of older individuals there is a tendency to portray one's self as having alternative personas ("imagoes") that compete or complement each other. The goal is to make sense of all of one's life, not just a period or *chapter* in it. In more recent publications, McAdams dubs this process, *selfing*.[35]

Kenneth and Mary Gergen, both experimental psychologists, have joined the chorus of those who believe that the traditional concept of individual selves is fundamentally flawed. In their view, one's current identity is "the result of a life story" in which the meanings of events have been "negotiated with others" and in which "the actions of others contribute vitally" to the narrative sequence.[36]

Hubert Hermans and his colleagues have put forward an account of the self that they call the "dialogical self." They claim that this has its roots in James's distinction between the *I* and the *me*, but that it also depends on Bakhtin's (1973) theory of the polyphonic novel.[37] Each *me* in James becomes a character in the polyphonic novel of self, and each of these *me*s has, not a thinking *I*, but a point of view relative to other characters. The authors state:

> In order to become dialogical, personal meanings (e.g., an idea, a thought about something, a judgment) must be embodied. Once embodied, there is a "voice" which creates utterances that can be meaningfully related to the utterances of another voice. It is only when an idea or thought is endowed with a voice and expressed as emanating from a personal *position* in relation to others that dialogical relations emerge.[38]

Hermans and Kempen, in *The Dialogical Self* (1993) indicate that because of dominance relations among different characters or selves, some voices will be undeveloped relative to others. They also suggest that when we adopt a narrative and reflective stance above selves, we become a "Self" that is relatively free to move the I-position among characters or selves, even to weaker ones, so that each can express its own view in the first person and can comment on and evaluate various points of view of other selves.[39]

Among philosophers in the continental tradition, Paul Ricoeur's view is that self and other are so intimately connected as to defy separation. The self as character in one's narrative is the other. So the self as author and the self as character are in constant dialectical relation.

In Anglo-American philosophy, the most influential narrative theorists of the self have been Alasdair MacIntyre and Daniel Dennett. In *After Virtue* (1981), MacIntyre articulates a "central thesis" about human nature, which is that humans, in their actions and practice, as well as in their fictions, are story-telling animals:

> I can only answer the question 'What am I to do?' if I can answer the prior question 'Of what story or stories do I find myself a part?' We enter human society, that is, with one or more imputed characters—roles into which we have been drafted—and we have to learn what they are in order to be able to understand how others respond to us and how our responses to them are apt to be construed.

It is through hearing such stories, he says,

> that children learn or mislearn both what a child and what a parent is, what the cast of characters may be in the drama into which they have been born and what the ways of the world are. Deprive children of stories and you leave them unscripted, anxious stutterers in their actions as in their words. Hence there is no way to give us an understanding of any society, including our own, except through the stock of stories which constitute its initial dramatic resources. Mythology, in its original sense, is at the heart of things.

For such reasons, then, the narrative concept of selfhood requires that "I am the *subject* of a history that is my own and no one else's, that has its own peculiar meaning."[40]

When someone complains, say while contemplating suicide, that his or her life is meaningless, typically the complaint is that "the narrative of their life has become unintelligible to them, that it lacks any point, any movement toward a climax or a *telos*." Hence, they may no longer be able to discover a reason for doing one thing rather than another. In sum, personal identity "is just that identity presupposed by the unity of the character which the unity of narrative requires. Without such unity there would not be subjects of whom stories could be told."[41]

In Daniel Dennett's view, consciousness should be understood as consisting of narrations, produced by the brain, the point of which is to interpret objects and events in some coherent way.[42] At any given time, the brain generates multiple interpretations of differing degrees of inclusiveness, some of which are in competition with one another. In the more inclusive of these competing narrations, the self shows up as a "center of narrative gravity." In this way of looking at things, the self is not a real object but a fiction about which it is convenient to talk, in the same sense in which any material object's center of gravity is not something real in the world but merely a useful fiction.

Sometimes the brain's goal of achieving overall coherence within a single, inclusive narrative may be unattainable. The result is mental pathology, such as dissociative-identity disorder. In such cases, the brain may have to posit more than one "self." In other words, there may be so much inconsistency among alternative, inclusive narratives that it is impossible for the brain to integrate them around a single center of narrative gravity, that is, a single self. The brain then generates two or more "selves," each the "center of gravity" of its own independent narrative.

Neurophysiology and the Self

Two noteworthy features of the current theoretical landscape are, first, that the notion of self has gained ascendancy both in neurophysiological theorizing and in robotics and, second, that theorizing about the self has become increasingly interdisciplinary, involving philosophers, cognitive and developmental psychologists, neurophysiologists, linguists, physicists, computer scientists, and roboticists, all of whom to a greater extent that ever before are becoming aware of and utilizing one another's results.

For over a century, scientists tried to develop a map of the psychological functions of the human brain. In the 1960s, Roger Sperry and his colleagues did research on "split-brain" patients that linked this approach to the question of how we should understand self-consciousness. The backdrop for Sperry's research is that in the late 1930s, neurosurgeons in the United States had begun performing an operation in which they severed the corpus callosums of severe epileptics in the hope of confining seizures to one hemisphere of the brain, thus reducing their severity. To their surprise, the procedure was doubly successful, often reducing not only the severity of the seizures but their frequency. But the operation had a truly bizarre side effect, unnoticed until many years later.

The side effect is that the operation created two independent centers of consciousness within the same human skull, each one associated with a different hemisphere of the brain. As Sperry and his colleagues demonstrated, these centers of consciousness lacked introspective access to each other and could be made to acquire and express information independently. Most dramatically, they sometimes differed volitionally, expressing their differences using alternate sides of the same human bodies that they jointly shared. In one case, for instance, a split-brain patient reportedly hugged his wife with one arm while he pushed her away with the other; in another, a patient tried with his right hand (controlled by his left, verbal hemisphere) to hold a newspaper where he could read it, thereby blocking his view of the TV, while he tried with his left hand (controlled by his right, nonverbal hemisphere) to knock the paper out of the way.[43]

Among other findings, researchers have noted that in split-brain patients, under experimental conditions, the left hemisphere, which controls verbal production, devises interpretations, consistent with its own information, of right-hemisphere-produced actions and emotions, weaving together autobiographical fact and inventive fiction to produce a personal narrative that sustains the sense of a continuous self. Some have speculated that this behavior in split-brain patients mimics the narrative inventiveness of the brain, in normal humans in smoothing over discontinuities in experience.[44]

Antonio Damasio, a neurologist, has, on the basis of reports from his patients who have suffered brain damage, proposed the existence of a *neural self*.[45] He claims that these patients, deprived of current information about parts of their bodies, have sustained damage to the neural substrate of the self. By contrast, healthy people use their senses of self to access information about the slowly evolving details of their autobiographies, including their likes, dislikes, and plans for the future. They also use them to access representations of their bodies and their states. Damasio calls a person's representations, collectively, his or her *concept of self*, which, he says, is continually reconstructed from the ground up. This concept is an evanescent medium of self-reference. It is reconstructed so often that the person whose self-concept it is never knows it is being remade unless problems arise.

In a more recent book, Damasio, proposed that consciousness represents a relationship between the self and the external world.[46] The self model that actually shows up phenomenologically as a more or less constant feature of our consciousness is not the robust self of our narrative reveries but what he calls the *core self*. It is a representation of a regulatory system in the brain and brain stem, the function of which is to monitor and maintain certain of the body's internal systems, such as respiration, body temperature, and the sympathetic nervous system.

He calls the system being represented, *the protoself*. In his view, all states of consciousness are bipolar in that they include a representation of the core self *in relation to* the external world. In this representation, he says, the core self remains relatively stable, while sensory input from the external world changes dramatically and often. Thus, in almost every conscious state, there is something relatively stable, namely the core self, and something changeable, the external world. This fact about consciousness, he claims, generates the "illusion" that there is a relatively constant self that perceives and reacts to the external world.

Analytic Philosophy

From the 1950s to 1970, fission examples had been discussed sporadically by analytic philosophers.[47] Around 1970, the discussion of them, together with the high visibility experimentation done on split-brain patients, began to provoke a revolution of sorts in analytic personal-identity theory. There have been three major developments. One of these is that the *intrinsic*-relations view of personal identity has been largely superseded by the *extrinsic*-relations view (also sometimes called the *closest-continuer view* and the *externalist view*). According to the older intrinsic-relations view, what determines whether a person at different times is identical is just how the selves at these times are physically or psychologically related to *one another*. According to more recent extrinsic-relations views, what determines whether a person at different times is identical is not just how the two selves are physically or psychologically related to *one another*, but also how they are related to *others*. For instance, in Locke's intrinsic-relations view, you right now are the same person as someone who existed yesterday if you remember having experienced or having done things that person of yesterday experienced or did. In an extrinsic relations version of Locke's view, one would have to take into account not only whether you remember having experienced or having done things that that person of yesterday experienced or did but also whether, besides you, anyone else remembers having experienced or having done things that that person of yesterday experienced or did.

Fission examples are largely responsible for the recent move from an intrinsic- to an extrinsic-relations view. In the sort of fission examples that have been most discussed, a person somehow divides into two (seemingly) *numerically* different persons, each of whom, initially, is *qualitatively* identical to the other and also to the prefission person from whom they both descended. For example, imagine that all information in human brains is encoded redundantly so that it is possible to separate a human's brain into two parts, leaving each half-brain fully functioning and encoded with all it needs to sustain the original person's full mental life just as (except for the elimination of underlying redundancy) his whole brain would have sustained it had his whole brain never been divided. Now suppose that in some normal, healthy human we perform a brain-separation operation, removing the two fully functioning half-brains from his body, which is then immediately destroyed. Suppose, further, that we immediately implant each of these half-brains into its own, brainless body, which, except for being brainless, is otherwise qualitatively identical to the original person's body, so that two people simultaneously emerge, each of whom, except for having only half a brain, is qualitatively identical—physically *and* psychologically—to the original person whose brain was divided and removed and, of course, to each other.

Are these two fission descendants the same person as each other? On an intrinsic view of personal identity, such as Locke's, they would be. Each would remember having experienced things and having performed actions that the original person experienced and performed. If in deciding whether a person at one time and one at another are the same person, we have to consider *only* the relations between the two of them, then it would seem that they might be related so as to have all that is required to preserve identity. Obviously, the problem with supposing that we have to consider *only* the relations between the two of them is that the other fission descendant has an equal claim to be the original person.

Many contemporary philosophers believe that, in such a case, the prefission person—the brain donor—would cease, first, because identity is a transitive relationship—which implies that if one of the fission descendants were the same person as the brain donor, and the brain donor were the same person as the other fission descendant, then the former fission descendant would be the same person as the latter fission descendant; second, because the fission descendants, at least once they began to lead independent lives, cannot plausibly be regarded as the same persons as each other (think, for instance, of the moral and legal complications if, five years down the road, one of them turns out to be a nice, law-abiding person and the other a nasty, criminal type); and, third, because it would be arbitrary to regard just one of the fission descendants but not the other as the same person as the donor (at the moment of "conception," the two are equally qualified to be the same person as the donor). Hence, in the view of these philosophers, it is more plausible to regard each of the fission descendants as different from the prefission person. Philosophers who reason this way accept an extrinsic-relations view of personal identity, according to which what determines whether a person at one time and one at another are the same person is not only how the two are physically or psychologically related to *each other* (which is all that would need to be considered on an *intrinsic relations* view) but *also* how the two are related to *others* (in the case of our example, especially the other fission descendant).

The fission examples that eighteenth-century philosophers considered were religious-fiction scenarios. The fission examples that in our own times philosophers have considered are science-fiction scenarios. Both sorts raise essentially the same issues for personal-identity theory. In the eighteenth century, many philosophers supposed that the religious-fiction fission examples had a counterpart in real life (postmortem) situations. In our own times, some of the science-fiction fission examples actually do have counterparts in real-life situations, in the case of the split-brain operations.

Since 1970 there has been another major development in personal-identity theory. Philosophers have begun again to question whether personal identity is primarily what matters in survival. That is, they have faced the possibility that people might cease and be continued by *others* whose existences they would value as much as their own and in pretty much the same ways as they would value their own. Imagine, for instance, that you have a health problem that will result soon in your sudden and painless death unless you receive one or the other of two available treatments. The first is to have your brain removed and placed into the empty cranium of a body that, except for being brainless, is qualitatively identical to your own. The second is to have your brain removed, divided into functionally identical halves (each capable of sustaining your full psychology), and then to have each of these halves put into the empty cranium of a body of its own, again one that is brainless but otherwise qualitatively identical to your own.

In the first treatment, there is a 10 percent chance that the transplantation will take. If it takes, the survivor who wakes up in the recovery room will be physically and psychologically like you just prior to the operation except that he will know he has had the operation and will be healthy. In the second there is a 95 percent chance both transplantations will take. If both take, each of the survivors who wakes up in the recovery room will be physically and psychologically like you just prior to the operation except that each of them will know he has had the operation and each will be healthy. If the transplantation in the first treatment does not take, the would-be survivor will die painlessly on the operating table. If either transplantation in the second treatment does not take, the other will not take either, and both would-be survivors will die painlessly on the operating table. Everything else about the treatments—suppose—is the same and as attractive to you as possible: both are painless, free of charge, and, if successful, result in survivors who recover quickly.

As we have seen, many philosophers believe that you would continue in the first (nonfission) treatment but cease and be replaced by others in the second (fission) treatment. As in the case of the previous fission examples, they think that you would cease and be replaced in the second treatment because they believe, first, that identity is a transitive relationship; second, that the survivors, at least once they begin to lead independent lives, cannot plausibly be regarded as the same people as each other; and, third, that it would be arbitrary to regard just one of the survivors but not the other as you. Hence, in the view of these philosophers, it is more plausible to regard each of the survivors as a different person from you.

Assume, for the sake of argument, that this way of viewing what will happen in the two treatments is correct. On this assumption, you would persist through the first treatment but in the second you would cease and be replace by others. So, given the circumstances specified in the example, only by sacrificing your identity could you greatly increase the chances of someone who initially would be qualitatively just like you emerging from the operation and surviving for years. The question is whether, in the circumstances specified, it would be worth it for you to have such an operation, that is, whether it would be worth it only from the point of view of what in more normal circumstances would be considered a totally selfish (or self-regarding) point of view. Many who consider examples like this one feel strongly that it would be worth it. So, for them at least, it would seem that ceasing and being continued by others can matter as much, or almost as much, as persisting, and in pretty much the same ways. But if ceasing and being continued by others can matter as much and in the same ways as persisting, then identity is not what matters primarily in survival.

Derek Parfit, perhaps the leading analytic personal-identity theorist of the twentieth century, has a neo-Lockean view of personal identity, according to which what binds the different stages of us into the individual people that we are is not just memory but psychological relations more generally (including beliefs, intentions, character traits, anticipations, and so on). Unlike Locke, Parfit thinks that it is not necessary for each stage of us to be *directly* related to every other stage. It is enough if each stage is *indirectly* related through intermediate stages. In sum, what binds us are psychological connections, overlapping "like the strands in a rope."[48] Thus, Parfit's view is not vulnerable to Thomas Reid's objection to Locke's view. In Parfit's view, if C, at t_3, is *directly* psychologically connected to B, at t_2, but *not* to A, at t_1, but B, at t_2, *is* directly psychologically connected to A, at t_1, then C, at t_3, is *indirectly* psychologically connected to A, at t_1, and that may be enough to preserve personal identity.

Parfit has also responded to those who think that the notion of *same person* enters into the proper analysis of various psychological relations, particularly memory. To avoid the charge that his analysis of personal identity is circular, he has formulated it in terms of specially defined senses of psychological relations that do not include the notion of *same person*. For instance, in the case of memory, Parfit has defined a notion of *quasi memory* (or, *q-memory*), which is just like that of *memory*, except that whereas the claim that someone *remembers* having experienced something *might* imply that the person remembers that *she herself* experienced that thing, the claim that someone *q-remembers* having experienced something implies—by definition—only that the person remembers that *someone* experienced that thing. Thus, Parfit's view may not be vulnerable to the argument Butler used to try to show that Locke's view is circular.

To illustrate how q-memory might work, Parfit gave as an example Jane's seeming to remember Paul's experience, in Venice, of looking across water and seeing a lightning bolt fork and then strike two objects.[49] Parfit claimed that in seeming to remember this experience, Jane might know that she was seeming to remember an experience that Paul (and not she) had had originally and that if Jane knew this, then she would know, *from the inside*, part of what it was like to be Paul on that day in Venice. In other words, Jane would know she was seeming to remember Paul's experience from the same sort of subjective, first-person point of view from which Paul actually had the experience originally and from which ordinarily Jane actually remembers only her own experiences. If one acknowledges that Parfit's hypothetical example is at least theoretically possible, as it seems we should (imagine, say, that part of Paul's brain had been surgically implanted into Jane's brain), then apparently it is possible, in analyses of personal identity, to substitute q-memory for memory and thereby avoid Butler's objection. In other words, even if simple memory analyses of personal identity are circular, it would not follow that q-memory analyses of personal identity are circular.

When Locke proposed his psychological-relations view, most philosophers subscribed to a soul view. In 1984, when Parfit proposed the fullest version of his theory, probably most philosophers subscribed to the view that the continuity of our bodies, or of some part of our bodies, is necessary for personal persistence. Parfit, by contrast, denied that bodily continuity is necessary for personal persistence. To support this denial, he supposed, first, that while someone's brain is healthy, his body is ridden with cancer and his only hope for survival is to have his entire healthy brain transplanted intact to another healthy body. He supposed also that this transplantation procedure is perfectly safe and that the body into which the donor's brain will be transplanted is better than his current body, not only in that it is healthy but also in many other respects that appeal to the donor. Parfit pointed out, surely correctly, that the donor has not lost much if he jettisons his old body and moves his brain to the better body that awaits it. Such an operation would not be as bad as staying in the old body and dying of cancer, even if the death were painless. In fact, vanity being what it is, if radical cosmetic surgery of this sort were available and safe, it is likely that many people would choose it, even if the old bodies they jettisoned were healthy. So, if physical continuity matters, Parfit concluded, it cannot be the continuity of the whole body but at most the continuity of the brain.

But, Parfit argued, the importance of our brains, like that of our other organs, is not intrinsic but derivative; that is, the brain's importance depends solely on the functions it serves. For most of us, if half of our brains were functionally equivalent to the whole, the preservation of our whole brain would not matter much. And, it would seem, the continuity even of any part of the brain is not necessarily important. If some other organ, such as the liver, sustained our psychologies and our brains served the functions this other organ now serves, then this other organ would be as important in survival as the brain now is and the brain only as important as this other organ now is. So, it would seem that if something else—anything else—could sustain our psychologies as reliably as the brain, then the brain (i.e., the physical organ that actually now functions as the brain) would have little importance in survival, even if this other thing were not any part of our bodies.[50]

A critic might object that even though the importance of an organ is derivative and based solely on its being the vehicle for preserving a person's psychology, given that it has always been that vehicle, then the preservation of that organ matters importantly, perhaps even primarily, in survival. In other words, it is possible that even though something else *might* have assumed that organ's function of preserving a person's psychology, once an organ actually has served the function of preserving a person's psychology, then it does matter importantly in survival. But even though this is possible, it is doubtful that the very organ that has actually sustained your psychology, merely in virtue of its having sustained your psychology, thereby matters all that importantly to you in survival.

Imagine, for instance, that competent doctors discover that you have both a brain disease and a brain abnormality. The disease has not impaired the functioning of your brain yet. But if it is untreated, it will result in your death in the near future. Because of the abnormality, there is a simple, effective, and painless cure. The abnormality is that you have two brains, the one now diseased, which is the only one that has ever functioned as a brain, and another, right beside it, lying dormant—healthy and perfectly capable of performing a whole brain's functions should the need arise, but nevertheless never yet functioning as a brain and not currently encoded with any of your psychology. There is a simple procedure the doctors can perform to switch the roles of your two brains: All of the encoded psychology on your diseased brain will be transferred to the healthy one; as it is transferred, it will be erased from your diseased brain, whereupon your healthy brain will begin to function just as the diseased one did (and would have continued to function had it been healthy and left alone).

Suppose that the procedure is as quick and as simple (and as abrupt) as flipping a switch, that it will not affect subjective psychology, and that consciousness will be continuous throughout the procedure. Indeed, suppose that you (and the person who emerges from the procedure) will not even notice any change. Once the transfer is completed, almost instantaneously, your diseased brain will become dormant and pose no further threat to your organism's physical or psychological health. In these imagined circumstances, how much would it matter to you that the brain of yours that has always sustained your psychology will no longer sustain it, while another that has never sustained it will sustain it from now on? Probably not much. The procedure would not be as bad as death. Unless the procedure caused existential anxiety, it would not even be as bad as a root canal. So much for the derivative value of the organs that have actually sustained our psychologies.

Those who are skeptical of this response might imagine that whereas the procedure described is the simplest way of disabling the threat to the organism posed by your diseased brain, it is not the only way. An alternative procedure the doctors can perform is to repair your diseased brain through a series of twenty brain operations spread over the next twenty years of your life. Each operation will cost about one-half of your annual salary (suppose that insurance does not and probably never will cover the procedure) and will require two months of hospitalization. In addition, the operations will be disfiguring. When they are finally completed, you will be healthy enough, but your life will have been seriously disrupted and your body and face will be somewhat deformed. We assume that on your scale of values, the disruption, expense, and disfigurement, while bad, are not as bad as death. (If they are as bad as death, reduce their severity to the point where they are not *quite* as bad as death.) So, if the first procedure is as bad as death, then the second procedure is a better choice. Which procedure would you choose? We think most people would choose the first procedure.[51]

Finally, a critic might object that even though the preservation of one's body might not matter in survival, it still might be necessary for personal persistence. However, in Parfit's view, in the case of many of the exotic examples under discussion in the personal-identity literature, including the one just discussed, the question of whether one persists is an *empty question*. Once one knows all of the physical and psychological ways in which the earlier and later persons are related, and how the earlier person evolved (or transformed) into the later person, one knows everything there is to know about the situation that is relevant to the question of personal persistence. There is no *further fact* to know—say, whether or not in such circumstances one actually persists. That is, in the case of such examples there may be no truth of the matter about whether one persists.

In one of Parfit's most controversial claims—his notorious *branch-line* example—he asks you to put yourself imaginatively into the place of a person on Earth who is trying to teletransport to Mars.[52] You enter the teletransportation booth and push the button, activating the process. You succeed in producing a replica of yourself on Mars. But because the teletransporter has malfunctioned, you fail to dematerialize on Earth. A few minutes later, on Earth, you emerge from the teletransporter and are told believably that due to its malfunction your heart has been damaged and you have only two more days to live. Parfit argues that in such a case you should not be too concerned. Rather, you ought to regard your replica's persistence—now taking place on Mars—as an adequate surrogate for what might have been your own persistence on Earth. While not many philosophers have followed Parfit in taking this line, explaining why one should not take it without returning to the view that identity is what matters in survival has not been easy.[53]

The final of the three major developments since 1970 in analytic personal-identity theory has been a challenge to the traditional three-dimensional view of persons, according to which a person can be wholly present at a given moment—for instance, you are wholly present right now. Some philosophers have argued that we should replace this three-dimensional view with a four-dimensional view, according to which only time-slices or "stages" of persons exist at short intervals of time. On this four-dimensional view, persons are aggregates of momentary person stages, beginning with the person stage that came into being at a person's birth and ending with the person stage that exists when the person dies, and including every person stage between birth and death.

To see why it might matter which of these two views is correct, consider again any of the fission examples (except the branch-line case) discussed above. In commenting on each of those examples, it was suggested that the prefission person is not identical with either of his postfission descendants. That was a three-dimensional way of describing the situation. A four-dimensionalist would have said that what we are calling "the prefission person" is really not a person but rather a person stage and that what we are calling "the postfission descendants" are also person stages. According to a four-dimensionalist, in a fission example the prefission person does not cease. Rather, what happens is that the prefission person stage becomes a shared person stage. That is, two persons, each of whose postfission person stages are separate from the other's overlap prior to fission and, thus, share their prefission person stages.

Philosophers have used this four-dimensional way of conceptualizing fission examples to argue that they cannot be used as evidence that identity is not what matters in survival. The reason, according to these philosophers, is that in a four-dimensional model, no one ceases in a fission example (and, hence, identity is never traded for other benefits). Rather, what happens before fission is that "the prefission person" is really a shared stage of two persons. After fission, these two persons no longer share any present or future stages. On this view, a given person stage may be part of two or three (or potentially any number) of persons. So, it is sometimes called the multi-occupancy view of persons. Although it has its defenders, most personal identity theorists either have remained with the traditional three-dimensional view or alternate between the two views, depending on which way of conceptualizing a situation is clearest in the context under discussion.[54]

So ended the twentieth century. Before World War II, the self seemed to be a unified subject of investigation. Although theorists did not agree on what to say about it, most seemed to agree that it was something about which something might be said. When they talked about the self, it was as if they agreed that in talking about it they were talking about the same thing, and about just one thing. By the end of the century, there were no such presuppositions.

XIV

EVERYTHING THAT HAPPENED
AND WHAT IT MEANS

We began by suggesting that what we really want to know about theories of the self and personal identity—indeed about any part of the past that truly interests us—is "everything that happened and what it means." We've now completed our account of "everything that happened." It's time, then, to say "what it means."

It is obvious that at the most fundamental level, theories of the self and personal identity are an expression of concern with the self and its ability to endure. As we have seen, Christianity played a decisive role in connecting that concern, as it played itself out in the West, with philosophical theorizing. But the concern itself did not begin with Christianity. It did not even begin with the Greeks or Hebrews, or even the Egyptians. Rather, it began much earlier, perhaps with the Neanderthals, who twenty thousand years ago, in what is now France, Israel, and China, left remains of their dead in shallow graves, with carefully arranged, small, uniformly sized stones around them. No one knows exactly what these stones meant to the Neanderthals who put them there. But since the stones were purposefully and carefully arranged, it seems likely that they meant something. Most anthropologists think that the stones were arranged to express the Neanderthals' belief that those who were buried in this fashion continued to live beyond their bodily deaths.

If the Neanderthals really did believe that bodily death is sometimes not the end of personal existence, then it would seem that they differed in this respect from their predecessors. Other early hominids and nonhuman animals may have mourned particular deaths, but their concern with death was bound to the present and to the world of the senses. The Neanderthals, on the other hand, seem to have originated a future-oriented concern with death—and if not the Neanderthals, then some group of early hominids or humans. It does not matter for the point we want to make exactly who did it. What matters is that it was done very early, in prehistoric times.

Assuming that it was the Neanderthals who came up with this innovation, what could have motivated them to suppose that at least some among them would survive the demise of their gross physical bodies? The study of traditional cultures suggests two possible answers: visions and dreams. In our own times, people in traditional cultures, throughout the world, have visions and dreams in which they are visited by ghostly entities, mostly with humanlike bodies that seem to be made not of flesh and blood but of something ethereal.

Such visitations by ghostly others is associated in the minds of many people in traditional cultures with what anthropologists sometimes refer to as belief in "doubles," that is, in ghostly selves. Some people in traditional cultures even believe that their physical shadows are these selves. In addition, many traditional people believe in astral travel, that is, in their ability to leave their gross physical bodies behind and travel to another location, particularly while asleep. Closely related is the idea of reincarnation, in which selves go back and forth between the normal world and the afterlife. As we have seen, such beliefs may have exerted a powerful influence on Greek philosophy, particularly on Pythagoras and through him on Plato and through Plato on all subsequent Western thought.

Yet, so far as one can tell, most people in traditional cultures do not have deep longings to have doubles or even to survive bodily death. Of course, they do not want to die in the first place, but that is a different matter. Within such cultures it tends just to be accepted that some or all people do have doubles and do survive their bodily deaths. For instance, in many traditional cultures, even today, ancestors are part of one's social world. People communicate with them daily on a variety of subjects and seek advice from them on how to deal with life's problems. However, becoming an ancestor is not something that traditional people long for, just one of the things that they believe happens—a fact of life, if you will, or of death.

By contrast, in today's Western industrialized cultures many people take a *personal* interest in their *own* survival of bodily death and are curious about whether they *themselves* will survive. Often they *long* to survive, particularly in some way that is better than their earthly lives. Often they are *anxious* about whether their postmortem fates will be better, for instance, whether they will go to heaven or hell. When did such attitudes toward survival of bodily death begin?

In Western philosophy, one of the earliest expressions of sustained *curiosity* about survival of bodily death occurs in Plato's *Phaedo* where, while Socrates awaits the hemlock, he devotes a great deal of time and energy trying to prove that all people survive their bodily deaths and, hence, that he too will survive. But on that occasion, even though Socrates believes that he will survive his bodily death and even looks forward to certain postmortem pleasures that he expects, he does not seem to be *longing* to survive. Nor is there any suggestion that he is *anxious* about his survival. He has a positive attitude about life after death in that he thinks that it will be free of the distractions of the body and, hence, ideally suited to philosophical contemplation. But, for the same reason that he has a positive attitude about the prospects of his surviving bodily death, he recommends that philosophers "practice death" while they are still alive by trying to minimize the distractions of the body.[1] In a myth that appears toward the end of the *Phaedo*, people who live improperly are saddled with demeaning reincarnations. Even so, Socrates does not recommend that anyone give up any earthly pleasures in order to avoid such a fate. In sum, there is no indication that he is fearful of death.[2]

Compare Socrates' attitude toward life and death with that of St. Paul, whom we quoted earlier as saying, "If the dead are not raised, 'Let us eat and drink, for tomorrow we die.'"[3] Here St. Paul seems to have been expressing the thought that were there no postmortem price to pay, it would be better to live one's current life hedonistically. But in view of the effect on *one's own* afterlife of living that way, he thinks that each of us is better off refraining from indulging ourselves. There is no hint of any such future-oriented concerns in Socrates, who recommends "practicing death," not living it up, as the best way to live, and not primarily because it will make one's *afterlife* better but because it will make one's *current* life better. The same sort of lack of concern with one's afterlife tends also to be true of the other pagan philosophers in the West.

So, in Christianity, it would seem, a new element has entered the picture, at least new in the West: the anxious recommendation that one forgo certain pleasures now so that *one's own afterlife* will be better. What seems to have been of primary importance to early Christians is not how best to live, either for one's own sake or for others, in this life, but how best to live in this life for *one's own* sake *in the afterlife*—that is, for the sake of bettering one's own condition in the afterlife: for instance, "Do not store up for yourselves treasures on earth, where moth and rust destroy, and where thieves break in and steal, but store up for yourselves treasures in heaven" (Matt. 6:19–20). This recommendation, it would seem, expresses not just curiosity about one's own postmortem fate, or even just concern, but *anxious* self-concern. The message is that in the afterlife, one may have it personally better or worse and it is up to each one of us to live now so as to have it personally better. And what it will take to do that is self-sacrifice: postponing the good life. In other

words, you can pay now or pay later, but it is cheaper—infinitely cheaper, in fact—
to pay now. In sum, whereas Greek and Roman philosophers tended to be much
more preoccupied with living well now, Christians were much more preoccupied
with living well later. This major change in focus was deeply consequential for
theories of the self and personal identity.[4]

Early Christians were not only preoccupied with living well in the afterlife,
but they had a specific view about how this was going to happen: it involved
bodily resurrection. Initially, to those early Christian apologists, who were materialists, that's all that one's afterlife involved. But once Platonism came to the fore,
Christian survival meant the continuation of one's immaterial soul *together with*
one's reconstituted material body in a way that preserved one's *personal* persistence. Having to explain all of this posed several serious philosophical problems.
Among them were the problems of how to explain the relationship between the
immaterial soul and the material body and how to explain how a body that does
not remain intact can nevertheless be identical to a body that will exist in the
afterlife. And, of course, one had to explain these things so that personal identity
is preserved, or else death would not have been defeated, as early Christians
claimed that it was by Christ's Resurrection, and the distribution of rewards and
punishments in the afterlife would make no sense. Explaining these things has
been a perennial problem for Christian philosophers, from the Patristic Period
until modern times.

In early times, so far as Christianity is concerned, and even today among most
Christians, dualism reigned supreme. Earlier, the idea of an immaterial soul had
been introduced by Plato, but it then became somewhat superseded in classical
antiquity by the views of Aristotle and the atomists. But in the Hellenistic Period,
the idea of an immaterial soul rose again, at first independently of Christianity
but later in concert with it. Yet it would be Christianity that would thrust this
idea into the mainstream of European intellectual life. Even so, the idea of an
immaterial soul, as a respectable theoretical postulate, could not long survive the
arrival of modern physical science. It had grave difficulty even surviving the
arrival of Aristotelian science.

As we have seen, it was not just the notion of an immaterial soul that ran into
trouble. Eventually, even the more scientifically friendly notion of self ran into
trouble. However, the notion of self ran into trouble for somewhat different reasons. For one thing, the status of the self as a real entity, rather than a convenient
fiction, was an issue at least from the time of Locke. In addition, the unity of the
self and its potential to explain other unities, such as the alleged unity of consciousness, soon gave way to fragmentation that itself was in need of explanation.
As a consequence, the notion of self ran into trouble as something to which one

could appeal in accounting for survival not just of bodily death but of day-to-day, even moment-to-moment survival, while one is alive. That is basically why we refer in the title of this book to the fall of the soul *and* the self. However, whereas these days the fall of soul as a scientifically useful notion can more or less be taken for granted, the claim that the self also fell has to be put more delicately. In particular, the unified self as a scientifically useful notion has to be distinguished from the self as a practically useful notion. It also has to be distinguished from notions of various hyphenated self-activities, such as self-discovery, self-acceptance, self-modeling, and so on.

In saying that the self has fallen, we do not mean to say that ordinary folk beliefs or day-to-day practices of self-reference are in trouble. Rather, we mean to say something about the notion of self as a scientifically useful notion. It's worth pausing here briefly to explain the difference between the practical and the theoretical uses of the notion of the self.

It is obvious that before the development of philosophical and scientific theories of the self and personal identity, people understood themselves to be continuing entities with various sorts of capacities. They had linguistic ways of expressing this understanding, for instance, by saying things like, "When I was a boy ..." and "I lent you money ..." And when they said such things they understood themselves, and were understood by others, to be saying something about themselves at an earlier time.

Almost as certainly, people believed themselves to be, or to have, souls prior to the advent of philosophical theories of self and personal identity. From an early time, probably even ordinary people thought that souls, perhaps as breath, are intimately connected with life, often by being what it is in a living thing that accounts for its being alive. Ancient people had words, such as *psyche* (Greek), *ka* (Egyptian), and *hun* (Chinese), which they used to refer to what Christians and their cultural descendants later came to think of as souls. Obviously, the views of such prephilosophical peoples about souls were theoretical in a sense, but not in the same sense as the postulated theoretical entities in deliberately constructed philosophical or scientific theories. The primitive notions of self and soul were not part of anyone's consciously chosen theory. Rather, they were tacitly implicated in folk beliefs and practices. Ordinary people did not have to study philosophy in order to know about selves and souls. They got that knowledge at their mother's knee.[5]

Unlike the holders of folk beliefs and practices, Greek philosophers—Plato and Aristotle, for instance—did not just *use* the concept of *psyche* (soul) in the ordinary folk-theoretical and -practical ways in which everyone in their culture used it. Rather, they used it in a special sense to provide theoretical explanations.

In particular, in their views, *psyche* came to be understood as something that at least in part is an immaterial thing that gives unity to living beings and that survives bodily death. For instance, in Plato and among those who followed him, *psyche* as an immaterial thing was thought to be a vehicle for one's individual, personal persistence before birth, during life, and after bodily death; in Aristotle and among those who followed him, *psyche* was the form of the body and hence a source of unity in living things. But because of *psyche*'s tie to the body, it was less clear in Aristotle's thought whether it could be a vehicle for one's individual, personal persistence before birth or after death.

For present purposes, the important point is that in the sense in which we understand the notion of some concept's being *scientifically useful*, by the time of Plato the notion of *psyche* was, in some Greek philosopher or other's view, a scientifically useful notion. The immaterial, immortal soul, which was a Christianized version of *psyche*, persisted as a scientifically useful notion until well after the seventeenth century, even though once modern physical science arrived on the scene, its explanatory usefulness began to wane. Descartes, for instance, retained the notion of an immaterial soul, which he equated with mind (*mens*) and self, but he abandoned the previously held idea that the notion of soul could be used to explain life. He held that animals, which are alive, have no souls, or selves, since animals do not think and thinking is essential to soul and self. In animals at least, he explained life mechanistically. Ultimately, as thinkers eventually came to believe that the brain, rather than the soul, is the seat of the mind, the soul as a scientific concept became marginalized, and the brain moved to center stage. The notion of soul continued to have a life in religious thought and in ethical theory, but for scientific purposes it was all but dead.[6]

What about the notion of a unified *self*? The story of its rise as a theoretically useful notion parallels that of the soul, except for one thing: when the notion of the soul was introduced as a scientifically useful notion, it was posited as a real thing. There was never any suggestion that it might merely be a useful fiction. Not so, in the case of the notion of the self, which came into its own theoretically in Locke's attempt, in the second edition of his *Essay*, to give an empirically grounded account of personal identity. But while the self posited there plays a theoretically prominent role, it did so alongside the suggestion that it may merely be a useful fiction—"a forensic term."

In general, as various eighteenth-century thinkers began to marginalize or drop the notion of the soul, they tended to retain Descartes's association of the self with consciousness and his suggestion that a unified self plays a role in the production of human action. Even so, in the case of many eighteenth-century thinkers, it is difficult to tell whether they are employing the notion of the self merely pragmatically, as a useful fiction, or as a realistically understood scientific postulate.

Many eighteenth-century thinkers who rejected the idea that the soul is an immaterial substance and the idea that the notion of an immaterial substance is useful scientifically did not then automatically turn around and explicitly use a naturalized notion of the self scientifically. Rather, they tended to talk in terms of mind and consciousness, more than self.[7] Significantly, when they did turn, in scientific contexts, to the notion of a unified self, they tended to use it not to explain but as something that itself needed to be explained. So, for instance, Hartley and then Hazlitt did not appeal to the unified self to explain anything but instead suggested developmental accounts of the acquisition of self-concepts. The closest either of them got to appealing to the self to explain something was to appeal to the belief people had in the self to explain other beliefs or attitudes that people also had. For instance, both of them appealed to the belief people had in the self to explain the phenomenon of self-interested behavior.

After Kant, the notion of the self as a real, unified entity that does some explanatory work continued to play a robust role primarily in *philosophical*, as opposed to scientific, theories. Think, for instance, of Schopenhauer and Husserl. However, from the end of the nineteenth century, to the extent that the notion of a real self shows up at all in *scientific* theories, it tends to get divided up into more manageable concepts. In Freudian psychology, for instance, the self is divided into the three theoretical postulates of id, ego, and superego. And in contemporary neurophysiology, the notion of the self shows up, if at all, only in the guise of a neurologically encoded self-model. An exception to this trend is the pre-1970s thought of existentialists and humanistic psychologists, from Kierkegaard to Carl Rogers, in which the hunt was on for the *true* or *inner* self. Otherwise, after World War II the self as a theoretically useful unitary object of activity or reflection more or less vanished. William James, at the end of the nineteenth century, divided the self mercilessly, in spite of his wanting to retain it as a useful theoretical notion. By dividing it so mercilessly, he was among the first to foreshadow its demise.

In James's account, after elevating the "personal self" to a very high status, even claiming that no psychology that hopes to stand can question its existence, he immediately conceded that in cases of dissociation an individual human can have more than one personal self. Moreover, he continued, each personal self may be regarded both as an object and as a subject (a *me* and an *I*). The self as object may be further divided into the material self, the social self, and the spiritual self, each of which may be still further divided. He said, for instance, that *"a man has as many social selves"* as there are individuals and groups *"who recognize him* and carry an image of him in their mind." He said that a person's *spiritual self* may be regarded as a set of "psychic dispositions," including the abilities to argue and discriminate and to have "moral sensibility," "conscience," and an "indomitable will." Alternatively, he elaborated, one's spiritual self can be seen as "the entire stream of our personal consciousness," or more narrowly as the "present 'segment' or 'section' of that stream." When James speaks of the *I*, he further parceled the stream into thoughts, adding that the *I*, a thought, is at each moment a different thought "from that of the last moment, but appropriative of the latter, together with all that the latter called its own."[8]

In a similar fashion, but more self-consciously, after World War II and increasingly into the last third of the twentieth century, psychologists and cultural theorists not only demoted the self, but dismantled it as a unitary object of study. Currently, in scientific contexts, which so far as the notion of self is concerned are almost always psychology contexts, when the notion of self shows up, it tends to show up in one of its many hyphenated roles, such as self-image, self-conception, self-discovery, self-confidence, self-esteem, self-knowledge, self-acceptance, self-reference, self-modeling, self-consciousness, self-interest, self-persistence, self-control, self-denial, self-deception, and self-actualization.[9] While the notion of identity is not quite analogous, to some extent it has suffered a similar fate, as notions of racial identity, ethnic identity, sexual identity, gender identity, social identity, political identity, and so on have come in scientific contexts to take prominence over the notion of personal identity.

The ontological status of these various hyphenated notions of self is often unspecified. Psychologists rarely explain whether the *self-* notions they employ are supposed to be interpreted realistically or as explanatory fictions, such as the notion of a center of gravity. Moreover, even as theories that employ such hyphenated *self-* notions in an individually manageable way have proliferated, there has been no concerted attempt to unify *self-* theories with one another. The result has been fragmentation not only within theories but among theories.

So, where does that leave us? The notion of a unified self was introduced into scientific theory in the seventeenth century, particularly in the theories of Descartes and Locke, as a replacement for the notion of soul, which had fallen on hard times. But eventually the notion of a unified self fell onto hard times of its own. Its demise was gradual, but by the end of the twentieth century the unified self had died the death if not of a thousand qualifications, then of a thousand hyphenations.

Of course, researchers working in different traditions or on different aspects of the self have continued to share a common focus of inquiry in that they all study the behaviors of the human organism. But, lacking a refined understanding of how the human organism unifies hyphenated self-behaviors and self-phenomena, researchers have lost touch with anything that deserves to be called a unified self. Surprisingly, it has not seemed to matter. In order to get on with their research, psychologists have found little need to relate hyphenated self-behaviors and self-phenomena to a unified self, as James had tried so heroically to do. As a result, the unified self, if indeed there ever was such a thing, has receded from view. Those who seek it today in both the philosophical and psychological literatures soon discover that none but the carefully initiated can wade into the waters of theoretical accounts of the self without soon drowning in a sea of symbols, technical distinctions, and empirical results, the end result of which is that the notion of the unified self fades from view.

Consider, for instance, a recent paper by Ulrich Neisser that many psychologists, especially, but also many philosophers, hold in high regard.[10] Neisser characterizes what he has done as having identified five mechanisms of self-knowledge or "five kinds of self." The five in question are the ecological, social, private, extended, and conceptual selves. Nothing of importance seems to hinge on which of these—mechanisms or selves—we take Neisser to have revealed. Either way, each involves a different mechanism in the organism—and these mechanisms have distinctive material bases, temporal spreads, developmental profiles, and pathologies.

Neisser himself did little of the research he characterizes. Instead, he fit the research that others have done into an overarching framework. The others include different groups of psychologists, each of which worked on one or another source of self-knowledge, more or less independently of the others. The framework Neisser provides for organizing their discoveries does not account—does not even try to account—for the unity of selfhood or of self-knowledge, even supposing either of these is unified.[11] It may seem, then, that, in his paper at least, fragmentation wins the day. But does it?

Even though Neisser does not explain how his five sources of self-knowledge work together to provide information in a *coordinated* way to the organism, implicit in his account is the suggestion that there must be some way in which they do so. After all, the organism copes. It would seem then that the sources of self-knowledge must all work *together* to help it cope. If they did not, the organism would quickly perish, or at least run into more trouble than it does. If the sources of self-knowledge do work together to help the organism cope, then to that extent at least the organism would seem to be unified. And since in some views, the self just is the organism, at the end of the day, the forces of unification may win after all.

It may be, of course, that although the forces of unification win at the deepest scientific levels of description and analysis, fragmentation still prevails at shallower levels and that we will want or need to retain talk of some of these levels either for the purpose of doing scientific psychology or of engaging in practical conduct. This might happen, for instance, if at a physiological level of analysis and description, science yields an account of a unified organism even though, at a cognitive level, there is no unification in sight.

In an earlier time, the suggestion that the self should be identified with the organism would have been rejected due to the self's supposed immateriality. Today, few secular theorists are substance dualists. Without anyone's having a very clear idea of what materialism is, most theorists believe that whatever it is, it must be true. But a different sort of problem looms on the horizon: the possibility that the self cannot be identified with the organism and hence unified by means of the organism's unity—not because the self is immaterial but because it is social. The impetus for this idea stems originally from Hegel but resonates in a variety of later thinkers, such as James, Baldwin, Royce, Mead, Vygotsky, Lacan, Foucault, Derrida, gender-identity theorists, and social constructivists, among others. James, for instance, seems to have committed himself to each person's having "social selves" that extend beyond the boundaries of his or her organism. A similar idea, often based on the alleged social dimension of self-expressions, is a staple of deconstructionist and postmodernist thought.

Even Neisser seems to think that one or two of the selves that he characterizes is inherently social. For instance, he *defines* what he calls *the interpersonal self* as a self that is "engaged in immediate unreflective social interaction with another person," and he says that most of the information that this self-mechanism gathers "comes into existence when two (or more) people are engaged in personal interaction."

> [When the two are in sync with each other,] the mutuality of their behaviour exists in fact and can be perceived by outside observers; more importantly, it is perceived by the participants themselves. Each of them can see (and hear, and perhaps feel) the appropriately interactive responses of the other. Those responses, in relation to one's own perceived activity, specify the interpersonal self.[12]

In addition, Neisser's *conceptual self* also seems to contain a social component.

In sum, it may be that if unity enters the picture, it comes in at the level of the organism, not at the level of the self. In ancient Greece, selves, in their earlier incarnation as *psyches*, were introduced in order to explain life. In that capacity, they were a *source* of unity, not a *result* of unity. When, in the eighteenth century, selves replaced souls, in the view of some theorists, selves retained this unifying

function.[13] Eventually, however, as selves lost this role, they lost their explanatory force. Now, instead of being thought to generate unity, they have become a
major symptom of fragmentation.[14] Instead of something that explains, they
have become something that needs to be explained.

Where will it all end? One possibility is that the multifaceted threads of
debate and theorizing are never going to be woven together. We may have passed
from an era, such as the eighteenth century was, in which an important source of
concern was unwelcome answers and both the hope and fear of new knowledge
to an era in which so far as a unified self is concerned there are in scientific contexts no comprehensive questions, let alone answers, nor any prospect of finding
them. Instead of comprehensive questions and answers, we are left to harvest
only continually increasing, albeit fragmenting additions to knowledge. Yet
progress occurred and is still occurring on localized fronts, seemingly at an accel-
erated rate. In other words, in the absence of a theoretically useful notion of a
unified self, researchers are continually learning more about the pieces. Whatever else may happen, it is almost a sure thing that, in the foreseeable future,
theorizing will continue down the road it is on. In light of this, perhaps one
should just concede that there is nothing to do about theoretical fragmentation
except perhaps to get over the feeling that there is anything that needs to be done
about it.

Of course, it is always possible that there will be a grand synthesis of the various strands of contemporary theorizing about self-behaviors and self-phenomena
that will win the allegiance of most theorists, thereby drawing everything together
again. But there is no such synthesis in sight. And, although it may be objection-
ably speculative even to have an opinion on this subject, it seems to us that the
only sort of theory that might be compelling enough that, later, most everyone
might take it as their point of departure in elaborating further theories of the self
would be an integrated, detailed physiological theory of how those portions of the
brain function that control how we represent ourselves to ourselves and to others.
It will be a long time, if ever, before we have such a theory. But, at this point, even
if we did have one, it would still not weave together such disparate concerns as
the traditional question of personal identity and the newer one of what matters
primarily in survival. Nor would it provide a mechanism for containing the social
dimensions of the self. So it seems likely that well before any such unifying theory
emerges, current occasional expressions of concern about the problem of fragmentation and the still-lingering hope for eventual reintegration will be replaced
by the recognition that the multifaceted threads of debate and theorizing are
never going to be woven together completely, whether or not their being woven
together would yield a unified self.

Is fragmentation, then, the end of the story? In reflecting on Hitchcock's *Rear Window*, we assumed that what we want from historians is an account of everything that happened and what it means. On that assumption, is the ultimate truth about self and personal-identity theory the somewhat deflating one that while we will no doubt continually learn more and more details about self-behaviors and self-phenomena, a comprehensive overview of a unified self will elude us? What, then, of persistent "existential" concerns, such as "Who am I?" that historically have brought and even today continue to bring many people to the consideration of self and personal identity in the first place?[15] Can such concerns be answered without a comprehensive overview? Can they be answered without a unified self? Or should they be dismissed as overly naive?

These are difficult questions to answer. Our view, in brief, is that such concerns have an important role to play in life but cannot be taken at face value. It would be too much of a digression to try to develop this view here.[16] Instead, we want to consider very briefly two hopeful possibilities. One of these is that we are better off without a unified theory and approach. The reason for this is that what we characterized somewhat ominously as theoretical fragmentation could instead have been characterized more benignly as healthy pluralism.[17] The basic idea behind this suggestion is that what can seem nostalgically to have been eras of beneficent theoretical coherence came at a price. At such times, legitimate points of view and approaches were excluded. Yet not all pluralisms are healthy; some are merely chaotic. So, to sustain this optimism, at the very least a case would have to be made that the current state of theoretical and methodological pluralism is healthy. In our view, a strong case for this could be made. Whether ultimately it would prevail is another question. It is also another question whether theoretical coherence and healthy pluralism are incompatible.

A second somewhat hopeful possibility stems from the perhaps disturbing realization that what we characterized as a unified self is not something that we once had and then lost sight of but, rather, something that we never had to begin with. To whatever extent it may have seemed like we had it, this was an illusion. In this view of things, a better way of characterizing what happened as a consequence of the development of theory is not that we lost something valuable that we once had but that we became better positioned to shed an illusion and finally see what we had—and have—for what it truly is. Shedding an illusion, even the comforting one that there is a unified subject matter of self and personal-identity theory and we can grasp it whole, is a kind of progress. It is not progress of a sort that is internal to any theory but, rather, progress in gaining a better synoptic understanding of the development and current state of theory—metaprogress, if you will. Arguably, it is a sign of the importance of the shedding of the illusions of a unified self and of theoretical closure that it may be psychologically impossible to embrace wholeheartedly that there may be no knowable comprehensive truth about who and what we are and about what lies at the root of our egoistic concerns.

Nevertheless, each of us seems to have a kind of direct, experiential access to him- or herself that makes the development of theories of the self and personal identity, however interesting, seem somewhat beside the point. This feeling of special access is what fueled Descartes's contention that one's own self is first in the order of knowing. The truth, however, seems to be that nothing is first in the order of knowing, that is, that there is no single privileged place to begin the development of theory, no single privileged methodology with which to pursue it, and no practical way to unify the theories that result from starting at different places using different techniques. This was not so apparent until recently, but it seems abundantly clear now. In sum, as we have already suggested, if there is unity in sight, it is the unity of the organism, not of the self or of theories about the self.

But while most may agree that the soul has fallen, many people may doubt that the self has fallen. After all, one might object, the role of self-reference in our purposes, intentions, emotions, and thoughts remains—and likely will remain—pretty much what it always has been. It would remain thus even if our theoretical view of the self were to lack coherence overall or we were to decide that a unified self is a fiction. This is true for pretty much the same reason that our practical ways of thinking about time seem to be impervious to advances in the understanding of time in physics. So far as the self is concerned, regardless of theory we still have to decide what to do *now*, *here*, with *this body*, in *this social world*, with *these people*, and so on. And each of us has to decide this for him- or herself. Our commonsensical world, with its apparently enduring entities, is the arena in which most of our practical projects arise and are pursued. That is not going to change anytime soon, if ever. So, in what sense has the self fallen?

Our answer is that the notion of a unified self has fallen in pretty much the same sense in which the soul fell. Both notions began as folk-theoretical notions long before they acquired theoretical importance in science. Both notions then acquired great theoretical importance in science and then eventually lost it. Neither notion then went away. In North America today, most people, mainly for religious reasons, believe that they have an immaterial soul that is their essence and that their souls will survive the demise of their bodies. Similarly, even though the unified self has fallen as a scientifically useful notion, it too is still around. But unlike in the case of the soul, the self's status as a useful notion does not depend on its role in religious views. Rather, there are a great many very fundamental practices, of great importance to society, that depend on the integrity of the notion of a unified self. Among these practices are self-reference, ownership, responsibility, personal persistence, and belief in the rationality of prudence. But the persistence and importance of these practices does not show that the notion of a unified self is alive and well in the relevant sense. It was once thought to be a scientifically useful notion. It no longer is, certainly not to anything like the extent to which it once was. In that sense, it has fallen. And what made it fall was fragmentation and the widespread belief among theorists that the unified self is a fictional entity.

But there is a difference in the fates of soul and self. Notwithstanding the use of the word *soul* in popular culture, its persistence as a notion that lays claim to theoretical or even practical importance depends almost entirely on its role in religious belief. Not so with the notions of self and personal identity, which have great practical importance in social arrangements and in everyday life. We could give up religion and get along just fine without the notion of soul. But we could not as easily give up what we would need to give up in order to get along without notions of self and personal identity. To get along without these, we would have to withdraw from modern social arrangements and virtually all of the ways in which we narrate our histories to ourselves and others.

If we are right about this, then what can the history of theories of the self and personal identity tell us about the human quest, in the West, for self-understanding? So far as *theory* is concerned, what it tells us is that in understanding the self, progress has been made, at the cost of fragmentation, which may or may not be a surface phenomenon and, hence, the end of the story. So far as *practice* is concerned, things are pretty much as they always have been. For many central and persistent purposes of everyday life, theory and practice are and are likely to remain autonomous, at least when it comes to theories of the self. We do not need to understand ourselves theoretically to get on in the world.

From our present vantage point, it is hard not to read the history of theories of the self and personal identity as a story of how religious dogma can retard scientific understanding. Christianity is primarily responsible, with its dogma of resurrection and its decision to cast its theology in a Platonic mold. Without the encouragement of Christianity, substance dualism might never have gotten its vicelike grip on the imagination of European thinkers. The Enlightenment, seemingly like a new dawn, began to loosen that grip. But Christian dogma had become so intertwined with theoretical common sense that it continued to cast a shadow over the next two hundred years of science and philosophy. Materialism, with its inevitable marginalization and fragmentation of the self, had to claw its way into theoretical ascendancy. However, today, without meaningful theoretical support from religion or science, the unified self stands naked and exposed, revealed for the first time for what it is: a misleading, albeit socially indispensable and incredibly useful fiction.

At the end of the day, it is clear, just as it always was, that each of us humans is indeed fairly unified, just as we always thought that we were. But we are not unified by the soul or the self. We are unified by our bodies. Some day we may understand how. When that day comes, what it is to be a self, and to be the same self over time, may not seem like important theoretical issues. However, they will continue to be important practical issues. At the very beginning of Western theorizing about the self and personal identity, Epicharmus seems to have glimpsed this important truth: whether or not, in theory, persons or selves persist through changes, in practice, they do; lenders still expect debtors to repay their debts and debtors are still obligated to repay them.

Stepping back and looking at Western theorizing about the self and personal identity as a whole, an important part of what it means that theory took the course that it did is that in the West, from the earliest beginnings of theory until fairly recently, thinkers have been preoccupied with elevating the self—the "I"—to an exalted status. The soul was created importantly for this purpose, and when the soul ceased to be useful, the unified self was called in to fill the void. Seemingly very different notions, but essentially the same game: to show that the self—the I—is a demigod of sorts, reigning unopposed over its domain, the human person. From a selfish point of view, much of what matters most to humankind was linked to this demigod: one's essence, free will, consciousness, personal survival, the defeat of death. What the history of theory thus shows is that there has been a persistent effort, from beginning to end, to make this case—to show that a unified self is a secure repository of many of humankind's most glorious conceits and aspirations. And what history also shows is that in the face of continuing scientific development, the case for many of these conceits and aspirations cannot be made.

In the seventeenth and eighteenth centuries, science undermined the soul. The self was recruited to take its place, including providing unity and direction to the human person, as well as being the vehicle for persistence both during life and after bodily death.[18] In effect, science took the I, as soul, out of heaven and in the guise of a unified self brought it down to earth. Like the soul, the self was to be the source of unity, power, freedom, control, and persistence. But the fly in the ointment was analysis. So, soon enough what had been one—the I—became many. What had been real became fiction. And what had been a source of explanations became itself in need of explanation. Analysis has been the self's undoing. As a fragmented, explained, and illusory phenomenon, the self could no longer retain its elevated status. And it is hard to see how it might ever again regain that status. It is as if all of Western civilization has been on a prolonged ego trip that reality has finally forced it to abandon. If this interpretation is plausible, then what happens next may be a new phenomenon in history, a kind of dark night of the "soul": not necessarily a bad thing, but a different thing.

So what does it all mean? The story of Western theorizing about the self and personal identity is not only, but centrally, the story of humankind's attempt to elevate itself above the rest of the natural world, and it is the story of how that attempt has failed. It is another illustration, as if another were needed, of how pride goeth before the fall.

NOTES

Introduction

1. Her actual words: "Start from the beginning and tell me everything you saw and what you think it means."

2. Of course, there will be competing interpretations of this relevant and helpful information according to some of which there has been a murder and according to others not. What the Grace Kelly character really wants to know is whether there is *an* interpretation in either group that is better than *any* interpretation in the other group. In her view, an interpretation will be better only if it is more likely to correctly answer the question of whether there has been a murder.

3. This remarkable exchange was known to Plato (*Theaetetus* 152e) and subsequently widely discussed in late antiquity as "the Growing Argument." See David Sedley, "The Stoic Criterion of Identity," *Phronesis* 27 (1982): 255.

4. It may not have been until after the appearance of Christianity that this thought came to be used as a basis for suggesting that some (but only some) of the ways in which atoms come together and pull apart in an organism or thing are compatible with its remaining the same. An additional question suggested by Greek materialistic atomism is whether the change and stability of selves, or people, is to be understood on the same model as would be used to understand change and stability in general, or whether people are special, so that their change and stability is to be explained differently. So, for instance, at the end of the seventeenth century John Locke gave one account of the identity of inanimate objects, another of the identity of animate objects, and another of the identity of persons. Some other philosophers, by contrast, have given just one account for everything.

1. From Myth to Science

1. For a discussion of the origins of psychological terms in Greece, see, e.g., E. R. Dodd, *The Greeks and the Irrational* (Berkeley: University of California Press, 1951); Julian Jaynes, *The Origin of Consciousness in the Breakdown of the Bicameral Mind* (Princeton, N.J.: Princeton University, 1976); R. P. Onians, *The Origins of European Thought About the Body, the Mind, the Soul, the World, Time, and Fate* (Cambridge: Cambridge University Press, 1988); and Paul S. MacDonald, *History of the Concept of Mind: Speculations About Soul, Mind, and Spirit from Homer to Hume* (Burlington, Vt.: Ashgate, 2003).

2. See, for instance, the essays on this topic in James C. M. Crabbe, ed. *From Soul to Self* (London: Routledge, 1999).

3. Thomas Metzinger has recently suggested that out-of-body experiences (OBEs) may have played an important role in the prehistory of the concept of soul as a substance separate (and separable) from body. See Metzinger, "The Pre-Scientific Concept of a 'Soul': A Neurophenomenological Hypothesis About Its Origin," in *Auf der Suche nach dem Konzept/Substrat der Seele. Ein Versuch aus der Perspektive der Cognitive (Neuro-) Science*, ed. M. Peschl (Würzburg: Königshausen und Neumann, 2003), 185–211.

4. Or perhaps merely removing the illusion of separateness.

5. Kathleen Freeman, ed., *Ancilla to The Pre-Socratic Philosophers: A Complete Translation of the Fragments in Diels, Fragmenta der Vorsokratiker* (Oxford: Basil Blackwell, 1971), fragments 129, 81, 89, and 45.

6. Freeman, *Ancilla*, fragment 91; and Plato, *Cratylus*, in *The Collected Dialogues of Plato*, ed. Edith Hamilton and Huntington Cairns (New York: Pantheon Books, 1961), 421–74. In Cratylus's view, in order to speak truly, one needs a world that is stable. This aspect of his view is not so different from Plato's own view, except that Cratylus thought that no stable world exists. Plato, of course, posited nonmaterial "Forms," or "Ideas," as the stable objects of knowledge.

7. Plato, *Symposium*, 207d–208b, ed. and trans. C. J. Rowe (Warminster, England: Aris & Phillips, 1998), 91, 93.

8. In most of the *Phaedo*, Plato seems to be thinking of survival as the persistence of a naturally immortal, indivisible, individualistic soul, whether extended or not. Yet, at the end of the dialogue, he presents a myth in which the ideas of reincarnation, "guardian angels," and "purgatory" are introduced. If one takes this myth seriously or goes beyond the *Phaedo* and attends to everything Plato said on the topic of survival of bodily death, a confusing picture emerges. In the *Republic*, for instance, Plato proposed what today we would call an empirical psychology, in which he recognized an irrational factor within the mind itself. And, in contrast to the *Phaedo*, where the passions are depicted as a distraction from without, in the *Republic* they are an integral part of the mind and even a source of needed energy for sensuous or intellectual activity. Interestingly, in the *Phaedo* Plato uses the same passage from Homer to illustrate the soul's struggle with the body that he uses in the *Republic* to illustrate an internal dialogue between two "parts" of the soul.

9. Plato, *Timeaus*, in *The Dialogues of Plato*, trans. Benjamin Jowett (1871), 4th ed. (Oxford: Clarendon Press, 1953), 69b–70b.

10. But if Plato were a dualist in the modern sense, he would then be faced with the problem of explaining how what is material and extended can be affected by what is immaterial and unextended. Specifically, in the case of humans, he would be faced with the problem of explaining how a human's immaterial, unextended part—the soul—and his or her material, extended part—the body—interact. This is the Achilles heel of dualism. No substance dualist, as holders of this view are called, has ever proposed a plausible solution to this problem. That is the main reason why there are so few substance dualists among professional philosophers today.

11. Two other aspects of Plato's view of the soul deserve brief mention. First, in the *Theaetetus,* he endorses the view that different sense organs—eyes, ears, sense of touch, etc.—are responsible for conveying to the mind different data of sensation, such as sights, sounds, and feels. He claimed that these data then need to be combined in the mind in some appropriate way in order for the organism to perceive physical objects in an external world. To effect this combination, he supposed that the mind has a special faculty whose job it is to do this combining. Second, toward the end of the *Cratylus*, Plato comes close to introducing into the discussion of personal identity the hypothetical possibility of fission, which from the eighteenth century on has proved to be a potent source of theoretical development. In the *Cratylus*, fissionlike issues arise in the context of a conversation about names and other representations, such as images. The question is raised whether only a perfect image can represent or whether imperfect images also represent. Socrates says:

> Let us suppose the existence of two objects. One of them shall be Cratylus, and the other the image of Cratylus, and we will suppose, further, that some god makes not only a representation such as a painter would make of your outward form and color, but also creates an inward organization like yours, having the same warmth and softness, and into this infuses motion and soul and mind, such as you have, and in a word copies all your qualities, and places them by you in another form. Would you say that this was Cratylus and the image of Cratylus, or that there were two Cratyluses?

Cratylus answers, "I should say that there were two Cratyluses." Socrates replies:

> Then you see, my friend, that we must find some other principle of truth in images, and also in names, and not insist that an image is no longer an image when something is added or subtracted. Do you not see that images are very far from having qualities which are the exact counterpart of the realities which they represent?

Cratylus answers: "Yes, I see." Socrates continues,

But then how ridiculous would be the effect of names on things, if they were exactly the same with them! For they would be the doubles of them, and no one would be able to determine which were the names and which were the realities.

(Plato, *Cratylus* 432a–e; 466, in *The Collected Dialogues*)

12. Plato, *Phaedrus* 245c–e; 492–93, in *The Collected Dialogues*.

13. There are passages in Aristotle, in the so-called exoteric writings—especially the *Eudemus, or On the Soul*—which some scholars attribute to a very early stage in Aristotle's career (an attribution other scholars have disputed). In these passages, Aristotle seems to take a Platonic view of human nature: the real human is simply the incorporeal soul; the body is at best an instrument of the soul and at worst its prison or mortal tomb. See Werner Jaeger, *Aristotle: Fundamentals of the History of His Development* (1934; reprint, New York: Oxford University Press, 1967), 39–53.

14. Aristotle, *De anima* book 1, 1 (408b), and 3, 5, (430a, 10–25). This and subsequent translations of Aristotle are from Richard C. Dales, *The Problem of the Rational Soul in the Thirteenth Century* (Leiden: E. J. Brill, 1995), 9–10. Because of the inscrutability and importance of these passages, they bear another translation:

[Mind] seems to be an independent substance implanted within the soul and to be incapable of being destroyed. And in fact mind as we have described it is what it is by virtue of becoming all things, while there is another which is what it is by virtue of making all things.... Mind in this sense of it is separable, impassible, unmixed, since it is in its essential nature activity.... When mind is set free from its present conditions it appears as just what it is and nothing more: this alone is immortal and eternal (we do not, however, remember its former activity because, while mind in this sense is impassible, mind as passive is destructible), and without it nothing thinks.

(In *Works of Aristotle*, vol. 1, trans. W. D. Ross, Great Books of the Western World, vol. 8 [Chicago: Encyclopedia Britannica, 1952], 638, 662)

The main puzzle about Aristotle's conception of *nous* (i.e., intellect or mind), which arises in both of these translations, is whether to equate the *nous* capable of "becoming all things" (i.e., *nous tō panta ginesthai*, the possible or potential intellect) with the *nous* capable of "making all things"(i.e., *nous tō panta poein*, the active or agent intellect) or, instead, to equate it with the "passible intellect" (i.e., *ho pathōtikos nous*, passive intellect). Most current scholars equate the possible intellect with the passible intellect, thus implying that it is corruptible. On this interpretation, only the agent intellect is incorruptible and immortal. But a number of medieval commentators, most notably Thomas Aquinas, held the view that the possible and agent intellects are one and the same intellect, which is incorruptible and immortal, and that the passive intellect is just another name for imagination. A recent defender of this latter view is Mark Ambrose, "Aristotle's Immortal Intellect," *Proceedings of the American Catholic Philosophical*

Association: Person, Soul, and Immortality, Vol. 75, 2001 (New York: American Catholic Philosophical Association, 2002). We will see further discussion of this issue in later chapters.

15. Aristotle, *De Generatione Animalium* 2, 3 (736a)

16. According to Richard Sorabji, 700 years after Aristotle's death Neoplatonists invented the view that according to Aristotle *nous* is immortal. They did this, he said, in order to counter the criticism, made by Christians, that pagan philosophers were inconsistent. See, Sorabji, "Soul and Self in Ancient Philosophy," in *From Soul to Self*, ed. M. James C. Crabbe (New York: Routledge, 1999), 10.

17. Aristotle, *Metaphysics*, ed. and trans H. Tredennick, 2 vols., Loeb Classical Library (London: William Heinemann, 1936), 12.8, 1074a; see also *Metaphysics* 5.6, 1016b3. See also Udo Thiel, "Individuation," in *The Cambridge History of Seventeenth Century Philosophy*, vol. 1, ed. Daniel Garber and Michael Ayers (Cambridge: Cambridge University Press, 1998), 212–62.

18. In his *Errors of the Philosophers*, Giles of Rome (1247–1316 C.E.) relies on this passage from Aristotle to argue that Aristotle would deny the possibility of resurrection; in *Medieval Philosophy: Selected Readings from Augustine to Buridan*, ed. H. Shapiro (New York: Random House, 1964), 384–413.

19. Quoted by Diogenes Laertius. Quoted here from David Sedley, "Epicurus," in *Routledge Encyclopedia of Philosophy*, ed. E. Craig (London: Routledge, 1988), http://www.rep.routledge.com/article/A050.

20. Epicurus, *Letter to Menoeceus* 124, cited by Tad Brennan, "Immortality in Ancient Philosophy," in *Routledge Encyclopedia of Philosophy*, ed. E. Craig (London: Routledge, 2002), http://www.rep.routledge.com/article/A133.

21. We are indebted in this paragraph especially, but also in this entire section, to A. A. Long, "Stoic Philosophers on Persons, Property-Ownership, and Community," in *Aristotle and After*, ed. Richard Sorabji (London: Institute of Classical Studies, 1997), 13–32. Long explains that in the quotations included in this section, the selection and translation of which is due to him, he has translated the Greek word, "*oikeiosis*," as "appropriation," with the understanding that "the forcible connotations of appropriation should be discounted" and that "the word [*oikeiosis*] primarily refers to a process or activity, innate in all animals, which explains why, from the moment of birth, they behave in self-regarding ways."

22. Diogenes Laertius, *Lives of the Philosophers*, book 7, in Long, "Stoic Philosophers," 25.

23. Seneca, *Epistle*, 121.14, in Long, "Stoic Philosophers," 25.

24. Hierocles, *Elements of Ethics*, col. VI, 23–53, in Long, "Stoic Philosophers," 26.

25. Hierocles, LS57G, in Long, "Stoic Philosophers," 27.

26. David Sedley, "The Stoic Criterion of Identity," *Phronesis*, 27 (1982): 255, 259.

27. Hippocrates, "On the Sacred Disease," in "Hippocratic Writings," in *Great Books of the Western World*, vol. 10 (Chicago: Encyclopedia Britannica, 1952), 154, 156.

28. See Heinrich von Staden: "Body, Soul, and Nerves: Epicurus, Herophilus, Erasistratus, the Stoics, and Galen," in *Psyche and Soma—Physicians and Metaphysicians*

on the Mind-Body Problem from Antiquity to Enlightenment, ed. John P. Wright and Paul Potter (Oxford: Oxford University Press, 2000), 79–116.

29. Galen (130–200 C.E.), for instance, in explaining the operations of the nervous system in thought and action, found it expedient to give at least lip service to the possible role of an immaterial soul. In general, however, he was more strongly influenced by Aristotle than by Plato and usually rejected even the hint of dualism found in Aristotle. For instance he asserted, "If the reasoning part of the soul exists, it is mortal, because it also represents the mixtures of the humours in the brain." He went on to suggest that reasoning is not a defining feature of the human soul but just another function of brain activity that is present in various degrees among animals, including human animals. See Gregory Zilboorg, *A History of Medical Psychology* (New York: W. W. Norton, 1941); and Rudolph E. Spiegel, *Galen on Psychology, Psychopathology, and Function of Diseases of the Nervous System* (New York: S. Karger AG, 1973), 130.

30. The Skeptics Pyrrho (c. 360–c. 272 B.C.E.) and Sextus Empiricus (c. 150–c. 225 C.E.), for instance, distinguished sharply between what is known directly and what must be inferred.

31. On these issues see Voula Tsouna, *The Epistemology of the Cyrenaic School* (Cambridge: Cambridge University Press, 1998); Tim Crane and Sarah Patterson, eds., *History of the Mind-Body Problem* (London: Routledge, 2000); Anita Avramides, *Other Minds* (London: Routledge, 2001); as well as John P. Wright and Paul Potter, eds. *Psyche and Soma—Physicians and Metaphysicians on the Mind-Body Problem from Antiquity to Enlightenment*, (Oxford: Oxford University Press, 2000).

2. Individualism and Subjectivity

1. Heraclitus, (fragment 11), in *Ancilla to the Pre-Socratic Philosophers: A complete Translation of the Fragments in Diels, Fragmenta der Vorsokratiker*, ed. and trans. Kathleen Freeman (Oxford: Basil Blackwell, 1971).

2. Cicero, *De Offices*, trans. Walter Miller (New York: MacMillian, 1908), book 1, 30:107, 110, 35:126; De Finibus Bonorum et Malorum, trans. H. Rackham (New York: MacMillian, 1914), book 3, 75.

3. Epictetus, *The Manual*, part 17, in *The Discourses of Epictetus*, trans. P. E. Matheson (New York: The Heritage Press, 1968), 279, with some emendations by the authors.

4. Epictetus, *Discourse* 1.2, in *The Discourses of Epictetus*, trans. P. E. Matheson (New York: The Heritage Press, 1968), 9–10.

5. Marcus Aurelius, *Meditations*, trans. George Long (London: Collins' Clear-Type Press, n.d.), book 2, 14:104.

6. The translations in the passages quoted are from Lucretius, *De Rerum Natura*, trans. R. E. Latham (Harmondsworth: Penguin, 1951).

7. Other scholars who translate these crucial passages in *De Rerum Natura* differently include: William H. D. Rouse, "Even if time shall gather together our matter

after death and bring it back again as it is now placed, and if once more the light of life shall be given to us, yet it would not matter one bit to us that even this had been done, when the recollection of ourselves has once been broken asunder" (Cambridge, Mass.: Harvard University Press, 1924; 3rd rev. ed. reprint, 1966); H. A. J. Munro, "And if time should gather up our matter after our death and put it once more into the position in which it now is, and the light of life be given to us again, this result even would concern us not at all, when the chain of our self-consciousness has once been snapped asunder" (in Whitney J. Oates, ed., *The Stoic and Epicurean Philosophers* [New York: The Modern Library, 1940]). However, even though the word "*repetentia*," which Latham translated as *identity*, is translated by Rouse as *recollection of ourselves* and by Munro as *self-consciousness*, the point of Lucretius's reflections remains basically the same. It is that one's body and spirit, including one's memories, must be united and exist *continuously* into a future about which it is rational for one to feel egoistic concern. Once this continuity is broken, as it is at bodily death, then rational egoistic concern is no longer possible. A natural way to express this point is that once this continuity is broken, then rational egoistic concern is no longer possible because one no longer exists.

8. Quoted in D. J. Enright, ed., *The Oxford Book of Death* (Oxford: Oxford University Press, 1983), 28. In this connection, see the fascinating remark on Lucretius by Pierre Bayle, *A General Dictionary, Historical and Critical*, trans. J. P. Bernard, T. Birch, and J. Lockman, 10 vols. (London: J. Bettenham, 1734–1741): "The same atoms which compose water are in ice, in vapours, in clouds, in hail and snow: those which compose wheat are in the meal, in the bread, the blood, the flesh, the bones etc. Were they unhappy under the figure or form of water, and under that of ice, it would be the same numerical substance that would be unhappy in these two conditions; and consequently all the calamities which are to be dreaded, under the form of meal, concern the atoms which form corn; and nothing ought to concern itself so much about the state or lot of the meal, as the atoms which form the wheat, though they are not to suffer these calamities under the form of wheat" (note Q). In addition, according to the late-eighteenth-century philosopher Abraham Tucker, Lucretius was forced to consider the objection that "the atoms, some thousands of years hence, after infinite tumblings and tossings about, would fall into their former situation, from whence a thinking, feeling soul must necessarily result: but he denied that this would be the same soul. Just as when a company of dancers assemble together and dance for six hours, the whole is one ball: but if they leave off at the end of three hours, and a fortnight afterwards a second party is proposed whereon they meet to dance for three hours again, this is a ball too, but another ball distinct from the former. So the soul, which is but a dance of atoms, cannot be the same . . . [and] therefore, whatever wretched fortune may befal it, we, that is, our present souls, have no concern therein" (Tucker, *The Light of Nature Pursued*, 7 vols. [1805; reprint, New York: Garland, 1997], 7:11–12).

9. Plotinus, *Ennead* 4.2.1.2, in *Great Books of the Western World* (Chicago: Encyclopedia Britannica, 1952), 17:140.

10. *Ennead* 5.3.3, *Great Books*, 17:217.

11. *Ennead* 4.3.27, *Great Books*, 17:156.

12. *Ennead* 4.3.32, *Great Books*, 17:158.

13. *Ennead* 4.4.2, *Great Books*, 17:159.

3. People of the Book

1. Christianity emerged from Judaism and adopted the Hebrew Bible as its Old Testament. And Islam, in the Qur'an, accepts the Hebrew prophets and Jesus as precursors of Muhammad and recounts the basic storyline in the earlier scriptures. All three religious traditions trace their ancestry to Abraham.

2. For example, "He that toucheth the dead body of any man shall be unclean seven days" (Num. 25:16–17).

3. As translated in Neil Gillman, *The Death of Death: Resurrection and Immortality in Jewish Thought* (Woodstock, Vt.: Jewish Lights Publishing, 1997), 135. Note that the passage quoted suggests the identification of self with dead body, not soul.

4. Philo, "The Unchangeableness of God," *The Works of Philo Judaeus, the Contemporary of Josephus*, trans. Charles Duke Yonge (London: H.G. Bohn, 1854–1890), 36:176.

5. For details, see Raymond Martin, *The Elusive Messiah: A Philosophical Overview of the Quest for the Historical Jesus* (Boulder, Colo.: Westview Press, 1999).

6. Ibid. Also see E.P. Sanders and Margaret Davies, *Studying the Synoptic Gospels* (Philadelphia: Trinity Press International, 1989), 7–15, 21–24.

7. Gal. 3:27–8.

8. 1 Thess. 4:17.

9. 1 Cor. 2.

10. Our account is based in part on Theo K. Heckel, "Body and Soul in St. Paul," in *Psyche and Soma—Physicians and Metaphysicians on the Mind-Body Problem from Antiquity to Enlightenment*, ed. John P. Wright and Paul Potter (Oxford: Oxford University Press, 2000), 117–32.

11. "Beloved Pan, and all ye other gods who haunt this place, give me beauty in the inward soul; and may the outward and inward man be at one." Plato, *Phaedrus*, 15:279b, in *The Dialogues of Plato*, trans. Benjamin Jowett, 4th ed. (Oxford: Oxford University Press, 1953).

12. 2 Cor. 4:16.

13. 2 Cor. 5:9.

14. 1 Cor. 15:20–1.

15. As noted by Paul (Acts 26).

16. 1 Cor. 15:17, 32.

17. 1 Cor. 15:35.

18. 1 Cor. 15:36–38.

19. 1 Cor. 15:40, 42, 44, 50.

20. See Caroline Walker Bynum, *The Resurrection of the Body in Western Christianity, 200–1336* (New York: Columbia University Press, 1995), 23 ff.

21. Cited in ibid., 24.

4. Resurrected Self

1. More graphically, the Christian apologist Arnobius (fl. 300) characterized the body as "a disgusting vessel of urine" and "a bag of shit." See Caroline Walker Bynum, *The Resurrection of the Body in Western Christianity, 200–1336* (New York: Columbia University Press, 1995), 31, 61.

2. Athenagoras, *On the Resurrection of the Dead*, in *The Ante-Nicene Fathers*, ed. A. Roberts, J. Donaldson, and A. C. Coxe (Grand Rapids, Mich.: W. B. Eerdmans, 1977), 2.8:153.

3. On Chrysippus, see Aphrodisias, *On Prior Analytics*, 180, 33–36: 181, 25–31. Simplicius, *Physics*, 886, 12–16, writes: "The Stoics say that the same I comes into existence in the recurrence. But unsurprisingly they ask whether the present and former I are numerically one through being the same in essence (*ousia*), or whether I differ because of the different location in time of different cosmogonies." Also see Origen, *Against Celsus*, 4.68; 5.20. All of these are cited in and translated by Richard Sorabji, in unpublished material, from whom we learned of the existence of these passages. For more on Stoic views, see Richard Sorabji, "Soul and Self in Ancient Philosophy," in *From Soul to Self*, ed. M. James C. Crabbe (New York: Routledge, 1999), 22–23. Also see Origen, *Contra Celsum*, trans. and intro. Henry Chadwick (Cambridge: Cambridge University Press, 1986), 4.68, 5.20.

4. Minucius Felix, *Octavius*, in *Ante-Nicene Fathers*, ed. A. Roberts, J. Donaldson, and A. C. Coxe (Peabody, Mass.: Hendrickson, 1995) , 4.6:179.

5. Ibid., 4.34:194.

6. Tertullian, *On the Resurrection of the Flesh*, in *Ante-Nicene Fathers*, ed. A. Roberts, J. Donaldson, and A. C. Coxe (Peabody, Mass.: Hendrickson, 1995), 3.8:551, 3.57:590.

7. Origen, *On First Principles*, in *Ante-Nicene Fathers*, vol. 4, ed. A. Roberts, J. Donaldson, and A. C. Coxe (Peabody, Mass.: Hendrickson, 1995), 1.5:260.

8. Ibid., 1.5:67.

9. Arnobius (c. 303), who wrote at about the same time as Origen, affirms in opposition to the Platonic doctrine of preexistence that souls are created. However, he makes the creating agent a being inferior to God, and he asserts the *gratuitous* character of the soul's immortality, denying that it is naturally immortal. In effect, he claimed that we survive bodily death not because of the kinds of beings we are but due to God's grace.

10. Origen, fragment on Psalm 1.5, cited by Bynum, *The Resurrection of the Body*, 64.

11. Ibid., 66.

12. See, for instance, Bynum, *The Resurrection of the Body*.

13. Origen, *On First Principles*, 10.3:294.

14. Methodius of Olympus, *From the Discourse on the Resurrection*, in *Ante-Nicene Fathers*, ed. A. Roberts, J. Donaldson, and A. C. Coxe (Peabody, Mass.: Hendrickson, 1995), 4.6:365 (italics added).

15. Methodius, De resurrectione, B 2, chap. 6, cited by Bynum, *The Resurrection of the Body*, 70.

16. Gregory of Nyssa, *On the Soul and the Resurrection*, in *Nicene and Post-Nicene Fathers*, ed. P. Schaff and H. Wace, 2nd ser. (Peabody, Mass..: Hendrickson, 1995), 5:433.

17. Ibid., 5:462.

18. Ibid., 5:467.

19. Ibid., 5:446.

20. In the last years of the fourth century, Jerome wrote a ferocious polemic against John of Jerusalem (fl. 390), in large part for John's having been a follower of Origen on the question of resurrection. Jerome's attack was a continuation of an earlier critique of Origen by Epiphanius (315?–403), which was itself based on Methodius' critique of Origen. Although the tone of Jerome's letter is arrogant and contemptuous, for more than a thousand years it had an profound influence on Christian theologians.

21. Jerome, letter to Pammachius against John of Jerusalem, in *Nicene and Post-Nicene Fathers*, ed. P. Schaff and H. Wace, 2nd ser. (Peabody, Mass..: Hendrickson, 1995), 6:436–8.

22. Saint Augustine, *The Confessions*, trans. Maria Boulding (New York: Vintage Books, 1997), 152–62.

23. Ibid., 163.

24. Ibid., 165.

25. Augustine, *De Vere Religione*, in *Nicene and Post-Nicene Fathers*, ed. Philip Schaff, 1st ser. (Peabody, Mass.: Hendrickson, 1995), 39.72.

26. Augustine, *City of God*, in *Nicene and Post-Nicene Fathers*, vol. 2, ed. Philip Schaff, trans. Rev. Marcus Dods, 1st ser. (Peabody, Mass.: Hendrickson, 1995), 13.24.2:259.

27. Augustine, *The Confessions*, 213.

28. Augustine, *City of God*, 22.20:498.

29. In addition to worries about resurrection, Christians had two other reasons to be interested in the notion of person. The first of these was to explain how Jesus could be both god and man. The second was to make sense of the doctrine of the Trinity. From the second to the sixth century, the theological and philosophical work that these puzzles generated would be the center of debates, both between Christians and pagans and among Christians, who would vie with each other for doctrinal domination of the church. The question about Christ's nature, which arose soon after the initial reports of his Resurrection, was posed first. It was not settled until the Council of Calcedon, in the sixth century. The doctrine of the Trinity was doctrinally resolved at the Council of Constantinople, in the latter part of the fourth century.

In general, interpretations of the Trinity take one of two forms. The first is that of the Greek fathers and of the Latin fathers before Augustine, who start from the plurality of persons and proceed to the assertion that the three persons are really one God. Their problem is how to arrive at one from three, their answer is "consubstantiality" of the Son and Holy Spirit with the Father. Dangers to be avoided, in this approach, are tri-theism and Arianism (the subordination of one or more persons of the Trinity). The other form of interpretation starts out from the unity of God and moves to the trinity of persons. Now the problem is how to arrive at three from one and how to show that the three are equal in stature to one another and to the one. The problem on this approach is how to ensure that the three are not merely modes of the one (modalism, or Sabellianism). Augustine, who presented his view of the Trinity in a number of works, but principally in *On the Trinity*, assumed that God is a single unified mind, and then looked for analogies between the Trinity and the human mind that would throw light on the mystery. The importance of the Trinity debate for the more central concerns of the present book is basically that the church fathers and subsequent Christian philosophers and theologians, in trying to make sense of the dogma that God is both three and one, were forced to make distinctions and identify questions that subsequently nourished thinking about more mundane issues having to do with the nature and status of earthly persons.

5. The Stream Divides

1. Not much of Plato or Aristotle had been translated into Latin. There was more, but not a great deal, that had been translated from the works of Greek Stoics, Epicureans, and Skeptics. Even prior to this period, it seems unlikely that Aristotle's works were known to Lucretius, Seneca, and Augustine. Cicero was acquainted with some works of Aristotle that are now lost, but he barely mentions the writings that would come into prominence in Europe in the thirteenth century. During the Early Middle Ages there was a vigorous development of Arab and Jewish philosophy, but it occurred mostly outside of Europe. Almost all of Aristotle's writings, but only a few works of Plato, including the *Republic*, the *Laws*, and the *Timaeus*, were translated into Arabic. A number of Neoplatonist writings were also translated into Arabic. In general, Arab philosophers learned about Plato mainly from Aristotelian commentators, but Alfarabi wrote a paraphrase of Plato's *Laws*, and Averroës, a paraphrase of Plato's *Republic*. Under the influence of the Arabs, medieval Jewish thinkers, including Avicebron (Ibn Gabirol) and various Jewish mystics, were strongly influenced by Neoplatonism.

2. During the thirteenth century, when Aristotelianism was becoming dominant among Latin philosophers, Latin translations were being made of Plato's *Phaedo* and *Meno*, as well as of a number of works by Neoplatonists.

3. Earlier, Cicero had summarized the positions of a number of schools of Greek philosophy and had even translated one of Plato's dialogues. Victorinus, a contemporary of Augustine, had translated Plotinus and some texts of Aristotelian and Stoic logic. Many of the works available at this time, such as those of Lucretius and the translation of Plotinus, were no longer available during the High Middle Ages and had to be rediscovered and translated again in the Renaissance. For instance, Plotinus was available only in fragments collected by the Arabs in what was called *Aristotle's Theology*. The full works of Plotinus were eventually translated into Latin again by Ficino, in 1492. See H. J. Blumenthal, *Aristotle and Neoplatonism in Late Antiquity: Interpretations of the* De anima (Ithaca, N.Y.: Cornell University Press, 1996), 173.

4. Commentaries on Aristotle's views on the soul that would eventually pass to the Scholastics and Renaissance scholars were of two sorts: those by the Aristotelians themselves, in particular Alexander of Aphrodisias and later Themistius; and those by Neoplatonic commentators, such as Philoponus and Simplicius. Alexander and Themistius, in particular, would significantly influence the direction that Arab philosophy would take,

especially with respect to theories of the intellect. These works, as well as a fragment of Philoponus commenting on *De anima*, 3.4–3.8, were available to Aquinas, when developing his own Aristotelian view. Other writings of Philoponus and Simplicius would be translated only during the Renaissance.

5. Themistius concluded by remarking that while it was reasonable of Aristotle to pose for himself the problem of why we do not remember after death whatever we think before death, "the solution," entailed by Aristotle's statements, is "that the productive intellect is unaffected, while the passive intellect is perishable" (430a24–25). Themistius, *Themistius' Paraphrase of Aristotle De anima 3.4-8*, in *Two Greek Aristotelean Commentators on the Intellect: The De Intellectu Attributed to Alexander of Aphrodisias and Themistius' Paraphrase of Aristotle De anima 3.4-8*, ed. and trans. Frederic M Schroeder and Robert Todd (Toronto: Pontifical Institute of Mediaeval Studies, 1990), 94–95.

6. In their attempts to deal with the Aristotelian corpus, the Scholastics had also to deal with their own previous development of Christian Neoplatonism. Augustine, of course, was the major source and the transmitter of Plotinian Neoplatonism. But there were other Neoplatonic sources: most importantly pseudo-Dionysius, who presented a cosmological "celestial hierarchy," which was a thinly veiled version of Proclus's *Elements of Theology*. As we shall see shortly, these works influenced John Scotus Eriugena and, through him, the Scholastics. In addition, the Scholastics also had the works of a Christian Neoplatonic commentator on Aristotle, John Philoponus (c. 490–c. 575), who read into Aristotle's *De anima* that the rational soul is a substance that is also the form of the human body. Unlike Themistius, he was certain that each individual has his own rational soul, which is immortal. He also had an interesting view of resurrection, according to which no material from the original body is recovered. Rather, at the resurrection, there will be a new immortal body of entirely different material. In making this suggestion, he was not bothered about whether the resurrected person was a new person, so long as it had the same soul as one who died.

7. John Scotus Eriugena, *On the Division of Nature*, vol. 8, in *Medieval Philosophy: From St. Augustine to Nicholas of Cusa*, ed. J. F. Wippel and A. B. Wolter (New York: Free Press, 1969), 137.

8. Moses Maimonides, *Guide for the Perplexed*, trans. M. Friedlander (London: Routledge & Kegan Paul, 1904), 395.

9. Ibid., 106

10. Quoted in Colin Morris, *The Discovery of the Individual, 1050–1200* (New York: Harper & Row, 1972), 81–82.

11. As quoted in ibid., 66.

12. Abelard and Heloise, *The Letters of Abelard and Heloise*, trans. Betty Radice (Harmondsworth: Penguin, 1974) 132–33, 115.

13. Quoted in Michel Foucault, *The History of Sexuality*, trans. Robert Hurley, vol. 1, *An Introduction* (New York: Vintage Books, 1980), 20.

14. A century earlier, in Muslim Spain, Ibn Hazm (994–1064), in *The Dove's Necklace*, analyzed and celebrated romantic love, which he saw as a physical, moral, and spiritual union with the beloved. In twelfth-century Europe, William of Saint Thierry,

in *The Nature and Dignity of Love* (1120?), distinguished five kinds of love, all of which he said might be good to varying degrees. By contrast, Augustine, the most introspective writer of his era, gave little attention to psychological nuance for its own sake and usually depicted differing human motives simply as choices between good and evil.

15. Dostoevsky, for instance, was the first to write what is now called a *polyphonic novel*, in which there is no overarching authoritative account of the events depicted in the story (Mikhail Bakhtin, *Problems of Dostoevsky's Poetics*, trans. R. W. Rotsel [Ann Arbor, Mich.: Ardis, 1973]). For a contemporary historian who deals with much the same issue, see J. E. Goodman, *Stories of Scottsboro* (New York: Pantheon, 1994).

16. Augustine, *The Confessions*, 61.

17. C. S. Lewis was prompted to remark, "Real changes in human sentiment are very rare—there are perhaps three or four on record—but I believe that they occur, and that this is one of them." Quoted in Morris, *Discovery*, 108.

18. Honorius Augustodunensis, *Clavis Physicae*, ed. Paolo Lucentini (Rome: Edizioni di Storia e Letteratura, 1974), 307:60; as translated by Caroline Walker Bynum, *The Resurrection of the Body in Western Christianity, 200–1336* (New York: Columbia University Press, 1995), 147.

6. Aristotelian Synthesis

1. To add to the confusion, a variety of related problems came to the fore that had not previously seemed so pressing: Is the rational soul passed from parents to children biologically? If, as almost everyone believed, it is not transmitted biologically, how is it related to the vegetative and sensitive souls, which *are* transmitted biologically? Is the rational soul different in kind from the souls of beasts? Can individual humans have more than one soul? And so on.

2. Cited by Richard C. Dales, *The Problem of the Rational Soul in the Thirteenth Century* (Leiden: E. J. Brill, 1995), 26.

3. Ibid., 39–40.

4. Ibid., 70.

5. Albert set himself the task of translating into Latin an authentic version of Aristotle. As a teacher of theology at Cologne and Paris, he had among his students Thomas Aquinas, whose genius he recognized and whose future greatness he foretold. The disciple accompanied his master on his travels, returning with him, in 1248, to Cologne, where Albert was a professor and Aquinas secured his first academic appointment. Subsequently, they parted company physically but never spiritually. In 1274, as Albert was on his way to the Council of Lyons, he was informed of the death of his former and much-beloved student, which prompted him to declare that "the Light of the Church" had been extinguished.

6. Albert, *Summa Theologica*, part 1, tract 12, question 69, ad. 2, cited in Dales, *The Problem of the Rational Soul*, 98.

7. Bonaventure, *Breviloquium*, 7.5.2, cited in Dales, *The Problem of the Rational Soul*, 99–100.

8. Cited in Caroline Walker Bynum, *The Resurrection of the Body in Western Christianity, 200–1336* (New York: Columbia University Press, 1995) , 236–37, 240–41.

9. Thanks to Aquinas's having been a student of Albert, he had access early on to a better text of Aristotle than had been available to others. He thought that many of the problems that conservatives had with Aristotle were due to their working from a corrupt text. To the conservatives, his break with Augustinianism was so shocking that in 1270, and again in 1277, they persuaded the bishop of Paris to condemn some propositions to which he subscribed.

10. Aquinas, *Summa Theologica*, 1.118.2, ad. 2, cited in Dales, *The Problem of the Rational Soul*, 110.

11. Aquinas, *Summa Theologica*, 1.77.8, in *Great Books of the Western World*, vol. 19, part 1 (Chicago: Encyclopedia Britannica, 1952), 406.

12. From a contemporary, secular point of view, it's hard even to understand what this doctrine of Aquinas could possibly mean. Whatever it means, he borrowed it from *Liber de Causis*, which he knew was based on Proclus's Neoplatonic *Elements of Theology*. Aquinas, *On Being and Essence*, trans. A. Maurer (Toronto: The Pontifical Institute of Medieval Studies, 1949), 4:44.

13. Commentary to I Corinthians 15:17–19, lect. 11, cited in Carl N. Still, "Do We Know All After Death? Thomas Aquinas on the Disembodied Soul's Knowledge," in *Proceedings of the American Catholic Philosophical Association: Person, Soul, and Immortality, Vol. 75* (New York: American Catholic Philosophical Association, 2002), 108.

14. Cited in Bynum, *The Resurrection of the Body*, 236.

15. Thomas Aquinas, *Summa Contra Gentiles*, trans. Charles O'Neil (Notre Dame, Ind.: Notre Dame University Press, 1975), 4.80–81:307.

16. In December 1273, toward the end of his life, Aquinas, while saying mass, had a mystical experience. Subsequently, he suspended work on the third part of his *Summa Theologica* and resolved to write no more, saying: "All I have written seems to me like so much straw compared with what I have seen and with what has been revealed to me." F. C. Copleston, *Aquinas* (1955; reprint, Baltimore, Md.: Penguin Books, 1961), 10.

17. Dales, *The Problem of the Rational Soul*, 133.

18. Thomas Aquinas, *Aquinas Against the Averroists: On There Being Only One Intellect*, trans. Ralph McInerny (West Lafayette, Ind.: Purdue University Press, 1993), para. 69. It is worth noting that Aquinas's argument here, which relies, at least in part, on our consciousness of personal ownership of our acts of understanding, is not entirely successful as an argument against the Averroists. This is because intuitive self-consciousness can be accounted for in different ways, without requiring that the soul, itself, be unified. Deborah Black, "Consciousness and Self-Knowledge in Aquinas's Critique of Averroës's Psychology," *Journal of the History of Philosophy* 31 (1993): 349–85, argues that on Aristotelian principles, which Aquinas shares with Averroës, the nature of soul can be known only indirectly, through its activities, rather than directly, through self-consciousness. As Aquinas says in

the *Summa Theologica*, "the presence of the mind does not suffice" for knowledge of the soul, "but rather, diligent and subtle inquiry is required" (1.87.1; cited in Black, 357). And this "subtle inquiry" into the powers and activities of soul can lead to different conclusions. Black suggests that Averroës could answer Aquinas by arguing that it is the imagination, or passive intellect, by which we take ownership of acts of the material/agent intellect. For, on Aristotelian assumptions, an image is always perfectly correlated with any act of the intellect, and the image is formed wholly by corporeal activities of the human soul. So even if the intellect comes from without and is singular, any abstract understanding of the particular, is associated with a particular image and thereby can be experienced as owned by the particular soul.

19. Dales, *The Problem of the Rational Soul*, 136.

20. Udo Thiel, "Individuation," in *The Cambridge History of Seventeenth-Century Philosophy*, vol. 1, edited by Daniel Garber and Michael Ayers (Cambridge: Cambridge University Press, 1998), 215.

21. Dante, *Convivio*, 2.8.8; as cited in Nancy Lindheim, "Body, Soul, and Immortality: Some Readings in Dante's *Commedia*," *MLN* 105, no. 1 (1990): 5.

22. Even Averroës would agree that "some part of us is immortal."

7. Care of the Soul

1. Quoted in Paul Oskar Kristeller, *Renaissance Thought: The Classic, Scholastic, and Humanist Strains* (New York: Harper & Row, 1961), 125. Throughout this chapter we are indebted to Kristeller.

2. Giannozzo Manetti, for instance, toward the middle of the fifteenth century, wrote in reply to Pope Innocent III's treatise on the miserable condition of people a lengthy essay on human dignity and excellence, embellishing his points with classical quotations.

3. There was, however, a downside. Theory languished. The humanists failed to provide new insights into natural philosophy, theology, law, medicine, and mathematics. Instead, their influence on these fields was external and indirect, due almost entirely to their providing new classical source materials.

4. Ficino, *Platonic Theology*, book 3, chap. 2, trans. and quoted in Kristeller, *Renaissance Thought*, 129.

5. Marsilio Ficino, *Platonic Theology*, trans. Josephine L. Burroughs, quoted in Paul Kristeller, "Ficino and Pomponazzi on the Place of Man in the Universe," *Journal of the History of Ideas* 5 (1944): 228.

6. Kristeller, "Ficino and Pomponazzi," 230.

7. Marsilio Ficino, from *De Vita Libri Tres* (1489), quoted in Paul S. MacDonald, *History of the Concept of Mind: Speculations about Soul, Mind, and Spirit from Homer to Hume* (Burlington, Vt.: Ashgate, 2003), 232.

8. Paul Kristeller, *The Philosophy of Marsilio Ficino*, trans. Virginia Conant (New York: Columbia University Press, 1943), 327.

9. Ficino, *Platonic Theology*, book 14, chap. 3, quoted in Kristeller, *Philosophy of Marsilio Ficino*, 238.

10. Quoted in Kristeller, "The Philosophy of Man," 133.

11. Ibid., 129.

12. Ibid., 136–37.

13. Francesco Piccolomini, *Librorum ad scientiam de natura attinentium* (Frankfurt, 1597), 876–77, quoted and trans. in Emily Michael, "Renaissance Theories of Body, Soul, and Mind," in *Psyche and Soma*, ed. John P. Wright and Paul Potter, (Oxford: Clarendon Press, 2000), 161.

14. John H. Randall Jr. *The Career of Philosophy: From the Middle Ages to the Enlightenment* (New York: Columbia University Press, 1962), 85.

15. Quoted in Rudolf Steiner, *Eleven European Mystics*, trans. Karl E. Zimmer (New York: Rudolf Steiner, 1971), 201.

16. Ibid., 203.

17. Paracelsus, *The Hermetic and Alchemical Writings of Paracelsus*, 2 vols., ed. and trans. A. E. Waite (Berkeley: Shambala, 1976), 1:176.

18. Ibid., 1:161.

19. Paracelsus, *The Diseases That Deprive Man of His Reason, Such as St. Vitus Dance, Falling Sickness, Melancholy, and Insanity, and Their Correct Treatment*, trans. G. Zilboorg, in *Four Treatises of Theophrastus von Hohenheim, Called Paracelsus*, ed. and trans. C. L. Temkin, G. Rosen, G. Zilboorg, and H. E. Sigerest (Baltimore, Md.: John Hopkins University Press, 1996), 142.

20. According to Francis Yates, *Giordano Bruno and the Hermetic Tradition* (London: Routledge and Kegan Paul, 1964), Bruno's philosophy was based on second-century Hermetic texts that had been translated by Ficino. More recently others have argued that Pythagorean doctrines are more fundamental to Bruno's views. See, for instance, H. Gatti, *Giordano Bruno and Renaissance Science* (Ithaca, N.Y.: Cornell University Press, 1999).

21. Giordano Bruno, *The Expulsion of the Triumphant Beast*, trans. A. D. Imerti (Lincoln: University of Nebraska Press, 1964), 76.

22. Ibid., 76–77.

23. Quoted in Peter Burke, "Representations of the Self from Petrarch to Descartes," in *Rewriting the Self: Histories from the Renaissance to the Present*, ed. Roy Porter (London: Routledge, 1997), 19.

24. As Burke has pointed out, "the advice that Polonius gives to Laertes in *Hamlet* "to thine own self be true" may have been a commonplace, but it was a relatively new commonplace" (ibid., 20).

25. Montaigne, "Three Kinds of Association" (1588), in *The Complete Works of Montaigne*, ed. and trans. Donald M. Frame (Stanford, Calif.: Stanford University Press, 1957), 629.

26. Montaigne, "On Experience," in *Essays*, ed. and trans. J. M. Cohen (Harmondsworth: Penguin, 1958), 344.

27. Montaigne, "To the Reader," in *The Complete Works of Montaigne*, ed. and trans. Donald M. Frame (Stanford, Calif.: Stanford University Press, 1957), 2.

28. Montaigne, "On Giving the Lie," in *The Complete Works of Montaigne*, ed. and trans. Donald M. Frame (Stanford, Calif.: Stanford University Press, 1957), 504.

29. Montaigne, "On Friendship," in *Essays*, ed. and trans. J. M. Cohen (Harmondsworth: Penguin, 1958), 102.

30. Montaigne, "On Cannibals," in *Essays*, ed. and trans. J. M. Cohen (Harmondsworth: Penguin, 1958), 106.

31. Timothy Reiss, *Mirages of the Selfe: Patterns of Personhood in Ancient and Early Modern Europe* (Stanford, Calif.: Stanford University Press, 2003), has argued for a competing view of Montaigne, according to which subjectivity, which in his view requires modern individualism with its encapsulated inner self, does not emerge until late in the seventeenth century, in the *Penses* of Pascal and in the possessive individualism of Locke. Reiss claims that virtually all previous thinkers, including Montaigne and even Descartes, who is a kind of transition figure, viewed the self within the context of relations to ever widening circles of social life and hence were not really concerned with subjectivity at all. In Reiss's Montaigne, for instance, there is no concern with subjectivity but only private reflection. We see no reason to think of subjectivity so narrowly. Doing so robs one of the ability to track the incremental ways in which concern with subjectivity expanded in stages over nearly two thousand years. In our view, in addition to what Reiss thinks concern with subjectivity involves, it involves also such things as concern with differing inner perspectives on the same outer events, and it may be found in such figures as Augustine, Avicenna, Abelard and Heloise, Petrarch, Montaigne, and Descartes, among others. In addition, thinking of subjectivity in Reiss's way obscures the contribution made by the Christian dogma of personal survival of bodily death to the growth of individualism in the West.

8. Mechanization of Nature

1. Galileo Galilei, *The Assayer* (1623), in *Discoveries and Opinions of Galileo*, ed. and trans. Stillman Drake (Garden City, N.Y.: Doubleday Anchor Books, 1957), 237–38.

2. Mechanization, at the theoretical level, was a goal, rather than a reality. In Newton's original view, gravitational attraction was an exception, an idea that Cartesians, in particular, strongly resisted.

3. Descartes thus replicated in a more general form Galileo's more local invention of the subjective. To the present day, philosophers of mind as a whole have not resolved this issue. The nub of the difficulty is that after Descartes it has not been possible *merely* to assume that the mind and body are unified. It has become necessary to explain both *how* they are unified and how we can reliably acquire knowledge of body and mind. This has not been an easy task. Even so, this dual project, performed against the backdrop of a mechanized nature, is what was primarily responsible intellectually for transforming the premodern into the modern world.

In finding a place for the self in such a world, Descartes opted for a basically Platonic (intuitive) view of the origins of knowledge, relinquishing whatever faith he may have had in the senses. He argued, as Augustine and Avicenna had argued earlier, that it is possible to doubt altogether the existence of body but not to doubt one's own existence, for the very act of doubting requires that one exist as a doubter. In other words, while experience seems to ensure that an experiencer exists, it does not seem to ensure that an external world of material objects exists—for all we know, the world of our experience could be part of an elaborate dream. All that is revealed in the immediate testimony of consciousness seems to be mental, not the external objects that everyone naturally believes are the causes of our experiences. This seeming realization elevated the task of proving the existence of the external (material) world—including one's own body—into a major metaphysical and epistemological problem.

Descartes tried to solve this problem—that is, to prove that external, material objects exist—first, by proving that God exists and is not a deceiver and then by arguing that if there were no external world and had God not given us any faculty the proper exercise of which would enable us to discover that our natural belief in an external world is mistaken, then God would be a deceiver. It follows, he claimed, that there must be an external world. Many subsequent thinkers thought that the problem of how to prove the existence of an external world is genuine but were unimpressed with Descartes's solution. This, together with epistemological foundationalism, were among the main ways in which Descartes set the agenda for the next three hundred years of philosophy of mind.

4. Some recent commentators on Descartes doubt that he made this mistake. In their view, his point was that if extension were an essential attribute of the nature of humans, humans would know this intuitively. Since they do not, extension cannot be an essential attribute of humans. Hence, it is at best only an accidental, or contingent, attribute. See, for instance, Marleen Rozemond, *Descartes's Dualism* (Cambridge, Mass.: Harvard University Press, 1998).

5. Descartes to Marquess of Newcastle, 23 November 1646, and to More, 5 February 1649, in *The Philosophical Writings of Descartes*, ed. and trans. John Cottingham, Robert Stoothoff, Dugald Murdoch, and Anthony Kenny, 3 vols., vol. 3, *The Correspondence* (Cambridge: Cambridge University Press, 1991), 302–4, 565–66.

6. Descartes, *The Seventh Set of Objections with the Author's Replies*, in *The Philosophical Writings of Descartes*, vol. 2, ed. and trans. John Cottingham, Robert Stoothoff, and Dugald Murdoch, 3 vols. (Cambridge: Cambridge University Press, 1984), 382. Even so, Descartes sometimes teetered on the brink of discussing self-concepts developmentally, particularly in distinguishing between the consciousness of infants and adults. For instance, in a letter to Arnauld, written seven years after the *Meditations*, Descartes made a distinction between "direct and reflective thoughts." As an example of the former, he cites "the first and simple thoughts of infants," such as "the pleasure they feel when nourished by sweet blood." On the other hand, he continued, "when an adult feels something, and simultaneously perceives that he has not felt it before," we should call this "second perception *reflection*" and attribute it "to the intellect alone, in spite of its being so linked to sensation that the two occur together and appear to be indistinguishable from each other" (*The Philosophical Writings*, 3:357).

7. See, for instance, the 1643 correspondence between Descartes and Elisabeth of Bohemia, in John J. Blom, trans. and ed., *Descartes: His Moral Philosophy and Psychology* (New York: New York University Press, 1978), 107–14.

8. Descartes, *Meditations on First Philosophy: Sixth Meditation*, in *The Philosophical Writings of Descartes*, ed. and trans. John Cottingham, Robert Stoothoff, Dugald Murdoch, and Anthony Kenny, 3 vols. (Cambridge: Cambridge University Press, 1991), 2:56.

9. Descartes, *Meditations on First Philosophy: Second Meditation*, in *The Philosophical Writings of Descartes*, vol. 2, ed. and trans. John Cottingham, Robert Stoothoff, and Dugald Murdoch, 3 vols. (Cambridge: Cambridge University Press, 1991), 2:20.

10. Although officially Descartes subscribed to a doctrine of personal immortality, how personal it was is open to question. He held, for instance, that after bodily death people will continue to possess "intellectual memories" but they will cease to possess "corporeal memories." In a letter of 1642 to the bereaved Huygens, Descartes said that after death people will persist in "a sweeter and more tranquil life" than they enjoyed on earth and "shall still remember the past," for they "have, in my view, an intellectual memory which is certainly independent of the body." But Descartes does not further explain how, in his view, such intellectual memories of particulars are possible (Descartes, *The Philosophical Writings*, 3:216); quoted in J. Sutton, *Philosophy and Memory Traces: Descartes to Connectionism* (Cambridge: Cambridge University Press, 1998); see also Descartes, *The Philosophical Writings*, 1:42, 1:106–7, quoted in M. Bobro, "Prudence and the Concern to Survive in Leibniz's Doctrine of Immortality," *History of Philosophy Quarterly* 15 (1998): 306.

11. In favor of the first answer, Hobbes said that "it is pleaded that a lump of wax, whether it be spherical or cubical, is the same wax, because the same matter." In favor of the second, "that when a man is grown from an infant to an old man, though his matter be changed, yet he is still the same numerical man," in virtue of having retained the same "form." And, in favor of the third, that when something acquires a "new accident," that is, a new property, "a new name is commonly imposed on the thing."

Hobbes then raised for each proposal what he took to be a decisive objection. On what might be called the *same-matter* proposal, "he that sins, and he that is punished, should not be the same man, by reason of the perpetual flux and change of man's body." On the *same-form* proposal, "two bodies [with the same form] existing both at once, would be one and the same numerical body"—for instance, if in continually repairing the ship of Theseus by replacing old planks with new ones, one saved the old planks and then eventually made out of them a ship that was identical in form to the other, then the ship reconstructed out of the original planks "without doubt, had also been the same numerical ship with that which was in the beginning; and so there would have been two ships numerically the same, which is absurd." On the third proposal, all it would take for something to change into something else is its acquisition of a new property, so "nothing would be the same it was; so that a man standing would not be the same with that which he was sitting; nor the water, which is in the vessel, the same with that which is poured out of it." Quotes here and in next paragraph are from Thomas Hobbes, "De Corpore," also known as *Elements of Philosophy*, 2.11, in *The English Works of Thomas Hobbes*, ed. W. Molesworth, vol. 1 (London: J. Bohn, 1839), 135. We profited in our account of Hobbes's views from William Uzgalis's excellent World

Congress of Philosophy paper, "Paideia and Identity: Meditations on Hobbes and Locke," available at http://www.bu.edu/wcp/Papers/Mode/ModeUzga.htm.

12. In distinguishing here between a human and its body, Hobbes was apparently assuming, first, that a human's body simply consists of the matter of which it's composed and, second, that its persistence conditions are the same as a randomly arranged collection of matter, such as a pile of sand. In the case of the sand pile, change one grain, one might say (and Locke later did say), and one has a different pile. In the case of the human body, change one property, and one has a different human body. So, on Hobbes's rather implausible view, while a human may last for quite a while, his body will not.

13. Hobbes, "De Corpore," 2.1:137.

14. Spinoza, *Ethics*, 5.23, in *The Collected Works of Spinoza*, vol. 1, ed. and trans. Edwin Curley (Princeton, N.J.: Princeton University Press, 1985), 607.

15. In his discussion of the case of a Spanish poet of whom he had heard who suffered from amnesia, Spinoza seems to commit himself to the view that the human body cannot persist without memory. One would have thought that while memory might be required for an individual mind to persist, it would not be required for an individual body to persist. *Ethics*, 4.39.

16. Spinoza, *Ethics*, 5.42:616.

17. Spinoza, *Ethics*, 4.67, trans. W. H. White, rev. A. H. Sterling, in *Great Books of the Western World*, vol. 31 (Chicago: Encyclopedia Britannica, 1952), 444.

18. Leibniz, *Discourse on Metaphysics* (1686), in *Philosophical Essays*, ed. and trans. Roger Ariew and Daniel Garber (Indianapolis: Hackett, 1989), 65.

19. Ibid.

20. Leibniz, letter to Arnauld, May 1686, in *Philosophical Essays*, ed. and trans. Roger Ariew and Daniel Garber (Indianapolis: Hackett, 1989), 75.

21. Ibid., 75, 73.

22. Leibniz, *New Essays Concerning Human Understanding* (1765), trans. A. G. Langley (New York: Macmillan, 1896), 255–56.

23. See, for instance, Roderick Chisholm, "Identity Through Possible Worlds: Some Questions," *Noûs* 1 (1967): 1–8; reprinted in *The Possible and the Actual*, ed. Michael J. Loux (Ithaca, N.Y.: Cornell University Press, 1979), 80–87; Hilary Putnam, "The Meaning of 'Meaning,'" in *Language, Mind, and Knowledge*, ed. K. Gunderson (Minneapolis: University of Minnesota Press, 1975), 131–93; Saul Kripke, *Naming and Necessity* (Cambridge, Mass.: Harvard University Press, 1980); David Lewis, *On the Plurality of Worlds* (Oxford: Blackwell, 1986); and James Ballie, "Personal Identity and Mental Content," *Philosophical Psychology* 10 (1997): 323–33.

9. Naturalizing the Soul

1. This empiricist principle, while it might sound similar to the Aristotelian principle that all knowledge comes first through the senses, is based on different presuppositions.

Unlike Aristotle, who took the objective world as a given, the empiricists followed Descartes in doubting the existence and nature of anything not immediately presented to the mind. Thus all knowledge of an external world must be inferred based on immediate states of mind. The empiricists also differed from rationalists like Descartes in holding that the mind is originally a "tabula rasa," or blank tablet, totally devoid of original innate ideas.

2. John Locke, *An Essay Concerning Human Understanding* (1690–94), 4.3.6, ed. Peter H. Nidditch, pbk. ed. (Oxford: Oxford University Press, 1979), 4.3.6:540–41. The citation refers to book, chapter, section, and page, and subsequent references to Locke's *Essay* should be understood similarly.

3. Locke, *Essay*, 2.27.9:335, 17:341.

4. Ibid., 2.27.26:346

5. Ibid., 2.27.16:341.

6. See Michael Ayers, *Locke*, 2 vols. (London: Routledge, 1991), 2:266–67. Why did Locke think that appropriation and accountability go hand in hand? There is an admittedly speculative but still, we think, plausible reason why he might have thought this. He might have thought that, analogous to the way in which people come under the rule of their government by constituting themselves as a body politic and hence accept civil responsibility for what they do, humans become subject to ethical norms by constituting themselves as persons and hence accepting ethical responsibility for what they do. That is to say, humans, merely by virtue of being alive and, hence, by virtue of being humans, do not, as it were, accept accountability for their pasts. But humans (or persons) do accept accountability for their pasts, or at least for those parts of their pasts that they remember, when, through consciousness, they declare ownership of the various parts that collectively constitute themselves.

7. Strictly speaking, mere cohesive collections of atoms, such as lumps of gold, would be "collective substances," while things such as oak trees, horses, and persons, would not be substances at all but, rather, particular mixed modes, that is, functional organizations of particular substances.

8. The self constituted by appropriation of one's past, present, and also future acts, in Locke's legal theory, became the self-possessing individual who "appropriates" and owns his own "person" as a form of property and whose labor is to be used as he wishes: "Man . . . hath by Nature a Power . . . to preserve his property, that is his Life, Liberty, and Estate": *Second Treatise on Government*, sect. 87, cited by C. B. MacPherson, *The Political Theory of Possessive Individualism: Hobbes to Locke* (Oxford: Clarendon University Press, 1962), 198; see also 200–201. It is this aspect of modern individualism that Timothy Reiss focuses on in *Mirages of Selfe: Patterns of Personhood in Ancient and Early Modern Europe* (Stanford, Calif.: Stanford University Press, 2003), discussed in chapter 7, note 31. The individual, in this modern view, is not, a priori, a member of society, as in the premodern view, but becomes such a member only through social contract. But in this regard it is interesting to compare Locke's view with that of Chrysippus and other Stoics, discussed toward the end of chapter 1.

9. Locke, *Essay*, 2.27.18:342.

10. Samuel Clarke, *The Works of Samuel Clarke*, 4 vols. (1738; reprint, New York: Garland, 1978), 3:720–913.

11. Ibid., 3:750.

12. Ibid., e.g., 3:769–73.

13. Ibid., 3:784–87.

14. Ibid., 3:790.

15. Ibid., e.g., 3:807–9.

16. Ibid., 3:809, 870.

17. Ibid., 3:844–45.

18. Ibid., 3:860, 890, 894.

19. Ibid., 3:844–45, 852.

20. See C. Fox, *Locke and the Scriblerians* (Berkeley: University of California Press, 1988).

21. R. Burthogge, *An Essay Upon Reason and the Nature of Spirits* (1694; New York: Garland, 1976), 264–65.

22. Alexander Pope et. al., *Memoirs Of the Extraordinary Life, Works, and Discoveries of Martinus Scriblerus* (1714), ed. C. Kerby-Miller (New York: Russell and Russell, 1966). At the time, George Berkeley was a good friend of Arbuthnot and so may well have read *Scriblerus* and probably at least knew of its contents. In the nineteen century, Thomas Brown, in his influential *Lectures on the Philosophy of the Human Mind*, 2 vols. (Boston: Glazier and Co., 1828), quotes approvingly from *Scriblerus*, 1:118–19, 2:489–90. Denis Diderot (1713–1784) comments interestingly on different, real-life conjoined twins, which he characterized not as an example of two immaterial souls bound together, but as "an animal which had in theory two senses and two consciousnesses": "D'Alembert's Dream," which was written in 1769, though published much later, in Denis Diderot, *Dialogues*, trans. F. Birrell (New York: Capricorn Books, 1969), 78.

23. For instance, Thomas Brown, Reid's leading successor early in the nineteenth century and an important influence on James Mill, John Stuart Mill, and William James, wrote, "Although the constant state of flux of the corporeal particles furnishes no argument against the identity of the principle which feels and thinks, if feeling and thought be states of a substance, that is, essentially distinct from these changing particles, the unity and identity of this principle, amid all the corpuscular changes,—if it can truly be proved to be identical,—furnishes a very strong argument, in disproof of those systems which consider thought and feeling as the result of material organization. Indeed, the attempts which have been seriously made by materialists to obviate this difficulty, involve, in every respect, as much absurdity, though certainly not so much pleasantry, at least not so much *intentional* pleasantry, as the demonstrations which the Society of Freethinkers communicated to Martinus Scriblerus.... The arguments which they are represented as urging in this admirable letter, ludicrous as they may seem, are truly as strong, at least, as those of which they are the parody; and, indeed, in this case, where both are so like, a very little occasional change of expression is all which is necessary to convert the grave ratiocination into the parody, and the

parody into the grave ratiocination" (Brown, *Lectures*, 1:118–9). William James quotes from Brown's remarks about *Scriblerus* in "The Consciousness of Self," in *Principles of Psychology*, 2 vols. (1890; reprint, New York: Henry Holt, 1918), 1:372.

24. Joseph Butler, *The Analogy of Religion, Natural and Revealed* (1736; London: Henry G. Bohn, 1852), 86.

25. Ibid., 87–88

26. Ibid., 328.

27. Ibid., 330.

28. Ibid., 331–2.

29. Ibid., 332, 334.

30. David Hume, *Treatise of Human Nature* (1739), ed. L. A. Selby-Bigge ed. (Oxford: Clarendon Press, 1888).

31. Another, perhaps more charitable, way of understanding Hume's division of labor in the *Treatise* is that in book 1 he is studying reason and what reason can discover. In doing so, he isolates reason from the rest of our mental capacities. It is seen to self-destruct. In book 2, on the other hand, he introduces consideration of the passions. Here there are no pretensions that need to be redressed. Instead, Hume turns to more constructive projects, such as providing a social account of the self.

32. Hume, *Treatise*, 253.

33. Ibid.

34. In and of itself, Hume suggested, our supposing that objects persist is not so bad. But "in order to justify to ourselves this absurdity," we make up a story, often one in which the principle character is the notion of substance; that is, we invent the fictions of "soul, and self, and substance to disguise the variation" in our perceptions. When, as in the case of "plants and vegetables," we cannot fool ourselves into believing that the persistence of an underlying substance accounts for the persistence of the organism, we invent an equally "unknown and mysterious" surrogate—presumably, "life"—to connect the successive and different perceptions (ibid., 254–55).

35. Ibid., 255.

36. Ibid., 261.

37. Ibid., 261–62.

38. Ibid., 262.

39. Ibid., 262.

40. Ibid., 258.

41. David Hume, "Essay on the Immortality of the Soul" (1755/1783), in *The Philosophical Works of David Hume*, 4 vols. (Boston: Little, Brown and Company, 1854), 4:547–48.

42. "For when we attribute identity, in an improper sense, to variable or interrupted objects, our mistake is not confin'd to the expression but is commonly attended with a fiction, either of something invariable and uninterrupted, or of something mysterious and inexplicable, or at least with a propensity to such fictions." And further: "The identity which we ascribe to the mind of man is only a fictitious one, and of a like kind with that which we ascribe to vegetable and animal bodies. It cannot, therefore, have a different

origin, but must proceed from a like operation of the imagination upon like objects" (ibid., 255, 259).

43. Thomas Reid, *Essay on the Intellectual Powers of Man* (1785), in *Philosophical Works of Thomas Reid*, ed. W. Hamilton (1895; reprint, Hildesheim: George Olms, n.d.), 1:444.

44. Although Reid assumed that the need for substance is an argument for immaterial substance, his argument actually, so far as it goes, shows at most only the need for substance of some sort. In any case, Reid, the immaterialist about the mind, here criticized Hume, whom Reid regarded as an immaterialist about everything, for not being able to explain, on immaterialist grounds, the difference between impressions and ideas. This is one of the few places in Reid's published work where his metaphysics of the soul may have made a substantive difference to the scientific account he was trying to develop.

45. Reid, *Essay on the Intellectual Powers of Man*, chapter 6, "Of Memory." Although Reid is famous for this criticism of Locke, he is thought to have got it from Bishop George Berkeley. Actually, he got it from George Campbell, although Berkeley had come up with a similar criticism earlier; see J.C. Stewart-Robertson, "Thomas Reid and Pneumatology," in *The Philosophy of Thomas Reid*, ed. M. Dalgarno and E. Matthews (Dordrecht: Kluwer Academic Publishers, 1989), 397. But even Berkeley was not the first. Henry Grove had come up with it earlier, though he did not publish it. For more details, see R. Martin and J. Barresi, *Naturalization of the Soul: Self and Personal Identity in the Eighteenth Century* (London: Routledge, 2000), 70–73.

46. Reid, *Essay*, 1:344.

47. David Hartley, *Observations on Man, His Frame, His Duty, and His Expectations* (1749), 2 vols., reprint, intro. T. L. Huguelet, 1 vol. (Gainesville, Fla.: Scholars' Facsimiles & Reprints, 1966), 1:511–12.

48. Cf. Hume, *Treatise*, 326.

49. Joseph Priestley, *Disquisitions Relating to Matter and Spirit, and the Doctrine of Philosophical Necessity Illustrated* (1777; reprint, New York: Garland, 1976), 163.

50. Ibid, 165.

51. Ibid., 166–67; emphasis added.

52. This idea was not key in the context of his own theory. Following Isaac Watts, he thought that some material core of self persists.

53. Thomas Cooper, *Tracts, Ethical, Theological, and Political*, 2 vols. (London: J. Johnson, 1789). See John Barresi and Raymond Martin, "Self-Concern from Priestley to Hazlitt," *The British Journal of the History of Philosophy* 11 (2003): 499–507; see also Udo Thiel, *Lockes Theorie der personalen Identität* (Bonn: Bouvier Verlag Herbert Grundmann, 1983), 196–97, and Thiel, ed., *Philosophical Writings of Thomas Cooper* (Bristol: Thoemmes Press, 2000).

54. Cooper, *Tracts*, 1:456–58.

55. Ibid., 462–63.

56. Ibid., 463–64.

57. Thomas Belsham, *Elements of the Philosophy of Mind, and of Moral Philosophy* (London: J. Johnson, 1801), 162–63.

58. William Hazlitt, *An Essay on the Principles of Human Action and some Remarks on the Systems of Hartley and Helvetius* (1805), reprint, intro. J. R. Nabholtz (Gainesville, Fla.: Scholars' Facsimiles & Reprints, 1969).

59. Ibid. 133–39.

60. Ibid. 110–11.

61. "[Imagination] must carry me out of myself into the feeling of others by one and the same process by which I am thrown forward as it were into my future being and interested in it. I could not love myself, if I were not capable of loving others. Self-love, used in this sense, is in its fundamental principle the same with disinterested benevolence" (ibid., 3).

62. Ibid., 33–34.

63. Ibid., 48–49.

64. Ibid., 34–35.

65. For more on Cooper, see Barresi and Martin, "Self-Concern."

66. Jean-Jacques Rousseau, *Emile* (1762), trans. Barbara Foxley, intro P. D. Jimack (London: Dent, 1974), book 1. See also Jean A. Perkins, *The Concept of the Self in the French Enlightenment* (Geneva: Librairie Droz, 1969), 95.

67. Perkins, *The Concept of the Self*, 124–25.

68. Hume, *Treatise*, 317.

69. Hazlitt, *Essay on the Principles*, 140.

70. Ibid., 10–11.

71. Ibid., 6, 10–11, 27–29.

72. Ibid., 31.

73. Ibid., 135–36.

74. Ibid., 138–40.

10. Philosophy of Spirit

1. Kant's view of the noumenal and phenomenal self combines the Cartesian project of positing the self as a knower of the world that is not itself an object within the world with the empiricist project of positing a self as just one of many objects within the world.

2. Immanuel Kant, *Critique of Pure Reason* (1781; rev., 1787), ed. and trans. Norman Kemp Smith (New York: St. Martin's Press, 1965), A364n:342.

3. Ibid., B157:168.

4. For an accessible explanation of this difficult idea, see Simon Blackburn, *Think* (Oxford: Oxford University Press, 1999), 138–40.

5. Kant, *Critique of Pure Reason*, B408:369.

6. Husserl, to take another example, retained Kant's notion of the transcendental ego, but with two differences. He attributed metaphysical reality to it, and he seemed to want to claim that there is a different transcendental ego corresponding to each different person. How Husserl could have known this is a mystery.

7. Gary Hatfield, "Remaking the Science of Mind: Psychology as Natural Science," in *Inventing Human Science: Eighteenth-Century Domains*, ed. Christopher Fox, Roy Porter, and Robert Wokler (Berkeley: University of California Press, 1995), 211.

8. The anecdotes are related in Ernst Cassirer, *Rousseau, Kant, and Goethe*, trans. James Gutmann, Paul Kristeller, and John Randall (Princeton, N.J.: Princeton University Press, 1945), 1.

9. Jean-Jacques Rousseau, "The First Walk," in *Reveries of the Solitary Walker*, trans. Peter France (Harmondsworth: Penguin, 1979), 27.

10. Rousseau, "The Tenth Walk," in *Reveries*, 153–55.

11. Rousseau, "The Fifth Walk," in *Reveries*, 88.

12. Jean-Jacques Rousseau, *The First and Second Discourses* (1755), trans. R. Masters (New York: St. Martin's Press, 1964), 195.

13. Friedrich von Schiller, *Letters on the Aesthetic Education of Man*, in *Literary and Philosophical Essays: French, German, and Italian*, Harvard Classics 32 (New York: Collier, c. 1910), letter 6.

14. Samuel Taylor Coleridge, *Biographia Literaria* (1817), ed. James Engell and W. Jackson Bate (Princeton, N.J.: Princeton University Press, 1983), 1:118–9.

15. Ibid., 1:304.

16. Samuel Taylor Coleridge, *Collected Letters*, 6 vols., ed. Earl Leslie Griggs (Oxford: Clarendon Press, 1956–71), 2:1197.

17. Samuel Taylor Coleridge, *Opus Maximum: Collected Works*, 16 vols., ed. Thomas McFarland with Nicholas Halmi (Princeton, N.J.: Princeton University Press, 2002), fragment 2 ff., 15:121.

18. Ibid., 15:132.

19. Ibid.

20. Johann Fichte, *Foundations of Transcendental Philosophy (Wissenschaftslehre), Nova Methodo* (1796–99), ed. and trans. Daniel Breazeale (Ithaca, N.Y.: Cornell University Press, 1992), 112.

21. Ibid., 110–11.

22. Ibid., 112.

23. Ibid., 111.

24. Quoted in translation in Frederick Neuhouser, *Fichte's Theory of Subjectivity* (New York: Cambridge University Press, 1990), 155.

25. G. W. F. Hegel, *The Phenomenology of Spirit* (1807), trans. A. V. Miller (Oxford: Oxford University Press, 1977), 130.

26. Subsequent quotations are from ibid., 111–19.

27. Arthur Schopenhauer, *The World as Will and Representation* (1818, 1844, 1859) trans. E. F. J. Payne (New York: Dover, 1966).

28. Arthur Schopenhauer, "Immortality: A Dialogue," in *Studies in Pessimism: A Series of Essays*, trans. T. Bailey Saunders, 4th ed. (London: Swan Sonnenschein & Co., 1893; reprint, St. Clair Shores, Mich.: Scholarly Press, 1976), 53–58; this is the source of subsequent quotations.

29. Søren Kierkegaard, *Sickness Unto Death*, ed. and trans. Howard B. Hong and Edna H. Hong (Princeton, N.J.: Princeton University Press, 1980), 13.

30. Ibid., 29–30.

31. Friedrich W. Nietzsche, *Ecco Homo: How One Becomes What One Is* (1888), in *The Philosophy of Neitzsche*, ed. Geoffrey Clive, trans. A.M. Ludovici (New York: New American Library, 1965), 49.

32. Friedrich W. Nietzsche, *Ecce Homo: How One Becomes What One Is* (1888), trans. R. J. Hollingdale (Harmmondworth: Penguin, 1979), 75.

33. Friedrich W. Nietzsche, *Human, All Too Human: A Book for Free Spirits*, ed. and trans. R.J. Hollingdale (New York: Cambridge University Press, 1996), 267–68.

34. Friedrich W. Nietzsche, *The Will to Power* (1901), trans. Walter Kaufmann (New York: Vintage, 1968), note 492. This book of Nietzsche's was selectively edited and altered by his sister after his death and is widely regarded as corrupt. However, it seems likely that the passages that we quote, which have nothing to do with politics or race, accurately represent his views.

35. Ibid., 485.

36. Ibid.

37. Ibid., 526.

38. Ibid., 489.

39. Ibid., 490.

40. Ibid., 484.

41. Ibid., 529.

42. Ibid.

43. Ibid., 548.

44. Ibid., 549.

45. Wilhelm Dilthey, *The Human World: Introduction to a Philosophy of Life*, trans. Jeremy J. Shapiro, cited in Jürgen Habermas, *Knowledge and Human Interests* (Boston: Beacon Press, 1971), 145.

46. Wilhelm Dilthey, *Gesammelte Scriften*, 18 vols. (Stuttgart: B. G. Trubner, 1914–77), 4:59; quoted by the translator in Michael Ermarth, *William Dilthey: The Critique of Historical Reason* (Chicago: University of Chicago Press, 1978), 319–20.

47. Dilthey, *Gesammelte Scriften*, 7:280; Ermarth, *William Dilthey*,137.

48. Josiah Royce, "Some Observations on the Anomalies of Self-Consciousness," pp. 169–97 in *Studies of Good and Evil* (1898; Hamden, Conn.: Archon, 1964), 169.

49. Josiah Royce, *The World and the Individual: Second Series: Nature, Man, and the Moral Order* (New York: Macmillan, 1901–13), 263.

50. Royce, "Some Observations," 196.

51. F. H. Bradley, *Appearance and Reality: A Metaphysical Essay* (1893, 1897; Oxford: Oxford University Press, 1978), 72.

52. Ibid., 73.

53. Ibid.

11. Science of Human Nature

1. In Newton's theory, gravitational attraction is action at a distance, so his theory is not straightforwardly mechanistic. Nevertheless, the overwhelming impression that his theories left on most thinkers is that because of the simplicity and regularity of nature that his theories revealed, the universe as a whole is genuinely clocklike.

2. See Jonathan Israel, *Radical Enlightenment* (New York: Oxford University Press, 2002), part 2.

3. Julien Offray de la Mettrie, *Man the Machine* (1748), trans. Gertrude Bussey (LaSalle, Ill.: Open Court, 1912).

4. Pierre Cabanis, *Relations of the Physical and the Moral in Man* (1802), ed. George Mora, trans. Margaret Duggan Saidi (Baltimore, Md.: John Hopkins University Press, 1981).

5. By such as A.L. Wigan (fl. 1844), Jean-Pierre-Marie Flourens (1794–1867), Paul Broca (1824–1880), John Hughlings Jackson (1835–1911), and David Ferrier (1843–1928). Thomas Willis in the seventeenth century had proposed localization, but this view lost ground in the eighteenth century, only to reappear in the nineteenth.

6. J. Chadwick and W.N. Mann, *The Medical Works of Hippocrates* (Oxford: Blackwell, 1950), 183.

7. As quoted in Joseph E. Bogen, "Mental Duality in the Anatomically Intact Cerebrum," paper presented as the Presidential Address to the Los Angeles Society of Neurology and Psychiatry, January 1983; published, in part, as "Partial Hemispheric Independence with Neocommisures Intact," in *Brain Circuits and Functions of Mind*, ed. C. Trevarthen (Cambridge: Cambridge University Press, 1990), 215–30.

8. Anne Harrington, *Medicine, Mind, and the Double Brain: A Study in Nineteenth-Century Thought* (Princeton, N.J.: Princeton University Press, 1987), 7–10.

9. Other advances included the development by Charles Bell (1774–1842) of new ways of distinguishing between sensory and motor nerves; Johannes Müller's (1801–1858) doctrine of specific nerve energies that systematized the epistemological role of the nervous system as intermediary between mind and world; and the beginnings of a sensory phenomenology of vision and of touch. In Müller's view, for instance, the doctrine of specific nerve energies involved two principles: that the mind is directly aware not of objects in the physical world but of states of the nervous system, which serve as intermediaries between the world and the mind; and that the qualities of the sensory nerves of which the mind receives knowledge in sensation are specific to the various senses, the nerve of vision being normally as insensible to sound as the nerve of hearing is to light.

10. We are talking here of serious empirical research on brain physiology. Phrenology did come under popular notice, but by the time it did, interpreting "bumps on the head" as reflecting underlying brain functions had become pseudoscience, not science.

11. Charles Darwin, *Autobiography*, in *Charles Darwin, His Life Told in an Autobiographical Chapter, and in a Selected Series of His Published Letters*, ed. Francis Darwin (London: John Murray, 1892), 40.

12. John Tyndall, *Fragments of Science for Unscientific People: A Series of Detached Essays, Lectures, and Reviews.* (London: Longmans, Green and Co., 1871) pp. 119-120.

13. Some of the material in this and the next section has been adapted from Robert H. Wozniak, *Mind and Body: René Descartes to William James* http://serendip.brynmawr.edu/Mind/Table.html.

14. Puységur's techniques and Mesmer's explanations were promulgated in the United States by the Frenchman C. P. de Saint Sauveur.

15. James Braid, *Neurypnology; or, the Rationale of Nervous Sleep, Considered in Relation with Animal Magnetism* (London: John Churchill, 1843), 94.

16. Braid may not have been the first to have done this. The Scottish physician James Esdaile (1808–1859) published a book three years after Braid's in which he claimed to have performed over 3,000 operations in Calcutta using only hypnosis as an anesthetic.

17. Theodule Ribot, *Diseases of Personality* (1891), reprint, in *Significant Contributions to the History of Psychology, 1750–1920, Series C: Medical Psychology: T. A. Ribot*, ed. D. N. Robinson, vol. 1 (Washington, D.C.: University Publications of America, 1997), 1.

18. Ibid., 3–6, 8.

19. Ibid., 154–56.

20. Ibid.

21. In his youth, Comte was influenced by the *ideologues*, a group of radical French thinkers that included Cabanis and Condorcet (1743–1794), author of *Sketch for a Historical Picture of the Progress of the Human Mind*. In their work, Comte found an optimistic, developmental philosophy of history. He was also influenced by the utopian socialist Claude Saint-Simon (1760–1825), who dreamt of a society led by scientists and industrialists in which there would be a division of labor that would ensure social harmony.

22. Thomas Kuhn, *The Structure of Scientific Revolutions* (Chicago: University of Chicago Press, 1962).

23. Auguste Comte, *The Postive Philosophy of Auguste Comte*, 3 vols., trans. and compiled by Harriet Martineau (London: George Bell & Sons, 1896), 2:100–101.

24. *Theses on Feuerbach*, VI, in K. Marx and F. Engels, *Selected Works*, Vol. I, (Moscow: Progress Publishers, 1969), p. 14.

25. Karl Marx and Friedrich Engels, *The German Ideology* (Moscow: Progress Publishers, 1976), 42.

26. Karl Marx, preface to *Critique of Political Economy*, in K. Marx and F. Engels, *Selected Works* (New York: International Publishers, 1975), 1:503.

27. Thomas Brown, *Lectures on the Philosophy of the Human Mind*, 2 vols. (Boston: Glazier & Co., 1828), 1:133.

28. James Mill, *Analysis of the Human Mind*, 2 vols., ed. A. Bain, A. Findlater, and G. Grote (London: Longman's Green Reader and Dyer, 1869), 2:168.

29. Brown and James Mill were more psychological than philosophical or biological in their theories, and for that reason, their thinking has been appreciated subsequently more by nineteenth-century psychologists than by philosophers. For instance, in *Principles of Psychology* William James applauded Brown's discussions of connectedness in the stream of consciousness. Likewise, psychologists at the end of

the century regarded James Mill's associative psychology as an important advance on Hartley's approach. By contrast, they tended to consider John Stuart Mill's psychology, which has been greatly appreciated by twentieth-century analytical philosophers, as too philosophical.

30. J. S. Mill, *Auguste Comte and Positivism* (1866; Ann Arbor: University of Michigan Press, 1968), 64.

31. Mill, *Analysis*, 2:174.

32. Ibid., 2:174–75.

33. J. S. Mill, *An Examination of Sir William Hamilton's Philosophy* (1865; London: Longman's, Green, Reader, and Dyer, 1878), 262–63; William James, *Principles of Psychology*, 2 vols. (1890; reprint, New York: Henry Holt & Co., 1918), 1:358.

34. James, *Principles*, 1:358–59.

35. Ibid., 1:359–60.

36. H. Sidgwick *The Methods of Ethics* (1874), 7th ed. (Chicago: University of Chicago Press, 1907), 162, 418.

37. Alexander Bain, *The Emotions and the Will*, 3rd ed. (New York: Appleton and Co., 1876), 203–4.

38. James M. Baldwin, *Mental Development in the Child and the Race* (New York: Macmillan, 1894), 2–4.

39. James M. Baldwin, *History of Psychology: A Sketch and an Interpretation*, 2 vols., (London: Watts & Co., 1913), 2:108–9.

40. James, *Principles*, 1:365–66.

41. Ibid., 1:224.

42. Ibid., 1:225.

43. Ibid., 1:226–27.

44. Ibid., 1:227.

45. Ibid., 1:291–92.

46. Ibid., 1:294.

47. Ibid., 1:296–97.

48. Ibid., 1:297–98.

49. Ibid., 1:301–2.

50. Ibid., 1:319.

51. Ibid., 1:320.

52. Ibid., 1:333.

53. Ibid., 1:335–37.

54. Ibid., 1:338.

55. Ibid., 1:338–39.

56. Ibid., 1:339–40.

57. Ibid., 1:340–41.

58. Ibid., 1:344–6.

59. Ibid., 1:371.

60. Ibid., 1:373.

61. Ibid., 1:400.

62. Ibid., 1:400–401.

12. Before the Fall

1. Quoted from Martin Kusch, *Psychologism: A Case Study in the Sociology of Philosophical Knowledge* (New York: Routledge, 1995), 191.

2. During the first half of the century, both phenomenology and analytic philosophy abandoned foundationalism in epistemology. Phenomenologists abandoned it in making the transition from Husserl to Heidegger, who looked back over Husserl's head to Nietzsche. Analytic philosophers began making the change somewhat later.

3. W. V. O. Quine's extraordinarily influential paper, "Two Dogmas of Empiricism," *The Philosophical Review* 60 (1951): 20–43, marked a turning point in analytic philosophy. Those who accepted Quine's argument, which included quite a few analytic philosophers, abandoned the logical-positivist idea that the a priori analysis of concepts is the main task of philosophy.

4. Husserl, who began as a student of Franz Brentano (1838–1917), was subsequently influenced by Gottlob Frege (1848–1925) to move away from "psychologism" toward a more logical style of analysis.

5. Quoted from Kusch, *Psychologism*, 179.

6. Edmund Husserl, *The Crisis of European Sciences and Transcendental Phenomenology*, trans. and intro. David Carr (1954; Evanston, Ill.: Northwestern University Press, 1970), 3B.60:212. In section 3B.62:216, Husserl tried to distill a basis for the "I" by tracing this activity of self-appropriation back to those structures of experience on which the very activity of being aware of things and their meanings depends. He asked whether souls are spatial and concluded that in some sense they must be since "all objects in the world are in essence 'embodied,' and for that very reason all 'take part' in the space-time of bodies"; "this applies to spiritual objects of every sort," including souls.

7. Ibid., 3B.62:217.

8. Ibid.

9. Ibid., 3B.62:218–19.

10. Heidegger does not try to prove the existence of others. Instead, he takes himself to have demonstrated, in three ways, that others are among the necessary conditions of human existence. First, since everything that a human does refers to others in some fashion, others are always implicated in one's actions; even when one is alone, one experiences the absence of others. Second, typically one conceptualizes oneself in an "impersonal" way—as a generalized or impersonal other—that derives from one's culture. Finally, one's mode of existence as authentic or inauthentic is influenced by others. One is drawn toward authenticity in the presence of authentic others and toward inauthenticity in the presence of inauthentic others.

11. Martin Heidegger, *Being and Time* (1927), trans. John Macquarrie and Edward Robinson (New York: Harper & Row, 1962), 2.3.64:368.

12. Ibid.

13. Ibid., 2.3.64:370.

14. Jean-Paul Sartre, *Transcendence of the Ego: An Existentialist Theory of Consciousness* (1936), trans. Forrest Williams and Robert Kirkpatrick (New York: Noonday Press, 1957), 104.

15. Sartre, *Transcendence*, 49.

16. Jean-Paul Sartre, *Being and Nothingness* (1943), trans. Hazel E. Barnes (New York: Citadel Press, 1964), 200.

17. Ibid., 222.

18. Russell's lectures bear titles like, "Facts and Propositions," "Particulars, Predicates, and Relations," and "The Theory of Types and Symbolism."

19. Bertrand Russell, *Logic and Knowledge*, ed. R.C. Marsh (London: George Allen & Unwin Ltd., 1956), 277.

20. Ludwig Wittgenstein, *Tractatus Logico-Philosophicus* (1921), trans. D. Pears and B. McGuiness (London: Routlege & Kegan Paul, 1961), 5.6:56, 5.63:57, 5.632:57, 6.4311:72.

21. Ibid., 6.4312:72.

22. A.J. Ayer, *Language, Truth, and Logic* (New York: Dover Publications, 1946), 125–26.

23. Ludwig Wittgenstein, *The Blue and Brown Books* (Oxford: Blackwell, 1958); Ludwig Wittgenstein, *Philosophical Investigations*, ed. G. Anscombe and Rush Rhees, trans G. Anscombe (Oxford: Blackwell, 1953).

24. Wittgenstein, *The Blue Book*, 61–62.

25. Ibid., 62.

26. Ibid.

27. John Austin, "Other Minds," *Aristotelian Society Supplementary 20* (1946). Reprint, in *Classics of Analytic Philosophy*, ed. Robert Ammerman (New York: McGraw-Hill, 1965), 374.

28. Gilbert Ryle, *The Concept of Mind* (Chicago: University of Chicago Press, 1949).

29. Robert C. Solomon and Kathleen M. Higgins, *A Short History of Philosophy* (New York: Oxford, 1996), 286. Although on this occasion Ryle was sarcastic, earlier he had written a respectful review of Heidegger's *Being and Time*, and he shared Heidegger's insistence on the primacy of *knowing how* over *knowing that*.

30. May had studied briefly with Adler, after Adler had broken with Freud, and with Paul Tillich (1886–1965), the existentialist theologian. Then, during a three-year period when May was gravely ill and faced the possibility of death, he read Kierkegaard. Subsequently, he studied psychoanalysis with Harry Stack Sullivan (1892–1949) and Erich Fromm (1900–1980).

31. Rollo May, "The Origins and Significance of the Existential Movement in Psychology," in *Existence: A New Dimension in Psychiatry and Psychology*, ed. Rollo May, Ernest Angel, and Henri F. Ellenberger (New York: Basic Books, 1958), 7.

32. Maslow studied psychology at the University of Wisconsin, where he worked with Harry Harlow, who is famous for his studies of the social-attachment behavior of baby rhesus monkeys. Later, while teaching at Brooklyn College, he came into contact with European intellectuals who were immigrating to the United States, including Adler, Fromm, and Karen Horney. Later still, he met Kurt Goldstein, who introduced him to the idea of self-actualization. It was then that Maslow began his crusade for a humanistic psychology.

33. We profited in organizing our account of Mead from the excellent summary (author unknown) of Mead's views in The Internet Encyclopedia of Philosophy, http://www.iep.utm.edu/m/mead.htm#top.

34. G. H. Mead, *Mind, Self, and Society from the Standpoint of a Social Behaviorist* (1934), ed. Charles W. Morris (Chicago: University of Chicago Press, 1962), 135.

35. Ibid., 225.

36. Ibid., 225.

37. Ibid., 195.

38. Ibid., 154.

39. Ibid., 160.

40. Ibid., 197.

41. Ibid., 210–11.

42. Ibid., 210.

43. Lev Vygotsky, *Thinking and Speech* (1934), 293; quoted and trans. in Ivana Markova, "The Development of Self-Consciousness: Baldwin, Mead, and Vygotsky," in *Reconsidering Psychology: Perspectives from Continental Philosophy*, ed. J. Faulconer and R. Williams (Pittsburgh: Duquesne University Press, 1990), 151–74.

44. L. Vygotsky, "Consciousness as a Problem in the Psychology of Behavior," *Soviet Psychology* 17 (1979): 29.

45. Max Horkheimer and Theodore Adorno, *Dialectic of Enlightenment*, trans. John Cumming (New York: Herder and Herder, 1972), 3–4.

46. Max Horkheimer, *Die Juden in Europa* (1939), in *Wirtschaft, Recht und Staat im Nationalsozialismus. Analysen des Instituts für Sozialforschung 1939–1942*, ed. H. Dubiel and A. Söllner (Frankfurt: Suhrkamp, 1984), 33.

13. Paradise Lost

1. See, for instance, Claude Lévi-Strauss, *Structural Anthropology* (1958), ed. Allen Lane, trans. Clair Jacobson and Brooke Grundfest Schoepf (Harmondsworth: Penguin, 1968); and Roland Barthes, *Mythologies* (1957; Paris: Seuil, 1970).

2. We have profited in this section from Mary Klages's lucid and succinct "lecture notes" on Lacan at http://www.colorado.edu/english/ENGL2012Klages/lacan.html.

3. In Foucault's own words, "the death of the subject, of the Subject in capital letters, of the subject as origin and foundation of Knowledge, of Liberty, of Language and History": Michel Foucault, "The Birth of a World," interview with Jean-Michel Palmier, *Le Monde*, 3 May 1969, reprint, in *Foucault Live*, ed. S. Lotringer, trans. L. Hochroth and J. Johnson (New York: Semiotext(e), 1989), 61. Recounted in Hubert Dreyfus, "Heidegger and Foucault on the Subject, Agency, and Practices," an unpublished MS (2002) that we drew upon in interpreting Foucault.

4. Michel Foucault, "What Is an Author?" (1969), in *The Foucault Reader*, ed. P. Rabinow, trans. Josué V. Harari (New York: Pantheon, 1984), 118, 102.

5. Ibid., 114.

6. Quoted by Foucault, in *The History of Sexuality*, trans. Robert Hurley, vol. 1 (New York: Vintage, 1980), 20.

7. Ibid., 78.

8. Michel Foucault, "The Return of Morality," in *Foucault Live*, ed. S. Lotringer, trans. L. Hochroth and J. Johnson (New York: Semiotext(e), 1989), 466. More precisely, he said that before *The Care of the Self* (1984), the final volume of his *History of Sexuality*, he had tried to do this.

9. Michel Foucault, "The Concern for Truth," in *Foucault Live*, ed. S. Lotringer, trans. L. Hochroth and J. Johnson (New York: Semiotext(e), 1989), 458.

10. Cited by Paul Rabinow in Michel Foucault, *Ethics: Subjectivity and Truth*, ed. Paul Rabinow, trans. Robert Hurley et al. (New York: The New Press, 1994), xxxix.

11. Jacques Derrida, *Of Grammatology* (1967), trans. Gayatri Chakravorty Spivak (Baltimore, Md.: Johns Hopkins University Press, 1976), 158.

12. Jacques Derrida, "Structure, Sign, and Play in the Discourse of the Human Sciences," in *Writing and Difference* (1970), trans. Alan Bass (Chicago: University of Chicago Press, 1978), 278–79.

13. Jacques Derrida, *Positions*, trans. Alan Bass (Chicago: University of Chicago Press, 1981), 39.

14. Derrida, "Différance" (1968), in *Margins of Philosophy*, ed. J. Derrida, trans. David Allison (Chicago: The University of Chicago Press, 1982), 3–27.

15. Derrida, *Writing and Differance*, 286.

16. W. E. B. DuBois, *The Souls of Black Folk* (1903), in *Three Negro Classics*, ed. and intro. John Hope Franklin (Chicago: Avon, 1965), 213, 215.

17. Frantz Fanon, *The Wretched of the Earth* (1961), trans. Constance Farrington (New York: Grove Press, 1963), 36.

18. Frantz Fanon, *Black Skins, White Masks* (1952), trans. Charles Markmann (New York: Grove Press, 1967), 16. Recognizing the positionality of his own view, Fanon remarked, "Since I was born in the Antilles, my observations and my conclusions are valid only for the Antilles—at least concerning the black man *at home*."

19. Ibid., 17–18.

20. Ibid., 112.

21. Ibid., 109.

22. Amina Mama, *Beyond the Masks: Race, Gender, and Subjectivity* (London: Routledge, 1995), 48.

23. There are, of course, many other important theorists of ethnicity and race that deserve to be mentioned, among them: Homi K. Bhabha, Stuart Hall, Gayatri Spivak, Edward Said, Frank Chin, Hortense Spillers, Lisa Lowe, David Palumbo-Liu, Cornell West, and Henry Louis Gates Jr.

24. Whereas postmodernism has nourished many feminist theories of the self, its challenge to the idea of a stable self and to the validity of the category *woman* has also encouraged the view that there is nothing that all women have in common and, hence, brought into question whether there is anything for feminism to be about. In response to this challenge, Linda Alcoff has construed femininity as "positionality," which she says

has two dimensions: a social context that deprives women of power and mobility, and a political point of departure from which women can affirm their right to take charge of their own identities. Alcoff, "A Philosophical Dialogue with 'Dialogue with the Other,'" *Gender-Nature-Culture* (1994): 5–22. Sally Haslanger, on the other hand, has advocated a politicized, "critical analytical" approach to gender. In her view, the principal task for feminist theory is to provide an analysis of gender not in terms of the experience of sexed embodiment but in terms of a "pattern of social relations that constitute the social classes of men as dominant and women as subordinate." She advocates that women adopt whatever conception of gender best serves their emancipatory aims; see Haslanger, "Gender and Race: (What) Are They? (What) Do We Want Them to Be?" *Nous* 34, no. 1 (March 2000): 31–55. We have been aided in this section by Diana Meyers, "Feminist Perspectives on the Self," in *Stanford Encyclopedia of Philosophy* (Stanford, Calif.: Stanford University Press, 2004), which can be found at http://plato.stanford.edu/entries/feminism-self.

25. Judith Butler, *Gender Trouble* (London: Routledge, 1990), 9.

26. Sandra Bartky, "Sympathy and Solidarity: On a Tightrope with Scheler," in *Feminists Rethink the Self*, ed. Diana Meyers (Boulder, Colo.: Westview, 1997), 177.

27. Ibid.

28. Butler, *Gender Trouble*, 25.

29. N. Humphrey, "The Social Function of Intellect," in *Growing Points in Ethology*, ed. P. P. G. Bateson and R. Hinde (Cambridge: Cambridge University Press, 1976), 303–17, reprint, in Humphrey, *Consciousness Regained: Chapters in the Development of Mind* (Oxford: Oxford University Press, 1984).

30. D. Premack and G. Woodruff, "Do Chimpanzees Have a Theory of Mind?" *Behavioral and Brain Sciences* 1 (1978): 516–26.

31. Some have argued that even newborns mimic adults, but it is controversial whether the phenomena to which they point is genuine mimicry.

32. M. L. Hoffman, "Empathy, Its Development and Prosocial Implications," in *Nebraska Symposium on Motivation*, ed. C. B. Keasey, vol. 25, *Social Cognitive Development* (Lincoln: University of Nebraska Press, 1977).

33. H. Wimmer and J. Perner, "Beliefs About Beliefs: Representations and Constraining Function of Wrong Beliefs in Young Children's Understanding of Deception," *Cognition* 13 (1983): 103–28.

34. Henry A. Murray, *Explorations in Personality* (Oxford: Oxford University Press, 1938), 49.

35. D. McAdams, "What Do We Know When We Know a Person?" *Journal of Personality* 63 (1995): 365–95; D. McAdams, "The Case for Unity in the (Post) Modern Self: A Modest Proposal," in *Self and Identity: Fundamental Issues*, ed. R. Ashmore and L. Jussim (New York: Oxford University Press, 1997), 46–78.

36. K. J. Gergen and M. M. Gergen, "Narrative and the Self as Relationship," *Advances in Experimental Social Psychology* 21 (1988): 18.

37. H. Hermans, T. Rijks, and H. Kempen, "Imaginal Dialogues in the Self: Theory and Method," *Journal of Personality* 61 (1993): 210.

38. Ibid.

39. Yet, in apparent contradiction to this general principle, they concede that even this "Self" can *sometimes* be dominated by subselves, so that it might be better to conceive the Self as "in the middle of a highly dynamic field of criss-cross dialogical relationships among possible positions, subjected to influences from all sides": H. Hermans and H. Kempen, *The Dialogical Self: Meaning as Movement* (New York: Academic Press, 1993), 98.

40. Alasdair MacIntyre, *After Virtue*, 2nd ed. (South Bend, Ind.: University of Notre Dame Press, 1984), 216–17.

41. Ibid., 217–18.

42. See Daniel Dennett, "The Origin of Selves," *Cogito* 1 (1989): 163–73; and Nicholas Humphrey and Daniel Dennett, "Speaking for Ourselves: An Assessment of Multiple Personality Disorder," *Raritan* 9 (1989): 68–98. Both essays are reprinted in D. Kolak and R. Martin, eds., *Self and Identity* (New York: Macmillan, 1991), 144–61, 355–63. See also the development of these earlier ideas in Daniel Dennett, *Consciousness Explained* (Boston: Little, Brown, & Co., 1991).

43. For discussion of both the medical and philosophical aspects of these cases, see R. Sperry, "Hemisphere Deconnection and Unity in Conscious Awareness," *American Psychologist* 23 (1968): 723–33; R. Puccetti, "Two Brains, Two Minds? Wigan's Theory of Mental Duality," *British Journal for the Philosophy of Science* 40 (1989): 137–44; T. Nagel, "Brain Bisection and the Unity of Consciousness," in *Mortal Questions* (Cambridge: Cambridge University Press, 1979); and D. Parfit, "Divided Minds and the Nature of Persons," in *Mindwaves*, ed. C. Blakemore and S. Greenfield (Oxford: Basil Blackwell, 1987). All four of these essays are reprinted in D. Kolak and R. Martin, eds. *Self and Identity* (New York: Macmillan, 1991), 55–88.

44. See Michael Gazzaniga, *The Mind's Past* (Berkeley: University of California Press, 1998).

45. Antonio R. Damasio, *Descartes' Error : Emotion, Reason, and the Human Brain* (New York : G. P. Putnam, 1994).

46. Antonio R. Damasio, *The Feeling of What Happens : Body and Emotion in the Making of Consciousness* (New York: Harcourt Brace, 1999).

47. Fission examples had been discussed earlier in the twentieth century, in A. N. Prior, "Opposite Number," *Review of Metaphysics* 11 (1957–58): 196–201; Prior, "Time, Existence, and Identity," *Proceedings of the Aristotelian Society* 57 (1965–66): 183–92; J. Bennett, "The Simplicity of the Soul," *Journal of Philosophy* 44 (1967): 648–60; R. Chisholm and S. Shoemaker, "Identity," in *Perception and Personal Identity: Proceedings of the 1967 Oberlin Colloquium in Philosophy*, ed. Norman Care and Robert H. Grimm (Cleveland: Press of Case Western Reserve University, 1967).

48. Derek Parfit, *Reasons and Persons* (Oxford: Oxford University Press, 1984), 222.

49. Ibid., 220.

50. Ibid., 284–85.

51. For more on this example, see Raymond Martin, *Self-Concern: An Experiential Approach to What Matters in Survival* (New York: Cambridge University Press, 1998), 80–85.

52. Parfit, *Reasons*, 200–201.

53. For more on this, see Martin, *Self-Concern*, chaps. 6 and 7.

54. Derek Parfit's views may be found mainly in "Personal Identity," *Philosophical Review* 80 (1971): 3–27, and in *Reasons and Persons*. David Lewis's explanation and defense of the four-dimensional view of persons is in his "Survival and Identity," in *The Identities of Persons*, ed. Amelie Rorty (Berkeley: University of California Press, 1976), 17–40; and in Lewis, "Postscript to 'Survival and Identity,'" in *Philosophical Papers*, vol. 1 (New York: Oxford University Press, 1983). Other important work since 1970 that would have been discussed in a more complete survey includes papers by Sydney Shoemaker, Robert Nozick, John Perry, Peter Unger, Ernest Sosa, and Thomas Nagel. Copies of important papers by these and other authors can be found in Kolak and Martin, eds., *Self and Identity*, and Raymond Martin and John Barresi, eds., *Personal Identity* (New York: Blackwell, 2002).

14. Everything That Happened and What It Means

1. What Socrates means by continually dying is continually removing oneself in thought from as many bodily distractions as possible so that mentally one communes only with what is ideal and immaterial—the eternal verities, if you will.

2. Yet, in Socrates' time, and no doubt earlier, people must often have been afraid of death, or else Epicurus and other philosophers would not have spent so much time encouraging people to overcome their fears. In the late sixteenth century, Montaigne, too, exhorted people to overcome their fear of death:

> Let us deprive death of its strangeness, let us frequent it, let us get used to it; let us have nothing more often in mind than death.... We do not know where death awaits us; so let us wait for it everywhere. To practice death is to practice freedom. A man who has learned how to die has unlearned how to be a slave.
> (Michel de Montaigne, "To Philosophize Is to Learn How to Die," in *The Complete Essays*, ed. and trans. M. A. Screech ([New York: Penguin, 1993]), book 1, essay 20, 96)

The point of this seems to be that to live freely, we must free ourselves of the fear of death, which fear is all but universal. Recall Spinoza's famous pronouncement, "A free man thinks of nothing less than of death." See chapter 8, note 18.

3. See 1 Cor. 15:17, 32.

4. It was, of course, also deeply consequential for the question of how to live a good life.

5. It is an interesting question when organisms first developed a sense of themselves as beings that are distinct from others and when they first developed a sense of themselves as beings that persist over time. Some claim that every biological creature has a sense of itself as a being distinct from others. The basis for this suggestion is that in order to survive, living things have to be sensitive to their own boundaries, or else when they go

to eat something they might eat themselves. See Daniel Dennett, "The Origin of Selves," *Cogito* 1 (1989): 163–73, reprint, in *Self and Identity: Contemporary Philosophical Issues*, ed. D. Kolak and R. Martin (New York: Macmillan, 1991), 355–64.

6. Some eighteenth-century, empirically minded philosophers, such as Thomas Reid, tried to retain for the soul a place in scientific theory, often with an implicit suggestion that the notion of soul that they employed scientifically is the very same notion as the one that they and others employed religiously. However, by the end of the nineteenth century, such pretentious attempts to link science and religion were abandoned.

7. There were exceptions. Locke, for instance, tended to use *self* and *person* more or less interchangeably in what he took to be his empirically grounded account of personal identity over time. Hume, by contrast, thought of the self as a bundle of perceptions and tried sometimes to make use of this more empirically respectable notion of self in his scientific thoughts. But the bundle idea never actually does much work in Hume's scientific theories, such as in his account of the origin of sympathy.

8. William James, *Principles of Psychology*, 2 vols. (1890; reprint, New York: Henry Holt & Co., 1918), 1:294–401. After James, it is not obvious that theories of the self any longer have a unified object of study, that is, that there is a self that is sufficiently cohesive that it can be studied by just one disciplinary approach or as a unified thing. As we have seen, theorists continued to talk about the self at least until World War II as if it were cohesive. However, when the notion of the self did clearly seem to be functioning as a scientifically useful explanatory notion, often the theories in which it plays this role, such as psychoanalytic theory and existential or humanistic psychology, are ones that, from the perspective of many in our own times, are on the margins of science.

9. Hendericus Stam, in "The Dialogical Self, Meaning, and Theory: Making the Subject," paper presented at the First International Conference on the Dialogical Self, Nijmegen, Netherlands, June 2000, suggested that in psychological research the self as a unitary entity had all but been replaced by the study of hyphenated self-functions.

10. Ulrich Neisser, "Five Kinds of Self-Knowledge," *Philosophical Psychology* 1 (1988): 37–59, reprint, in *Self and Identity: Contemporary Philosophical Issues*, ed. D. Kolak and R. Martin (New York: Macmillan, 1991), 386–406.

11. By taking a synoptic view, Neisser seems to have freed psychologists to pursue their studies of one or the other of his sources of self-knowledge with a clearer conscience and less likelihood of getting confused. See, for instance, Chris Moore and Karen Lemmon, eds., *The Self in Time: Developmental Issues* (Hillsdale, N.J.: Erlbaum, 2000).

12. Neisser, "Five Kinds of Self-Knowledge," in Kolak and Martin, 391.

13. Abraham Tucker, who wrote late in the eighteenth century, is an excellent example. See R. Martin and J. Barresi, *Naturalization of the Soul: Self and Personal Identity in the Eighteenth Century* (London: Routledge, 2000), chap. 5.

14. Still, some philosophers continue to insist on something like the unity of the self. See, for instance, Peter Unger, *Identity, Consciousness, and Value* (New York: Oxford University Press, 1991), chap. 6. But see Owen Flanagan, *The Problem of the Soul: Two Visions of Mind and How to Reconcile Them* (New York: Basic Books, 2002), chap. 6.

15. In a recent interview, Derek Parfit remarked that what interests him most "are those metaphysical questions," such as personal identity, free will, and the passage of time, "whose answers seem to be relevant—or to make a difference—to what we have reason to care about or to do, and to our moral beliefs"; Andrew Pyle, ed., *Key Philosophers in Conversation: The Cogito Interviews* (London: Routledge, 1999), 180.

16. Charles Taylor, *Sources of the Self* (Cambridge: Cambridge University Press, 1989), traces the history of the self with the aim of answering questions of this sort.

17. See, for instance, Robert Solomon, *Continental Philosophy Since 1750: The Rise and Fall of the Self* (New York: Oxford University Press, 1998), 110.

18. Think, for instance, of the theories of Locke and Priestley.

REFERENCES

Abelard and Heloise. *The Letters of Abelard and Heloise*. Trans. Betty Radice. Harmondsworth: Penguin, 1974.

Alcoff, Linda. "A Philosophical Dialogue with 'Dialogue with the Other.'" *Gender-Nature-Culture* (1994): 5–22.

Ambrose, Mark. "Aristotle's Immortal Intellect." In *Proceedings of the American Catholic Philosophical Association: Person, Soul, and Immortality, vol. 75, 2001*, ed. Michael Baur, 97–106. New York: American Catholic Philosophical Association, 2002.

Ammerman, Robert, ed.. *Classics of Analytic Philosophy*. Indianapolis: Hackett, 1990.

Aquinas, Thomas. *Aquinas Against the Averroists: On There Being Only One Intellect*. Trans. Ralph McInerny. West Lafayette, Ind.: Purdue University Press, 1993.

——. *On Being and Essence*. Trans. A. Maurer. Toronto: The Pontifical Institute of Medieval Studies, 1949.

——. *Summa Contra Gentiles*. Trans. Charles O'Neil. Notre Dame, Ind.: Notre Dame University Press, 1975.

——. *Summa Theologica*. In *Great Books of the Western World*, vol. 19, parts 1 and 2. Chicago: Encyclopedia Britannica, 1952.

Aristotle. *Metaphysics*. Ed. and trans. H. Tredennick. 2 vols. Loeb Classical Library. London: William Heinemann, 1936.

——. *Works of Aristotle*. Trans. W. D. Ross. *Great Books of the Western World*. Chicago: Encyclopedia Britannica, Vol. 8, 1952.

Athenagoras. *On the Resurrection of the Dead*. In *The Ante-Nicene Fathers*, ed. A. Roberts, J. Donaldson, and A. C. Coxe, 2:149–62. Grand Rapids, Mich.: W. B. Eerdmans, 1977.

Augustine. *City of God*. In *Nicene and Post-Nicene Fathers*, vol. 2, ed. Philip Schaff, trans. Rev. Marcus Dods, 1st ser. Peabody, Mass.: Hendrickson, 1995.

——. *The Confessions*. Trans. Maria Boulding New York: Vintage Books, 1997.

Augustine. *De Vere Religione*. In *Nicene and Post-Nicene Fathers*, ed. Philip Schaff, 1st Series. Peabody, Mass.: Hendrickson, 1995.

Augustodunensis, Honorius. *Clavis Physicae*. Ed. Paolo Lucentini. Rome: Edizioni di Storia e Letteratura, 1974.

Aurelius, Marcus. *Meditations*. Trans. George Long. London: Collins Clear-Type Press, n.d.

Austin, J. L. "Other Minds." *Aristotelian Society Supplementary* 20 (1946). Reprint, in *Classics of Analytic Philosophy*, ed. Robert Ammerman, 353–78. New York: McGraw-Hill, 1965.

Avramides, Anita. *Other Minds*. London: Routledge, 2001.

Ayer, A. J. *Language, Truth, and Logic*. New York: Dover Publications, 1946.

Ayers, Michael. *Locke*. 2 Vols. London: Routledge, 1991.

Bain, Alexander. *The Emotions and the Will*. 3rd ed. New York: Appleton and Co., 1876.

Bakhtin, Mikhail. *Problems of Dostoevsky's Poetics*. Trans. R. W. Rotsel. Ann Arbor, Mich.: Ardis, 1973.

Baldwin, James M. *Mental Development in the Child and the Race*. New York: Macmillan, 1894.

———. *History of Psychology: A Sketch and an Interpretation*. 2 vols. London: Watts & Co., 1913.

Ballie, James. "Personal Identity and Mental Content." *Philosophical Psychology* 10 (1997): 323–33.

Barresi, John, and Raymond Martin. "Self-Concern from Priestley to Hazlitt." *British Journal for the History of Philosophy* 11 (2003): 499–507.

Barthes, Roland. *Mythologies*. 1957. Paris: Seuil, 1970.

Bartky, Sandra. "Sympathy and Solidarity: On a Tightrope with Scheler." In *Feminists Rethink the Self*, ed. Diana Meyers, 177–96. Boulder, Colo.: Westview, 1997.

Bayle, Pierre. *A General Dictionary, Historical and Critical*. Trans. J. P. Bernard, T. Birch, and J. Lockman. 10 vols. London: J. Bettenham, 1734–1741.

Belsham, Thomas. *Elements of the Philosophy of Mind, and of Moral Philosophy*. London: J. Johnson, 1801.

Bennett, J. "The Simplicity of the Soul." *Journal of Philosophy* 44 (1967): 648–60.

Benson, D. F., and E. Zaidel, eds.. *The Dual Brain*. New York: Guilford, 1985.

Black, Deborah. "Consciousness and Self-Knowledge in Aquinas's Critique of Averröes's Psychology." *Journal of the History of Philosophy* 31 (1993): 349–85.

Blackburn, Simon. *Think*. Oxford: Oxford University Press, 1999.

Blom, John J., ed. and trans. *Descartes: His Moral Philosophy and Psychology*. New York: New York University Press, 1978.

Blumenthal, H. J. *Aristotle and Neoplatonism in Late Antiquity: Interpretations of the* De anima. Ithaca, N.Y.: Cornell University Press, 1996.

Bobro, M. "Prudence and the Concern to Survive in Leibniz's Doctrine of Immortality." *History of Philosophy Quarterly* 15 (1998): 303–22.

Bogen, Joseph E. "Mental Duality in the Anatomically Intact Cerebrum." Paper presented as the Presidential Address to the Los Angeles Society of Neurology and Psychiatry,

January 1983. Published, in part, as "Partial Hemispheric Independence with Neocommisures Intact." In *Brain Circuits and Functions of Mind*, ed. C. Trevarthen, 215–30. Cambridge: Cambridge University Press, 1990.

Bradley, F. H. *Appearance and Reality: A Metaphysical Essay*. 1893, 1897. Oxford: Oxford University Press, 1978.

Braid, James. *Neurypnology; or, the Rationale of Nervous Sleep, Considered in Relation with Animal Magnetism*. London: John Churchill, 1843.

Brennan, Tad. "Immortality in Ancient Philosophy." In *Routledge Encyclopedia of Philosophy*, ed. E. Craig. London: Routledge, 2002. Online version: http://www.rep. routledge.com/article/a133.

Brown, Thomas. *Lectures on the Philosophy of the Human Mind*. 2 vols. Boston: Glazier & Co., 1828.

Bruno, Giordano. *The Expulsion of the Triumphant Beast*. Trans. A. D. Imerti. Lincoln: University of Nebraska Press, 1964.

Burke, Peter. "Representations of the Self from Petrarch to Descartes." In *Rewriting the Self: Histories from the Renaissance to the Present*, ed. Roy Porter, 17–28. London: Routledge, 1997.

Burthogge, R. *An Essay Upon Reason and the Nature of Spirits*. 1694. New York: Garland, 1976.

Butler, Joseph. *The Analogy of Religion, Natural and Revealed*. 1736. London: Henry G. Bohn, 1852.

Butler, Judith. *Gender Trouble*. London: Routledge, 1990.

Bynum, Caroline Walker. *The Resurrection of the Body in Western Christianity, 200–1336*. New York: Columbia University Press, 1995.

Cabanis, Pierre-Jean-Georges. *Relations of the Physical and the Moral in Man*. 1802. Ed. George Mora. Trans. Margaret Duggan Saidi. Baltimore, Md.: John Hopkins University Press, 1981.

Cassirer, Ernst. *Rousseau, Kant, and Goethe*. Trans. James Gutmann, Paul Kristeller, and John Randall. Princeton, N.J.: Princeton University Press, 1945.

Chadwick, J., and W. N. Mann. *The Medical Works of Hippocrates*. Oxford: Blackwell, 1950.

Chisholm, Roderick. "Identity Through Possible Worlds: Some Questions." *Noûs* 1 (1967) 1–8. Reprint, in *The Possible and the Actual*, ed. Michael J. Loux, 80–87. Ithaca, N.Y.: Cornell University Press, 1979.

Chisholm, R., and S. Shoemaker. "Identity." In *Perception and Personal Identity: Proceedings of the 1967 Oberlin Colloquium in Philosophy*, ed. Norman Care and Robert H. Grimm. Cleveland: Press of Case Western Reserve University, 1967.

Cicero. *De Offices*. Trans. Walter Miller. New York: Macmillan, 1908.

———. *De Finibus Bonorum et Malorum*. Trans. H. Rackham. New York: Macmillan, 1914.

Clarke, Samuel, and Anthony Collins. *A Letter to Mr. Dodwell, and etc*. In *The Works of Samuel Clarke*, 4 vols., 1738, 3:720–913. Reprinted, New York: Garland, 1978.

Coleridge, Samuel Taylor. *Biographia Literaria*. 1817. Ed. James Engell and W. Jackson Bate. Princeton, N.J.: Princeton University Press, 1983.

Coleridge, Samuel Taylor. *Collected Letters*. 6 vols. Ed. Earl Leslie Griggs ed. Oxford: Clarendon Press, 1956–71.

———. *Opus Maximum: Collected Works*. Vol. 15. Ed. Thomas McFarland with Nicholas Halmi. 16 vols. Princeton, N.J.: Princeton University Press, 2002.

Comte, Auguste. *The Postive Philosophy of Auguste Comte*. 3 vols. Trans. and compiled by Harriet Martineau. London: George Bell & Sons, 1896.

Condorcet, Marie Jean Antoine Nicolas de Caritat. *Sketch for a Historical Picture of the Progress of the Human Mind*. N.p. 1765.

Cooper, Thomas. *Tracts, Ethical, Theological, and Political*. 2 vols. London: J. Johnson, 1789.

Copleston, F. C. *Aquinas*. 1955. Reprint, Baltimore: Penguin Books, 1961.

Corlish, Marcia. *Medieval Foundations of the Western Intellectual Tradition, 400–1400*. New Haven, Conn.: Yale University Press, 1998.

Crabbe, James C. M., ed. *From Soul to Self*. London: Routledge, 1999.

Craig, Edward, ed. *Routledge Encyclopedia of Philosophy*. 10 Vols. London: Routledge, 1998.

Crane, Tim, and Sarah Patterson, eds. *History of the Mind-Body Problem*. London: Routledge, 2000.

Dales, Richard C. *The Problem of the Rational Soul in the Thirteenth Century*. Leiden: E. J. Brill, 1995.

Damasio, Antonio R. *Descartes' Error : Emotion, Reason, and the Human Brain*. New York: G. P. Putnam, 1994.

———. *The Feeling of What Happens: Body and Emotion in the Making of Consciousness*. New York: Harcourt Brace, 1999.

Darwin, Charles. *Autobiography*. In *Charles Darwin, His Life Told in an Autobiographical Chapter, and in a Selected Series of His Published Letters*, ed. Francis Darwin. London: John Murray, 1892.

Dennett, Daniel. *Consciousness Explained*. Boston: Little, Brown, 1991.

———. "The Origin of Selves." *Cogito* 1 (1989): 163–73. Reprint, in *Self and Identity: Contemporary Philosophical Issues*, ed. D. Kolak and R. Martin, 355–64. New York: Macmillan, 1991.

Derrida, Jacques. "Différance." 1968. In *Margins of Philosophy*, ed. J. Derrida, trans. David Allison, 3–27. Chicago: The University of Chicago Press, 1982.

———. *Of Grammatology*. 1967. Trans. Gayatri Chakravorty Spivak. Baltimore, Md.: Johns Hopkins University Press, 1976.

———. *Positions*. Trans. Alan Bass. 1972. Chicago: University of Chicago Press, 1981.

———. "Structure, Sign, and Play in the Discourse of the Human Sciences." 1970. In *Writing and Difference*. Trans. Alan Bass, 278–93. Chicago: University of Chicago Press, 1978.

Descartes, René. *The Philosophical Writings of Descartes*. Ed. and trans. John Cottingham, Robert Stoothoff, Dugald Murdoch, and Anthony Kenny. 3 vols. Cambridge: Cambridge University Press, 1991.

Diderot, Denis. *Dialogues*. Trans. F. Birrell. New York: Capricorn Books, 1969.

Dodd, E. R. *The Greeks and the Irrational.* Berkeley: University of California Press, 1951.

Dreyfus, Hubert. "Heidegger and Foucault on the Subject, Agency, and Practices." Unpublished MS, 2002 .

Dubiel, H., and A. Söllner, eds. *Wirtschaft, Recht und Staat im Nationalsozialismus. Analysen des Instituts für Sozialforschung 1939-1942.* Frankfurt: Suhrkamp, 1984.

DuBois, W. E. B. *The Souls of Black Folk.* 1903. In *Three Negro Classics*, ed. John Hope Franklin. Chicago: Avon, 1965.

Edwards, Paul, ed. *Encyclopedia of Philosophy.* 8 Vols. Macmillan & Free Press, 1967.

Enright, D. J., ed. *The Oxford Book of Death.* Oxford: Oxford University Press, 1983.

Epictetus, *The Manual.* In *The Discourses of Epictetus*, trans. P. E. Matheson, 273–92. New York: The Heritage Press, 1968.

Eriugena, John Scotus. *On the Division of Nature.* In *Medieval Philosophy: From St. Augustine to Nicholas of Cusa*, ed. J. F. Wippel and A. B. Wolter. New York: Free Press, 1969.

Ermarth, Michael. *William Dilthey: The Critique of Historical Reason.* Chicago: University of Chicago Press, 1978.

Fanon, Frantz. *Black Skins, White Masks.* 1952. Trans. Charles Markmann. New York: Grove Press, 1967.

———. *The Wretched of the Earth.* 1961. Trans. Constance Farrington. New York: Grove Press, 1963.

Felix, Minucius. *Octavius.* In *Ante-Nicene Fathers*, ed. A. Roberts, J. Donaldson, and A. C. Coxe, 4:173–98. Peabody, Mass.: Hendrickson, 1995.

Fichte, Johann. *Foundations of Transcendental Philosophy (Wissenschaftslehre), Nova Methodo.* 1796–99. Ed. and trans. Daniel Breazeale. Ithaca, N.Y.: Cornell University Press, 1992.

Flanagan, Owen. *The Problem of the Soul: Two Visions of Mind and How to Reconcile Them.* New York: Basic Books, 2002.

Faulconer J., and R. Williams, eds. *Reconsidering Psychology: Perspectives from Continental Philosophy.* Pittsburgh: Duquesne University Press, 1990.

Foucault, Michel. "The Birth of a World." Interview with Jean-Michel Palmier, *Le Monde*, 3 May 1969. Reprint, in *Foucault Live*, ed. S. Lotringer, trans. L. Hochroth and J. Johnson, 65–67. New York: Semiotext(e), 1989.

———. "The Concern for Truth." In *Foucault Live*, ed. S. Lotringer, trans. L. Hochroth and J. Johnson, 455–64. New York: Semiotext(e), 1989.

———. *Ethics: Subjectivity and Truth.* Ed. Paul Rabinow. Trans. Robert Hurley et al. New York: The New Press, 1994.

———. *The History of Sexuality.* Trans. Robert Hurley. 3 vols. New York: Vintage, 1980.

———. "The Return of Morality." In *Foucault Live*, ed. S. Lotringer, trans. L. Hochroth and J. Johnson, 465–73. New York: Semiotext(e), 1989.

———. "What Is an Author?" In *The Foucault Reader*, ed. P. Rabinow, trans. Josué V. Harari, 101–20. Pantheon, 1984.

Fox, C. *Locke and the Scriblerians.* Berkeley: University of California Press, 1988.

Fox, C., R. Porter, and R. Wokler, eds., *Inventing Human Science: Eighteenth-Century Domains.* Berkeley: University of California Press, 1995.

Freeman, Kathleen, ed. *Ancilla to The Pre-Socratic Philosophers: A Complete Translation of the Fragments in Diels, Fragmenta der Vorsokratiker*. Oxford: Basil Blackwell, 1971.

Galilei, Galileo. *The Assayer*. 1623. In *Discoveries and Opinions of Galileo*, ed. and trans. Stillman Drake, 229–80. Garden City, N.Y.: Doubleday Anchor Books, 1957.

Gatti, H. *Giordano Bruno and Renaissance Science*. Ithaca, N.Y.: Cornell University Press, 1999.

Garber, Daniel, and Michael Ayers, eds.. *The Cambridge History of Seventeenth Century Philosophy*. 2 Vols. Cambridge: Cambridge University Press , 1998.

Gazzaniga, Michael. *The Mind's Past*. Berkeley: University of California Press, 1998.

Gergen, K. J., and M. M. Gergen. "Narrative and the Self as Relationship." *Advances in Experimental Social Psychology* 21 (1988): 17–56.

Giles of Rome. *Errors of the Philosophers*. In *Medieval Philosophy: Selected Readings from Augustine to Buridan*, ed. H. Shapiro, 384–413. New York: Random House, 1964.

Gillman, Neil. *The Death of Death: Resurrection and Immortality in Jewish Thought*. Woodstock, Vt.: Jewish Lights Publishing, 1997.

Goodman, J. E.. *Stories of Scottsboro*. New York: Pantheon, 1994.

Gregory of Nyssa. *On the Soul and the Resurrection*. In *Nicene and Post-Nicene Fathers*, ed. P. Schaff and H. Wace, 2nd ser., 5:430–68. Peabody Mass: Hendrickson, 1995.

Habermas, Jürgen. *Knowledge and Human Interests*. Boston: Beacon Press, 1971.

Harrington, Anne. *Medicine, Mind, and the Double Brain: A Study in Nineteenth-Century Thought*. Princeton, N.J.: Princeton University Press, 1987.

Hartley, David. *Observations on Man, His Frame, His Duty, and His Expectations*. 1749. 2 vols. Reprint, intro. T. L. Huguelet. 1 vol. Gainesville, Fla: Scholars' Facsimiles & Reprints, 1966.

Haslanger, Sally. "Gender and Race: (What) Are They? (What) Do We Want Them to Be?" *Nous* 34, no. 1 (2000): 31–55.

Hatfield, Gary. "Remaking the Science of Mind: Psychology as Natural Science." In *Inventing Human Science: Eighteenth Century Domains*, ed. Christopher Fox, Roy Porter, and Robert Wokler, 184–231. Berkeley: University of California Press, 1995.

Hazlitt, William. *An Essay on the Principles of Human Action and some Remarks on the Systems of Hartley and Helvetius*. 1805. Reprint, intro. J. R. Nabholtz. Gainesville, Fla.: Scholars' Facsimiles & Reprints, 1969.

Heckel, Theo K.. "Body and Soul in St. Paul." In *Psyche and Soma—Physicians and Metaphysicians on the Mind-Body Problem from Antiquity to Enlightenment*, ed. John P. Wright and Paul Potter, 117–32. Oxford: Oxford University Press, 2000.

Hegel, G. W. F. *The Phenomenology of Spirit*. 1807. Trans. A. V. Miller. Oxford: Oxford University Press, 1977.

Heidegger, Martin. *Being and Time*. 1927. Trans. John Macquarrie and Edward Robinson. New York: Harper & Row, 1962.

Hermans H., and H. Kempen. *The Dialogical Self: Meaning as Movement*. New York: Academic Press, 1993.

Hermans, H., T. Rijks, and H. Kempen. "Imaginal Dialogues in the Self: Theory and Method." *Journal of Personality* 61 (1993): 207–235.

Hippocrates. "Hippocratic Writings." In *Great Books of the Western World*. Vol. 10. Chicago: Encyclopedia Britannica, 1952.

Hobbes, Thomas. "De Corpore." Also known as *Elements of Philosophy*. In *The English Works of Thomas Hobbes*, ed. W. Molesworth. Vol. 1. London: J. Bohn, 1839.

Hoffman, M. L. "Empathy, Its Development and Prosocial Implications." In *Nebraska Symposium on Motivation*, ed. C. B. Keasey. Vol. 25, *Social Cognitive Development*. Lincoln: University of Nebraska Press, 1977.

Horkheimer, Max. *Die Juden in Europa*. 1939. In *Wirtschaft, Recht und Staat im Nationalsozialismus. Analysen des Instituts für Sozialforschung 1939–1942*, ed. H. Dubiel and A. Söllner, 33–53. Frankfurt: Suhrkamp, 1984.

Horkheimer, Max, and Theodore Adorno. *Dialectic of Enlightenment*. Trans. John Cumming. New York: Herder and Herder, 1972.

Hume, David. *Treatise of Human Nature*. 1739. Ed. L. A. Selby-Bigge. Oxford: Clarendon Press, 1888.

——. "Essay on the Immortality of the Soul." In *The Philosophical Works of David Hume*, 4 vols., 4:547–55. Boston: Little, Brown and Company, 1854.

Humphrey, N. "The Social Function of Intellect." In *Growing Points in Ethology*, ed. P. P. G. Bateson and R. Hinde, 303–17. Cambridge: Cambridge University Press, 1976. Reprint, in N. Humphrey, *Consciousness Regained: Chapters in the Development of Mind*. Oxford: Oxford University Press, 1984.

Humphrey, Nicholas, and Daniel Dennett. "Speaking for Ourselves: An Assessment of Multiple Personality Disorder." *Raritan* 9 (1989) 68–98. Reprint, in *Self and Identity: Contemporary Philosophical Issues*, ed. D. Kolak and R. Martin, 144–61. New York: Macmillan, 1991.

Husserl, E.. *The Crisis of European Sciences and Transcendental Phenomenology*. 1954. Trans. and intro. David Carr. Evanston, Ill.: Northwestern University Press, 1970.

Israel, Jonathan. *Radical Enlightenment*. New York: Oxford University Press, 2002.

Jaeger, Werner. *Aristotle: Fundamentals of the History of His Development*. 1934. Reprint, New York: Oxford University Press, 1967.

James, William. *Principles of Psychology*. 2 vols. 1890. Reprint, New York: Henry Holt, 1918.

Jaynes, Julian. *The Origin of Consciousness in the Breakdown of the Bicameral Mind*. Princeton, N.J.: Princeton University Press, 1976.

Jerome. "Letter to Pammachius against John of Jerusalem." In *Nicene and Post-Nicene Fathers*, ed. P. Schaff and H. Wace, 2nd ser., 6:436–38. Peabody Mass: Hendrickson, 1995.

Kant, Immanuel. *Critique of Pure Reason*. Ed. and trans. Norman Kemp Smith. New York: St. Martin's Press, 1965.

Kierkegaard, Søren. *Sickness Unto Death*. Ed. and trans. Howard B. Hong and Edna H. Hong. Princeton, N.J.: Princeton University Press, 1980.

Kolak, Daniel, and Raymond Martin, eds. *Self and Identity: Contemporary Philosophical Issues*. New York: Macmillan, 1991.

Kripke, Saul. *Naming and Necessity*. Cambridge, Mass.: Harvard University Press, 1980.

Kristeller, Paul Oskar. *Eight Philosophers of the Italian Renaissance*. New York: Harper Collins, 1964.

——. "Ficino and Pomponazzi on the Place of Man in the Universe." *Journal of the History of Ideas* 5 (1944): 220–39.

——. *The Philosophy of Marsilio Ficino*. Trans. Virginia Conant. New York: Columbia University Press, 1943.

——. *Renaissance Thought: The Classic, Scholastic, and Humanist Strains*. New York: Harper & Row, 1961.

Kuhn, Thomas. *The Structure of Scientific Revolutions*. Chicago: University of Chicago Press, 1962.

Kusch, Martin. *Psychologism: A Case Study in the Sociology of Philosophical Knowledge*. New York: Routledge, 1995.

La Mettrie, Julien Offray de. *Man the Machine*. 1748. Trans. Gertrude Bussey. LaSalle, Ill.: Open Court, 1912.

Leibniz, Gottfried Wilhelm. *New Essays Concerning Human Understanding*. 1765. Trans. A.G. Langley. New York: Macmillan, 1896.

——. *Philosophical Essays*. Ed. and trans. Roger Ariew and Daniel Garber. Indianapolis: Hackett, 1989.

Lévi-Strauss, Claude. *Structural Anthropology*. 1958. Ed. Allen Lane. Trans. Clair Jacobson and Brooke Grundfest Schoepf. Harmondsworth: Penguin, 1968.

Lewis, David. *On the Plurality of Worlds*. Oxford: Blackwell, 1986.

——. *Philosophical Papers*. 2 vols. New York: Oxford University Press, 1983.

——. "Postscript to 'Survival and Identity.'" In *Philosophical Papers*, vol. 1. New York: Oxford University Press, 1983.

——. "Survival and Identity." In *The Identities of Persons*, ed. Amelie Rorty, 17–40. Berkeley: University of California Press, 1976.

Lindheim, Nancy. "Body, Soul, and Immortality: Some Readings in Dante's Commedia." *MLN* 105 (1990): 1–32.

Locke, John. *An Essay Concerning Human Understanding*. 1690–94. Ed. Peter H. Nidditch. Pbk. ed. Oxford: Oxford University Press, 1979.

Long, A.A. "Stoic Philosophers on Persons, Property-Ownership, and Community." In *Aristotle and After*, ed. Richard Sorabji, 13–32. London: Institute of Classical Studies, 1997.

Lucretius, Carus. *De Rerum Natura*. Trans. R. E. Latham. Harmondsworth: Penguin, 1951.

——. *De Rerum Natura*. Trans. H. A. J. Munro. In *The Stoic and Epicurean Philosophers*, ed. Whitney J. Oates. New York: The Modern Library, 1940.

——. *De Rerum Natura*. Trans. William H. D. Rouse. Cambridge, Mass.: Harvard University Press, 1924. 3rd rev. ed., reprint, 1961.

MacDonald, Paul S. *History of the Concept of Mind: Speculations About Soul, Mind, and Spirit from Homer to Hume*. Burlington, Vt.: Ashgate, 2003.

MacIntyre, A. *After Virtue*. 2nd ed. South Bend, Ind.: University of Notre Dame Press, 1984.

MacPherson, C. B. *The Political Theory of Possessive Individualism: Hobbes to Locke*. Oxford: Clarendon University Press, 1962.

Maimonides, Moses. *Guide for the Perplexed*. Trans. M. Friedlander. London: Routledge & Kegan Paul, 1904.

Mama, Amina. *Beyond the Masks: Race, Gender, and Subjectivity*. London: Routledge, 1995.

Markova, Ivana. "The Development of Self-Consciousness: Baldwin, Mead, and Vygotsky." In *Reconsidering Psychology: Perspectives from Continental Philosophy*, ed. J. Faulconer and R. Williams, 151–74. Pittsburgh: Duquesne University Press, 1990.

Martin, Raymond. *The Elusive Messiah: A Philosophical Overview of the Quest for the Historical Jesus*. Boulder, Colo.: Westview Press, 1999.

——. "Locke's Psychology of Personal Identity." *Journal of the History of Philosophy* 38 (2000): 41–61.

——. *Self-Concern: An Experiential Approach to What Matters in Survival*. Cambridge: Cambridge University Press, 1998.

Martin, Raymond, and John Barresi. "Hazlitt on the Future of the Self." *Journal of the History of Ideas* 56 (1995): 463–81.

——. *Naturalization of the Soul: Self and Personal Identity in the Eighteenth Century*. London: Routledge, 2000.

——, eds. *Personal Identity*. New York: Blackwell, 2002.

——. "Personal Identity and What Matters in Survival: An Historical Overview." In *Personal Identity*, ed. R. Martin and J. Barresi. Oxford: Blackwell, 2003.

Martin, Raymond, John Barresi, and Alessandro Giovannelli. "Fission Examples in the Eighteenth- and Early-Nineteenth-Century Personal-Identity Debate." *History of Philosophy Quarterly* 15 (1998): 323–48.

Marx, Karl. *Critique of Political Economy*. In K. Marx and F. Engels, *Selected Works*, vol. 1. New York: International Publishers, 1975.

Marx, Karl, and Friedrich Engels. *The German Ideology*. Moscow: Progress Publishers, 1976.

——. *Theses on Feuerbach*. In K. Marx and F. Engels, *Selected Works*, vol. 1. Moscow: Progress Publishers, 1969.

May, Rollo. "The Origins and Significance of the Existential Movement in Psychology." In *Existence: A New Dimension in Psychiatry and Psychology*, ed. Rollo May, Ernest Angel, and Henri F. Ellenberger, 3–36. New York: Basic Books, 1958.

May, Rollo, Ernest Angel, and Henri F. Ellenberger, eds. *Existence: A New Dimension in Psychiatry and Psychology*. New York: Basic Books, 1958.

McAdams, D. "The Case for Unity in the (Post) Modern Self: A Modest Proposal." In *Self and Identity: Fundamental Issues*, ed. R. Ashmore and L. Jussim, 46–78. New York: Oxford University Press, 1997.

——. "What Do We Know When We Know a Person?" *Journal of Personality* 63 (1995): 365–95.

Mead, G. H. *Mind, Self, and Society from the Standpoint of a Social Behaviorist*. 1934. Ed. Charles W. Morris. Chicago: University of Chicago Press, 1962.

Methodius of Olympus. *From the Discourse on the Resurrection*. In *Ante-Nicene Fathers*, ed. A. Roberts, J. Donaldson, and A. C. Coxe, 4:364–77. Peabody, Mass.: Hendrickson Publishers, 1995.

Metzinger, Thomas. "The Pre-Scientific Concept of a 'Soul': A Neurophenomenological Hypothesis About Its Origin." In *Auf der Suche nach dem Konzept/Substrat der Seele. Ein Versuch aus der Perspektive der Cognitive (Neuro-) Science*, ed M. Peschl, 185–211. Würzburg: Königshausen und Neumann, 2003.

Meyers, Diana. "Feminist Perspectives on the Self." In the *Stanford Encyclopedia of Philosophy* (Stanford, Calif." Stanford University Press, 2004). http://plato.stanford.edu/entries/feminism-self.

——, ed. *Feminists Rethink the Self*. Boulder, Colo: Westview, 1997.

Michael, Emily. "Renaissance Theories of Body, Soul, and Mind." In *Psyche and Soma*, ed. John P. Wright and Paul Potter, 147–72. Oxford: Clarendon Press, 2000.

Mijuskovic, B. *The Achilles of Rationalist Arguments: The Simplicity, Unity, and Identity of Thought and Soul from the Cambridge Platonists to Kant: A Study in the History of an Argument*. The Hague: Martinus Nijhoff, 1974.

Mill, James. *Analysis of the Human Mind*. 2 vols. Ed. A. Bain, A. Findlater, and G. Grote. London: Longman's Green Reader and Dyer, 1869.

Mill, J. S. *Auguste Comte and Positivism*. 1866. Ann Arbor: University of Michigan Press, 1968.

——. *An Examination of Sir William Hamilton's Philosophy*. 1865. London: Longman's, Green, Reader, and Dyer, 1878.

Montaigne, Michel de. *The Complete Works of Montaigne*. Ed. and trans. Donald M. Frame. Stanford, Calif.: Stanford University Press, 1957.

——. *Essays*. Ed. and trans. J. M. Cohen. Harmondsworth: Penguin, 1958.

——. "To Philosophize Is to Learn How to Die." In *The Complete Essays*, ed. and trans. M. A. Screech, book 1, essay 20. New York: Penguin, 1993.

Morris, Colin. *The Discovery of the Individual, 1050–1200*. New York: Harper & Row, 1972.

Moore, Chris, and Karen Lemmon, eds. *The Self in Time: Developmental Issues*. Hillsdale, N.J.: Erlbaum, 2000.

Murray, Henry A. *Explorations in Personality*. Oxford: Oxford University Press, 1938.

Nagel, T. "Brain Bisection and the Unity of Consciousness" In *Mortal Questions* Cambridge: Cambridge University Press, 1979. Reprint, in *Self and Identity: Contemporary Philosophical Issues*, ed. D. Kolak and R. Martin, 75–82. New York: Macmillan, 1991.

Neisser, Ulrich, "Five Kinds of Self-Knowledge." *Philosophical Psychology* 1 (1988): 37–59. Reprint, in *Self and Identity: Contemporary Philosophical Issues*, ed. D. Kolak and R. Martin, 386–406. New York: Macmillan, 1991.

Neuhouser, Frederick. *Fichte's Theory of Subjectivity*. New York: Cambridge University Press, 1990.

Nietzsche, Friedrich W. *Ecco Homo: How One Becomes What One Is*. 1888. In *The Philosophy of Neitzsche*, ed. Geoffrey Clive, trans. A.M. Ludovici. New York: New American Library, 1965.

——. *Ecce Homo: How One Becomes What One Is*. 1888. Trans. R. J. Hollingdale. Harmondsworth: Penguin Books, 1979.

——. *Human, All Too Human: A Book for Free Spirits*. Ed. and trans. R. J. Hollingdale. New York: Cambridge University Press, 1996.

——. *The Will to Power*. 1901. Trans. Walter Kaufmann. New York: Vintage, 1968.

Onians, R. P. *The Origins of European Thought About the Body, the Mind, the Soul, the World, Time, and Fate*. Cambridge: Cambridge University Press, 1988.

Origen, *Contra Celsum*. Trans. and intro. Henry Chadwick. Cambridge: Cambridge University Press, 1986.

——. *On First Principles*. In *Ante-Nicene Fathers*, vol. 4, ed. A. Roberts, J. Donaldson, and A. C. Coxe (Peabody, Mass.: Hendrickson Publishers, 1995), 239–382.

Paracelsus. *The Diseases That Deprive Man of His Reason, Such as St. Vitus Dance, Falling Sickness, Melancholy, and Insanity, and Their Correct Treatment*. Trans. G. Zilboorg. In *Four Treatises of Theophrastus von Hohenheim, Called Paracelsus*, ed. and trans. C. L. Temkin, G. Rosen, G. Zilboorg, and H. E. Sigerest. Baltimore, Md.: John Hopkins University Press, 1996.

——. *The Hermetic and Alchemical Writings of Paracelsus*. 2 vols. Ed. and trans. A. E. Waite. Berkeley: Shambala, 1976.

Parfit, Derek. "Divided Minds and the Nature of Persons." In *Mindwaves*, ed. C. Blakemore and S. Greenfield. Oxford: Basil Blackwell, 1987. Reprint, in *Self and Identity: Contemporary Philosophical Issues*, ed. D. Kolak and R. Martin, 82–88. New York: Macmillan, 1991.

——. "Personal Identity." *Philosophical Review* 80 (1971): 3–27.

——. *Reasons and Persons*. Oxford: Oxford University Press, 1984.

Perkins, Jean A . *The Concept of the Self in the French Enlightenment*. Geneva: Librairie Droz, 1969.

Philo. *The Works of Philo Judaeus, the Contemporary of Josephus*. Trans. Charles Duke Yonge. London, H. G. Bohn, 1854–1890.

Plato. *Cratylus*. In *The Collected Dialogues of Plato*, ed. Edith Hamilton and Huntington Cairns, 421–74. New York: Pantheon Books, 1961.

——. *The Dialogues of Plato*. Trans. Benjamin Jowett. 1871. 4th ed. Oxford: Oxford University Press, 1953.

——. *Symposium*. Ed. and trans. C. J. Rowe. Warminster, England: Aris & Phillips, 1998.

Plotinus. *Ennead*. In *Great Books of the Western World*. Vol. 17. Chicago: Encyclopedia Britannica, 1952.

Pope, Alexander, et al. *Memoirs of the Extraordinary Life, Works, and Discoveries of Martinus Scriblerus*. Ed. C. Kerby-Miller. New York: Russell and Russell, 1966.

Porter, Roy. *Flesh in the Age of Reason: The Modern Foundations of Body and Soul*. New York: W. W. Norton, 2004.

——, ed. *Rewriting the Self: Histories from the Renaissance to the Present*. London: Routledge, 1997.

Premack D., and G. Woodruff. "Do Chimpanzees Have a Theory of Mind?" *Behavioral and Brain Sciences* 1 (1978): 516–26.

Priestley, Joseph. *Disquisitions Relating to Matter and Spirit, and the Doctrine of Philosophical Necessity Illustrated*. 1777. Reprint, New York: Garland, 1976.

Prior, A. N. "Opposite Number." *Review of Metaphysics* 11 (1957–58): 196–201.

——. "Time, Existence, and Identity." *Proceedings of the Aristotelian Society* 57 (1965–66): 183–92.

Puccetti, R., "Two Brains, Two Minds? Wigan's Theory of Mental Duality." *British Journal for the Philosophy of Science* 40 (1989): 137–44. Reprint, in *Self and Identity: Contemporary Philosophical Issues*, ed. D. Kolak and R. Martin, 68–74. New York: Macmillan, 1991.

Putnam, Hilary. "The Meaning of 'Meaning.'" In *Language, Mind, and Knowledge*, ed. K. Gunderson, 131–93. Minneapolis: University of Minnesota Press, 1975.

Pyle, Andrew. ed. *Key Philosophers in Conversation: The Cogito Interviews*. London: Routledge, 1999.

Quine, W. V. O. "Two Dogmas of Empiricism." *The Philosophical Review* 60 (1951): 20–43. Reprinted in W. V. O. Quine, *From a Logical Point of View*. Cambridge, Mass.: Harvard University Press, 1953.

Randall, John H, Jr. *The Career of Philosophy: From the Middle Ages to the Enlightenment*. New York: Columbia University Press, 1962.

Reed, E. S. *From Soul to Mind: The Emergence of Psychology from Erasmus Darwin to William James*. New Haven, Conn.: Yale University Press, 1997.

Reid, Thomas. *Essay on the Intellectual Powers of Man*. 1785. In *Philosophical Works of Thomas Reid*, ed. W. Hamilton, 1895, 1:213–508. Reprint, Hildesheim: George Olms, n.d.

Reiss, Timothy J. *Mirages of the Selfe: Patterns of Personhood in Ancient and Early Modern Europe*. Stanford, Calif.: Stanford University Press, 2003.

Ribot, Theodule. *Diseases of Personality*. 1891. Reprint, in *Significant Contributions to the History of Psychology, 1750–1920, Series C: Medical Psychology: T. A. Ribot*, ed. D. N. Robinson, vol. 1. Washington, D.C.: University Publications of America, 1997.

Rousseau, Jean-Jacques. *Emile*. 1762. Trans. Barbara Foxley. Intro P. D. Jimack. London: Dent, 1974.

——. *The First and Second Discourses*. Trans. R. Masters. New York: St. Martin's Press, 1964.

——. *Reveries of the Solitary Walker*. Trans. Peter France. Harmondsworth: Penguin, 1979.

Royce, Josiah. "Some Observations on the Anomalies of Self-Consciousness." In *Studies of Good and Evil*, 169–97. 1898. Hamden, Conn.: Archon, 1964.

——. *The World and the Individual: Second Series: Nature, Man, and the Moral Order*. New York: Macmillan, 1901–13.

Rozemond, Marleen. *Descartes's Dualism*. Cambridge, Mass.: Harvard University Press, 1998.

Russell, Bertrand. *Logic and Knowledge*. Ed. R. C. Marsh. London: George Allen & Unwin., 1956.

Ryle, Gilbert. *The Concept of Mind*. Chicago: University of Chicago Press, 1949.

Sanders, E. P., and Margaret Davies. *Studying the Synoptic Gospels*. Philadelphia: Trinity Press International, 1989.

Sartre, Jean-Paul. *Being and Nothingness*. 1943. Trans. Hazel E. Barnes. New York: Citadel Press, 1964.

———. *Transcendence of the Ego: An Existentialist Theory of Consciousness*. 1936. Trans. Forrest Williams and Robert Kirkpatrick. New York: Noonday Press, 1957.

Schmitt, C. B., Quentin Skinner, Eckhard Kessler, and Jill Kraye, eds. *The Cambridge History of Renaissance Philosophy*. Cambridge: Cambridge University Press, 1988.

Sedley, David. "Epicurus." In *Routledge Encyclopedia of Philosophy*, ed. E. Craig. London: Routledge, 1998. http://www.rep.routledge.com/article/A050.

———. "The Stoic Criterion of Identity." *Phronesis* 27 (1982): 255–75.

Schiller, W. *Letters on the Aesthetic Education of Man*. In *Literary and Philosophical Essays: French, German and Italian*, Harvard Classics 32. New York: Collier, c. 1910.

Schopenhauer, Arthur. "Immortality: A Dialogue." In *Studies in Pessimism: A Series of Essays*, trans. T. Bailey Saunders, 4th ed., 53–58. London: Swan Sonnenschein & Co., 1893. Reprint, St. Clair Shores, Mich.: Scholarly Press, 1976.

———. *The World as Will and Representation*. 1818, 1844, 1859. Trans. E. F. J. Payne. New York: Dover, 1966.

Sidgwick, H. *The Methods of Ethics*. 1874. Chicago: University of Chicago Press, 1907.

Smith, Roger. *The Norton History of the Human Sciences*. New York: W. W. Norton, 1997.

Solomon, Robert C. *Continental Philosophy Since 1750: The Rise and Fall of the Self*. New York: Oxford University Press, 1998.

Solomon, Robert C., and Kathleen M. Higgins. *A Short History of Philosophy*. New York: Oxford, 1996.

Sorabji, Richard, ed. *Aristotle and After*. London: Institute of Classical Studies, 1997.

———. "Soul and Self in Ancient Philosophy." In *From Soul to Self*, ed. M. James C. Crabbe, 8–32. New York: Routledge, 1999.

Sperry, R. "Hemisphere Deconnection and Unity in Conscious Awareness." *American Psychologist* 23 (1968): 723–33. Reprint, in *Self and Identity: Contemporary Philosophical Issues*, ed. D. Kolak and R. Martin, 55–68. New York: Macmillan, 1991.

Spiegel, Rudolph E. *Galen on Psychology, Psychopathology, and Function of Diseases of the Nervous System*. New York: S. Karger AG, 1973.

Spinoza, Benedictus (Baruch) de. *Ethics*. In *The Collected Works of Spinoza*, vol. 1, ed. and trans. Edwin Curley. Princeton, N.J.: Princeton University Press, 1985.

———. *Ethics*. Trans. W. H. White. Rev. A. H. Sterling. In *Great Books of the Western World*, vol. 31. Chicago: Encyclopedia Britannica, 1952.

Staden, Heinrich von. "Body, Soul, and Nerves: Epicurus, Herophilus, Erasistratus, the Stoics, and Galen." In *Psyche and Soma–Physicians and Metaphysicians on the Mind-Body Problem from Antiquity to Enlightenment*, ed. John P. Wright and Paul Potter, 79–116. Oxford: Oxford University Press, 2000.

Stam, Hendericus. "The Dialogical Self, Meaning and Theory: Making the Subject." Paper presented at the First International Conference on the Dialogical Self, Nijmegen, Netherlands, June 2000.

Steiner, Rudolf. *Eleven European Mystics*. Trans Karl E. Zimmer. New York: Rudolf Steiner, 1971.

Stewart, M. A., ed. *Studies in the Philosophy of the Scottish Enlightenment*. Oxford: Oxford University Press, 1990.

Stewart-Robertson, J. C. "Thomas Reid and Pneumatology." In *The Philosophy of Thomas Reid*, ed. M. Dalgarno and E. Matthews, 389–411. Dordrecht: Kluwer Academic Publishers, 1989.

Still, Carl N. "Do We Know All After Death? Thomas Aquinas on the Disembodied Soul's Knowledge." In *Proceedings of the American Catholic Philosophical Association: Person, Soul, and Immortality, Vol. 75*, 107–19. New York: American Catholic Philosophical Association, 2002.

Sutton, J. *Philosophy and Memory Traces: Descartes to Connectionism*. Cambridge: Cambridge University Press, 1998.

Taylor, Charles. *Sources of the Self: The Making of the Modern Identity*. Cambridge: Cambridge University Press, 1989.

Tertullian. *On the Resurrection of the Flesh*. In *Ante-Nicene Fathers*, ed. A. Roberts, J. Donaldson, and A. C. Coxe, 3:545–94. Peabody, Mass.: Hendrickson Publishers, 1995.

Themistius. *Themistius' Paraphrase of Aristotle De anima 3.4-8*. In *Two Greek Aristotelean Commentators on the Intellect: The De Intellectu Attributed to Alexander of Aphrodisias and Themistius' Paraphrase of Aristotle De anima 3.4-8*, ed. and trans. Frederic M Schroeder and Robert Todd. Toronto: Pontifical Institute of Mediaeval Studies, 1990.

Thiel, Udo. "Individuation." In *The Cambridge History of Seventeenth-Century Philosophy*, vol. 1, ed. Daniel Garber and Michael Ayers, 212–62. Cambridge: Cambridge University Press, 1998.

——. *Lockes Theorie der personalen Identität*. Bonn: Bouvier Verlag Herbert Grundmann, 1983.

——. "Personal Identity." Ch. 26 in Daniel Garber and Michael Ayers eds.,*The Cambridge History of Seventeenth Century Philosophy,* Vol. 1, pp. 868–912. Cambridge: Cambridge University Press, 1998.

——, ed. *Philosophical Writings of Thomas Cooper*. Bristol: Thoemmes Press, 2000.

Trevarthen, C., ed. *Brain Circuits and Functions of Mind*. Cambridge: Cambridge University Press, 1990.

Tsouna, Voula. *The Epistemology of the Cyrenaic School*. Cambridge: Cambridge University Press, 1998.

Tucker, Abraham. *The Light of Nature Pursued*. 7 vols. 1805. Reprint, New York: Garland, 1997.

Tyndall, John. *Fragments of Science for Unscientific People: A Series of Detached Essays, Lectures, and Reviews*. London: Longmans, Green and Co., 1871.

Unger, Peter. *Identity, Consciousness, and Value*. New York: Oxford University Press, 1991.

Uzgalis, William. "Paideia and Identity: Meditations on Hobbes and Locke." Available at http://www.bu.edu/wcp/Papers/Mode/ModeUzga.htm.

Vygotsky, L. "Consciousness as a Problem in the Psychology of Behavior." *Soviet Psychology* 17 (1979): 3–35.

Wiener, P. P., ed. *Dictionary of the History of Ideas: Studies of Selected Pivotal Ideas*. 4 Vols. Chicago: Charles Scribner's Sons, 1973–74.

Wimmer, H., and J. Perner. "Beliefs About Beliefs: Representations and Constraining Function of Wrong Beliefs in Young Children's Understanding of Deception." *Cognition* 13 (1983): 103–28.

Wittgenstein, Ludwig. *The Blue and Brown Books*. Oxford: Blackwell, 1958.

——. *Philosophical Investigations*. Ed. G. Anscombe and Rush Rhees. Trans. G. Anscombe. Oxford: Blackwell, 1953.

——. *Tractatus Logico-Philosophicus*. 1921. Trans. D. Pears and B. McGuiness. London: Routlege & Kegan Paul, 1961.

Wozniak, Robert H. *Mind and Body: René Descartes to William James*. http://serendip.brynmawr.edu/Mind/Table.html.

Wright, John P., and Paul Potter, eds. *Psyche and Soma—Physicians and Metaphysicians on the Mind-Body Problem from Antiquity to Enlightenment*. Oxford: Oxford University Press, 2000.

Yates, Francis. *Giordano Bruno and the Hermetic Tradition*. London: Routledge and Kegan Paul, 1964.

Yolton, J. W. *Thinking Matter: Materialism in Eighteenth-Century Britain*. Minneapolis: University of Minnesota Press, 1983.

Young, Robert, M. *Mind, Brain and Adaptation in the Nineteenth Century: Cerebral Localization and Its Biological Context from Gall to Ferrier*. Oxford: Oxford University Press, 1990.

Zilboorg, Gregory. *A History of Medical Psychology*. New York: W. W. Norton, 1941.

INDEX OF NAMES

SUBJECT INDEX

motives, 160, 162, 164, 167, 169, 172, 252, 273, 319n. 14

multiple personality disorder. *See* extreme dissociative disorder

mystery cults, 9, 53

myth, 9–28, 30, 50, 264, 276–278, 292, 308n. 8

naturalism, 28, 92–108, 114, 117, 131, 140, 142–170, 201–228, 296

Neanderthals, 290–291

Neoplatonism, 16, 27, 35–38, 53, 75–77, 79, 82, 86, 93–94, 96–97, 99–100, 103, 111, 117, 119, 311n. 16, 317nn. 1, 2, 4, 318n. 6

nervous system, 27, 95, 124, 159, 161–163, 174, 194, 203, 206–207, 312n. 29, 334n. 9

neurohypnosis, 206. *See also* hypnosis

neuroscience, 133, 135, 206–207, 250, 279–281

neurosis, 207, 248, 256

neutral monism, 173, 205

nihilism, 196

noumenal selves. *See* selves, noumenal

objectivity, 123–126, 190. *See also* subjectivity

observers, 124, 228, 299

occasionalism, 134

ordinary language philosophy, 230–231, 240, 242–244

organism, 9, 25, 72, 79, 101, 116, 119, 127–128, 144–145, 150, 158, 187, 204, 208, 236, 250–251, 274, 287, 297–299, 302, 307, 329n. 34, 320n. 18

organ of generation, 149

organs, 9, 66, 74, 115, 127, 130, 149, 202, 205, 286–287, 309n. 11

other minds, 28, 139, 214, 244

out-of-body experience. *See* experience, out-of-body

ownership, personal, 13, 20, 25–26, 32, 70–73, 83, 87–88, 91, 102, 113, 118, 144,

157, 162–167, 212, 214–215, 219, 221, 223, 225–228, 231, 233, 250, 303, 310n. 18, 320n. 18, 321n. 19, 327nn. 6, 8. *See also* appropriation

pain, 12, 17–18, 25, 34, 66, 108, 130, 144, 158, 165, 179, 206, 223

Patristic Period, 2, 55–75, 293

perceptions, 37, 118, 127–128, 134, 153–155, 205, 223, 225, 248

persistence. *See* personal identity; survival

person, 2–5, 24, 30–32, 48–51, 55–64, 66–68, 70, 101, 105, 138–151, 160–163, 181, 192, 214–217, 228, 239–240, 242–245, 280–282, 286–289, 304; category of, 218; defined, 77, 105, 144; vs. human, 25; vs. self, 144; stages, 213, 242, 268, 288–289; strict sense of same, 3; three- vs. four-dimensional view of, 138, 289; unity, 95, 143

personal identity, 1–5, 7, 51, 54–62, 100, 102, 114, 131, 135–138, 140–157, 159–163, 167–169, 172–173, 199–200, 212, 219, 221, 239–242, 281–285, 289, 293–296, 300–305; and assimilation, 63; body-based, 213; closest-continuer view, 215, 281; connected-consciousness view, 147; as illusion, 161; intrinsic- vs. extrinsic-relations views, 281–284; vs. human identity, 26; as matter of degree, 199; memory analyses of, 143–145, 154–157, 173, 199, 213–214, 243, 284; philosophy vs. psychology of, 7; vs. question of what matters in survival, 33–35, 138, 160–170, 283–288; same-consciousness view, 143, 146–148, 168; substance vs. relational accounts, 27, 136, 138. *See also* immortality; persistence; survival

personality, 10, 30, 38, 69, 83, 108, 110–111, 137, 184, 206–208, 216, 221, 243–245, 247, 251–252, 274–276, 277